COUNSELING & THERAPY SKILLS

THIRD EDITION

COUNSELING & THERAPY SKILLS

THIRD EDITION

DAVID G. MARTIN
UNIVERSITY OF MANITOBA

WAVELAND

PRESS, INC.

Long Grove, Illinois

To Patti,

for sharing the vision

For information about this book, contact:
    Waveland Press, Inc.
    4180 IL Route 83, Suite 101
    Long Grove, IL 60047-9580
    (847) 634-0081
    info@waveland.com
    www.waveland.com

About the Author

Dr. David Martin is Professor of Clinical Psychology at the University of Manitoba, where he has been teaching for over thirty years. He is the author of numerous research papers and seven books on psychology, and he has won three teaching awards as a university teacher. In addition, he received the Clifford J. Robson Distinguished Psychologist in Manitoba award in 1995, and in 2007, he received the Excellence in Professional Training award from the Canadian Council of Professional Psychology Programs.

Contents

Part Two: Other Issues in Practicing Therapy

Part Three: Theory and Evidence

Preface

As with previous editions, the goal of the third edition of *Counseling and Therapy Skills* is to communicate more than an academic understanding of the principles of therapy. I want to give the reader skills that actually can be applied in the counseling setting, and I want to start the reader on the path to becoming a great therapist. There is a significant paradox in learning to be a therapist. Therapy involves an intuitive, almost artistic attunement with the client, and the best predictor of a successful outcome is having a good therapy relationship. If one approaches therapy as primarily a set of skills, it is very difficult to make the kind of connection that seems to be healing. However, the beginning therapist, like the beginning artist, must first learn some skills. Later, the great therapists and the great artists "lose" these skills in the sense that they don't need to think about them much. They don't "apply skills" to their work, they "simply do it." I hope this book provides a balance in which the beginning therapist can learn skills without losing sight of the art of therapy.

Beginning therapists approach the frightening task of counseling or therapy uneasily and usually with only some commonsense notions of how to be helpful to a person in emotional trouble. These commonsense notions seem to fall into one of two categories: on the one hand, therapists often have some idea that empathy is a passive sort of pleasant listening skill, or, on the other hand, they try to fill the role of expert advice giver and interpreter. There is a third alternative that therapists in training welcome as valid and useful and within their ability to do, once they understand it. *Evocative empathy* is a skill that draws from a long tradition of theory, therapeutic practice, and research evidence. After more than 30 years of teaching these skills, I now think I can teach how to be ahead of the client in a helpful way that brings to life the client's deep experiences without taking over control of therapy—a way that permits the client to be the problem solver but gives the therapist a truly helpful and active role.

This book is designed for the beginning counselor or therapist, either in courses dealing with skill development or in practicum settings. These courses and practica are often found in clinical psychology programs and in education departments that stress educational psychology or counseling. I believe the "how to do it" message of the book will appeal to trainees. It is likely that other programs that involve counseling skills, such as nursing, occupational therapy, and social work, will also use the book. Since the presentation is at a beginning level, virtually any of the helping professions would find it useful.

The first section of the book describes the fundamental skills, along with material aimed at developing the reader's skills through a number of devices that engage him or her in actual practice exercises. The written format is limited for communicating the practice of therapeutic communication, but transcripts of therapy sessions in Appendix A can be used as exercises—of a workbook nature—in which the trainee reads clients' statements and responses and then writes possible therapist responses. In addition, these transcripts provide an opportunity to "observe" other therapists doing therapy. The reader is also urged to practice the skills in role-playing with one or two others, and I give advice about how to do this on the basis of my experience with role-playing in my classes. The last chapter in this section tries to articulate some understanding of complex issues that are almost impossible to put into words. These are the issues that involve going "beyond skills," such as *experiential understanding, emergent modes of expressing empathy, mindfulness, presence,* and *being in the zone* as a therapist.

The second section of the book rounds out the treatment of what the beginning therapist needs to know. It is more formal in that it discusses issues and offers practical advice about beginning sessions, settings for therapy, ethical issues, different formats for therapy, and other such topics. These topics are often found at the beginning of books on therapy, but this practice sets the mood of a book in the direction of formality and pedantic understanding of concepts, rather than toward the excitement and flow of what one actually does as a therapist. I prefer to place this more structured material toward the end, so that the book starts out at a full run with the material that means the most to the reader. The second section includes new material on being a culturally competent therapist and on the importance of the therapist's self-care. Among the ways therapists can be attuned to themselves is to be a client in the therapy process. In Appendix B, which is new to this edition, Jo Ann M. Unger, a therapist in training, shares her experiences as a client and expresses meaningful conclusions about the process.

Although the emphasis of the book is on developing skills, the third section of the book includes research evidence that evocative empathy actually works. It also provides a theoretical understanding of the nature of emotional problems that gives the therapist a foundation for *understanding why* evocative empathy works. These explanations acknowledge that there are many ways to understand therapy theoretically and that many of them contain useful truth. All theories are just simplified "line drawings" of one part of a very complex reality and the theoretical model in this book is no different. It draws most heavily from a cognitive approach to general learning theory and provides a useful "line drawing" that explains why evocative empathy is effective, in words that a cognitive behaviorist would be comfortable with. Thus, this book grows out of the integration of the most influential streams of thought in counseling and therapy in academic settings in North America.

Starting with Carl Rogers' seminal work, therapist empathy has become recognized as essential in nearly all approaches to counseling and therapy. The essential truth that is often missed, however, is that truly accurate empathy goes far beyond simple reflection and is active, arousing, experiential, and evocative. It is this essential truth that this book tries to convey. The second tradition, learning theory, has usually found expression through behavior modification, but recent trends have placed greater emphasis on cognitive factors. This book argues that a perfectly respectable learning theorist can understand that both cognition and experiential knowing are important parts of behavior and that they are both deeply involved in counseling and therapy.

It is not a contradiction in terms to be an empathic learning theorist. As a general comment, one of the main differences between *Counseling and Therapy Skills* and other texts is the heavy emphasis here on presenting material that the reader can use—can translate into behavior. A second important emphasis is the clear message that therapy demands active involvement, that empathy must be evocative, and that the therapist must work at the leading edge of the client's experiencing. Therapy involves the integration of cognition and experiencing. Thus, my presentation is more personal and less academic. My students have often found that the material in other books is "testable" in the sense that they can write exam questions on the material but that the pedantic structure leaves them with only a vague understanding of what to do. They often are left with the common misunderstanding that empathy is relatively passive.

In order to offer readers a more complete understanding of conducting therapy using the evocative empathy approach, I have created a DVD called "Observing Therapy." The DVD is five hours long and contains an introduction and videotaped excerpts of actual therapy sessions with three clients. You can read more about the DVD in the "About the DVD" section at the very end of the book.

I would like to thank Jeni Ogilvie of Waveland Press for her remarkably perceptive, thorough editing that clarified material that otherwise might have been confusing to readers. More importantly, Jeni was consistently supportive and very empathic when I most needed to feel understood in the editing process. I am grateful for Neil Rowe's gentle but persistent encouragement that gave this book new life at Waveland Press. I also appreciate the support and enthusiasm of Claire Verduin, Raphah Berg, and Joan Marsh, who were involved in the birth of this book's first edition. I thank Caelin White for his help in writing chapter 14, "Taking Care of Yourself." I also thank my friend, great listener, and colleague, Ed Johnson, who made many helpful suggestions on the manuscript, especially for chapter 16, "The Nature of Emotional Problems," which now makes a lot more sense.

Finally, Patti Barss has given me essential feedback on the book, a place to discuss and understand therapy better, and—most importantly—a foundation place from which to go out and live life.

David G. Martin

Developing Basic Skills

The Third Alternative
Evocative Empathy

I hope that this book will start you on the way to becoming a great therapist. In the process of getting started, we will be learning some skills together, but the first thing I need to say is that approaching therapy as just a set of skills or techniques will probably get in the way of your becoming an excellent therapist. The quality of the therapeutic relationship is far more important than whatever techniques the therapist uses. Whiston and Sexton (1993) reviewed research on therapy outcome and said, "More than any other element to date, the therapeutic relationship is significantly related to positive client outcome" (p. 45). *The connection heals.* It almost seems too simple to be true, but the most powerful factor in therapy is that the client feels deeply known and accepted. The client will also be doing *emotional reprocessing* and *increasing self-awareness* on the path to healing, but this is unlikely to happen without a good therapeutic relationship.

We will see also see that there is an artistic, intuitive aspect to therapy that is difficult to understand and almost impossible to express on paper. A helpful analogy can be drawn with learning to draw or paint. Most people can learn to draw fairly well by learning skills such as perspective drawing and shading. Few people, however, can produce art. Becoming an artist probably has something to do with innate talent, and it certainly has much to do with hard work and practice. First, the artist learned the basic skills, but that only made him or her an adequate painter or drawer. Most of us can probably become fairly good therapists by learning basic skills. Becoming the excellent therapist you want to be will start with basic skills, but be careful not to confuse these "training wheels" with the artistry of therapy. Having said that, let's look at the foundational skill of psychotherapy.

It has been my experience that beginning therapists feel they have only two options in responding to their clients. Some see "empathy" as some kind of warm and supportive reflection of what the client has just said, and others think they need to gather evidence and give advice, reassurance, and clever interpretations. Neither of these approaches works very well, but they seem to be the only ones that life prepares us for. There is a third alternative, a skill

3

that will not be easy to learn and that will feel awkward at first, but one you need to master if you want to be a good counselor or therapist. The most important goal of this book is to get you started toward this mastery. There seems to be no clear label for this skill, but I think Laura Rice's (1974) "evocative empathy" comes closest. To say it plainly, this skill is the fundamental skill for doing therapy. There will be many other things you will have to do, and there will be many times when evocative empathy is not appropriate, but for any of the other things to work, you must first make your client feel deeply understood, especially at the emotional level.

I am about to give you a formal definition of empathy that will sound pretty simplistic, sterile, and cold, but I will spend a couple of hundred pages warming up that definition. Empathy is "communicated understanding of the other person's intended message, especially the experiential/emotional part." Every word counts in this definition. It is not enough to understand what the person said; you must hear what he or she *meant* to say, the intended message. It is not enough to understand, even deeply; you must communicate that understanding somehow. It is absolutely essential that the other person feel understood—that the understanding be perceived (Barrett-Lennard, 1993, 1997). The part of the intended message that will be critical is the emotional or experiential part of the message; therapy is both an intellectual and an emotional process, and it is dealing with feelings that will be the most trouble for your client (and maybe for you and me). You will be listening for what your client is trying to say, and one way you will be doing this is to hear the feelings implicit in his or her message.

The business of therapy often involves some pretty painful stuff, and it is easier to talk in cognitive terms. A client might say, "It's not fair when less-qualified people at work are given promotions." At one level, this is an entirely accurate statement of fact about simple justice. Obviously, however, it is a very feelingful message—implicitly. Your job as the therapist is to bring the feelings to life in a way that leaves your client with the sense that you understand what was meant. You might say, "I guess you're feeling cheated by that." Let me explain my thinking as the therapist here. There are two steps I went through: First, I had to understand what was meant, and so I was naming to myself several possibilities, such as feeling anger, hurt, and cheated. I tried to get a sense of which of these possible feelings the person wanted me to hear. Second, I had to find the words to let him know that I understood.

I could have been "behind" him with a simple reflection like "There's no justice in a situation like that." Although this response wouldn't do any damage, it wouldn't be much help either, because it does nothing with the client's *reactions*. It is easier to talk about things outside ourselves in objective ways, and this includes the way we talk about feelings. You might have been tempted to word your response as, "That kind of situation can certainly arouse feelings of being cheated." This is more effective than "There's no justice in a situation like that" but less effective than "I guess you're feeling cheated by that." The difference may be subtle, but it is crucial. In one case we are talking about feelings as things, objectively, as though they can be aroused. In the other, we are naming a particular person's particular reaction in the here and now. We are bringing an experience to life.

You might be thinking that my response to my client is pretty tame, since there are lots of other feelings that could be present, consciously or unconsciously. Besides, how do we know that he is not distorting the justice of the situation? Perhaps we should confront him with this or at least get some more information from him about whether the people promoted really were less qualified. You will have to trust me on this for now, but I guarantee you that the fastest way to get to your clients' truth, and to get there in a way that will help them, is by helping them face the leading edge of what they are trying to say but can't quite say. The critical guideline is the phrase "the intended message." Maybe my client does feel more than cheated. Maybe he feels furious or hopeless or vengeful, but I have to be able to sense what he is trying to say right now and help him articulate that.

■ Lead or Follow?

Sometimes therapy approaches can be described as "leading" or "following" styles, but this distinction is inappropriate for understanding the nature of evocative empathy. In one sense you are following your clients, because it is not your job to determine the content or topic of what is talked about. You are not urging certain issues to the front; you are listening with focused intensity for where your clients are trying to go. In another sense, you are leading, since to be most effective, you stay one step ahead by dealing with what your clients only implied.

I hope it is becoming clear that there is a critical region where therapy takes place. If you lead too far, you will get off the track, take over the direction of therapy, threaten your clients into needing their defenses against you, and probably start giving lousy advice. If you just repeat your clients' words (or worse, are behind them and deaden the process), they might as well be talking to their dog, who probably will do them more good just by being nonjudgmental. I'm being too harsh, of course, because sometimes you will have to give advice and offer opinions, and sometimes being right with your client will be just the right thing to do. My concern is, though, that these are the things you will do most of time, when effective therapy requires that you concentrate on making the implicit explicit.

A question that often arises here is whether the therapist has to wait for the client to say something before dealing with it, and isn't that inefficient? This question grows out of a misunderstanding of evocative empathy as passive. If you waited for your client to say everything explicitly, it would be inefficient and probably quite frustrating for both of you. If, however, you have "good ears" and can hear what the client is hinting at, you will seldom be repeating the client's words. In one sense, you will be leading, but in another you will not, because the ideas and emotions you articulate will be ones your client is thinking and will recognize them as such. One goal of your response is that your clients think, "Oh, right, exactly, . . . that's just what I meant." Or perhaps, "That is what I'm saying, but it hits hard to hear you put it that way." They don't always say this out loud, of course, but it is rewarding feedback to get. It lets you know that you're working well.

■ Levels of Empathy

Some writers have used terms like *additive responses* (Hammond, Hepworth, & Smith, 2002) and *advanced empathy* (Egan, 2004) to describe approximately what I am talking about. Usually, however, these responses are prescribed only for later in therapy, after a strong relationship has been established. Some (Carkhuff, 1969) caution that too much empathy early in therapy can create so much anxiety for the client that therapy is hampered. If you understand what I am saying, however, you will see that therapy doesn't progress in stages, with different kinds of understanding appropriate for different stages; it progresses along a continuum. Your guideline to this continuum is in the phrase "the intended message."

Of course, later in therapy the therapist can go a lot further and make much more emotionally poignant statements—because the client intends for the therapist to hear so much more then. The principle is still the same as it was early in the process; you articulate what the other person meant to be communicating. Early in the relationship, the other person will be cautiously building trust in you, not intending that you see or hear everything. But you still can go beyond the actual words spoken without threatening your client. Nearly every statement has some implicit meanings in its message. Whether you know the person well or have just met, your most effective response, the response that will make the other person feel most deeply understood, will be to put into words what he or she meant.

This means that you will sound quite different later in therapy, since the client will have given you so much more to work with. An outside observer might describe you as more passive earlier in therapy and almost interpretive later in therapy, but relative to what the client is trying to say, you will be doing about the same things in both situations.

■ Evocative Empathy and Interpretation

There are some strong resemblances between evocative reflections and what psychoanalytic therapists refer to as moderate interpretations or interpretations at the preconscious level. They are not the same thing, however, and it is important that you understand why. The intentions of the therapist who uses one of the techniques are different from the therapist who uses the other, and consequently, the process for the client is different.

When an interpretation is given to the client from the therapist's frame of reference in order to point out relationships and insights that the "more perceptive" therapist understands better than the client, the therapist is the source of the solution. The empathic therapist, in contrast, sees the client as the source, sees the client as the problem solver. Of course, the empathic therapist has to do some internal "interpreting" in the sense that hearing the implicit message requires drawing inferences, making connections, and seeing subtle relationships. This ability to hear with the "third ear" (Reik, 1948) is one of the two basic skills you must learn. (The other is finding the words to express your understanding.) The empathic therapist's *intent*, however, is not to guide the client cleverly toward the truth but to bring the client's experiencing to life, so the client will deal with it and find his or her own truth—accurately know his or her own experience.

Some of these differences are pointed out strikingly by Karl Menninger, a famous analytically oriented therapist. He says: "It is helpful to some young analysts to have it put thus: One tells a patient what the patient *almost* sees for himself and one tells him in such a way that the patient—not the analyst—takes the 'credit' for the discovery" (1958, p. 134). In some ways, Menninger's description of the timing of interpretations is remarkably similar to the process I have been describing, and I suspect that his therapy was effective and sounded very much like that of effective empathic therapists. The sharpest difference, of course, lies between Menninger's view of the therapist's role as the expert who really brings out the truth and the view that the client is capable of finding the truth with a specific kind of help from the therapist; the client truly does deserve the credit for the discovery.

Laura Rice (1974) says it well:

> Evocative reflection is not the same as an interpretation. Although a "good" interpretation and a "good" evocative response may sound very similar, the aim of the reflection is different; attempts to demonstrate their similarity only serve to blur a worthwhile distinction. . . . The aim of an interpretation is to go beyond the client's statement, to point out patterns and connections, and to offer to the client new ways of viewing his experience. The aim of an evocative reflection is to open up the experience and provide the client with a process whereby he can form successively more accurate constructions of his own experience. (p. 290)

Barkham and Shapiro (1986) studied reactions to therapists' responses that were categorized as reflection, exploration, or interpretation. They referred to "exploration" responses as "medium-depth" therapist comments characterized by "reformulation" and "nonjudgmental labeling." Exploration sounds very similar to evocative empathy because it is neither a simple reflection (following the client) nor an interpretation (leading the client), but it is both. Their research found a "considerably greater impact of exploration than of either reflection or interpretation on client-recalled understanding events for ongoing sessions. . . . The impact of exploration was even more marked during initial sessions" (p. 9).

It seems likely that if interpretive and empathic therapists really did sound just alike and differed only in their intentions, it would make little difference to clients or to the process of therapy. Clients' perceptions of their therapists as empathic, caring, and honest are among the best predictors of successful therapy, as we will see in chapter 18. Therapists' intentions, however, get reflected in behavior. Greenberg and Elliott (1997) offer a good example. "It may be that the same words (e.g., "You're feeling angry because therapy is ending") could be either an interpretation or an empathic response, depending on the therapist's intention" (p. 170). Differences in wording, inflection, and responses to content do appear between interpretive and empathic therapists, and these do affect therapy.

■ Empathy Is Not Sympathy

It is common to confuse empathy with a lot of other attributes, such as personal warmth, caring for another person, agreeing with the other person, and sympathy. These qualities may appear with empathy, but they are not the same as empathy (Irving & Dickson, 2006). I can be empathic with a person whose presence I can barely stand, who disagrees with me, and for whom I feel no sympathy. It would be difficult, but it could be done, because empathy just says: "I understand what you are trying to say and how you feel, and I would articulate it this way." The purpose of empathy is to help the other person face his or her experience—to face what he or she feels and thinks but can't quite look at clearly. In doing this, I am not saying that I see it the same way or that I agree with it. I am also not saying that I care for or respect the other person, just as a result of being empathic, although respect and dependable acceptance are crucial parts of therapy. We will talk about these relationship issues later; for now, I want to make it clear that empathy and acceptance are different from each other, even though they usually go together.

Most important, empathy is not sympathy. Sympathy implies pity; empathy implies trust. I am saying to my client that he or she is strong enough to solve problems, that I will not condescend pityingly, and that our work together is not just hand holding.

■ This Is Hard Work: Empathy Is Not Passive

Good therapy is an active process that demands concentration, feeling, quick thinking, and an ability to sense another person's emotions.

Probably the most common misunderstanding of empathy is that it is supposed to be passive. This misunderstanding is so pervasive that I almost hesitate to mention the enormous debt that empathy-oriented therapy owes to Carl Rogers. It has been my experience that people instantly associate his name with passivity, although that is clearly not what he meant his approach to imply. As long ago as 1942, he said:

> Often the client has attitudes which are implied in what he says or which
> the counselor through shrewd observation judges him to have. Recogni-

tion of such attitudes which have not yet appeared in the client's conversation may, if the attitudes are not too deeply repressed, hasten the progress of therapy. (p. 173)

He probably would be more comfortable with his later wording of the same thought.

[Empathy] involves being sensitive, moment to moment, to the changing felt meanings which flow in this other person, to the fear or rage or tenderness or confusion or whatever, that he/she is experiencing. It means temporarily living in his/her life, moving about in it delicately without making judgments, sensing meanings of which he/she is scarcely aware, but not trying to uncover feelings of which the person is totally unaware, since this would be too threatening. (Rogers, 1975, p. 4)

He gives a common-sense test for when empathy is accurately sensitive.

If the therapist has communicated a superficial understanding of the client's expression, the client's inner response and perhaps verbal response will be "Of course. That's what I just said." Clearly, this has not done much to advance self-exploration. When the therapist has communicated an effectively empathic response, the client's reaction is likely to be "That's exactly right! I didn't suppose anyone could understand what I really meant. Now I wish to tell you some more." When the therapist is exceptionally effective and has caught the subtle meanings on the edge of the client's awareness, the client's reaction is likely to be first a pause, then a gradual appreciation: "Yes, I think you're right! I had never thought of it in just that way before, but that is what I've been feeling and experiencing. And now I see some more." (Rogers, 1980, p. 2155)

There is an old and not very amusing joke about Rogers that illustrates this misunderstanding. Maybe I shouldn't tell it, but better you should hear it from me than from some kid on the street who will have it all wrong. The client says "I feel so depressed," and Rogers replies "Your feeling is unhappiness."

"I am going to end it all."

"You feel like committing suicide."

The client goes to sit on the ledge of an open window and says, "This is it. I'm going to jump."

"You feel like jumping right now."

The client jumps, and Rogers leans out the window and says "Plop." Rogers was asked about this joke, and as the interviewer (Hall, 1967) started to tell it, he replied (with, I would guess, barely muffled annoyance), "I know the story. My answer, for once and for all time, is that I would not have let him jump out the window" (p. 66). He has been "more than a little horrified at the interpretation of my approach which has sometimes crept into the teaching and training of counselors. . . . A wooden technique of pseudo-understanding in which the counselor reflects back what the client has just said" (Rogers, 1962, p. 420).

One interchange between client and therapist actually sounded like this:

CLIENT: All you ever do is repeat back what I just said.

THERAPIST: You feel that all I ever do is repeat your words to you.

C: There! You're doing it right now.

T: You feel that I am doing it right at this moment.

This painfully awful exchange continued for several more lines, but I can't stand it anymore. The therapist had read a little about "reflection," figured it was easy to do, and set out to do good. You, however, would have been listening for the implicit message in what the client said and would have responded with something like, "I think you mean I can be pretty frustrating, that I just leave you to wallow around in this stuff, which is pretty hard to deal with. I guess my passivity annoys you a lot." Actually, you likely wouldn't be in this fix, since your evocative responding would not have been "saying back what I just said." However, you will face similar situations when clients find you frustrating or annoying. It will be difficult to hear the attack on you because of your own feelings of being threatened, but you should listen for the implied meaning and put it into words.

A common feeling among new therapists is that they are redundant, that their clients really would do just as well talking to a nice cocker spaniel. The temptation is to start "doing more to the client" to feel that the therapist has a useful and powerful role to fill. This almost inevitably means offering interpretations, advice, confrontations, questions, homework assignments, and rational analyses. Then the therapist feels useful. When these don't work the therapist might drop back to passive reflections, until the frustration of uselessness sets in again. I can promise you two things. First, you probably don't yet know how to give evocative empathy (unless you are a very rare beginning therapist), and so you are not in a position to say it doesn't work and is frustratingly passive. Second, as you become better at it, you will find your contribution to the process rewarding and active and plenty difficult enough to satisfy your need to be "doing something."

It used to bother me when a client would say, at the end of therapy, "I feel good that I was able to do this myself. You didn't really solve my problems for me." Of course this is the perfect way for the client to feel, and my being bothered was just from my own need for recognition of the fact that I thought I had been working pretty hard. One goal of therapy is the client's independence, however, and it really did please me when one client said, "I did this myself. You never did anything but repeat back what I said, but you said it a little stronger." Perfect. He perceived what I said as really his message, just said in a little different way that made its impact stronger.

As a therapist, you will be an expert on a process, not on the nature and content of a particular person's problems.

One last thought about therapy being a demanding enterprise: some therapists do damage. I will discuss this at length in later chapters, but it is important that you know that therapy can be helpful or it can leave the client worse off than she or he would have been without therapy. This sobering thought should lead you to work hard at becoming as good as you can, to be as open as you can to the sometimes threatening process of the growth you face in becoming an effective helper.

■ Rating the "Core Conditions"

I have focused on evocative empathy in this chapter, partly because it is fundamental and partly because it is the most "teachable" of the fundamental approaches a therapist must offer his or her clients. I will be talking about many other aspects of being a therapist throughout the book, and a brief summary of part of what lies ahead will be helpful. A number of writers have built on Rogers' early work to outline the "core conditions" essential to good therapy (Carkhuff & Berenson, 1967, 1977; Elliott & Freire, 2007; Hammond, Hepworth, & Smith, 2002; Patterson, 1974; Patterson & Hidore, 1997; Rennie, 1998; Rogers, Gendlin, Kiesler, & Truax, 1967; Truax & Carkhuff, 1967). Another purpose of this summary section is to introduce you to one of the rating scales that have been designed to operationalize therapist empathy.

The core "helper dimensions," another term for the "core conditions," are accurate empathy, respect for the client, and genuineness. The core "helpee dimensions"—the client's jobs—are exploration, understanding, and action (Carkhuff & Berenson, 1967, 1977).

I have already discussed empathy to some extent. Briefly, *respect* is reflected in the dependable acceptance the therapist gives the client, a nonjudgmental openness to let the client think, feel, and say whatever he or she is experiencing without losing the sense that the therapist accepts him or her as a person with worth. *Genuineness* is difficult to define but generally means that the therapist is not phony and merely relating within a role. Many writers go beyond this definition to talk about "authenticity" and "openness," topics I will discuss in chapter 6.

Each of these dimensions involves therapist behavior that can be described operationally, and rating scales have been developed to permit quantified judgments of therapist behavior within the session. These scales were developed for research purposes, but they are also widely used for training, since they specify behaviors, rather than using only abstract descriptions. Because the empathy scale is especially useful for our purposes, we will look at it now.

■ One Way to Describe Empathic Behavior

Several empathy scales have been developed and validated (Burns, 1995; Carkhuff, 1969; Rogers, Gendlin, Kiesler, & Truax, 1967; Truax & Carkhuff, 1967; Vanaerschot & Lietaer, 2007), but I will draw most heavily from Robert

Carkhuff's (1969) five-point scale, which reduces some of the ambiguity of previous scales and is designed to be applicable to all human relations. The scale is based on observable behaviors, so that raters listening to tape recordings can reliably judge the degree of empathy being communicated, and this behavioral focus should also be helpful to you as you try to learn the skill. In chapter 18 we will learn some of the complexities and limitations of using these scales in research. We will also discover that clients' perceptions of understanding and acceptance in their therapist are more strongly related to successful therapy than are ratings done by observers using these scales. My only purpose now is to give you some idea of the skills you will be trying to learn.

Levels 1 and 2 describe nonempathic behavior, and so I will discuss them later. Briefly, a "1" is a response from the therapist's frame of reference that ignores the client's message, and a "2" is an attempt to understand that responds to the client's message but in a way that lessens its impact. Level 3 is what I would call a response right at or slightly behind where the client is working: the therapist responds only to the explicitly stated content and feeling of the client's response.

> *Level 3.* The expressions of the first person (therapist) in response to the expressed feelings of the second person(s) (client) are essentially *interchangeable* with those of the second person in that they express essentially the same affect and meaning. (Carkhuff, 1969, p. 316)

This level of responding is often called the "minimally facilitative" level. The therapist is responding to the surface expressions only and either does not hear or ignores feelings implicit in the client's response. This kind of response is not bad; it is just minimally facilitative. It can express the therapist's interest in a nonthreatening way and set the stage for later exploration. It is often the most appropriate response to make. The therapist who always responds at this level, however, will have disappointing results.

> *Level 4.* The responses of the first person add noticeably to the expressions of the second person(s) in such a way as to express feelings a level deeper than the second person was able to express himself. (p. 316)

Here the therapist is adding at least something new from what was implicit in the client's intended message. The therapist must have been able to hear what the client was trying to say. The client might have said, for example, "When I left home, my mother didn't even say good-bye." A level-3 response to the explicit content might have been, "Not even a good-bye at a time when good-byes were called for." The more deeply empathic therapist would have responded to the whole message, hearing nonverbal clues to what the client meant, clues we can't hear or see on paper. "Sounds like you were standing there waiting . . . for a good-bye that would mean she cared and then felt pretty empty when not even that came."

> *Level 5.* The first person's responses add significantly to the feeling and meaning of the expressions of the second person(s) in such a way as to (1)

accurately express feelings below what the person himself was able to express or (2) in the event of ongoing deep self-exploration on the second person's part, to be fully with him in his deepest moments. (p. 317)

The differences between levels 4 and 5 are largely differences in the degree to which the therapist has added to the client's message; a "5" brings the message to vivid life, restating it with precision, deep feeling, and the unique nuances that are part of the client's experience. It is critical that level-5 responses must still be responses to the client's intended communication if they are to be defined as empathic. Going beyond what the client can recognize as part of the message is going into interpretations. Accurate level-5 responses may be the most therapeutic, but they require considerable finesse at hearing the client accurately, and they are not common, even in the best therapy.

When the therapist goes beyond the intended message, he or she begins to respond from his or her own preconceived notions and enters what I would call interpretations and level 1 on the empathy scale. This includes introducing new material, pointing out inconsistencies, contradicting the client, and suggesting explanations that the client hasn't suggested. Occasionally, each of these approaches might be helpful, but only rarely. I will argue repeatedly that these are the easy things for us intellectually oriented therapists to do, but they are not the most helpful.

> *Level 1.* The verbal and behavioral expressions of the first person either *do not attend to or detract significantly* from the verbal and behavioral expressions of the second person(s) in that they communicate significantly less of the second person's feelings than the second person has communicated himself. . . . The first person may be bored or uninterested or simply operating from a preconceived frame of reference which totally excludes that of the other person(s). (p. 315)

A level-1 response simply shows no empathic intent on the therapist's part. A level-2 response, in contrast, is an attempt to be empathic but one that detracts from or distorts what the client communicates.

> *Level 2.* While the first person responds to the expressed feelings of the second person(s), he does so in such a way *that subtracts noticeable affect from the communications* of the second person. The first person may communicate some awareness of obvious surface feelings of the second person but his communications drain off a level of the affect and distort the level of meaning. The first person may communicate his own ideas of what may be going on but these are not congruent with the expressions of the second person. (p. 315)

Level-2 responses will slip into your therapy at times when you don't expect them. Your client might say "For the first time in my life, I'm feeling good about myself . . . liking myself." You respond "So you see real progress in the direction you're going." Your response is not inaccurate, but it is dampening. Your client was expressing feelings, and you responded with a cognitive generalization.

At the risk of making our discussions mechanistic, we can refer to therapist responses as "3s" or "just less than a 3," because it can be a useful shorthand if we all understand the complexity of what the shorthand means. This can get silly, though, with references to "threeish" therapists and "that's a 3.65." Actually, it can get more than silly if we lose sight of our real purpose—making the client feel deeply understood.

To close this section, Carkhuff and Berenson (1977) report a disconcerting study that should motivate you to work hard at developing your skills. It is not likely that these skills are a natural part of your behavior right now.

The modal (most common) level of functioning in interpersonal skills among general and professional populations was assessed. The general public and college freshmen scored at 1.5, nurses and teachers at 1.7, guidance counselors at 1.9, graduate students in psychology at 2.1, trained subprofessional and subdoctoral helpers at 2.7, and functioning professionals with advanced training in the skills at 4.0. If level 3 really is "minimally facilitative," we're in a little trouble.

■ What's Wrong with Rating Scales

The goal of evocative empathy is to make the client feel deeply understood. There are many ways to make a client feel understood, and we are in danger of losing sight of that now that we have a scale of "good responses." A five is only a good response if it makes the client feel understood. I have heard a few therapists say things like, "That was a pretty good session. I had a good number of fours." This puts the focus on the therapist's skillfulness and is not likely to make the client feel understood.

Under some circumstances, I can imagine a client feeling deeply understood if the therapist said, "I don't believe you." These would be rare circumstances, but the client might have been testing the therapist's honesty, and the therapist might have responded "I don't believe you" with a knowing smile that left the client feeling, "This person really knows me and will be straight with me. She knew exactly what I meant." This therapist response would receive a rating of one on the empathy scale, but it could have been the most empathic response possible. I certainly don't recommend saying "I don't believe you" to clients regularly, but I also don't want you "working to get more fours into my responses." Do whatever makes your client feel *known*.

CHAPTER 2

Learning to Hear

Responding effectively requires two abilities: you must be able to hear well and then you must be quick enough to articulate what you have heard. In addition, responding effectively means your client must perceive your understanding (Barrett-Lennard, 1993, 1997). These are difficult skills, and sometimes people who do one well have trouble with the others. Most people, however, have to work hard at each one until experience and practice make them come easily and naturally.

I can't decide which one beginning therapists have the more trouble with. Often, when role-playing therapy or listening to or watching a recording of a session, I have stopped to ask the struggling new therapist to sit and think for a minute what the client was feeling when he or she said the last response. Usually, the therapist can name, fairly accurately, some of the client's feelings but then says, "I knew that, but I couldn't find the words to say it right." So you may feel the most awkwardness and frustration at the task of learning to articulate. With practice (and only with practice, by the way), you will get better at this; articulating responses is a trainable skill.

Learning to hear the implicit message, however, may be easier only at the beginning, when it seems reasonably easy to name some general feelings such as anger, fear, and happiness. Your job is going to be to hear subtle nuances and the complexities of unique experiences. A psychiatrist I know says he can spot the new psychiatric residents who will be able to do therapy because they have a natural empathy that he doesn't think the others will be able to learn. I don't think the issue is quite this discouraging, but developing this sensitivity to the experiencing of others probably will take more time and experience than your other therapeutic skills. I can remember listening to a tape of one of the therapists who trained me and thinking, "Where did he get that? She didn't say that," when he responded to a client. The client answered something like "Exactly," and I knew I had a long way to go.

■ Basic Listening Skills

I have started this book at a full run, discussing evocative empathy in all its complexity. It is likely, however, that you have to start at a simpler level, and much of what you will do in therapy probably will be and should be at a simpler level. You will be using basic listening skills.

Attending

The first requirement for listening is that you pay attention to the other person. This may seem obvious, but many social interchanges are marked by a detached passivity in which the "listener" is just waiting for the other person to stop talking in order to get his or her next speech into the conversation. Attending is marked by a focused intensity. The listener's posture says, "I am interested. I am listening." Eye contact is frequent, and the therapist may be leaning a bit toward the client in an open and relaxed manner. Don't take this physical description too seriously, though. If you are thinking about the angle of your torso to the chair and your rate of eye-blinks, you won't be attending, no matter how good you look. Be focused, interested, and really trying to hear, and your body will take care of itself. OK, the truth is that I usually sit back, sometimes with my feet on the coffee table in my office. Sometimes I even tip back in my chair, in spite of the best efforts of my mother and my wife to teach me otherwise. But I am still attending with a focused intensity.

Even your voice's tonal quality will be communicating whether or not you're attending. If you are listening hard, your voice will come out more solid, and if you're not, there will be an empty, just-here-doing-my-job quality to it. Again, though, you cannot fake this quality; it will be there if you are attending.

I have been critical of passivity in the therapist, and rightly so, but in the process I have underestimated the power of focused attending. It is a rare thing in most human relationships to be listened to, and it can make a person feel valued and can free that person to explore new thoughts. The first client I ever saw said, at the end of fairly successful therapy, "I never knew it could be so much help just to have somebody listen to me." I was lucky, of course, to start out with such a good client, and this "compliment" really meant I wasn't all that hot as a therapist, but he was right in that focused listening can be helpful.

Acknowledgment Responses

Your goal is to make the client feel understood, and one way to do this, as he or she explores and thinks and feels, is to use short responses that simply say "I am with you, keep going." Phrases like "I see . . . I understand that . . . OK . . . Uh huh" can serve this function, and so can one- or two-word offerings that complete a sentence or are synonyms for something the client just said. Acknowledgment responses can include nods of the head and gestures. Acknowledgment responses say "I understand," but they don't prove it. The proof of understanding comes from articulated responses.

Reciprocal/Maintenance Responses

Probably the most frequent therapist response is the "reciprocal response" (Hammond, Hepworth, & Smith, 2002) or the "maintenance response" (Rice, 1974). These are level-3 responses from Carkhuff's rating scale; they are essentially interchangeable with what the client has said, both in feeling and in content. Sometimes maintenance responses are nearly exact repeats of what the client said, but those often sound so trite that the therapist usually paraphrases the client's message. One woman who didn't understand about paraphrasing tried to apply some of these skills in her home relationships (generally a good idea, since they are the foundation of all relationships) until her teenage daughter finally said, "Mother, what's wrong with you? Have you gone nuts? All you've been doing this last week is repeating everything I say."

The goal of a reciprocal response is to make the other person feel understood, and a good paraphrase is often the best way to do this. Hammond, Hepworth, and Smith (2002) say that reciprocal responses should be thought of as the therapist's "baseline" response and that "additive" responses (evocative empathy) should be done carefully and generally later in therapy. I agree that later in therapy the therapist will be using more complete and evocative language; an outside observer might say the therapist was being more "additive." *Relative to the client*, however, the therapist is working similarly in both instances. The goal is the same for the early as for the later responses—to articulate the intended message. It's difficult to do, but you need to be able to sense what it is that the client wants you to hear, what he or she is *trying to say*. Early in therapy, this will often be just about what the client has said explicitly, and a fancy response with lots of emotions and imagery could be beyond what was intended.

In chapter 1, I said that these level-3 responses are usually called "minimally facilitative" responses. This phrase seems derogatory unless we pay attention to the "facilitative." Very few people interact at a "3" level, and as we will discouragingly discover in chapter 18, research indicates that very few therapists operate at even this level. Reciprocal responses are facilitative. They hold up to the client what he or she has just said and help the client face the thoughts involved. Clients often will surprise you by denying that what you responded was what they said at all, even though you felt you were just repeating it back. Hearing another person say what we just said often makes us look at our statement from a different perspective.

Thus, paraphrasing what your client has said can be helpful, and even if this was all you ever did, you probably would have some success as a therapist. The problem is that it is slower than therapy needs to be. You certainly need to develop the ability to give your client reciprocal maintenance responses; in fact, this is probably the level at which you will start working. Then we can work on fine-tuning you, helping you learn to make the implicit explicit.

■ Hearing the Implicit Message

Learning to hear what another person has said is difficult. Hearing what the person was trying to say—what was meant—is even more difficult.

First Look for Reactions—Emotions Are the Foundation

If the client says, "People today just don't care about each other," you might paraphrase this as, "It's sort of a sign of the times how indifferent people are to each other." Not bad, but you haven't dealt with the *implicit reactions or emotions*. Stop reading for a minute and name the feelings intended by the client to be implicit in the comment. You might have said, "I guess it saddens you to see all that indifference," and I think the client would have had the internal reaction that we are aiming for. He would have recognized that as what he meant, and you would have taken him a step forward, because the statement was not only a cognitive observation; you named the feelings implied in it. That is your job.

We could have gone further with our response, of course. In our cleverness we might figure that actually the client is talking about loneliness and feeling not cared about, and ultimately we might be right. If we go beyond what our clients intended, however, we will slow therapy down by threatening them with our expertness and with their own thoughts that are frightening enough that they need to defend against them. The difficult trick is to be ahead of clients as far as we can get without going beyond what they will recognize as part of the intended message, as part of current experiencing.

Clear-cut examples are difficult to think of, and I am aware that this last example could be misleading. I can easily imagine a client I knew well saying "People today just don't care about each other" and meaning far more than "This indifference between people saddens me." I might well draw on things the client has said in the past and respond "And that's what gets to you so much . . . you reach out and ask to be cared about, and all you get is coldness back." Whether this response will be effective depends on what the client was trying to say and what he assumed I already knew. If he is assuming I know this past information, I have gone well beyond the client's factual statement, but I have not given an interpretation; I brought the implied experience to life.

Laura Rice says, "The first principle for evocative responding is that the therapist should listen for and respond to reactions, either explicit or implicit" (1974, p. 303). This is your first guideline for learning to hear. Read some of the client statements in Appendix A and, without looking at the therapist's response, name the feelings implicit in the statements. If you are able to, watch or listen to recordings of therapy and stop the recording after a client statement so you can practice naming reactions—feelings explicit and implicit. Try for a moment to suppress your own need for intellectual understanding of the causes of the client's behavior; stop trying to put some overall "sensible" structure on things; just practice knowing what another person is saying about his or her reactions in the present moment.

Understand the Impact on the Client

One helpful way to think of the client's message is to imagine it at three levels: (1) what is the story, (2) what are the implications of the story, and (3) what is the *impact* of the story on the client. The most powerful part of the message to hear is the third one. Many students find the word "impact" especially helpful in knowing what to listen for. How is this hitting the client?

I only recently realized how helpful the phrase "what is the impact on the client?" is to beginning therapists learning to "hear" at the experiential level. In supervision, I was using phrases like "what is going on inside the client right now?", "what is the client feeling?", "what is the client's emotion?", and these still are useful phrases. But a group of us were discussing how hard it is to listen at this third, experiential, level when I casually suggested the word "impact." Several students reacted immediately with some version of, "Now I get it in a powerful way." I asked them to write something about why the word "impact" was so helpful and would like to share some of their thoughts with you. We'll start with Karen O'Brien:

> The word itself, impact, has a feeling for me. I can feel it inside when someone says the word so I am immediately put into a "feeling" condition.
>
> The word "impact" implies action . . . how do I think what the client is saying "changed" their feelings? to indifference? to fear? to excitement? to optimism? What is the impact of saying whatever the client is saying having on them right now? Because there is always a reaction to impact (even if it is no reaction, which, in the world of feelings, is a reaction and can say a lot), and because I so clearly feel the word in that way, it gives me a way to feel myself into what the client is saying without having to think myself into it. I just have to let myself "feel" the impact of the client's words, experience, thoughts, expressions, body language, whatever . . . and then check with the client to see if I am with them in feeling the impact.
>
> Somehow, when the word "impact" is working well, it centers me in my feelings and gets me out of my head. When I am in the right frame of mind and consider the impact of what a client is saying, it seems to move me into an experiential sharing with the client. I can then move from there back into my head to respond.
>
> On a personal note, I have to work to get my head out of the way and to let this experiential sharing happen!

These students had watched me doing therapy live (with the client's permission, of course), and Tevya Hunter linked her observations about me doing therapy with her reaction to the word *impact*:

> We are taught to listen for the *emotion* . . . how the person is feeling. I think the difficulty with this stems from the fact that emotion is a loaded word for a few reasons:
>
> 1. People don't know emotion words, how to label them, or how to talk about them.
> 2. Emotions tend to scare a lot of people . . . they shy away from them.
> 3. We feel pressure (although we shouldn't) to respond after every statement, and we don't have enough emotion words for that.

I think the word *impact* opens up more options for the response. What is the client's story telling you, how is it affecting them? This may include emotions but it also involves other things. A client might be in a situation that makes them feel *mad* and they seem to be expressing *anger*, but as a whole the story they are telling is really making them frustrated (the overall impact is frustration). It's still about how they are feeling but it's in a broader sense. Personally, I feel looking for an emotion is too constraining, too specific. Impact is broader and more all encompassing.

I remember this impact comment stemming from an observation about how you do therapy. Your responses seldom actually involve emotion words. They are often observations about how a story and situation is making the client feel at that moment. . . . "that really touches you"; "that hurts." It seems to be about understanding the client at that specific moment—not about letting them know you understand the words that are coming out of their mouths, or the specific details of the narrative they are telling and the accompanying emotions, but about understanding the impact telling this story has on them. Maybe it's about how actually telling the story affects them more than how they felt at the time?

Emotion suggests a singular word (you are mad) whereas *impact* allows the therapist to expand beyond this to understand the entire situation probably often with many conflicting emotions.

Another thought: I think impact is a good mantra for the therapist to have. . . . I think it helps to consider the impact the client's story is having on you. It may be hard to feel another's emotions (especially if you have to do it daily), but to think about the impact the client's story is having on me helps me understand where they are coming from.

Finally, Kelley Robinson talked about trying to diminish intellectualizing and tune in to experiencing.

I guess the point is that two people could tell the exact same story but it would mean very different things to both of them. If a therapist's job was to be an expert, he or she would respond to both in the same way. But by tuning in and feeling what that story *means* to each client, by grasping the impact, they get into that emotional space where they can respond to the client's experience. Part of what was important to me in this was that if you do this properly, you don't have to try so hard not to intellectualize. It brings you into an experiencing space that makes the experiential responses more natural.

The Big Issue versus the Last 12 Words

One common error among beginning therapists is to lose sight of what the client means by focusing on the client's last few words, as though in making a "reflection" it would be illegal to go beyond what was just said. It is necessary to hear the whole message, which includes all the words actually said, as well as the tone of voice, the posture, and the assumed shared knowledge of what was said previously. Often, for example, a client will bring up an issue and then go into an elaborate illustration of it with the telling of an incident. The therapist is steadily following the story, responding to it, and articulating experiences within it, all the while having mentally "red flagged" the issue that brought the story up in the first place. The therapist is thinking, "What does all this mean to this person?"

Your client might start out talking about feelings of discouragement and then drift through a story about his best friend's father's depression over a business failure. You will be listening for the point of the story, red flagging the entry to the story so you can return to it. Then, not getting lost in details, you might say, "I see . . . what got you started on all this a few minutes ago was wondering whether all this studying is going to help you find anything meaningful in life. And then this story about your friend's father sort of illustrates how much life can be wasted. It's like you're asking, 'Am I going to waste my life?'" This response recognizes all of what the client was saying, but it stays on track by focusing on the main point of his message and by focusing on his reactions.

Nonverbal Communication

When I talked about attending, it was clear that much of your interest and caring will be expressed by the way you sit, where you are looking, and the tone of your voice. Similarly, much of the client's intended message will be expressed nonverbally, in subtle shadings of facial expression, in voice quality, in position and posture, and in small behaviors. Again, there is an important line between what are nonverbal parts of the intended message and what are meanings the therapist might be able to interpret from nonverbal cues that are not part of the message.

A client could say "She left without saying good-bye" in a tone of voice that communicated anger, indifference, hurt, pleasure, revenge, or any combination of these and other feelings. The words will be the same; the message will be entirely different in each case. Your client might say this with an angry voice and downcast eyes, and you might respond, "It's all a jumble of hurt and anger, isn't it?" You haven't said anything about anybody leaving without saying good-bye; it can be assumed that you heard that factual part of the message, because you went beyond it so accurately. You were able to go beyond it because you accurately read the voice tone and downcast eyes as part of what you were meant to hear.

What if your client grimly says, "When she left, she didn't even say good-bye, and I could not care less," but you pick up nonverbal cues that say there's a lot of caring going on? This is tricky. If you say, "Your words tell me one thing, that you don't care, and your clenched jaw tells me another, that you do care," you might be quite right and very clever, but the majority of times that you respond like this, you will slow your client down by being far enough ahead to threaten her. Actually, this technique of pointing out discrepancies will help occasionally, but the problem will be that you will remember the few times it worked and not notice the many times it slowed therapy down. There is an alternative, and it is not just passive acceptance of the verbal statement. Your job is to find some way to get as far ahead of the client as you can without losing what the client will recognize as part of the message. You might have said, "I guess you think about her leaving without even so much as the decency to say goodbye and feel 'Well, the hell with her,'" getting into your voice a strong hint of the feeling the client was expressing. This response does not intellectually point out discrepancies to the client; it does something far more powerful by holding up and bringing to life all of what the client has said. She has to recognize your response as a version of what she just said, and now there it is, in full color, and it has to be dealt with. You have used the nonverbal cues to hear the whole message and helped your client face it, without taking over as the expert showing the client the "truth."

Here and Now Can Include the Past

It should be obvious by now that this style of therapy is very much oriented toward present experiencing. The phrase "here and now" is most commonly used to describe this focus, and it captures the spirit of how therapy works. It is, however, often misunderstood to mean that we can deal only with issues in the historical present and leave the past for more psychoanalytically oriented therapists. This belief is based on a misunderstanding of both the empathic approach and more psychoanalytic approaches, which often do deal with the past but also stress activities like the reexperiencing of old hurts through "corrective emotional experiences" in therapy (Alexander, 1948).

I'll have to convince you later of the validity of this next statement but for now go along with me: your clients will try to talk about the things they need to talk about, and so you will not have to direct the topic of conversation. This may mean you will talk about issues in the present or in the past; that's not the point. What matters is reactions in the here and now. It happens very often that events from the past still have an enormous impact on a person, and it is this impact that is the focus of therapy. A memory from childhood can bring tears or pleasure in the present. If your client says, "Whenever I used to bring home something I made in school, my father would say, 'I don't want that junk around here,'" you might respond, "It sounds like, being back there in your mind, you can still feel the wanting-to-cry feeling of his not wanting something you were trying to please him with." You are helping your client live that experience over again, which will give him a chance to deal with the experience in a way he wouldn't have otherwise. The memory hurts and will normally be avoided, but if it is still affecting your client, the memory has to be dealt with.

Contrast what you have just done, bringing to life in the here and now the impact of a past experience, with what your response might have been. Many therapists would have heard the client's comment and made a causal connection, which probably is logically correct but which won't help the client reprocess an old experience. Such a therapist might have said, "So it makes sense why you don't think much of your own abilities now, with that kind of upbringing." Again, this is not a destructive response; it's just not as helpful as one that is experience-oriented.

■ Where Is the Leading Edge?

The Third Ear

Theodore Reik (1948) chose the title *Listening with the Third Ear*, because in this book he was trying to describe a process in which the therapist uses his or her own internal experiencing to hear meanings beyond the words the client uses. It seems that a few people are "naturals" at this kind of deep understanding; I remember one therapist in training who couldn't understand why I was so pleased at the quality of therapy she was doing with her first client, since this was the way she talked with her friends. Most of us, however, are not "naturals," but this does not mean we are doomed to lives of doing mediocre therapy. You can develop your "third ear," your ability to sense emotions and to draw inferences that accurately reflect the meaning in another person's words.

My first piece of advice will frustrate you: get lots of experience. There is no quick way to develop your ability to hear; it will grow as you do therapy, sharing in the experience of more and more people and getting more and more feedback on when you have heard accurately and when you have not. Experience by itself is obviously not the issue, since we all gain experience with others as we grow older. I'm sure you know some empathically dense people who have been talking with others for many years. There is an old joke that some people are getting 10 years' experience at the same time that others are getting the same year of experience 10 times. I am trying to make absolutely clear what you are aiming for in the interactions that will help you hear better: the experience you seek is that of trying to see things through another person's eyes, of sensing what that person is experiencing, and then putting your understanding into words that the other person will recognize as his or her view. Then you should humbly listen for feedback, and when you are wrong, try again, correcting your distortions and becoming sensitive to your own blind spots.

You may have noticed in the previous paragraph that I said "sensing" what your client is experiencing. I didn't say "figuring out" or even "hearing." As I often say to my students, your intellect has served you well and has gotten you this far in the educational system, but in becoming a great therapist, your intellect is going to be a mixed blessing. You need other, more intuitive sensing abilities. If you just try to "figure out" your clients cognitively, you're going to be terrible. We'll return to this issue many times; you need to *attune* yourself to your clients' experiencing. You need what Friedman (2005) calls *experiential listening*.

It is easy to understand that the client's process must be both cognitive and experiential, but it is less obvious that so must the therapist's process. An important theme in this book is that only part of the information we process is intellectual or cognitive. In fact, there is a great deal of evidence (which we will look at later) that much of our information processing is precognitive or preconceptual. Robert Shaw (2004) studied 90 experienced therapists and found that they reported "body empathy" as an important part of how they understood their clients. I think that this kind of bodily attunement to another person's experience usually comes with a lot of experience and is extremely rare in beginning therapists. But I at least want you aware of it as a possible part of how we can "hear" a client.

Another approach to getting experience in hearing meanings is more quickly available, although it is not as powerful as going through the process in a variety of circumstances over a long period of time. Chapter 7 and Appendix A give you the opportunity to read a client's comments and then put into words your understanding of the implicit message. The responses of the therapists (in Appendix A) will serve as feedback on your accuracy, but it would be more helpful if you could find a few friends to share in these exercises, each independently responding to the exercises and then discussing together your differences in perception. It may bother you how much disagreement there is among you about the meaning of some of the responses, and I would hope this humbles you a bit. Cockiness over your brilliance of understanding will detract more from your therapy than almost anything else. Get feedback.

The important thing is to go beyond your own limited experience and share in others' experience. If you enjoy good fiction, I hereby assign you to read lots of it, or experience good drama, or talk with your friends a lot.

How Far Is Too Far?

It may be a little intimidating to be told that there is a critical region, just ahead but not too far ahead of the client, where therapy takes place most efficiently. Most beginning therapists are better off to err a bit on the side of caution until they have developed their ability to hear the leading edge of the implicit message. The consequences of being too far ahead of the client (and often too far ahead in the wrong direction) are more serious than the slowness that comes from working right with the client. (Of course, working behind the client can be just as destructive as working too far ahead, since the client can give up in frustration.) The rule of thumb, as you know, is that the leading edge is the message that includes everything that the client intended as "signs." This includes verbal and nonverbal cues, as well as all the material that the client has "put on the table" and assumes you know from previous discussions. Thus, a very short response can be filled with meaning. It can be a strange experience to listen to a conversation between people who have known each other intimately for several years. What sounds to us like grunts and one-word comments can be to them a full and mutually empathic sharing; they have a huge pool of common experience that their words and grunts refer to. Similarly, as therapy progresses, the leading edge includes this common experience as assumed in what is said.

You can often tell after the fact when you have gone beyond the intended message, since the other person rejects what you have said or falls silent and withdraws or suddenly changes the topic. These experiences are feedback to you as you develop your ability to hear without going too far, an ability that you need because you want to know ahead of time how far is too far. Probably the most helpful guideline I can give you is to tell you to think how the person is going to react to what you are about to say. Will the person feel, "Yes, that's it exactly. That's what I was trying to say"? Occasionally, a client will "self-overdose," saying things that are horribly frightening and that she or he can't handle without running from therapy or building strong defenses that will slow therapy down. Part of the therapist's job is also to hear the next intended message, which is likely to be something that means, "This is too much . . . I have to back off," and so the therapist might say, "Things are going too fast . . . it's time to slow down, I guess." Even though the client did say the first things, they were beyond what she or he intended the therapist to hear. Usually, however, your sense of how much the client means for you to hear will help you define the leading edge of the message. *Your goal is to get as far ahead of the client as you can but have the client recognize what you say as part of what she or he meant.*

■ You Hear Selectively

So far I have been talking as though there will always be only one message in what the client says, and your job is to hear it. This is oversimplified, of course, since a client will convey many messages, sometimes in only a few words. "I see myself as an independent person who likes to be alone. I can accomplish more that way. My wife is different . . . so was my mother, come to think of it." What are you going to respond to—the importance of his aloneness and the good feeling that gives him, the implied incongruence between him and his wife, the just-noticed similarity between his wife and his mother, the newly implied incongruence between him and his mother, or his need and desire to accomplish? You really can't respond to it all without going into a very long speech, and so the first thing you must do is admit to yourself that you will respond selectively. Clearly, your selectivity will have an enormous influence on the course of therapy, and it is therefore incumbent on you to be aware of how you are being selective. There is a clear danger that you will subtly lead the client in your direction, rather than give him or her the opportunity to solve his or her unique problems.

Personal Needs and Theories

In chapter 6, I will discuss the therapist's own distortions and blind spots. For the issue of selectivity, it is important to recognize that you filter everything you hear and that you have theories of human behavior to which you have some personal commitment. The striking lesson of the literature on self-fulfilling prophecies (Rosenthal, 1994, 2002) is that not only do we distort our perceptions because we tend to see what we expect to see but we also influence others to fulfill our expectations by subtly expressing reinforcement when they behave as we expect them to. Ironically, we often reinforce them even when we believe we don't want them to behave this way.

It is not easy to know what to do about this problem, because the solution to it lies in the therapist's self-awareness—not a topic easily covered in this book. Personal therapy can help (be sure you get an evocatively empathic therapist for yourself), as can sharing your therapy with another therapist/ friend or two. You will probably have some kind of practicum experience, in which a supervisor will likely monitor you quite closely and perhaps listen to recordings of your therapy. Your need for this kind of outside feedback will not stop with the end of your training, however, and each therapist should seek out a similar arrangement for continuing feedback.

Limits of Your Experience

You might be wondering whether it is necessary that you have had the same experience as the client in order to be able to understand it. The answer is no and yes. Obviously, you can't possibly have experienced all the same things as all your clients or even, for that matter, one of your clients. It is impossible for one person to know what it is like to be another person. As in the title of Carson McCullers' (1940) poignant novel, "our hearts are all lonely hunters." We try to come close to understanding, and that isn't everything, but it is worth a lot. The more thoroughly you have lived, however, the easier it will be to sense similarities between your experience and your client's and to feel, with an "as if" quality, feelings that your client has. They do not then become your feelings, but you are more able to express your understanding of them.

The breadth of your own experience will come partly from your vicarious experiencing of clients' lives. The more therapy you do, the more experiences you will have to draw from to understand your current clients.

All this speaks to the problem of selectivity because you will respond selectively not only because of your own needs and theories but also because you will understand some things better than others. Your reaction to this should be to try to broaden your experience through sensitive living of your own life and seeking out vicarious sharing with others.

Selective, Not Manipulative

All I have said so far about therapist selectivity has implied that it is destructive and results from distortions and limited experience, but since selectivity is inevitable, there has to be a best way to approach it. Likely you do have notions about whether it is more important to deal with issues of independence or issues of commitment to relationships, notions that may grow out of a quite consciously held theory of human behavior. If you are aware of these notions, they might guide your selectivity as a therapist. The danger is that you will try to fit all your clients into a mold that makes sense to you but is not what is best for the client. For some people, independence at the expense of intimacy is better, and for others the opposite is true. Your solutions might be all right for you, but a lot of humility about what the Good Life is like is called for in a therapist.

A friend of mine calls this style of therapy "sneaky interpretation." I'm pretty sure he's kidding, but there is a disturbing possibility that the remarkable power of evocative empathy can be used manipulatively, to lead the client where you want in an insidious way. At least an interpretation is up front where it can be seen and possibly rejected. If, however, you respond to your client with what is in fact your analysis or emphasis, but you couch the response in language that says, "Here is what I think you're saying—I'm not trying to lay anything on you," you are being sneaky.

Poignancy

So how can you be honestly selective? Your goal is to capture, from all the complexity of what the client says, what is most important to him or her. You can trust that the person will try to talk about the important issues; your job is to hear this attempt—to hear what is most important.

Your first guideline is to listen for implicit and explicit reactions/emotions, to listen for the impact on the client. A second one that Rice (1974) discusses is *poignancy*. She says it well:

> The criterion of poignancy, or liveness, seems to be the therapist's best guide. How then is poignancy recognized? How can we recognize that the client is moving into an "unfinished" experience? . . . The most obvious sign is that the client feels something inconsistent or discomforting in the situation. In other cases, a kind of intensity comes through in the voice. On the other hand, the feeling may not be especially intense, but the client may feel that he somehow can't quite assimilate the experience. (p. 304)

Another way to say this is that you listen for the part of the message that seems invested with the most feeling, with the most sense of "there's something in this that I know is important and sort of understand but can't get into words."

Listening to Silence

Finally, in this chapter on learning to hear, I need to deal with silence. Silences are a lot harder on beginning therapists than they are on clients. One of my fellow students in graduate school wanted to shut off the tape recorder during silences even when we were role-playing, so as not to "waste tape." The tape wasn't being wasted, of course, but there was something so nerve-racking about all that unfilled time that he had to do something to stop the process. You will be tempted to fill silences at all costs, and likely you will start asking questions to get the client talking. There is a place for questions (see chapter 5), but it is no accident that beginning therapists ask more questions than experienced ones do (Ornston, Cicchetti, Levine, & Fierman, 1968). For one thing, experienced therapists can live through silences and even see them as constructive; for another, well-done evocative empathy makes it easy for the client to talk without being prompted by questions.

The question before us now, however, is how to listen to silences. It is common to think of silences in therapy as either "empty time" or an indication that the client is resisting, but there is evidence (Levitt, 2001) that silences can mean many different things. Sometimes the client is using the silence to think or explore or assimilate something, and your need to keep the chatter going will stop these processes. Sometimes the client is suffering and embarrassed at not being able to think of anything to say, and the most empathic response you could make would be something like, "It's hard to get things into words, huh?" or, "I guess you've hit a dead end" or, "I can tell it's hard to get going. I suppose it could be just not knowing where to start or going blank or something like that." In the first case, when the client is using the silence, your best response is to respect the silence and wait for the client to break it. In the second case, you are "listening" to mostly nonverbal cues and letting your client know you understand. You have to be well-attuned to your client to hear (sense?) the meaning of silences.

Levitt (2001) found three large categories of silences or pauses: productive silences, neutral silences, and obstructive silences. Understanding them might help you develop your "third ear" for the meaning of particular silences. Among productive silences, Levitt described (1) emotional silences, (2) expressive silences, and (3) reflective silences.

In an *emotional pause*, the client is experiencing sadness, joy, or some other emotion, or she is entering into contact with an emotion. When you see that your client is feeling a lot, it is often best just to "sit with it"—with your client, perhaps quietly offering a word or two to communicate, "I'm here in this with you . . . we're just being with your feeling." At other times, as your client is coming into contact with an emotion, you both may feel on the threshold of something new—kind of looking and waiting to see what's emerging. Often, when you fill an emotional silence with your chatter, you will stop the process. Emotional silences can be very powerful.

In an *expressive pause*, clients are silently searching for the words to capture their meaning accurately. This is an exploring process that can sound awkward, as the client tries a few words that aren't quite right and then tries again. Clients are often articulating something they haven't ever been able to express before, even to themselves. In this process, they are doing two important things. They are understanding a specific experience, and they are learning to explore themselves. Inexperienced therapists often interrupt expressive pauses by quickly offering words that are guesses at what the client is trying to articulate. I think that this often comes from the therapist's eagerness to be understanding, or to look understanding anyway, when the client's meaning isn't clear enough yet to either the client or the therapist.

Reflective pauses occur after a client makes a discovery, suddenly realizes how complex a problem is, or absorbs a new idea. Therapy includes moments of little discoveries, surprising new perspectives, and unexpected connections. Clients often react to these moments with something like, "wow" or "whoa" or "huh!" and then fall silent as they absorb and react to the moment. I love these moments and sometimes have to suppress my urge to rush in and articulate the new insight or discovery. It is important to let the client have the silence, as he reacts to it. One thing I often find helpful is just to say something like, "Wow, that surprised you."

Levitt described the neutral pauses as (1) mnemonic pauses and (2) associational pauses.

Mnemonic pauses are the moments when clients are trying to recall information and details about what they are discussing. This happens when the therapist has asked a question about past events or when the client is trying to make sure the story is accurate.

Associational pauses occur when a client shifts topics without making an explicit transition. For example, a client might be catching you up on what happened since the last session and just pause between unrelated events or stories.

You should be especially sensitive to the obstructive silences, which include (1) disengaged pauses and (2) interactional pauses.

Disengaged pauses happen when clients back away from a difficult emotion or topic. They disengage to avoid feeling too much pain, to distract the therapist from exploring painful material, or simply to withdraw from the situation. Responding to a disengaged pause requires great sensitivity because of some conflicting principles of therapy. In general, it is constructive for clients to face and deal with their emotions. On the other hand, this should be done in small steps, and if the pain to too intense the client can be frightened enough to build new defenses against the pain and against therapy. In general, we might be afraid that if we let the client "run away" from this experience, we are reinforcing running away. On the other hand, it is absolutely essential that our clients feel safe and that they are empowered to be in charge of their own healing. Usually, there is a way to respond to a disengaged silence that doesn't run away from the pain by pretending it isn't there but at the same time leaves the client feeling safe and empowered. You could gently say something like, "This is tough, huh?—Too tough?" Then, depending on what the client says, you might say, "OK, we'll go there now, as you're able to." Or, "There's something big here, but we'll get to it later. I hope you know that's your choice."

Interactional pauses are reactions to the therapist and what is going on in the relationship immediately. When clients sense pressure to talk or a change in the therapist's behavior, they often pause to try to figure out what's going on or how to respond to it. Sometimes therapists do or say awkward, surprising, or painfully obvious things, and most clients are reluctant to criticize or challenge their therapist (Rennie, 1994). They "pause to consider how best to safeguard the therapeutic alliance" (Levitt, 2001, p. 304).

I'm surprised that Levitt's study didn't discover one other kind of client silence, what we might call the "blank mind pause." Especially early in therapy, clients can hit a dead end and feel terribly awkward about not having anything to say. Sometimes they feel or say something like, "Well, that's my story. Now what?" Or they just fidget and squirm and look at the therapist silently for direction. If I am pretty sure we're in a blank mind silence, I usually break the silence with an acknowledgement of it. I possibly help with some guidance about how therapy works—how the client's job is just to talk about whatever is most on her mind right now and how my job is to help her explore it.

Levitt and her colleagues (Frankel, Levitt, Murray, Greenberg, & Angus, 2006) found that good-outcome therapy dyads had more emotional, expressive, and high reflective silences and fewer disengaged and interactional silences than poor-outcome dyads.

CHAPTER 3

Finding the Words

As mentioned in chapter 2, there are two steps in responding: first you must hear the message and then you must find the words to articulate what the client intended to convey. Most people are not used to responding with words that focus on what the other person said. We tend to ask questions, offer opinions, and make speeches. As an effective therapist, however, your job is to help your client face what he or she has just said. You might say that this seems silly in a way, since if the person just said it, there is no need to face it. The fact is, though, that the person often isn't feeling the full impact of what he or she is trying to say, especially when the material is difficult.

First, you will find it remarkable at times when you think you have just about repeated back the other person's words and the other person will say, "Is that what I said? I guess it is, but it sure sounds different to hear you say it." Even more striking are instances when the other person says, "No, that's not what I mean at all." Of course, some of these will be times that you have missed the message, but sometimes you truly will have only repeated back a level-3 response. We seem to be able to emit words but avoid their impact. The words have more impact when they come "reflected" back, since reflection might allow meaning to surface.

The second way you are helping your clients face what they have said is by being ahead of them, articulating what has been implied. We avoid what hurts, both in overt behavior and in our thinking, so that even when your client is talking about feelings, you might hear, "I know there is risk in my involvement with him." You respond, "Part of you is scared that if you care too much, you could really get hurt." Your response didn't really mean anything your client hadn't said, but by articulating the implied feelings, you are helping her face and experience a truth she couldn't quite stand to look at directly.

I will talk about how all this works in chapter 16, but for now it is useful to know that your client is in trouble partly because she fears her own thoughts, memories, and feelings, usually with little awareness of what it is she fears. Fearing these thoughts and feelings, she avoids them as much as possible, still being bothered by them but not able to do something wise about them because she is avoiding thinking and experiencing accurately. The only way to get rid of a fear is to face what is feared, feel the fear (in small doses), and have nothing bad happen. You are helping your client face feared thoughts and feelings—in small doses. How do you know what "size" these doses should be? By staying at the leading edge of what the client implies.

In the pages ahead, you will be told to "bring the client's experience to life" and to add "structure and focus" with your response. To give you some structure to hold on to right now, there are two general formulas that will help you find the words with which to respond. The general form of your response will be, "It sounds like you feel . . . because of. . . ." You name reactions and the causes of those reactions. When possible, you can go on to say, "I guess what you want is. . . ." This response goes on to focus on goals, on action, and on moving forward. Please don't cling to these formulas any longer than you have to, though; they are so simple that they are simplistic. Always remember that your goal is to make the client feel understood, not to apply a technique.

■ Bring It to Life

Your job is to find the words that will capture exactly your client's meaning and evoke (arouse, stimulate) the feelings your client is moving toward. You are to bring to life what is only being talked about. The word *evoke* means "to bring forth," and that is what you do when you bring the client's experiences to life. You do not *provoke* a response, since that would put you in control as the person who is deciding which experiences are to be felt. The client is the source of the experience, and your job is to evoke or facilitate the thoughts and experiences that come from the client—by bringing them vividly to life.

Painting the Picture

An image that some therapists find helpful is that of taking the raw material the client has laid on the table in bits and pieces and putting it all together as a whole scene—using it to paint a vivid picture and holding the picture up before the client, where he or she has to look at it. The therapist says with his or her actions, "Look, this is what you've said. We have to look at it in all its complexity and confusingness. Look." The therapist is not offering solutions or even suggesting which topics should be dealt with next but is just saying, "Look at all of what you are saying." Then the client has to deal with it, has to take the next step in exploring.

State All Sides of the Message

Part of "painting the picture" is painting the whole picture. Many therapists seem to think that only one thing can be true at a time and have difficulty acknowledging contradictory parts of their clients' experience. It is quite clearly our nature to have contradictory experiences, no matter how much that offends our need for logical order. Conflict is fundamental to human functioning and, as we will see later, underlies most human emotional problems. To deny conflict in our responding dooms us to incomplete understanding. A common helpful remark in therapy is something like, "You really feel both ways, don't you? It's like you want it more than anything but can't stand the thought of having it." And that's the truth for the client right now; further work and exploring and understanding might show a way out of the conflict, but not if some simple-minded therapist says, "Well, which is it? Do you want it or don't you?" I am not saying that every message contains conflict; I am saying that when you respond, you should listen for and put into words all the sides of the issue that the client is trying to deal with.

Several paragraphs ago, I mentioned your client who said, "I know there is risk in my involvement with him." The response I suggested was, "Part of you is scared that if you care too much, you could really get hurt," but my response missed an important part of the message. Actually, I hinted at the other part of the message by saying, "Part of you," but I hear this client's voice plaintively emphasizing the word *know.* A better response might have been, "Part of you is scared that if you care too much, you could really get hurt, and the other part is saying 'But I want him, and I do care.'"

Using the First Person

In the last response, I used a powerful tool of language for bringing the experience to life. Using the first person singular when articulating the client's own message makes it clear that the therapist is focusing on the client's experience and permits a more personally stated form of the response. There is a risk of being misunderstood when you do this, and a therapist who does it all the time can sound silly, but used sensitively, the *I* can help.

You will note in the transcript of Bob Lee's session (see Appendix A) that Bob often uses the first person as though he were the client speaking. He does it naturally and in a way that doesn't confuse the client about to whom the "I" refers. Many students have told me that they feel awkward using the first person this way. Speak this way only if it feels natural. When I do therapy, I tend to use the first person "I" to express a client's thoughts; I am more likely than Bob to preface my comment with "*So you're saying,* 'I want. . . .'" But that's only a matter of personal preference.

■ Starting Out

Finding the words to respond empathically looks a lot easier when you're reading about it than it really is. When you try to do it, I would anticipate a kind of blocking that might surprise you. When I teach these skills in groups, I often have the participants role-play different situations, with one of them as the talker and one as the empathic listener. To force the issue, I at first *prohibit* the listener's use of questions, reassurance, advice, talking about himself or herself, and suggestions. It is amazing how tongue-tied these rules leave people. These are the foundations of most social interchanges; we keep our conversations going by asking questions and telling people things. Life does not prepare us very well to be empathic (and I suspect this is one reason so few of us do well in relationships, but that's another book), and so we sit there at a loss.

Awkwardness

Unless you are a rare person, empathic responding will not feel smooth and natural at first. A useful analogy, though, is to think of playing tennis for 10 years, having evolved your own choppy forehand with no follow-through. This stroke serves you quite well and, along with your amazing reflexes, lets you maintain a respectable standing among your friends. Now, however, you have stopped improving and seek professional help. As the pro teaches you a better stroke, it feels terrible and awkward, and, worst of all, your arrogant friends have started to beat you. Only by forcing a change in style and by practicing will you become comfortable with a follow-through and eventually be a much better player. However, the temptation is overwhelming to give in to the awkwardness and go back to chopping.

One reason I will talk about role-playing in chapter 7 is that it gives you a chance to practice your new awkward empathy in a relatively low-threat situation. Only with practice will it become natural and start to feel "right." You will be rattled by silences that will seem 10 times as long as they are, and you will feel that you're looking foolish parroting back words. It will be tempting to start asking questions to fill in the time and get the other person talking, but it will be worth the effort to make yourself formulate your responses in the declarative form rather than the interrogative. This is not to say that questions are bad; they are often the most effective phrasing to use. The problem is that they are usually not as powerful as empathic responses, but they are what most of us use most of the time. You need practice with declarative empathic statements, and so I am advising you to force yourself to do this practice.

Another advantage of starting out with role-playing is that early attempts at developing these skills usually involve a lot of level-3 responding—that is, repeating back pretty much what the other person said. It is difficult to learn to find the words that stay just ahead of the other person, and when the skill is developing, it is easy to feel redundant or silly about repeating the other person's words. In role-playing or with a friend who knows what you are doing, this initial clumsiness won't matter so much or be so threatening.

Real-Time Responding

Another problem that beginning therapists often report is that they could come up with terrific responses if we could just build in a 15-second delay during which time stopped for the client so the therapist could think. The cure for this problem is also practice. If your tennis opponent's returns could be slowed to about one-third speed, your new forehand would be wonderful, but there just doesn't seem to be enough time for the backstroke before the ball gets there. Six months from now, of course, you will hardly be able to believe that the backstroke was ever a problem, since it seems to happen without your even thinking about it. It will just be natural. What's "natural" is what you've done so many times that it's overlearned. You will get faster, but for now it would be useful to use a recorder in several ways.

First, you can record your role-playing, or if you are already engaged in doing therapy, you certainly should record your sessions. With the recording and a supervisor or colleague, stop the session immediately after some client response, and take all the time you want to formulate a good response. Discuss different possible responses and then listen to what you actually said.

Second, when you read excerpts of therapy sessions in Appendix A, you can cover the therapist's responses with a piece of paper and write your own responses as though you were the therapist. Doing this with a friend or in a group will be a sobering experience, as you will become aware of the various kinds of messages other people perceive, and it will be good feedback on the accuracy of your own perceptions. You can then read what the original therapist actually said. Of course, the actual therapist response is not the only one or even the best possible one that could have been given, but these excerpts generally represent effective therapy, and it would be worthwhile to analyze what the therapists are doing. Appendix A also includes the therapists' discussion of what they see themselves doing.

Third, the process of supervision is an essential part of your training. Most people dislike hearing themselves on recordings, partly because nearly all of us misperceive ourselves to some extent, and the recording confronts us with ourselves. Your supervisor or colleague adds to this self-confrontation just by being there and articulating his or her own responses to your work. A supervisor or colleague can also comment and give you feedback on what you could have done.

The Inevitable Pause

Joseph Schubert (1977) has pointed out that there has to be *some* pause between the end of the client's response and the beginning of the therapist's because the therapist has to have some time to formulate a response. If the therapist is formulating a response while the client is still talking, she or he has to be forcing closure on the client's message and must miss some of the message. Schubert (as does Bourbonnais, 1980) presents some evidence that more experienced therapists demonstrate this momentary pause more than beginners do. If, however, you sit there silently counting, "One hippopotamus, two hippopotamus" in order to get the correct pause in before you respond, you probably have missed some of the finer points of our discussion.

■ Structuring and Focusing

Therapy is both a cognitive and an experiential process. There is a risk of overemphasizing one and losing the integration of both aspects of experience. I am afraid that I may have created the impression that only the emotional matters. In this section, and in chapter 5, I will dispel this impression as I discuss the cognitive, or intellectual, parts of therapy. I should explain that we are paying so much attention to the feeling part of therapy because most beginning therapists, perhaps even most people in our culture, are oriented toward the intellectual and the rational at the expense of the emotional and intuitive. The two must be integrated.

One way that you will help your client face what he or she is saying is to add sensible structure to it—not that you offer a logical analysis, but that you draw diffuseness together. Your client says, "A lot of the time it seems like people are . . . I don't know. . . really mean . . . no, not mean . . . they're loving, I guess . . . at least some . . . like some I know are." You might respond, "I'm not sure I got all that, but let me try. It sounds confusing . . . trying to know how you feel about the way people are toward you. The ones that matter to you seem to be loving, you guess, but at the same time that doesn't seem quite the whole truth because they seem mean in some ways too. Is that close to what you mean?"

We have to be careful not to impose meaning that the client didn't intend, and that is always a danger of working ahead of the person's explicit words, but let's assume for this time that the therapist's response was accurate. What is interesting is that it took the jumbled expressions of the client and stated them in a way that made sense, that was structured. The client still recognizes it as what he meant but now has a chance to look at it in a much clearer form, which means that he must confront what he said in a way that wouldn't have happened if the therapist hadn't been there to add the clarity.

Focus Rather than Elaborate

Another misunderstanding that often arises is that therapists think they should talk a lot, believing that in order to bring the client's experience to life they have to use many words and add elaborate verbal constructions. Your job is to hear the essence of the message and bring that to life. I talked in the last chapter about using "poignancy" as a guideline to what part of the message to respond to, and it can serve us here too. The client may be using many words and saying several things at once, but your job is to hear the central point. In fact, it is sometimes useful to be thinking, as you listen, what is the point here, as the client sees it? Another phrase I like is, "What is the heart of the matter?" You are listening for the "big issue" rather than the last 12 words. Then your words sharpen that issue by focusing and illuminating it, rather than going into a complex elaboration of your own. The client is supposed to be doing the work here, in an active and ongoing process. You are supposed to facilitate this process for the client, and if we have to stop and listen to your clever speeches, the client will lose the momentum of the exploring process.

Client Rambling

Clients ramble for many reasons. Sometimes rambling is a defense against fear of engaging in real contact with the therapist; sometimes it is a well-established defense against facing painful thoughts and feelings; sometimes it is just a casual verbal wandering that results from not feeling very much at all at the moment; sometimes it results from a habitually wordy style of talking; there are dozens of possibilities. Therapeutic growth results from exploration and self-confrontation, neither of which is likely during rambling, and one purpose of having the therapist in the room is to focus the process. The therapist facilitates exploration and self-confrontation by *fairly frequently* articulating the intended message.

When the client rambles, the therapist is still bringing focus to the process, but it can be more difficult to bring structure to what may seem like a swamp of details. The therapist is scrambling to keep the big issue marked with a red flag and to understand the details in the perspective of what the person is trying to get to among all the words. You might say, "OK, let me stop you for a minute to see if I've got what you're saying right so far. I think you mean that this story about how your aunt and uncle sold their house sort of illustrates what you were talking about before—that you wish there were something permanent—that you'd feel safer. Is that the point?"

Here you keep making it clear that you have *empathic intent*. Your behavior is not saying, "Here's what all this means." It is saying, "We are engaged in an intense exploration process in which I will try very hard to help you explore all this, through your eyes." However, you are not just a passive follower. Your words add structure and focus.

Interrupting Gently

Many beginning therapists are at a loss when a client talks rapidly and constantly, because they feel "rude" interrupting the client. You can, however, interrupt gently and empathically with a phrase like the one I used in the previous example. If you say some version of, "Can I stop you for just a second? I really want to be sure I'm getting what you've said," this almost always will give you a chance to say something, and it tells the client that you're really trying to understand. Thus, you can give some structure without shutting the client down or saying something that the client will feel as criticism of how he or she is talking.

Summarizing

Another kind of structure you can bring to the process results from summarizing responses. Again, of course, your job is not to add new material; it is to take what's on the table and pull it together, in an exploring, let's-see-if-I-understand-this-so-far way. In the process, you probably will be drawing in contradictory feelings and observations and will be putting together aspects of the whole issue that may not have entered the discussion together. The summarizing response is not formulated to draw these new relationships for the client or to confront him or her with contradictions that had better be resolved right now; rather, it is a way of painting a larger picture. The function it can serve is to present the client with a larger panorama to deal with, and if the connections are there to be made or the contradictions to be resolved, the client can do it. You help him or her look at the issue in a more complete way. Then the client can do the work.

Summarizing responses can be especially helpful when both you and the client seem to have hit a brick wall. You might say, "It's hard to know where to go from here? . . . Here's where I see us having gotten to so far . . ." (and then you draw together what's been said so far and bring it to life).

Frequency of Responding

In trying to decide how frequently to respond, we need to look at two effects we can have on the process of therapy. On one hand, the therapist needs to respond frequently because his or her function is partly to be the vehicle for self-confrontation by the client. Frequent responding keeps therapy going by giving feedback, by making the client feel understood, by preventing aimless circling, and by making mutual exploring the overall focus of therapy. All of these effects demand active participation by the therapist. A passive listener will leave the client to do all the exploring. As noted in chapter 2, passive listening can be a powerful influence, and many clients will eventually solve problems with it. But it is slow and frequently ineffective because it doesn't help the client break circles of avoidance behavior, and it doesn't help the client hear what he or she is implying. On the other hand, if the therapist responds too frequently, he or she can dominate the process, not letting the client do the work. The client is the problem solver, and the benefits of therapy are stronger and generalize more if the client goes through the steps of problem solving. Clearly, then, it is possible to respond too frequently.

In general, the answer to the question of how often to respond is "fairly frequently." Your role in therapy is an active one but not a dominant one. To guide yourself, be sensitive to whether you are letting the client work on issues, whether the client's self-exploring talk is increasing over the course of sessions, and whether you find yourself interrupting the client a lot. These are observations that usually require feedback through listening to recordings of your therapy and having someone else listen to you doing therapy.

I'm a little nervous having said "respond fairly frequently," because this could be taken as a "rule." It's only a general guideline. I've gone 15 minutes (or, in rare cases, longer) without saying anything in a session or even in total silence with the client. There are no "rules." There are only principles. The fundamental principle is: do whatever helps your client feel deeply known and accepted.

■ Bold, Forthright, Skillful Tentativeness

You may have noticed that many of the examples of dialogue in this book include phrases like, "I guess you mean . . . ," "I'm not sure this is right, but . . . ," and "I think I hear you. . . ." Each of these introduces a tentativeness that communicates that the client is the *source* of information about his or her own experience—that says to the client, "I am a fellow explorer going through this with you, but you are the final authority. I have things to add and things to share, but I offer them to you to use, rather than insist that I am right and am giving you the truth." This tentativeness is not permissive weakness; the therapist is quite insistent on staying with the process and confronting experience, but he or she is not insistent on one particular version of the "true content" of the client's life problems.

One function of this confident tentativeness is to give the client freedom to reject what the therapist says and to take some direction other than the one seen by the therapist. Many written examples of therapy seem to start out, "You feel. . . ." This can be an excellent way to start a response—usually when it is pretty obvious what the client has said. In this situation, the client clearly knows that you mean to put into words what he just tried to say. When you are working ahead of the client, however, starting out with "You feel . . ." can sound as if you are telling the client what he is feeling. I have found that the further ahead I am, the more I like to use skillful tentativeness, starting out with something like, "I guess you feel. . . ." Here there can be no doubt that I am not trying to take over the process and explain things but rather want to understand. Of course, this also eases matters when I have heard the client incorrectly. If our job is mutual exploring, and I miss the point, there is no great loss; I drop back a step and try again.

Empathic Intent

Even when you are ahead, even when you miss the point, even when the material is painful, as your client learns that your intent is consistently that of facilitating his or her thinking and feeling, an expectation of trust builds. If your intentions are perceived as empathic, the need for defenses against you lessens. The thoughts and feelings and things in the person's life become the sources of threat, not you. You are taking away the need for defenses in the therapy process itself. One way you do this is with skillful tentativeness.

Empathic Guesses

Once trust in your empathic intent is established, you have the foundation for making empathic guesses. These are just one way to be working ahead of the client when you are not very clear about what the implicit message is. You might start out with, "This is partly a shot in the dark, and tell me if I'm off base, but when you say 'I don't know if marriage is for me,' it sounds like there's some of that old fear of confrontation eating at you." Here I am using a lot of material the client has told me in the past, but I really don't know whether this is what he's saying right now. I think it might be, so I check it out. If our relationship is based on a mood of mutual exploration, he will tell me if I'm off. If I'm hearing correctly, we'll take a big step forward together.

The obvious danger is that empathic guesses can be used to disguise sneaky interpretations. Maybe it's my little theory that his reluctance to marry has a lot to do with his fear of anger, and I'm getting impatient with his not getting around to confirming my theory. Even if he is not implying this, I could make a sneaky interpretation by making it look as though I were being empathic with, "If I hear you correctly, what you're trying to say is that one thing that holds you back from marriage is that anger frightens you." It would be more honest of me just to say what my theory is. It wouldn't do much good if he's not ready for it, but at least he could deal with it as what it is—my interpretation. By dishonestly couching it in words that make it look like empathy, I make it a lot harder to deal with openly. I may even have a better chance of bringing him around to agree with me, but my experience has been that many clients recognize a sneaky interpretation as just that. How do I know this, you ask, if I haven't done some sneaky interpreting and been caught at it? Good question.

Done honestly with a client who trusts your empathic intent, empathic guesses can be a helpful occasional tool. Done dishonestly, they can undermine trust, insidiously lead the client toward incorrect beliefs and solutions (when you're wrong, which will be fairly often), and subtly lead the client toward correct beliefs and solutions (when you're right). Even this last benefit, however, is won at the price of the client's dependence on your wisdom rather than his or her own growing independence.

Lead-In Phrases

Much of the skillful tentativeness I am discussing is communicated in the first few words of the therapist's responses—in the "lead-in." This may seem a bit "techniquey," but many people have found it very useful to have a list of potential lead-in phrases. Hammond, Hepworth, and Smith (2002) present an excellent list, pointing out that it is too easy to fall into the habit of using a few favorite phrases that can come to sound artificial with overuse. In graduate school, I remember "You seem to feel . . ." as a big favorite that became so habitual with so many of us that it was silly: "You seem to feel that factor analysis would be the best approach to these data." Keep in mind that you are trying to convey skillfully tentative empathic intent, and then say what feels right.

As I told you earlier, one of the most useful lead-ins is "It sounds like . . ." When I was writing this book, one trainee said he couldn't wait for the book to come out; I had to give him a list of lead-ins right away. After we had spent one session discussing evocative empathy he started saying, "It sounds like . . ." so often that one client asked him whether he was learning a new technique. He clearly had missed the point. To help you with a variety of possible lead-ins, here is a list created by Hammond, Hepworth, and Smith (2002, pp. 114–115).

Empathic Response Leads

Kind of feeling . . .

Sort of saying . . .

As I get it, you felt that . . .

I'm picking up that you . . .

Sort of a feeling that . . .

If I'm hearing you correctly . . .

To me it's almost like you are saying, "I . . .

Sort of hear you saying that maybe you . . .

Kind of made (makes) you feel . . .

The thing you feel most right now is sort of like . . .

So you feel . . .

What I hear you saying is . . .

So, as you see it . . .

As I get it, you're saying . . .

What I guess I'm hearing is . . .

I'm not sure I'm with you, but . . .

I somehow sense that maybe you feel . . .

You feel . . .

I really hear you saying that . . .

I wonder if you're expressing a concern that . . .

It sounds as if you're indicating you . . .

I wonder if you're saying . . .

You place a high value on . . .

It seems to you . . .

Like right now . . .

You often feel . . .

You feel, perhaps . . .

You appear to be feeling . . .

It appears to you . . .

As I hear it, you . . .

So, from where you sit . . .

Your feeling now is that . . .

I read you as . . .

Sometimes you . . .

You must have felt . . .

I sense that you're feeling . . .

Very much feeling . . .

Your message seems to be, "I . . ."

You appear . . .

Listening to you it seems as if . . .

I gather . . .

So your world is a place where you . . .

You communicate (convey) a sense of . . .

Study this list, so that even if you never use one of these lead-ins exactly, you will understand how they convey empathic intent. I've noticed (and people who have watched me do therapy have commented) that I use many fewer of these lead-in phrases than I used to. I'm not sure why this is so, but I think it might be that I have developed other ways to communicate my empathic intent and willingness to be wrong.

■ Unique Language

The easiest kind of therapy to master is "five phrase therapy." All you have to do is memorize the following five phrases and intersperse them judiciously in what your client says: (1) "That seems to bother you." (2) "I guess you're pulled two ways about all that." (3) "I can't help wondering how much all this means to you." (4) "Under that anger I think I hear some hurt." (5) "Under that hurt I think I hear some anger."

There. This information alone is worth the price of the whole book.

Actually, these phrases are not too bad as therapist responses, and you will hear yourself using them at times. One beginning therapist I know really did use phrase 1 just about whenever he couldn't think what to say, and he reported that it usually worked quite well. The problem with the five phrases is that they are not exact—not specific to the experience of the client—and therefore are only weakly able to bring the client's experience to life.

Suppose a client said, "She has a particular nasal tone of voice that she comes at me with when I feel weak, and it is most unpleasant." Notice that your client has made entirely factual statements about things outside himself. There are no reactions; he says, "It is most unpleasant," rather than, "I hate it." Clearly, there are a lot of feelings implied here, but the client has trouble approaching them directly. Your job is to hear what is implied and to help your client experience it. Compare the impact of your saying, "That seems to bother you," with that of, "When she starts that condescending whine, you seem to feel like getting away and hitting back, all at the same time." The second response has several advantages. It clearly brings the feelings to life more vividly. You are trying to help your client confront his experience—to feel the impact of the incidents he only described. By naming the feelings and reactions, by painting the picture vividly, you are far more likely to arouse the emotions that your client is trying to get to and to face. You have used language that is specific and concrete, that captures the precise nuance of what the client was trying to say. Your job is to name the feelings he has only implied and to name them in ways that help him confront the experience he has hinted at. The second response does all this. Another way that the second response is more helpful is that it names not only the reaction but also the cause of the reaction very specifically. I can't convey the therapist's tone of voice on this page, but I picture the words "condescending whine" being said with a hint of the tone that upsets the client so, and then the words "getting away" being said more softly, with perhaps a slightly firmer tone to "hitting back." The uniqueness of the therapist's response lies in the pregnant words used and in nonverbal voice qualities.

I want to be careful that the last few lines not lead you to be conscious of "acting" with your voice quality. Working at having the "right" voice quality would almost certainly make you sound false. What I am trying to imply is that if you are interested, intensely listening, and trying to move within what the client is experiencing, then your voice will speak quite naturally with both words and tone.

Specific Rather than General

To share another person's experience, we are far more effective when we use language that is specific to that person. Truax and Carkhuff (1967) proposed the term *concreteness* to refer to avoidance of the vague and abstract in favor of the specific and personal. Therapists frequently classify and categorize what clients say, trying to draw broad generalizations. This seems to come from approaching therapy as an intellectual process in which correctly identifying the causes of the client's problems will somehow cure those problems. This intellectualized approach is bad enough, but when it is coupled with attempts to place the client into categories that fit some personality theory, meaningful emotional change for this particular client with this particular set of problems becomes less likely.

When the client says, with reddening eyes, "I'm just no good . . . people would be better off without me around, damn it," a disturbing number of therapists would say, "Anger, especially anger at oneself, is often an important part of depression." Finally, the therapist thinks, here's something I read about—aggression turned inward—now we're getting somewhere. But this generalized abstraction (which may be true in many cases, for all we know), with its finality, cuts off the client's exploration, as though the problem were solved; it moves the client away from current experiencing toward intellectualizing; it does not give the therapist a chance to get accurate feedback on whether he or she has heard the client correctly; and it teaches the client, by example, to deal in abstractions.

Conversely, an evocatively empathic therapist would have said something like, "You can hardly stand how you're feeling about yourself right now . . . like you're a burden on others . . . it's a sadness and anger at yourself all at once, I guess."

Rice (1974) offers three words that capture the richness of the unique language required better than concreteness does. She says that the evocative response is *particular, subjective,* and *connotative.*

Particular. The opposite of drawing generalizations and pointing out similarities among the client's experiences, the particular response focuses vividly on current experiences. Rather than draw relationships, as many therapists are fond of doing, the evocatively empathic therapist facilitates experiencing. "After a client has grasped an experience freshly in this way, he may begin to explore similarities and patterns, and get very excited about the new avenues that are opened up. However, the generalization follows rather than leads to a new experience" (Rice, 1974, p. 307).

Subjective. Subjective refers to the individual's internal processes and reactions, as opposed to *objective,* which refers to external, unprejudiced, detached perspectives. I have frequently noted the need to focus on reactions—to pay most attention to how the person feels in response to situations, rather than talk about the situations or even about the person's feelings.

Rather than the usual condensed feeling words like "anxious" or "guilty," one might pick up a sense of the client feeling "stretched tight" or of feeling "dubious and slimy." Or, rather than putting a facile label on the situation being described, the therapist might make an exploratory response—

"When he said that and you resigned—I'd like to get the flavor of that. Can you tell me more about what it is like?" (Rice, 1974, p. 308)

Connotative.   One student said that the most pleasant assignment she had been given all year was when I suggested that reading good fiction could be an important way to develop a precision of language for doing therapy. Powerful prose and poetry differ from common language in some way that makes them arouse us to experience things in fresh, new ways. They use the same old words that you and I do, but fresh, vivid metaphors make us see what the novelist sees; rhythm and sound make us feel what the poet feels; sensory images carry a richness of associations that make us know what it would be like to smell or touch or hurt in certain ways.

A client might be talking about feeling confused, isolated, and rejected, and you respond, "It sounds like being little and lost in a big store and feeling sick when people think it's all so funny." Or to another client, "You reach out and say 'please' and he cuts you, like he's slicing at you with a razor." Or, "I guess you try not to think about all this, but it haunts you . . . always somewhere behind something ready to grab your stomach with cold hands." Each of these examples assumes that you have accurately understood the intended message, of course.

Metaphoric Language

Some of the examples in the previous paragraphs used powerful metaphors. Metaphors can be powerful because they often express complex experiential meaning quickly and in a way that other words cannot (Cirillo & Crider, 1995). Kopp talks about doing "metaphor therapy," using client-generated metaphors to capture experiences (Kopp, 1995; Kopp & Eckstein, 2004). Angus and Rennie (1989) gathered evidence that suggested that "a metaphor is typically embedded within experiential networks of memories, incidents, images and feelings constituting an 'associated meaning context'" (p. 377).

A client of mine suffered a personal tragedy and was very worried that she was withdrawing from other people and felt unable to do as much as she felt she should be doing. We had previously talked about the part of her that was like a tiger in her strength and commitment to what she felt was right. In the context of our talking, I commented, "Right now you seem to me to be a wounded tiger. You've retreated to hide in your cave and lick your wounds." She later told me that this metaphor captured her experience at many levels and strongly resonated with how she felt in a way that helped her put words on feelings she barely knew she had. She was still a tiger, not a weakling, and it was natural and right that she retreat for a while.

Concise and Vivid—Not Necessarily Long or Dramatic

It is a lot to ask that you be particular, subjective, connotative, and metaphoric in the few seconds you have to respond, but it is important to remember that you do have only a few seconds. Some trainees interpret "particular," "subjective," and especially "connotative" and "metaphoric" to mean "elaborate, flowery, and dramatic." The most important principle is that your response accurately capture your client's experiencing, and this is more likely to happen if you respond concisely and vividly. Lots of words that finally get around to the issue are not nearly as effective as a few powerful ones. Your connotative language will use voice quality to heighten the power of the words, but here again, you must be sure not to "overact" and go beyond what the client will recognize as his or her experience.

I would especially caution you about not overdoing it with the use of metaphors. My experience has been that some beginning therapists "fall in love with" metaphors once they see how powerful they can be. Or maybe the problem is that metaphors can be one way therapists get to show off how clever they are, rather than bringing the client's experiencing to life. One student said that she finally realized that she "hides behind" metaphors; they gave her a way to sound like a therapist but still keep distance from the client's emotions. If you find yourself talking about "the winds of darkness tearing through the rended garment of your soul" you probably should get some extra supervision.

Successive Approximations

It is most likely obvious by now that therapy occurs in steps. The client is approaching thoughts and feelings, many of which are threatening, as closely as possible and then backing off when the discomfort starts. When you take each step with the person and "take the curse off" the threatening thoughts by talking about them openly and without discomfort of your own or rejection or judgment of the client, you help make that step less threatening. Now the person is able to go on to other material that used to be too threatening even to approach. The person is trying to get to "the truth," to accurately know his or her own experiencing. Likely we never know ourselves completely accurately, but the closer we can get, the more wisely and well we can live. You and the client are making evermore accurate explorations of what is true for the person, and you do this by successive approximations. You try to understand, and you are never completely accurate, but you get feedback and try again and explore a newly found path and try again. Since each approximation of "the truth" is bound to be inaccurate in some way, it is held only tentatively, as a more accurate one is searched for. An implicit rule of your relationship is that nothing gets written in stone; you and the client can change your minds next week without having to defend yourselves because the mood of therapy is one of mutual search.

After observing me doing therapy, a trainee pointed out one way I use successive approximations, although I was not aware I did it. The example she pointed out was something like, "I guess that makes you annoyed . . . angry, even." She said I seemed to have started out with a less strong word and "read" the client's reaction to it as I was talking. This nonverbal feedback gave clues about whether stronger words would still be within the intended message—whether the client would recognize them as part of what he or she meant to say. The trainee articulated a useful way to get as far ahead of the client as possible without taking over direction.

Vocabulary of Shadings

To capture accurately the complex nuances of meaning in what a particular person feels requires a large vocabulary of "feeling words." You can hardly articulate many successive approximations if your repertoire of hostile words is *mad, irritated,* and *angry.* I have often said something like, "That seems to make you angry" and had the client emphatically reject my statement and back off a bit, clearly threatened. A few moments later, though, we might quite comfortably be using the word *annoyed.* Perhaps I was right that what the client was experiencing was anger, but I clearly had gone beyond the intended message with a word that was too powerful. My guess is that, shortly, this client and I will be talking about anger, but we will have to approach it through more finely shaded gradations of meaning. You also have to be sensitive to what particular words mean to particular clients. With one client I remember, the word anger meant violent screaming and physical abuse, and it took me some time to figure out why some of my responses were so threatening.

In the last paragraph, I put *feeling words* in quotation marks because the job of developing a vocabulary of finely shaded meanings goes beyond what are traditionally thought of as "feeling words." Hostile words, for example, can include *miffed, irked, impatient, annoyed, irritated, resentful, bitter,* and *furious,* but they also can include *gagging on screams, twitching,* and *stretched tight,* depending on the person doing the feeling. Each of these words has a different meaning (which is why they all exist, obviously), and clearly you need to have the most complete vocabulary you can.

Following is a sample of common feeling words and their shadings taken from a thesaurus and dictionary of synonyms. All this list does, though, is give you a start toward developing a usable vocabulary. It would be a good exercise to work up your own list, including regional terms or faddish terms for various feelings. Study this list, and then choose one word and try to think of as many shadings of meaning as you can to that one word. Imagine a client in front of you describing the feeling.

Unhappy words: *dejected, low, sad, depressed, down, lost, blue, melancholy, brood, dreary, flat, joyless, downhearted, somber, gloomy, dreadful, dismal, empty, grim, desolate, hopeless, mourning, desperate, blah, glum, disappointed, aching, anguish, grieving, rotten, barren, awful, teary,* and *terrible.* Study this list or listen to lots of sad country songs.

Affection words: *love, friendly, caring, like, fond of, respect, admire, trust, close, adore, devoted, regard, tenderness, attachment, yearning, longing, infatuated, fellowship, attraction, favor, prize, hold dear, fall for, precious, passionate, woo, revere cherish,* and *idolize.*

Guilt words: *blame, regret, shame, embarrassed, at fault, reprehensible, wrong, remorseful, crummy, rotten, humiliated, unforgivable, mortified, ashamed,* and *disgraceful.*

Anger words: *resentment, irritation, rage, fury, annoyance, provoked, infuriated, inflamed, displeasure, animosity, wrath, indignation, exasperation, pique, huff, miff, sore, bitter, temper, hate, fume, dander, ferment, tiff, passion (sometimes), sullen, morose bristle, bridle, sulk, pout, frown, chafe, seethe, boil, rage, offend, rile, aggravate, rankle, worked up, cross, burning, pissed off, outraged, ticked off, hateful, vengeful,* and *mad.* There sure are a lot of these words.

Fear words: *timid, diffident, anxious, worried, apprehensive, misgiving, doubt, qualm, hesitant, fright, terror, horror, dismay, panic, consternation, scared, nervous, restless, trepidation, quivering, shaking, trembling, intimidated, cold sweat, dread, despondent, creeps, shivers, jitters, cower, afraid, tremulous, vulnerable, butterflies, jumpy, worried, uneasy,* and *unsure.*

Confused words: *bewildered, puzzled, flustered, overwhelmed, mixed up, muddled, perplexed, tumult, chaos, jumbled, uncertain, undecided, ambivalent, drifting, baffled, trapped, in a quandary, tangled, scrambled, unraveled, disjointed, swamped, drowning,* and *frustrated.*

Happy words: *contented, joyous, ecstatic, glad, cheerful, glee, optimistic, hopeful, alive, lively, merry, exhilarated, jovial, satisfied, comfortable, animated, inspired, elated, encouraged, heartened, refreshed, genial, light, buoyant, bright, saucy, jolly, playful, exultant, pleased, gratified, zest, bliss, thrilled, tickled, sensational, terrific, euphoric, enthusiastic, glowing, neat, good,* and *fine.* Actually there are a lot of these too.

Hurt words: *neglected, put down, rejected, demeaned, scorned, used, criticized, belittled, shot down, cast off, discarded, let down, disappointed, devastated, humiliated, betrayed, harmed, embarrassed, dumped on, ripped off, disillusioned, disparaged, maligned, laughed at,* and *exploited.*

Strength words: *responsible, confident, adequate, powerful, certain, sure, efficient, important, competent, effective, superior, cope, potent, able, lucid, adaptable, forceful, effectual, incisive, influential, growing, moving forward,* and *alive.*

This, quite obviously, is only a start. I have left out dozens of good words, and so you should make your own long list, in addition to reading all that good fiction. An important thing to note is that many of these words, although they carry useful nuances of meaning, are not common words, and particular clients may not know their meaning. If you are to communicate understanding, you obviously must match your words to your client. If you are being skillfully tentative, you will be getting regular feedback on your accuracy, and this will give you a chance to check out whether your words are the right ones for this person.

■ When You Miss

These first three chapters have set you a difficult task—not impossible, but difficult. You must hear well and you must articulate accurately and quickly. To top it all off, you will inevitably be wrong at times and must be ready to deal with these errors. The risk is that you will become defensive and worry about "losing face" when you miss, but this risk is greatly diminished if your goal really is to understand rather than to look like an expert. Your skillful tentativeness, for all the good things it does for the client, also covers you when you misunderstand. Because you make it easy for the client to disagree with you, you make it easy for yourself to say, "I missed on that one . . . say some more and let me try to understand it again."

In this case, *missing* means misunderstanding the intended message. When you say something that the client rejects or backs away from, you may have been quite right in some ultimate sense, but it won't do therapy any good to try to establish the accuracy of your opinion. It's not the truth that sets the client free nearly so much as it is the process of finding the truth. I had one client who told me about a dream in which he was forcing an ice cream cone down a woman's throat. I didn't have to be too clever or even very Freudian to see symbolism in this, and I gave in to the temptation to be clever, saying, "I wonder if there is some sexual and aggressive meaning to your dream." The client thought I was way off base and told me so, and I reluctantly backed off. About six weeks later, he said, "Do you remember that dream I had about the ice cream cone? I think I see something in it . . . I think it had a lot to do with how I see women and how anger and sex are mixed up together for me." I'll never know whether my comment delayed or speeded up his figuring this out (I suspect it slowed things down), but he saw it when he was ready. I am quite sure that if I had pursued the issue and convinced him of the accuracy of my interpretation, I could have made him agree with me intellectually but actually prevented his emotional growth by making him defend himself against me and against the feelings surrounding sex and aggression.

One last word of reassurance for when you miss: you can make a lot of mistakes and miss a lot of things, but your clients will repeatedly try to return to the issues that matter most. If you are consistently off, your clients will give up on you, but you can trust them to approach the things they need to deal with continually, as closely as they can stand to. Chapters 16 and 17 will discuss why you can trust your clients in this way.

Confronting Experience

One student described this approach to therapy as "continuously confronting the client. Each thing the therapist says is a little confrontation, even though it is said gently." He was right, and there are useful things to learn from what he said, as long as we are clear about what the word *confrontation* means. Most people seem to use confrontation to mean that the therapist is pointing out discrepancies in the client's thinking and presenting alternative views that the client hasn't seen or can't see for him- or herself. These discrepancies are presented in a challenging way. In contrast, the confrontation that occurs in evocatively empathic therapy is done by being at the edge of clients' experiencing and helping them face the meaning and emotion of what they said. In a sense, it is self-confrontation, done with the therapist as a strong companion. The therapist, however, is not passive. He or she confronts the client with the implied part of what the client says and thus helps the client confront his or her experiences. Patterson recognizes this when he says, "It is possible that confrontation should not be considered as a separate condition or dimension of psychotherapy. . . . The recognition and communication of discrepancies in the client's verbalizations and behaviors does seem to be an aspect of empathy" (1974, p. 77).

As has been true so often before in our discussion, much depends on the therapist's intent. An empathic confrontation does not communicate, "Here, let me point out to you things you should have seen but haven't"; it communicates, "You seem to feel many different ways all at the same time; let me put it all into words so we can look at it together." The therapist can help the client confront his or her own experience with a comment like, "As I hear you, you feel both ways—you think bosses are unfair, and you worry that you don't perceive other people, bosses included, accurately. It's hard to know what's true."

■ Combining Cognitive and Experiential

One of the most important lessons in this book is that effective therapy (effective living, for that matter) requires an integration of cognitive and experiential functioning. Some therapy approaches, most notably Ellis' (1994), assume that cognitions determine emotions, while other "experiential" approaches focus on unstructured feelings, "letting it all hang out." There is good reason to believe, however, that emotional reactions and preferences can be established independently of cognitive activity (Christianson, Saeisae, & Silfvenius, 1996; Damasio, 1999; Fox, 1996; Hermans, De-Houwer, & Eelen, 1995; Lambie & Marcel, 2002; Ohman, 2002; Pessoa, 2005; Phelps, 2006; Seeburger, 1992; Whalen, et al., 2004; White, 1996; Winkielman, Zajonc, & Schwarz, 1997; Zajonc, 1980, 1981; chapters 8 and 16 of this book), and it is clear that some degree of rationality is required to survive and live an effective life. Littrell (1998) points out that emotion is essential in treatment, but just expressing painful emotion without acquiring new responses to the pain can be harmful. I suspect that some of the "pure experience" approaches to therapy developed as a reaction against the powerfully intellectualized nature of more traditional therapy, and it is my impression too that much of the therapy practiced by professionals educated in our university systems tends toward "pure cognition." There is, in fact, strong interest in cognitive approaches, which have many strengths but which also seem to teach that cognition controls all, including emotional responses. Cognitive and emotional functioning are closely intertwined, but they can and do operate independently too. Fears, for example, are the result of complex conditioning experiences. Although "expectations" and "preferences" and other cognitions become involved in them, a well-established principle of conditioning is that *the only way to get rid of a fear is to feel it.* In other words, changing emotions requires emotional experiencing. Sometimes talking gets rid of fears but not because one can reason away the fear; rather, in the process of the talking, some of the fear is aroused and has a chance to be extinguished.

Therapy is both a rational process and a "corrective emotional experience" (Alexander, 1948). I like Bohart and Tallman's (1997, 1999) statement: "Change is cognitive-experiential. Learning and discovery that leads to change is experiential and not just intellectual. Experiencing is a different way of knowing than knowing through conceptual analysis or through thinking about" (1997, p. 397. See also Bohart, 1993 and chapter 8 of this book). When helping the client confront him- or herself emotionally, the therapist provides the client with an opportunity to feel fears and other emotions in a safe setting and to solve problems. Material that used to be too emotionally threatening to be clearly thought through becomes available to think with— to find new solutions that permit more effective living outside of therapy.

Whelton (2004) summarized the research on the role of emotion and cognition in a wide variety of approaches to therapy (humanistic, cognitive, behavioral, and psychodynamic). His conclusion can give you the comfort of knowing that research evidence supports doing therapy that is deeply experiential, tempered by reason and thinking, and given within a strong relationship.

> First, emotion and emotional processing are now widely perceived to be vital dimensions of therapy in all therapeutic modalities. Second, the cathartic idea, the idea that emotional expression, by itself, is always

inherently good, is now viewed as an incomplete and inadequate perspective. The value of emotional expression depends on several contextual variables and on the availability of support to process, explore and articulate the experience. Emotional arousal and expression can lead to constructive change for some clients and problems. Third, the acceptance of emotional experience is generally beneficial and the avoidance of emotional experience is generally harmful, even when the emotions are painful and negative. Fourth, when the client is productively engaged in therapy and is processing information in an experiential manner successful outcomes can be predicted. Fifth, exposure to difficult and fearful stimuli while emotionally aroused in a safe, supportive environment will restructure expectancies and reduce anxiety and symptoms of trauma. Finally, emotional engagement and arousal facilitates effective therapy but lasting personal change also requires cognitive reflection and the construction of new meaning. It is worth remembering as well that the bedrock of all therapy is the development of a relationship and emotional responsiveness is at the heart of this unique form of personal and professional intimacy. (Whelton, 2004, p. 67)

Conclusions versus Experiences

As I will say many times, many therapists tend toward intellectual solutions. This could reflect a North American cultural bias (Messer & Winokur, 1980) toward a belief in rationality and the pioneering spirit that believes there is a workable solution to every problem if we just lay out the steps and follow them. It certainly reflects the fact that to become a professional in our educational system, you must use intellectual prowess nearly exclusively. In therapeutic style, this seems to result in therapists who are constantly searching for *conclusions*. Conclusions and insights are important, let me repeat, but the therapist's job is to set up the conditions within which the client can come to the conclusions, and this is done by facilitating experiencing.

Shaping toward Experiencing

A therapist I know once said to me, "I just don't have the patience to shape clients the way you do." He meant this as a criticism and politely worded advice that therapy goes a lot faster if the therapist controls the process more and tells the client more from the therapist's point of view. I am quite sure that this particular therapist did not understand the nature of evocative empathy and saw it as relatively passive, and I am quite sure that the apparent speed of his more directive approach was an illusion, an observation I will discuss more in chapter 17. What really interested me, though, was his use of the word *shape*. He was using it, of course, in the operant conditioning sense of reinforcing small steps, or successive approximations of the final desired behavior. It would detract from therapy to be sitting there thinking in terms of delivering reinforcers for successive approximations, but in a sense that is what is happening when you see through the client's eyes and help him or her confront experiences.

One common way to move clients toward dealing with feelings is to ask, "How did you feel about that?" In this case, you might get to feelings, but they will be ones you drew out of the client, and, more important, your question implies that you did not hear whatever feelings were implicit in the client's message. By asking the question, you lose the facilitative effects of an empathic response. In contrast, you could articulate the reactions implied in what the client said, and now the client is emitting the feelings, rather than having them elicited by you. Most important, the client has been rewarded for making the approach to feelings, however subtle and incomplete that may have been. By responding in an empathic and accepting way to that part of the message, you are rewarding experiencing behavior—in a sense, "shaping" toward more complete experiencing.

While we're talking in these learning terms, consider for a moment the effect of your behavior in terms of modeling or imitation. When you use experience-oriented words, made more meaningful and poignant by nonverbal parts of your response, you are teaching by example that therapy is a process of exploration and experiencing. In contrast, when you ask questions, even questions like "How do you feel?", to some extent you are teaching by example that an intellectual approach is called for. This is especially true when the therapist consistently engages in rational analysis of feelings, searching for the "correct conclusions." Such a therapist resembles the parent who says "If you hit your sister one more time, I'm gonna hit you," teaching one lesson with the words and, unawares, the opposite lesson more powerfully with behavior.

Preventing Avoidance Gently

One reason your client is in trouble is that he or she fears his or her own thoughts, memories, feelings, and impulses—internal processes of which your client is only partly aware. (The word *fear* is used very broadly here and includes many aversive emotions, such as guilt, shame, depression, and anxiety.) The only way to get rid of a fear is to feel it, but we all avoid the things we fear, and this is one reason fears are so persistent. For your client, the feared thoughts and feelings are usually avoided too quickly to be dealt with, and so they can still cause bad feelings but never be faced directly. This also means that the client can't solve life problems wisely because some of the "truth" is too painful to look at.

You gently prevent the avoidance of these thoughts in a step-by-step way by articulating the implicit message. You put into words what the client *is trying to say and can't quite say* and thus help him or her face what he or she would normally have avoided. The client faces the mildly painful thoughts in the safe surroundings of your relationship, nothing bad happens, and the fear dissipates (extinguishes, actually), so that the client feels fear reduction.

Look at the powerful thing you have done. The client made some response *that came from him or her*, felt some fear, and then felt relief. Fear reduction is one of the most powerful reinforcers of human behavior, and what you have done is to help your client feel fear reduction immediately after an act of self-confrontation. If this happens hundreds of times in therapy, as it should, your client will become more and more self-confronting, more open to his or her own experience. You are empowering your client to become more emotionally independent.

Facing Fear, Facing Joy

There are good reasons why I focus so much on the role of fear in discussing therapy, but we must remember that one of our goals is an openness to *all* experiences—an openness that is necessary to live a full, complete life. As the therapist listens, he or she is not just trying to hear pain but is listening for *poignancy*, for the central part of whatever experience the client is moving toward. Often that will include pain, but sometimes it will be a mixture of pain and joy; sometimes it will be only joy or affection; sometimes it will be peaceful; sometimes it will be chaotic or angry. Your job is to facilitate experiencing, not to determine which experiences are the appropriate ones.

Reprocessing Experience

The last few paragraphs have used learning principles to explain how self-confrontation helps the client. The language of information-processing theory can give a different perspective on the same process. There is good reason to think (Searleman & Herrmann, 1994) that each person's perception and memory of reality is a "construction," a perceived version of reality that is not accurate but is limited by selective perception and by the distortions imposed by "schemes" (Rice, 1974) that we develop. These schemes are like templates onto which we fit reality; they are what we expect to perceive, and we tend to perceive what we expect to perceive. Bruner (1962) reports an experiment in which people saw playing cards flashed quickly and were told to name each card. Occasionally an "anomalous" card, such as a red six of spades, was flashed, and many subjects reported it as a six of hearts. They "saw" what they expected to see. Similarly, the schemes within which we perceive life are limited and sometimes prematurely close off our processing of experience. An evocative empathy response prevents this closing off and forces continued processing of the experience by "putting the person back into the situation" in a vivid way.

The Centrality of Emotion

Therapy must be both cognitive and experiential, and the hardest part of it to learn and deal with seems to be the experiential. There is a growing acknowledgement of the importance of emotion in psychotherapy research and writing that lays a foundation for the focus of this chapter (Burum & Goldfried, 2007; Ehrenreich, Buzzella, & Barlow, 2007; Goldman, Greenberg, & Pos, 2005; Magnavita, 2006)

Coombs, Coleman, and Jones (2002), for example, found that "collaborative emotional exploration" was significantly related to positive outcome in both Cognitive Behavioral Therapy and Interpersonal Therapy, but "educative/directive process" was not. Greenberg and his colleagues (Greenberg, Auszra, & Herrmann, 2007) reported that emotion is central to good outcome in therapy, but it's not just the expression of emotion that is important. The emotional work needs to be what they define as "productive emotion."

> The emotion expressed has to be primary; the emotion has to be experienced (a) in the present and (b) in a mindfully aware manner, meaning that (c) the emotion has to be owned by the client who experiences him- or herself as an agent rather than as a victim of the feeling and (d) the emotion is not overwhelming; the emotional process has to be fluid rather than blocked; and the emotion has to be on a therapeutically relevant theme. (p. 487)

Greenberg (2007) also argues that much emotional work operates "largely below conscious awareness" (p. 414) and that some emotional changes can result from deliberate conscious action but much of it can only come from "more implicit processes based on new emotional and/or relational experiences" (p. 414). This is a more complete and elegant version of my previous statement that the only way to change a fear is to feel it.

Therapy as a "Safe Emergency"

Therapy is like no other relationship or situation. It is tightly bound within limits such as having a set and limited time, prohibiting dual relationships between therapists and clients, and providing confidentiality. These limits serve a wonderful purpose; they permit both the client and the therapist to be fully present for the hour, to focus intensely on only the client's experience, and—most amazingly—to provide a place where it is safe to weep or to be furious or to tremble with fear. Therapy is most fundamentally emotional work, and the therapist shows his or her courageous willingness to "go into the pit" or "walk through the fire" with the client as he or she re-experiences and reprocesses emotion.

Experiential Focusing

Gendlin (1962, 1969, 1974, 1978, 1991, 1996) has emphasized as strongly as anyone that emotional growth requires both cognitive and experiential involvement. He argues that, "direct experiencing is implicitly rich in meanings, but is never equatable to words or concepts" (1974, p. 227). He thus makes it clear that we have a complex challenge in therapy: our tool is language, but much of what matters most cannot be adequately expressed in language. It can be felt, but the *felt sense* is a physical process that is only inadequately expressible in concepts. Gendlin has developed a method called *focusing* to help the therapist and client engage in a process that deals with direct experiencing. When the client directly experiences his or her felt sense, there is a noticeable sensation of resolution or falling-into-place that Gendlin calls a *felt shift*. Afterward, this felt shift might well be followed by better conceptual or intellectual understanding, but an enormous amount has happened at the experiential level that simply cannot be expressed.

Focusing involves an explicit procedure for paying attention to what's going on inside the person's body. Gendlin (1978) argues that anyone can learn to focus and that most therapists simply do not facilitate the process; in fact, they often hamper the client's experiencing process. In therapy, "if clients do not, of their own accord, engage in this every few minutes, I try to bring it about. I ask people to stop talking and to sense inwardly into themselves. Let it form and let it tell you what it isn't" (1974, p. 228).

Gendlin's writings seem to give the therapist a role as somewhat more directive of the process than what I have been recommending, and so it is important for me to clarify this issue. In practice, Gendlin strongly argues that whatever else a therapist does, she or he must constantly return to the "baseline" of empathic responding. "Only in this way can the therapist stay constantly in touch with what is occurring in the person, and thus know and help make good use of whatever beneficial results other therapeutic procedures might have" (1974, p. 216). He makes the "very serious charge . . . that most therapists leave their patients inwardly alone. . . . One does not know what is happening for the person just now. Thus, one is blind. [Empathy] is not just one of many ways, but a precondition for the other ways" (p. 217). Even when he is instructing the client to focus, the spirit of what he does quite clearly is designed to leave the control of the therapy process in the client's hands. My impression is that the only real difference in how Gendlin and I do therapy is that I think evocative empathy, done well, facilitates the same experiential focusing for the client as does his more explicitly guided focusing process.

More recently, Bohart (Bohart, 1993; Bohart & Associates, 1996; Bohart & Tallman, 1997) has argued that *experiential knowing* is fundamental to psychotherapy. In fact, he calls it "the basis of psychotherapy." One of the most important themes that we will keep returning to is that therapy is both a cognitive and an experiential process. Both are absolutely essential, and we will come back to understanding experiential knowing in more depth in chapter 8.

■ Therapist as Chicken— Intellectualizing Is Easy

After training therapists for several decades, I have come to believe that the most difficult part of learning therapy is becoming comfortable with, and responding to, clients' emotions. I know I'm repeating myself, but "the most difficult" is a strong statement. It is very likely that you will struggle with this issue.

One therapist in training was having trouble staying focused on emotional issues with his clients, and as we discussed how difficult therapy was, he suddenly realized that a lot of his difficulty came from his fear of dealing with feelings. He said he liked to offer explanations and make interpretations and look for causes and categorize things because that was what he knew how to do, and it kept him from getting too involved with the client. Meaningful as this insight was to him, however, it did not suddenly make it easy to plunge into evocative responding; understanding an emotional reaction is not enough by itself to change that reaction, for us as well as for our clients. You have heard this somewhere before, but the only way to get rid of a fear is to feel it, and only through practice and getting feedback and facing your own fears of feelings will you become comfortable with experience-oriented therapy.

The MUM Effect

We have a strong tendency to avoid giving bad news to others—the MUM effect (Tesser & Rosen, 1972). Partly, we fear negative reactions from the other person; partly, it makes us feel bad to feel like the cause of painful feelings in the other person. Egan (2004) has said that the MUM effect often keeps counselors and therapists from using confrontation, and if every evocatively empathic response is a self-confrontation, there will be many times when you will be making your clients face painful things. I remember vividly the first time a client started weeping in therapy. I was scared that maybe this process didn't really work, and what was I going to do if she couldn't stop, and what if I was making her worse somehow by making her feel so bad. Now I do trust the process (which may be small comfort to you when your clients start weeping), and many of my clients cry at some point in therapy—and not because I'm mean. Many therapists have said that this is one of the hardest aspects of doing therapy; it takes time and experience and personal strength to be able to go through intense emotional pain with another person who matters to you.

A student therapist recently told me that she figured out why she was comfortable with some clients' painful and intense emotion but not with others. If the client pretty much got herself into the emotion, it was no problem to stay with it. However, the therapist often pulled back when a client just hinted at something difficult or painful. The therapist said, "It's like I'm afraid to say this thing that the client has clearly implied because I'm afraid I'll hurt him or upset him. It's almost like I feel like the cause of the hurt."

The "Maybe It's Because" Game

The favorite refuge of cowardly therapists is to look for causes of problems in the past, and clients are only too happy to go along with the game. An example of a common stereotype of therapy is the male client suddenly having a blinding flash of insight in which it all becomes clear that his inability to deal with authority figures stems from the time his father beat him with a studded belt because he kissed his mother too often. I'm being a bit flip, but the stereotype is distressingly common. In fact, most clients make their progress and find their insights in small steps over a period of time. They often are surprised to find themselves much better as they look back on old problems that now seem so remote it is as though some other person had the problem. "I don't see how it could have been from therapy," they say, "because I didn't really have any big insights." The changes have come from incremental emotional and cognitive experiences, not from smashing insights.

Remarkable "aha" experiences of sudden insight do occur in therapy sometimes, and they probably stand out in our memories because of their power. The misleading part is if they lead us to think that it was the new knowledge that was the whole source of therapeutic gain. It is not the truth alone that frees the client but also the process of finding the truth. The client's problem has been that the truth was too painful to look at, and so the feelings must change, through gradual exposure to the thoughts and feelings, to permit the insight to occur. Sometimes the insight brings emotional growth; sometimes the emotional growth brings insight. Both cognitive and emotional processes are essential parts of therapy, and the therapist's search for causes is usually a way to avoid the emotional part of the process.

■ Confrontation

Much of this chapter has been an attempt to redefine the word *confrontation*. Its usual meaning carries an aggressive, shake-'em-up-good connotation that implies that the therapist is the expert who has to guide the client toward the truth.

Abuses of Confrontation

Things that some therapists say in describing their behavior with particular clients include, "What he needed was a good swift boot in the rear to get off that self-pitying stuff" and "I told him it was time to shit or get off the pot" and "I pointed out to her that for all her talk about wanting to make friends, the way she treated them was designed to drive friends away." To use the language of learning principles, these comments reflect a punitive approach to therapy. Evocatively empathic therapy uses confronting responses in a way that rewards (with fear reduction) problem solving by the client. Traditional confrontations are attempts to punish the failure to problem solve. Put this way, the long-term effects of the two approaches become clearer. Punishment is popular because it seems to work quickly, since the other person shows rapid behavior change *if the punisher holds sufficient coercive power.* Long-term change is unlikely, however, for several reasons. Punishment only teaches what not to do; it does not reinforce the more desired behavior. Punishment only suppresses the punished behavior; it does not weaken the behavior, since the only way to do that is through extinction. Punishment causes a lot of unintended aversive effects, such as punishing the child for being in school or the client for being in therapy, in addition to punishing the targeted behavior. Punishment often requires the continued presence of the punisher's coercive power.

Evocatively empathic therapy, in contrast, is based on principles of reward, of positive reinforcement. "People do what they are reinforced for doing" is a powerful truth. In contrast to the effects of punishment, positive approaches specifically establish desirable behavior, making the undesirable behavior unnecessary. Positive approaches reward interaction with the parent, teacher, friend, or therapist, in addition to rewarding particular behaviors. Positive approaches establish the independence of the other person.

In a way, I have been too harsh with the people who made the comments at the beginning of this section. I can share their frustration at passive acceptance of the client's evasive behavior, contradictory verbalizations and actions, and whining. But a direct attack on these will only bring, at best, a temporary compliance and, at worst, a building of new and stronger defenses against the therapist. I think some of this frustration grows out of a lack of familiarity with a workable alternative. Passive approaches seem so futile.

In the Spirit of Accurate Empathy

The alternative that evocatively empathic therapists seek is an active, confronting-of-experience, let's-explore-all-the-edges way of facing the client with what he or she has said. It is critical that this be done in the spirit of empathy. The therapist's intention is to make it clear that the client is the source of new knowledge, and the therapist's role is to keep the client working at the edges of his or her thinking and feeling. Cameron (1963) says it nicely:

> The good therapist does not of course coerce his patient to move too rapidly into sensitive areas. As French has often expressed it, the good therapist, like the good gardener, waits until he recognizes something which is struggling to emerge and then makes it easier for it to emerge. He never tries to drag anything up from the unconscious or deep preconscious into awareness. (p. 769)

Cameron speaks from a psychoanalytic viewpoint, but the attitude of the good therapist could hardly be better described.

Contradictions and Distortions

The traditional confrontation says, "Aha, I've caught you in a contradiction," while the empathic confrontation says, "I can understand your confusion when you feel both X and Y at the same time." Both responses focus on the contradiction, but the second one does not *judge* it. The second response just says, "We have to look at this to see where we're going next."

Similarly with distortions: only if distortions are based on a *lack of information* can you talk a person out of them. In most cases, distortions will be based on the inability to use information that, objectively, is just as available to the client as it is to you. Persuasion is probably worse than nothing because the client will have to defend the distortion or, worse, give you a "Yes, doctor" response and quietly withdraw. I remember a client whose problem clearly involved a sexual incident for which the police had threatened him with legal action. Early in therapy, the client said, "Well, I'm sure that sex doesn't have anything to do with all this." I nearly choked, since he had talked so much about the incident. My response was, "So the way you see it, sex isn't a central part of this . . . it looks now like the important part is worrying about losing control and doing something you don't even know you're doing." Notice that I haven't agreed with him or disagreed with him—my version of the truth is not an important part of our process together. I am sure that a direct confrontation would have stopped him dead, although I probably could have done better than I did by including in my response some reference to the incident, while still acknowledging that it was not central to him. This particular client was in therapy for a relatively long time, but it is interesting that near the end of therapy he said, "It's pretty obvious that all of this I've been through has centered around sex."

The fastest way to get to the truth is to make the truth bearable.

Arguing with Clients

One bind that you automatically avoid by adopting an empathic mutual-exploration stance is that of arguing with your clients in order to save your own face or pride. I hope no therapist would have an out-and-out argument with a client, but it is not uncommon for therapists to engage in subtle arguments, with what we might politely call "firm persuasion." If you have a pet theory or interpretation or piece of advice that the client rejects, you are in a position where you must either back down, in the sense of losing out, or argue the client into backing down and accepting what you say. As with most direct attacks, this forces the client to defend against you and what you say and is almost always counterproductive. If you win the argument, you will have intellectual compliance but you cannot have emotional change, as that comes from the client's experiencing. If you win the argument and are wrong, you will have led the client down, at best, a blind alley and, at worst, a destructive course. Unless you are irrationally arrogant, you must admit that at least some of what you would tell a client has to be wrong. What are the consequences when you impose such advice on a client?

You are an expert on the process of therapy but not on the content of this particular client's therapy. You keep the client working in a particular way but not on any particular content that you determine. Thus, you are never wrong; you may hear incorrectly, but if you do, you simply say so and try again. There is no need to argue.

The State of the Relationship

Earlier I referred to confrontation done in the spirit of accurate empathy and to confrontation being a part of evocative empathy. In the first chapter I also talked about different intensities of interaction at different stages of therapy. Both of these observations are related to how "confronting" the therapist can happen and still be facilitative.

Expertness versus Empathic Intent

A lot of your style as a therapist will have to do with how you picture your role. If it is important to you to be an expert, and one of your motives for being a therapist is to have direct control over others, you will have a lot of discomfort with this approach to therapy. In the direct sense, you must give up control and operate in an egalitarian way. Obviously, however, if all I have discussed is true, you will have an enormous influence, but as a facilitator, not a controller. This is not the place to examine your motives for being a therapist (although you should do that somewhere), but the need to be an expert is an important issue in understanding the place of confrontation in your therapy.

Advantages of Self-Confrontation

To summarize, then, your job is to help the client confront the implications of what he or she is saying. In doing this, you reward self-exploration, you help make frightening thoughts and feelings less frightening, you help the client become a strong problem solver, you reward him or her for talking to you, you help him or her open up to emotional sensitivity in general, and you facilitate the solving of immediate problems.

■ Defensiveness and Resistance

Some people come to therapy in great pain, while others come with life difficulties but little felt emotion. Therapy will usually go faster for the first than for the second group because the people in the first group are more strongly motivated to change and because they are more sharply feeling whatever it is that is bothering them. The well-defended client, in contrast, has worked out ways of avoiding emotional pain and will have difficulty giving up those defenses, and this behavior is discussed in detail in chapter 16. Briefly, this person has, consciously and unconsciously, developed avoidance behaviors that include partially inhibiting frightening thoughts and feelings. The therapy process asks that he or she give up these defenses and face pain, as a first step toward a better solution to life. This is a lot to ask and is the main reason therapy with highly defended people takes longer.

Mistrustful Clients

One subtle kind of resistance comes from a general mistrust of others. This doesn't have to be an obvious suspiciousness. It can be a fearful holding back; it can be a frustrated inability to think of anything to say—an inability that puzzles and confuses the client; it can be verbal diarrhea that never stops to let the therapist get close to anything. Intimacy of any kind inevitably involves vulnerability to the other person, who gains the power to hurt you to the extent that you reveal your weaknesses to him or her. Most human emotional problems have a lot to do with previous relationships in one way or another, and so it is no surprise that clients have trouble trusting their therapists enough to make themselves vulnerable. Trust must be earned through dependable acceptance, through respect, through being nonjudgmental, through not hurting the other person, and through dependable understanding. These things take time to develop, and to the extent that trust is a problem, therapy demands patience.

Deeply mistrustful, strongly suspicious clients are very difficult to work with, and it is especially important to be sensitive to the limits of the intended message. You can sometimes make "empathic guesses" with clients who trust you, but it is important to "stay close" to the message with very untrusting clients.

Intellectualizing

I have been pretty hard on therapists who intellectualize a lot, arguing that they don't do very good therapy. One reason they don't is that their style feeds right into one of the most effective of the defenses against feelings. If feelings are hard to handle, as they are for most people who seek therapy, there is great relief in dealing with everything at a cognitive level. You can even talk *about* feelings and analyze them to death without letting yourself know you are actually avoiding feelings. Surely, the person thinks, if I talk about feelings all the time and even join discussion groups where we discuss the nature of emotion, I'm a feeling person. Rational analysis does serve us well in controlling many aspects of life, and so we read books about positive thinking and try to talk ourselves out of and into different feelings.

The insidious thing about intellectualization by the client is that it can so easily draw the therapist into a similar style. Like the therapist mentioned earlier, we're comfortable with ideas and rational analysis. You survived the educational system this long not by being emotionally sensitive but by being an organized thinker. It is deeply ironic that we now are asking you to give up some of what has helped you survive and to become more experiential. Let's hope that graduate school doesn't ruin your naturally empathic ability.

To repeat, though, we are not going to abandon reason for "pure feeling"; we are going to try to integrate the two. When the client says, "There is an aspect of our marriage that fits the general notion of increasing isolation in the middle stages of a relationship," you will know that he has made an important emotional statement, but in intellectual terms. A direct attack might be to say, "You are talking about your marriage in intellectual terms. How do you feel about it?" Here you are trying to get him to the feelings, an excellent goal, but you have not acknowledged that he was trying to talk about feelings. He might say, in response to your question, "Well, the isolation is the hardest part." This is sort of a feeling response, but he is still talking about feelings rather than experiencing them. You might have said, "So you're pretty lonely for the way she used to love you." It's the same meaning as his statement but worded in a subtly different way that makes all the difference.

Taking Away the Need for Defenses

Therapy with well-defended clients can be frustratingly slow. Most writers on therapy agree that there is no fast way to do such therapy, although there is disagreement about what is the fastest of the slow approaches to use. The therapist's frustration often leads to a desire to attack the client's defenses directly, and some therapists recommend this technique for defensive clients (Carkhuff & Berenson, 1967; Davanloo, 1996; Ellis, 1994; Reich, 1949). Research (Beutler, Moleiro, & Talebi, 2002) strongly shows that raising a client's defensive resistance through such directive measures is related to poor therapeutic outcomes. Defensiveness, however, has developed for such clients through the process of anxiety reduction and has, in this sense, been "successful." To the extent that such defenses are anxiety reducing, they have been strongly established and can be given up only with considerable pain. Truax and Carkhuff (1967) say that the research literature suggests a poor prognosis for very defensive clients, regardless of the approach used.

The client will not give up the defenses as long as the need for them exists. We must somehow take away the need for the defenses, admitting to ourselves that this is going to take a long time.

The dilemma a therapist faces is how to respond empathically to the client whose verbalizations seem primarily defensive. The therapist might fear that empathic and accepting responses to defensive verbalizations will reinforce the client's defenses. To some extent this is possible. However, by confronting and attacking the defenses, the therapist is punishing the client's few self-exploratory responses and establishing him- or herself as a source of aversive feelings. The therapist's job can be described as taking away the client's need for defenses within the therapy hour by not being an anxiety arouser him- or herself and by offering understanding and acceptance without punishing the client for being defensive. It is unlikely that any client's verbalizations are entirely defensive. The client will be trying to approach troubling feelings and then backing off. It is the therapist's job to hear these attempts and to articulate them in a nonthreatening way.

I am saying all this more strongly than I did years ago (Martin, 1972) because I am now more convinced that defensive clients can benefit from therapy, but the therapist must enter such therapy with the knowledge that a commitment of time and effort is required. There are limits to what therapy can do, and there are limits on what you can do; this is one of the times when it is important to know what those limits are.

Confrontations That Imply Criticism to the Client

We have already talked about how arguing can damage therapy. This happens partly because arguing usually implies criticism of the other person. Strupp (1996) and his colleagues have gathered convincing evidence that

even a small number of pejorative communications by the therapist has highly deleterious effects on the patient-therapist relationship. Indeed, I believe that there are few things more important for therapists to learn than to avoid being drawn into conflict and power struggles with a patient, which is of course exactly what patients are typically impelled to bring about. (p. 136, italics in original quotation)

I hope it surprises you that we would even be worried that therapists might say pejorative, hostile, critical, or blaming things to clients. Some therapists do make such comments, sometimes openly, sometimes subtly, and sometimes as a matter of preferred technique. Davanloo (1996), for example, writes of the need for the therapist to be familiar with clients' "tactical defenses" and illustrates

> the therapist's immediate challenge of these defenses, and in some cases pressure leading to the head-on collision and breakthrough. . . . Only if a therapist can recognize them can he/she know how to challenge them, and only if he/she can recognize them instantly can he/she challenge them quickly enough to be truly effective." (p. 153)

Such challenges are probably made by the therapist with good intentions, but there is good evidence (Henry, Schacht, & Strupp, 1990) that this kind of "technical intervention" is often perceived by the client as carrying an accusatory meaning that is quite strongly related to lack of success (or even deterioration) in therapy. They say that "even well-trained professional therapists are surprisingly vulnerable to engaging in potentially destructive interpersonal process," but they also note that in their studies, the "good outcome cases [included] not a single instance of therapist blaming and belittling" (p. 773).

Assuming Good Intentions

There is something about these last few sections that is troublesome. I have been talking about "very defensive clients" as though they were a diagnostic group that is somehow different from other clients.

Like nearly all human problems, defensiveness is on a continuum. We are all defensive to some degree, for the same reasons that "very defensive" people are, and we all have difficulty giving up our defenses, in the very same way that "very defensive" people do. The principles are all the same; what I want to do is to alert you to the difficult issues that defensiveness brings, not to start you looking for a category of clients that are "very defensive" and should be either avoided or treated differently. The effective therapist (maybe even the effective person) assumes good intentions on the client's part. At the very least, it is clear that every client is trying to live the best life he or she can. Sometimes clients (and the rest of us too) do things that are destructive to themselves and others, but there are reasons for such behaviors.

The effective therapist believes in the importance of personal responsibility but has little use for the concept of blame in understanding human behavior. Seen this way, defensiveness loses some of its power to frustrate the therapist, whose job it is to facilitate the client's good intentions—the client's attempts to live the best life he or she can. If distortions block good living, it is our job to help take away the need for the distortions.

5

The Basic Principle
The Client Is the Problem Solver

The fundamental philosophical basis of this approach to therapy is that clients are responsible for their own lives and that they are capable of solving their own problems, with a special kind of help from the therapist. This principle has several implications for the therapist's role—implications that are not always obvious to therapists, implications that I will explore in this chapter.

I will also stress that therapy and counseling are very much problem-solving processes. I have been pretty hard on intellectualizing clients and therapists, and for good reason, but I must now repeat that therapy is neither a process of "pure reason" nor one of "pure feeling." Some approaches to therapy argue that cognitions determine emotions (Ellis, 1994), while others stress encountering current experiencing and even prohibit talking *about* feelings in an intellectual way (Perls, 1970). To repeat from chapter 4, cognitions do affect feelings to some extent, and feelings do distort cognitions to some extent. However, there is good reason to think that thinking and feeling can also operate independently of each other (Christianson, Saeisae, & Silfvenius, 1996; Fox, 1996; Damasio, 1999; Hermans, De-Houwer, & Eelen, 1995; Lambie & Marcel, 2002; Ohman, 2002; Pessoa, 2005; Phelps, 2006; Seeburger, 1992; Whalen et al., 2004; White, 1996; Winkielman, Zajonc, & Schwarz, 1997; Zajonc, 1980, 1981; chapters 8 and 16 of this book), and it seems clear that both are important—that effective therapy *integrates* them.

The client is trying to solve real-life problems, and the therapist facilitates this by helping the client face thoughts and feelings that are too painful for the client to face alone. Both thinking and feeling become clearer and lead to more effective living. The philosophy behind this book is expressed well by Bohart and Tallman in their book *How Clients Make Therapy Work* (1997). They say, "Learning and discovery that leads to change is experiential and not just intellectual" (p. 397). They say this within "the active-client perspective. . . . We believe that all power to effect change comes from the client. Interventions by therapists are impotent and useless until active clients invest their own creative energies in them to make them work" (p. 395).

■ Solving Problems, Getting Strong

All approaches to therapy are aimed at solving the client's problems, and nearly all say that one of their goals is increased independence and personal responsibility on the client's part. But there is a strange paradox here if the therapist is the primary problem solver. In a way, the therapist is saying, "You be independent because I am telling you to." In contrast, if the client does the problem solving, he or she gains two benefits. In the long run, the second benefit may be the more important. The person's current life problems get solved, and the person has gone through the process of problem solving—of facing internal experiences and successfully and independently thinking his or her way through. Like my client who said, "I did this myself! You never did anything but say back to me what I said, only you said it a little stronger," your clients will leave therapy stronger. Your goal as a therapist is never to be needed again.

The way you accomplish this goal is by creating the conditions in which the client can think independently. You say, sometimes explicitly but usually through your behavior, "You must solve your problems yourself. I can't do that for you, but I know how to help you solve your problems. What I have to offer is a powerful process in which I help you explore and think, and together we will find your solutions. In a sense, I don't know where we need to go together, but I know how to get there."

When I started doing therapy, I used to say only the first part of this statement, "You must solve your problems yourself. I can't do that for you," until I realized that this sounded weak and frightening to my clients, who must have wondered exactly why they were talking to me. Many clients come to therapy looking for advice and solutions to be provided by the therapist, and just to say I wouldn't be giving advice, without saying what I *would* do, probably sounded as if I didn't have a clue about what I was doing. The therapist's confidence in therapy is a powerful curative factor, and so you need to say what you can do as well as what you cannot.

When a client asks how therapy works, I often say, "Your job is to explore whatever is on your mind. It doesn't all have to fit together before you say it—just explore. And my job is to help you do that exploring. My experience has been that three things will happen as we do that exploring. You will discover things about yourself and your life that you didn't know before; as we talk, your feelings will change; and you will figure out new solutions." It is worth our while to look at these events and how they come about when we make the client the primary problem solver—processes that are made clearest by talking in learning terms for a minute.

Deconditioning Feared Thoughts

Anxiety constricts behavior, both internally and externally, so that the anxious person takes in less of what is happening in the environment and thinks and feels fewer of the processes that are happening internally. Anxiety can be fears of things in the environment, but it more powerfully and painfully results from fears of one's own memories, thoughts, and feelings (see chapter 16). The only way to get rid of fear is to feel it, in small doses, and not have bad consequences follow. Fear must be faced to be beaten, and what therapy does is to help the client face painful thoughts and feelings, making them less painful. The person comes to think and feel more accurately and fully, both knowing him- or herself more accurately and seeing solutions and information in the environment more clearly. Thus enter the discoveries of "things you didn't know about yourself" and "new solutions."

Thus, also, "the feelings change as we talk," because a lot of the internal pain the client brought to therapy will fade away as thoughts and feelings that used to be frightening lose their ability to frighten through exposure.

Reinforcing Thinking

A directive, advice-giving therapist could give a client some of the bene-fits mentioned in the last section if the therapist were exceedingly brilliant about what thoughts and feelings were frightening the client. He or she would directly expose the client to those thoughts and feelings, and extinc-tion would take place. The therapist would elicit the appropriate responses. Even assuming, however, that he or she was always right about what the appropriate responses were (no therapist ever is), the therapist is depriving the client of the process of independent problem solving. In a paradoxical irony, the therapist can make the client *dependent* on outside problem-solving help by doing the problem solving.

In evocatively empathic therapy, the client *emits* the appropriate responses—thinking and facing internal experiencing—and then the therapist responds in a way that helps the client face what he or she has approached. Think for a minute what is being reinforced. The client takes a step forward, trying to face something, trying to explore something. If the client were alone, he or she would have felt some threatening emotions, retreated from the pain, and felt some relief; unfortunately, the client will have been reinforced for the retreat and avoidance. With the evocatively empathic therapist, however, the client makes the attempt to explore and approach, feels some threatening emotions, but doesn't retreat, because the therapist puts the difficult material into words and the two of them face it together. Now the threatening emo-tions also diminish but not because of retreat; rather, facing them "takes the curse off them" (that is, extinction and counterconditioning take place). What has been reinforced is the approach, the attempt to face experience and to explore it. This process happens thousands of times in good therapy, and so the client is being reinforced thousands of times for independent thinking.

There are other ways that the person is rewarded for problem solving too, of course. Exploring pleasant emotions is obviously rewarding, and simply the thrill of succeeding at solving something challenging figures in too; ther-apy doesn't deal only with painful emotions and thoughts.

But the absolutely critical difference between evocatively empathic ther-apy and therapy directed by the therapist is that the client goes through the problem-solving process. It is not just the truth that makes the client free and strong; it is going through the process of finding that truth.

■ The Client's Job

Earlier I suggested telling the client that his or her job was to "explore whatever is on your mind." This wording seems to make the most sense to clients, but the client's work can be more fully described as including self-exploration, self-understanding, and taking effective action (Carkhuff & Berenson, 1967, 1977; Egan, 2004; Rice, 1984). Egan divides therapy into three overlapping stages and says that each of these is the primary client task for each of the stages.

It makes sense that the three tasks follow in the order listed, since understanding would grow out of exploration, and appropriate action would depend on first understanding the problem, but therapy is probably more usefully seen as a continuous process rather than occurring in stages. Clearly there will be proportionally more self-exploration early in therapy and proportionally more action-taking later, but both are important in every session. Clients often talk about trying solutions and changing behavior in the first few sessions, and continuing to explore experiencing is important in the last session. Come to think of it, there never is a "last session" to good therapy. The client and therapist stop meeting, of course, but the whole point of therapy was to start a continuous process of effective living, which will always involve self-exploration, new self-understanding, and taking action.

Exploration

Most clients come to therapy implicitly saying, "I'm in trouble and I don't know why." When we first ask the person what the problem is, we will get an answer that will reflect the client's current understanding, but it will inevitably be incomplete and inaccurate in many ways. If clients really knew what the problem was, they probably wouldn't need to be in therapy. So therapy is largely a shared search. The client's first job is self-exploration, without a need to make sense out of everything before it is said—with a need to feel around the edges of whatever comes to mind. In some ways this resembles the analyst's rule of free association, although the therapist obviously has a more active role in evocatively empathic therapy.

Clients are doing a lot of self-disclosing, both to their therapist and to themselves. They are saying new things and things that have never been put into words before. A gratifying statement that you will hear from clients, especially early in therapy, is "I've never told anybody this before. I'm amazed I was able to tell you." So self-exploration is difficult for clients because they are having to look at new demons in the fog and trust you to be able to accept and handle not only the awful things they could never share before but also the unknown ones that might suddenly emerge.

Rice (1984) stresses the importance of the client's exploration process as involving experiential reprocessing of his or her affective, inner, and idiosyncratic reactions. One goal of the exploration is discovery of "things you didn't know about yourself"—discovery that leads to new understanding.

Understanding

Dollard and Miller (1950) used the term *neurotic stupidity* to describe the unwise way that a person with anxiety-based problems often approaches life problems. Foolish, self-defeating behavior seems to follow from distorted beliefs about others and about him- or herself. As we shall see in chapter 16, this is largely because so much of the information needed for problem solving and living well is distorted or even not used by the person at all—not because the information isn't available to be seen and used, but because the person is unable to use it. You already know that this is partly the result of anxiety; internal processes such as thoughts and feelings are so threatening that they are avoided one way or another, and this avoidance behavior becomes habitual and persistent, since it works so well to reduce the intense discomfort of anxiety.

New understanding in therapy results partly from the discoveries made during self-exploration. Clients start to recognize, explore, and re-evaluate their self-schemas (Rice, 1984). Thoughts and feelings that were too threatening to be looked at lose their power to frighten, and the client says, "How stupid! Of course that's part of the problem: I'm afraid that if I stand up to him, he'll leave me, but if I really look at it, I know he won't." So a discovery has been made, and now the person has more information with which to think—more information with which to develop more complete understanding. She knows herself better, intellectually and emotionally, and can come up with wiser, more accurate solutions. For this client, the very thought that "he'll leave me" was so threatening that she couldn't think it in anywhere near complete form without becoming so scared that she stopped thinking. All she knew was that she couldn't stand up to him.

So, you are thinking, she had an insight. *Insight* is a widely used word that seems to capture one popular stereotype of what therapy is. In fact, London (1964) separated therapies into "insight therapies" and "action therapies." He probably would call evocatively empathic therapy an "insight" approach, although I hope it is clear to you by now that this reflects a superficial understanding of evocative empathy. The popular stereotype is that all that is necessary is talking and understanding, and every now and then the client will have a dramatic insight that will cause progress to happen in therapy. Generally, *insight* has been used to describe the process of seeing new knowledge or gaining new understanding in a relatively sudden way and with relatively strong emotion. These "aha" flashes are dramatic and important but, probably because of their intensity, have attracted attention disproportionate to their frequency in therapy. Most growth and progress in therapy is quite gradual, with step-by-step increases in understanding, but the experience of insight is often associated with moments of therapeutic growth, and this leads many people to think that the insight causes the growth. They then try to provide their clients with directly given new knowledge as a therapeutic technique. The problem that nearly all therapists have faced then is the diffi-cult-to-explain fact that this clever new knowledge almost never brings the hoped-for flash of new understanding.

The insight often comes as the old painful knowledge becomes less pain-ful—the therapeutic growth and emotional experiencing may cause the "insight," not the other way around. An emotional release occasionally accompanies the sudden realization of a new understanding as anxiety reduc-tion takes place.

Thus, the natural aftermath of exploration is understanding, as the client clears away the fog by facing it and grappling with it. New ideas start coming; new solutions to old problems become apparent; the person feels a new strength and knows him- or herself better.

Taking Action—Talk Is Not Enough

But talk is not enough. Another part of the stereotype of therapy is that it is a cerebral exercise sometimes described as "navel-gazing," in which the cli-ent and therapist wallow around in words and feelings and self-understand-ing for their own sakes. Above all else, however, therapy should be a problem-solving process. Although some therapists may encourage navel-gazing, the stereotype is wrong or at least incomplete. Our goal is to do therapy that helps clients both think better and live better.

The client comes to therapy with serious problems in living and wants new solutions to problems—wants to live differently. Facile advice will do no good, and neither will teaching, if the person has an anxiety-based problem. The problem is not the unavailability of better solutions but the person's inability to use what's available. The goals of therapy are to help the person become more able to think and feel and find new solutions more success-fully—in his or her life outside therapy. New understanding needs to be struc-tured and operationalized and applied in the client's life. These new solutions emerge as the client becomes aware of new options (Rice, 1984).

Egan (2004) calls the final stage of therapy "strategies for action." It is true that effective action will follow accurate understanding, but an emphasis on action and new solutions should be mixed in throughout therapy.

Before we lose sight of evocative empathy, let me say that this action-ori-ented emphasis grows out of the client's attempts to solve problems. The cli-ent will try to approach what he or she needs to deal with and will get as close as he or she can, and then will back off. These approaches will include the experiencing and emotions we talked about so much in the previous chapters, and they will also include attempts to solve problems. If you are evocatively empathic, you will hear and respond to all of this.

Your client might say, "I always sit near the door in any classroom, so I can leave if the situation arises that I really have to." Again, this can be seen as a purely factual statement devoid of feeling and of any attempt to solve problems, but to see it this way would be to hear none of the *intended message*. You could both bring the experiencing to life and respond to an implicit attempt to solve problems by saying, "So one way you try to handle that sudden trapped panic in class is by clearing the way to run. It sounds like you really think about all this a lot—about how much you want to find some way to manage and to make things different." The client implied all of this, although he said it obscurely. Your response recognized both feelings and attempts at problem solving.

Another client might say, "I can't seem to make friends. Nothing works . . . if you smile . . . or listen . . . or try to be interesting . . . all that sucking up to people that's supposed to be so charming . . . they just put you down anyway." Most people would respond to this person with some advice about how to win friends and influence people, advice the person has heard a dozen times already. Or they might pick up the hostility in her voice and point out that she probably drives people away, advice that, of course, will drive this person away. The evocatively empathic therapist will hear a lot of implicit feeling in this remark and will also hear some implicit goals and some implicit attempts at problem solving. Does all that seem unlikely to be in this one comment? How about responding, "It's frustrating to reach out—even irritating, it sounds like—wanting people to like you but feeling like you have to sort of crawl to please them . . . and then even that doesn't work and you feel shunned . . . What *will* work!?"? (This last "What *will* work!?" is said in a tone of voice that clearly means the therapist is speaking as though he or she were the client.)

Many therapists are terribly "task-oriented." They want specific goals with specific solutions, and they want them right now, so that advice about possible solutions rolls easily off their tongues with, "You could try joining a group where you'll meet people who share your interests, or how about starting to jog at the Y?" Only advice columnists can solve human problems this easily; the rest of us are stuck with tedious methods like building therapeutic relationships and exploring and facilitating the client's own problem solving. Likely you are thinking that it would at least be useful to suggest alternatives for the client to think about. But the most common client response you will get then is, "Yeah, I thought about that, but. . . ." Offering suggestions this way will be useful only if there is information available to you that is not available to the client. Ask yourself whether the "suggestions" you are offering are things that are not available to the client to think of. Does she know about the "Y" or that you can meet people jogging or taking dancing lessons? Obviously, in most cases, the problem is not a lack of information; it is an inability to use the information available.

Getting Bogged Down

One student who read a draft of this book said that one of the most useful things to him was advice on how to go from talking and understanding to action. He would feel his therapy bog down, get uneasy, and "frantically start designing action programs for the client." Students do seem to have trouble seeing the talking-to-action transition; part of the problem seems to be that "action programs" seem as if they have to be very structured and identifiable as programs (often with some way to keep score, such as on charts). Your clients are constantly in an action program; every waking minute they are doing something that affects their lives. They will frequently be talking about how they live those lives day to day; this talk is about the real action that they are taking to live—far more than a "program" would be.

As practical advice, refer back to our second "formula response," on page 32 in chapter 3. When you say, "I guess what you want is . . . ," you focus on goals and action. The point is not that you should use this particular wording all the time. (You don't want a client to ask whether you're learning a new technique.) Understand the principle behind this formula. Clients are nearly always implying something they want or want to change; be sure to respond to these hints. Your job is to facilitate the *client's* problem solving, and you do this most powerfully by hearing and acknowledging the client's experiencing and attempts at problem solving. If you ask rhetorical questions ("How about trying . . .?") or make suggestions, you are focusing on the solutions to the current problems, but you are ignoring and thus failing to reinforce the attempts that the client is making. You are helping solve a particular problem (assuming you give good advice, which will be true only part of the time), but you are not working toward the second major benefit of therapy—the client's own independent strength as a thinker and problem solver.

Acceptance

There is a danger in describing "the client's job." We can come to think of exploration, understanding, and action as some kind of prescription that the client *must* go through. My experience has been that we therapists are especially likely to push the client toward overt action. An extremely important and common experience in successful therapy is that the client comes to a sense of *acceptance*—acceptance of self, of others, of circumstances, of the wisdom of not taking overt action sometimes. The client is discovering all kinds of experiences that were only vaguely known, and part of this discovery may bring the insight that nothing new needs to be done, now that the client feels differently.

We need to trust the process. The client will do the problem solving. If that means making internal changes, then we do a serious disservice by urging toward some particular solution, such as taking overt action.

■ Trusting Your Client—A Bit of Theory

We need to look briefly at an important theoretical question here if we are going to be comfortable with the amount of control that this approach to therapy gives the client. How can you trust your client to talk about the things he or she needs to talk about? Many people would say, "It's all very well to be empathic and warm, and every therapist should demonstrate these qualities— they are necessary but surely not sufficient for therapy to take place. The client is confused and troubled and can't think clearly, while the therapist is the expert who knows a great deal more about effective living than the client and knows a great deal more about the nature of anxiety-based problems."

First, this comment reflects a serious misunderstanding of the process of evocative empathy; it reflects the common misunderstanding of empathy as passive. More important for this discussion, however, is it confuses the therapist's greater knowledge of the process of therapy and the nature of anxiety-based problems in general with expertness about *this particular client's problems.* Only the client can really know his or her own problems, although the therapist can know the process to deal with those problems. The client is confused and is distorting things, but two general principles make it clear that he or she can be trusted to solve problems, given that the problem is distortions. (I will tentatively limit this statement to people with anxiety-based problems [see chapter 16] and discuss special difficulties with psychopathic and psychotic problems, in chapter 10.) Second, it is the nature of anxiety-based problems that the person is constantly approaching the sources of anxiety and backing off in the face of the emotional pain. Detailed discussion of this is included in chapters 16 and 17, but trust me for now. Your client *will* try to deal with the things he or she needs to deal with. If you hear these attempts and respond to them, you will help break the vicious circle of suffering and avoidance.

■ Using Questions

I have been pretty harsh about therapists who ask a lot of questions, pointing out how inexperienced therapists ask more than experienced therapists and how questions fail to acknowledge the client's message, implying that the client hasn't done things right. Questions, however, are sometimes appropriate and helpful.

Questions Are Easy

The use of questions is clearly a big issue for beginning therapists. When, as a learning exercise, I prohibit the use of questions by the person role-playing in the therapist-in-training sessions, an almost universal reaction is that he or she feels helpless to keep the discussion going in the "therapy." We depend on questions to get responses from other people, to fill in awkward silences, to gather information, and to solve problems. Questions are easy to depend on because they demand a response, and so we use them often. Sometimes, however, they don't facilitate the other person's own processes as much as an evocatively empathic response. An evocatively empathic response also virtually demands a response when it takes what the other person almost said and puts it right back in front of him. In fact, trainees often accuse me of asking questions when I am role-playing the therapist or when they observe me doing therapy, but when we listen back to what was actually said, the response is clearly a statement of understanding. "But," they then say, "it sure *felt* like a question." It felt like a question because an evocative response *evokes* a reaction.

Empathic Questions

Most questions are attempts to elicit information from the other person, but there is a kind of question that serves the purpose of skillful tentativeness and conveys empathy. Clearly this is what the therapist intends with, "Are you saying that you don't care but you want to care?" Other examples of empathic questions will be less clear in print because their accuracy will depend on their context, the tone of voice, and the therapist's intent. Asking "Are you scared right now?" could be a marvelous response in which the therapist is clearly with the client, or it could be straight off the wall.

An empathic question is often the best way to word a response when you are working quite far ahead of the client and think you understand but aren't sure. You make it clear that you are groping and exploring with the client and that control of therapy is still in his or her hands.

Empathic questions can also give the client "emotional permission" to talk about difficult material. If you can tell that your client is trying to tell you something that is embarrassing or frightening or painful and just can't quite get the words out, but both of you have a pretty good idea of where the story is going, it can be an enormous relief for you just to ask about the story in a calm, accepting way. Asking for the details can be a softer way to get the words on the table than if you used a declarative statement.

One potential problem is that the form of empathic questions is also an easy way to do sneaky interpretations. In fact, a very common manipulative trick in discussions is to preface a statement of personal opinion with, "Don't you think that . . . ?" In form, this preface implies that the speaker isn't expressing a position but rather putting into words the other person's position. Watch your friends and point this out to them when they do it. I'm sure they'll really appreciate your charm and helpfulness.

Evidence-Gathering Therapy

In one training clinic, therapists were required to write up a detailed report on their clients after the fourth interview. For many of the therapists in training, this requirement changed the process of therapy from facilitating problem solving by the client to information gathering and diagnosis by the therapist, who *had* to have a lot of very specific information in a very short time. Learning to write such reports is probably important, but as a goal they distort the process of therapy. In this situation it was possible to have the therapists just ignore the requirement for detailed facts, do therapy, and then set aside a specific time after the fourth interview just to gather information from the client. The point is that this report writing exaggerated a tendency that already exists in most beginning therapists—the tendency to gather information and facts. Presumably, the expert therapist simply needs enough such facts to formulate an accurate appraisal of the problem, and this will lead to effective solutions. This tendency, like our intellectualization, almost certainly comes from a lifetime of solving problems academically by gathering facts. I know you're sick of hearing this, but it is not the truth that matters nearly so much as the process of the client's finding the truth.

In "evidence-gathering therapy," the therapist sets out looking for the facts, asking lots of questions. This question asking, especially in the first interview, creates a powerful "set" for the client. The client is learning how to do therapy and how therapy works by the example set by the therapist in this early encounter; it is not reasonable of the therapist to expect to ask a lot of questions and the have the client suddenly start self-exploration.

Genuine, Reality, Chatty, and Manipulative

Schubert (1977) describes four kinds of questions therapists ask and argues that only one of them is really facilitative. "Genuine questions" ask for the client's personal view of an event or experience and can be answered only by the client. A therapist might ask, "How do you feel when you fail at something?" Schubert then would insist that the therapist respond to the answer with intent listening and empathic responding. "Reality questions" ask for information that anyone could provide—that do not depend on the client's personal frame of reference. "Chatty questions" ask for therapeutically irrelevant small talk. These two are neither very helpful nor very hurtful of therapy. "Manipulative questions," however, are like the sneaky interpretation questions discussed earlier—their goal is to win a point. The questioner is not interested in the answer but in getting the other person to reach a certain conclusion or to admit he or she is wrong or inadequate.

These are useful ways to categorize questions if we add "empathic questions" (which really may be questions only in grammatical form). Genuine questions can be very helpful in therapy because they communicate a desire to understand without taking control. They are asked within the atmosphere of mutual exploration and often permit the therapist to formulate a response when there is little material to respond to. They leave the direction of therapy in the client's hands and are asked tentatively. The risk is that the therapist will disguise manipulative questions as genuine questions, carefully selecting questions to lead the client in some particular direction, but the risk also exists for sneaky interpretations disguised as evocative empathy.

I do ask a fair number of genuine and empathic questions in therapy, but given a choice, I usually use a similarly worded evocatively empathic response if I can think of one. Rather than ask, "How do you feel when you fail?", you could say, "I guess part of what you feel when you fail is fear of something, but it sounds like there's more to it, too." This response shows that you understood some and gives the client "credit" for an attempt to talk about feelings, and it also leaves the door wide open for further exploration— accomplishing what the question would accomplish and more.

■ The Content of Therapy

Many books on therapy, especially psychoanalytic books, discuss a great deal about the content of therapy—what particular emotional issues are dealt with—and have little to say about specific techniques—the process of therapy. This book has focused nearly exclusively on the process and neglected the content, even though content is extremely important. This neglect has been intentional, because it is my conviction that each client's conflicts and problems are extremely complicated and unique to him or her, and the therapist's job is to understand this uniqueness with great precision.

Uniqueness and Commonalities

There clearly are commonalities among human needs and problems; behavior does seem to be lawful; and knowledge of human psychology and psychopathology can help you be a better therapist. But it can also make you a worse therapist. Think back to our discussion of the need for specificity of language, for particularity and subjectivity. A particular client's growth comes out of experiencing the unique felt nuances of his or her own life. We do a disservice when we try to generalize the client's process to fit some principle like "Depression is aggression turned inward" or "People catastrophize disapproval from others."

There is truth in these general principles (and hundreds of others), and understanding them can help the therapist hear implicit messages earlier than she or he would have heard them without the theoretical knowledge. The more you know about human behavior, the better your chance of developing a "third ear." The other edge of this sword, though, is that you might cling to the few hundred principles you know and hear *only* within their framework. Depression isn't always aggression turned inward. Being hurt by rejection isn't always the result of catastrophizing. We all perceive reality imperfectly, and there is reason to think that you will hear what you expect to hear. Even worse, you will tend to draw out from others what you expect to hear. If you are not victim to these distortions, you are the first person in history to be so perceptive; the rest of us have to admit to them and try to hold our understanding of the nature of life tentatively.

Directive in Process, Not Content

One unfortunate word that was used to describe empathy-oriented therapy in the 1940s was *nondirective*. It was meant to distinguish this approach from therapy in which the therapist guided the client through particular emotional and developmental issues and was clearly the superior expert. *Nondirective,* however, sounds pretty wimpy and led to a lot of misunderstanding. Evocatively empathic therapy is clearly quite directive about the general process of therapy, but it leaves in the client's hands the discovery of the specific content of his or her problems.

I Have Never Had a Client Who Didn't Surprise Me

All the therapists I have talked with about this (including myself) have said that they are constantly formulating "little theories" about their particular client, even when they are trying to listen and stay with the person and stay as flexible and tuned in and open as possible. Just like your knowledge of principles of behavior, these "little theories" can both help and hinder you as a therapist. It seems inevitable that you will be thinking about the implications of what your client is saying, as you listen and respond, and your own personal intuitions and understandings can serve you well *if* they tune you in to hear better. You might hear a theme developing and see a number of possible implications and future directions ahead of where your client is. When your client tries to go toward these things, you will be ready to hear the attempt and to go with him or her sooner than you would have been otherwise.

There are at least two ways these "little theories" can do damage, however. First, even if you are as brilliant as your mother says you are and accurately know what direction your client needs to go in, responding ahead of the intended message will threaten the client and slow therapy down. Second, much of the time you will not only be ahead of the client, you will also be going in the wrong direction. Again, you will be vulnerable to confirming your notions through selective listening and self-fulfilling prophecies, and this may be an especially serious problem if you feel a commitment to the ideas you develop about the client. They become "my insights" and evidence of expert cleverness, and it will be threatening to you to have to hear contradictory evidence from the client.

When the client starts therapy, he or she reports certain things as the problem, but it seldom turns out that those things were the "real" problem. The client isn't lying, of course, but neither of you knows ahead of time what the "real" problem is. The beauty of evocatively empathic therapy is that you, as the therapist, aren't required to know the truth for this particular client ahead of time. You know the process for finding the truth. Hard as I try not to, I sometimes succumb to the temptation to formulate my "little theories" about clients, especially ones that look as if they fit some category I've read about. But this clearly grows out of my own need for structure, because every category we have for human behavior is only a crude approximation of any one individual. Every time I start to get committed to one of these formulations, I get startled when the client goes to some completely unexpected place. One client seemed quite clearly to me to be having trouble leaving home because her mother had her in a complex guilt conflict over dependency, and in my mind this became "the problem." I heard evidence for it everywhere in what the client said and was amazed when she cried for the first time in therapy when her older sister left home. I hadn't been entirely wrong; she had tried to talk about her mother. But I had been so intent and become so narrow in my expectations that I could now look back over weeks of therapy in which she had been trying to talk about her sister and see that I, in my cleverness, had not heard her.

The best protection against this kind of distortion is probably to formulate lots of "little theories"—to think ahead, which seems to be inevitable, but constantly to realize that there are dozens of possible directions to go in and implications to see and to listen for as many of them as possible. I really have never had a client who didn't surprise me.

You and I Are Not That Smart

I hope that you are self-actualized and living a meaningful, full life in which you never do self-defeating things, and your relationships are filled with mutual understanding and unconditional acceptance. A bit more realistically, I hope that things are all right for you and that the solutions you have for your life are working pretty well, even though sometimes you can feel pretty bad. It's hard enough trying to live one life well and to see through your own distortions and to find workable solutions for yourself. It really is overwhelmingly unlikely that your solutions are what is best for another person. Giving advice and solving other people's problems doesn't work—not just because the other person resists but also because nobody is smart enough to do such an incredibly complicated task for another person. The advice giver will inevitably give destructive advice as well as helpful advice. Because only the other person can fully know his or her own experience, only he or she can ever have all the necessary information to find wise solutions.

The beauty of evocatively empathic therapy is that you don't have to be an expert about your client's life. You only have to be an expert about a process.

Personality Theories

A lot of your training has probably included the study of different theories of personality—study that has no doubt made you a better person or at least taught you a lot of new terms. There are dozens of such theories, and many of them offer brilliant and helpful insights into human functioning. Each of them makes some sweeping claims about the fundamental nature of humans, however, and many of them flatly contradict each other. They obviously can't all be right, and it is likely that none of them is right in any kind of a complete way. It's a cliché to say that psychology is an infant science dealing with incredibly complex matters, but it's true, and this truth must humble the therapist.

You probably know what I am about to say, because I've said it twice before in this chapter, but personality theories can both help and hinder you as a therapist. Their valid insights can help you hear implicit messages sooner than you would have if you knew nothing about "idealized self-images" or "oedipal conflicts" or "the child talking to the adult within you." Study personality theories carefully. But the danger is that you will become so committed to a theory that you will try to fit everybody into it. Our theories are crude; our categories are crude; nobody really fits any theory exactly. Historically, schools of personality theory have been very much like religions, with a guru who has disciples and followers who attack the followers of other gurus as clearly wrong and probably even infantile. The schools are even named after the guru, so that you know what I mean when I say something like, "I know a Skinnerian who calls Freudians followers of Sigmund Fraud." They're all wrong, but that's OK because they're all partly right too, and you don't have to sort it all out before you can do good therapy, which is a very good thing. I never know what to say when someone asks me what school of thought I subscribe to, and I usually give such a long answer that the person leaves before I'm finished. He or she wanted a label with which to put me in a category, and I want to resist that. "Eclectic" is a reasonably good answer, but it can mean anything from, "I fly by the seat of my pants" to "I'm a closet Jungian, but I'd rather not say so." The fact is, though, that all of us do have some notions about human nature and the kinds of problems that people face. It is probably useful to give a lot of thought and discussion to just what this implicit personality theory is that you hold, because it is going to guide your therapy to some extent; it will make you tend to select certain parts of the client's message over others.

But We Already Talked about That

One last comment on the content of therapy will be from a slightly different perspective. Your client will be talking about his or her unique content in exploring a particular problem and then will leave it to talk about other things. If this particular issue, however, is still not resolved or is still the cause of discomfort, the client will return to it. Often the same general topic will arise repeatedly in therapy. The client is taking repeated runs at the problem, dealing with it a bit differently each time, leaving it for a while, and then returning to it. Sometimes in discussing one of your therapy sessions with you, another therapist or your supervisor might observe, "It sounds like he's worried about whether his son likes him," and you might respond, "Yeah, but we already talked about that." It seems to feel redundant to the therapist; the issue has been tabled and dealt with, so why return to it? Trust the process; if the client is trying to return to the issue or is still troubled by it, it still needs to be faced. The person with anxiety-based problems *will* try to approach the issues that are causing the trouble, and if he or she is making that approach, your job is to hear it—to know that here is the appropriate content of therapy.

If your client says, "Well, I've told you the whole story, and I understand it, and I'm still paralyzed. I still don't know what to do, and I still feel awful," you can safely say, "If it still hurts so much and is still all so confusing, we don't know the whole story; there must still be things we don't understand." Actually, of course, this usually wouldn't have been the most helpful thing to say, since it doesn't prove that you understood. A better response might have been, "I hear you sort of reaching out . . . where do I go from here . . . I'm stuck . . . help me with this, please." Most of the time, the client would go on talking after this. If he or she didn't, I might say something about there still being things we don't know and let's explore them further together.

■ Influencing the Process

To say that this approach is directive in process does not mean that the therapist gives directions like, "You have made an intellectual statement; now tell me the feelings behind that statement." It is directive only in the sense that the therapist behaves in a particular way that keeps the client looking at what he or she has said—that says that this is a process of intense mutual exploration. Thus, you don't usually have to do much in the way of direct teaching of the process—it just flows and happens if you start right out responding empathically after some general opener like, "What can I do for you?" or, "What's on your mind?" or, "How are you?" Good evocative empathy is so rewarding to the client and so quickly feels productive that questions like, "What am I supposed to do?" and "What's the point in this?" may not come up.

Teaching the Process

Sometimes, however, clients do ask these questions, and some clients have little or no idea what therapy is like. They may have been sent to you for help with their "nerves" and expect an examination and advice. They may not be oriented toward verbal problem solving. They may want to please you and be at a loss how to start. Or a client may spill words easily for a while and then get stuck, asking, "Now what?" It can be helpful to teach something about the general process of therapy with words like, "Yeah, it must be puzzling to know how talking is supposed to help—even to know what to talk about. I'll tell you a little about how I work, and if I miss something you'd like to know about, just ask. I see you having come here hurting and confused over how your wife seems to be changing so fast and really not knowing what to do or think or feel about that. Very complicated stuff, and something has to be done soon. What you and I can do together is to explore and talk and try to figure this out. My experience has been that if you will talk about whatever is most on your mind—the feelings, the ideas, whatever—then my job will be to help you explore that, and together we will discover things we don't understand now." If the client seems interested, I will very explicitly say just what it is that I do. "I think a lot of times a person can sort of vaguely understand and feel things, and what I'll do is try to hear what you're trying to say, and I'll help you get that into words—to get that clearer. Sometimes I'll be guessing as I try to understand, and I want to count on you to tell me when I miss. If I can count on you to do that, it'll be easier for me to make some guesses." I seldom would make such a long speech in a session, but all these ideas might come out at one time or another. Anything about the process that the client wants to know is legitimate.

Getting a Word in Edgewise

One problem that arises occasionally is that a client will talk so rapidly and continuously that there are virtually no natural pauses in which the therapist can respond. In most cases, when this happens the therapist is not providing any evocative empathy, and the client is not going through much self-confrontation. As we discussed in an earlier chapter, there is a way to intervene in the process without giving orders that violate the spirit of therapy. You can say, in a supportive but firm tone, "Can I stop you for a minute? . . . I want to make sure I'm understanding this part. If I understand what you mean, you want to be a calmer person, but you want life to be meaningful, too." You might have to be fairly persistent sometimes, but by intervening this way you clearly are expressing an intention to understand, and you are not making the client feel judged in the way you would if you said, "Wait . . . you're talking so much I can't get a word in edgewise."

Requests for Advice

A more common problem is what to do with direct requests for advice. Many people come to therapy expecting to get advice and can be quite frustrated when they don't get it. It is easy to give in to the urge to give advice, especially under the pressure of the client's expectations and hopes. But if the client really does have to take responsibility for his or her own life, and if evocative empathy really is as powerful as it is supposed to be, there has to be a better way to handle the question, "Well, I've told you what the problem is. What do you think I should do?" Or, even worse, "Nobody cares enough even to give me suggestions about what I could do differently. Please don't you be like everybody else and not help me." (Can't you feel the guilt as you say you don't give advice?)

You need a response that shows you understand the need for advice, that says you can't solve the client's problems, that says he or she is responsible for his or her own life, but that says that you *will* help—that there is hope. You could say, "It would really feel good if I could tell you 'Here, do this' and you could go do it and the problem would be solved. (Note: This empathic statement will probably help your clients to look at what they are asking for and to know that even if you did say, "Here, do this," they wouldn't do it.) I don't think I'm smart enough to solve your problems for you, but I think I do know how to help you solve them. I guess right now you feel so much at a loss that it seems like you could never figure anything out alone. Let's do that together." You are expressing both hope and confidence in yourself and in therapy as well as understanding and a trust of the client's capacity to take personal responsibility.

I had one client who must have asked me, "What do you think I should do?" at least 100 times. There are just so many ways to say you don't give advice, and after a while he started following his question with, "Never mind, I know what you're going to say." Later in therapy he said, "I still wish you could do this for me, but I really do know that it has to come from me. I know what I have to do, and nobody can do it but me." (Remember that teaching is appropriate in therapy if the problem is simply a lack of information, but this is a much different matter from giving advice.)

■ Setting Goals

Clients come to therapy because they want change. So one goal of therapy is always that things be different than they are. The difficult question is: change to what?

Goals Are Values

Just like the content of therapy, the goals of therapy can be stated in general ways, and this is a useful, even a necessary, thing to do. The particular goals of a particular client's therapy, however, are unique to that client and reflect that client's values. When we ask for the goals of therapy, we are asking for a description of the Good Life, and any such description is inevitably relative to the individual's culture and circumstances. Is individual accomplishment good? Most people in our culture would say that it is, but there are cultures in which the group good is valued more, and to praise a child for an individual accomplishment would be to humiliate him or her. Is it good to be open and honest in your intimate relationships? "Sure," you say, but the truth is more like, "That depends." You aren't *completely* open and honest in your relationships; why not? Are you espousing values for your client that you don't really live by yourself? There are people for whom openness and honesty would be terribly self-defeating under some circumstances. How will you respond when your clients express goals for themselves that you disagree with, especially if you have a personal investment in the issue? You might feel strongly about sexism and have a client who says, "I think women were meant to be passive. I don't want some woman who'll sacrifice her family for some ideal about independence." This client is struggling to define and pursue goals for his life. Can you let him do that? Your solutions are not the best solutions for everybody, and a therapist is called on to let the client find his or her own best solutions. There are limits beyond which each of us will not go—values whose violation we can't participate in—but these limits have to be wide for an effective therapist.

Describing the effective person is so difficult that only a few humanistic theorists—and, more recently, the "positive psychology" movement (Allport, 1969; Resnick, Warmoth, & Serlin, 2001; Seligman & Csikszentmihalyi, 2000)—have made a serious effort at it (Maslow, 1954; Pfaffenberger, 2005; Rogers, 1961). One way to summarize these descriptions of the effective person that is meaningful to me (Martin, 1991) is to say that she or he has four general characteristics: (1) a quiet sense of personal worth; (2) autonomy and a sense of competence; (3) accurate, full openness to feelings and thoughts; and (4) the capacity to be intimate. In a sense, these describe the goals of therapy for me, although each individual will find his or her own expression of these characteristics.

Another way to state the general goals of therapy that I will discuss in chapter 17 is less positive in tone. It is to name the problems that bring people to therapy and say that the goals are the relief of these problems: (1) reducing painful emotions, (2) improving problem-solving ability, (3) reducing maladaptive behavior, and (4) improving self-esteem.

These general guidelines are helpful, but each client determines the specific goals of therapy.

The Hierarchy Emerges

So the client finds the goals; how does this happen? It is quite clear that anxiety-based problems are so complex that the person entering therapy often does not know what the problem is, and so goals set at one point in therapy frequently change. A client recently said to me, "I remember telling you I was a trusting person, and I really meant it. But I guess I'm not . . . I guess that's a big part of the problem." So now one of his goals is to become more trusting. To have said this was a goal at the beginning of therapy would have made no sense, because he saw himself as an unusually trusting person. It was threatening to him to know that he didn't trust very much, and only as we worked through other, less threatening material could we get close to this particular bit of truth. We worked on successive approximations of the truth—on a series of threatening thoughts and feelings naturally arranged in a hierarchy of how threatening they were.

Sorenson, Gorsuch, and Mintz (1985) refer to clients' goals (or "presenting complaints") as "moving targets" that change over the course of therapy. In their study, more than half of the clients reported new problems as therapy progressed, and dealing with these problems was significantly related to outcome. Yalom (2002) says that, "psychotherapy consists of a gradual unfolding process wherein the therapist attempts to know the patient as fully as possible" (p. 4).

The goals of therapy emerge from the therapy process. This does not mean that goals are unimportant or that there really are no goals. It means that goals are held and worked toward energetically but with the flexibility to know that they can change with new understanding. This flexibility seems essential to effective living and effective problem solving; your client will need both strength and flexibility to live well, and you give the client the chance to get both when you help him or her be the problem solver.

What Is a "Cure"?

I am concerned that what I have been writing will sound naive, as though evocatively empathic therapy were the key to the golden door that will let your clients live happily ever after. Human life is essentially a difficult process, with ups and downs and conflicts both within and between people. It is possible to live well and meaningfully, and good therapy can contribute to that. But there is no "cure," no goal to reach. Life is a process that one can live more or less effectively and rewardingly. You will enter your clients' lives for a limited time and have an influence that may change directions for them in some ways by helping them be stronger.

6

Relationship Issues

The power of the therapeutic relationship comes from its nonjudgmental nature. The therapist dependably accepts and values the *person* as worthwhile but does not judge what the client says as *either* good or bad. The therapist says, through behavior, that anything can be said or thought, without being either praised or punished. (There are, of course, limits on overt behavior that must be set.) The client is free to explore all of his or her experiences and to find whatever solutions are best. It may surprise you that being nonjudgmental means not giving approval, just as much as it means not giving disapproval. As soon as you approve of a particular way of thinking or feeling, you are saying that you are in a position to approve and disapprove and that not feeling or thinking this particular way is not acceptable. For example, your client is having trouble crying in front of you because he is embarrassed and ashamed, and you say, "Go ahead; it's good to cry; it's not to be ashamed of; feel free." Your intentions are helpful and supportive, but you have failed to understand what the client is trying to say, and you have said that it is not acceptable to feel ashamed of crying. You have, probably unintentionally, taken over the direction of therapy and subtly prohibited certain feelings. You could have given the support you wanted to give, without making the judgment, by saying, "This is pretty painful stuff, and I guess it brings the hurt up into your eyes . . . but then you want to stop because it would feel so crummy for tears to come. I want you to know that it's OK with me if you cry, but I realize that's not the issue—it's not OK with you."

Clients will sometimes say to you, "It really helped when I told you all that stuff about what I think, and you didn't even flinch. I guess I expected you to laugh or think I was crazy or awful or something." We all think disgusting things sometimes, and a common feeling that clients bring to therapy is, "Although people may like me, if they could really know what goes on in my mind, that liking would turn to disgusted rejection." This fear leaves the person feeling unlovable and unworthy because what he or she *really is* feels unacceptable.

If I had only two words to describe a good relationship, they would be *understanding* and *acceptance*. To be accepted by someone who really knows you as you are may be life's most releasing experience, and that is what therapy provides. The therapist *proves* that she or he understands through evocative empathy and also communicates a dependable, nonjudgmental acceptance of the client. The client feels safe, and without that safety, therapy won't happen. Timulak and Lietaer (2001) found that clients' positive experiences in therapy were most related to empowerment, safety, and insight. I once asked an adolescent client why some staff at his treatment facility were helpful and some were not. He said, "It's a trust thing. Some of them aren't safe." In therapy, this essential safety comes from being dependably accepted.

This chapter is about the nature of the relationship that communicates that acceptance. So far, this book has focused on evocative empathy skills, implying that they constitute almost all of therapy. Evocative empathy will work, though, only in the context of a *good relationship*, and that easy-to-say phrase "good relationship" will lead us into incredibly complex areas. Now the going starts to get tough. I write this chapter uneasily, knowing that we are only going to scratch the surface of the issues and fearing that I am going to mislead you with some simplistic descriptions—knowing that I can only introduce a topic that you will be resolving for yourself for years. Evocative empathy is partly a complex and difficult art, but it is also partly an ability that can be fairly well defined and taught and learned with practice. Relationship skills, however, depend much more on the kind of person you are and on the needs and distortions that you bring to doing therapy.

I started this book by saying that the clearest evidence we have is that the quality of the therapeutic relationship is the best predictor of the effectiveness of therapy. To be a great therapist, you must be able to establish a strong connection with another person. Only part of that process involves evocative empathy.

Remember all the things that evocative empathy is not: It is not sympathy or love or caring or agreement or disagreement. It is making the client feel deeply known by communicating an experiential understanding of the other person's intended message. It often does imply caring and respect, but it is important that it not be confused with these other things. You could be evocatively empathic with a person with whom you totally disagreed and whose presence you could hardly stand, difficult as that might be to do. The relationship involves more than evocative empathy, and we have to tackle what that "more" is.

■ The Therapeutic Alliance

Because the therapy relationship has been demonstrated to be the most important part of therapy, many researchers are studying it, usually under the general term *therapeutic alliance*. In chapter 18, we will discuss the evidence for a strong relationship between the therapeutic alliance and successful outcome in therapy. Well over a hundred studies and meta-analyses find a significant, consistent relationship between the therapeutic alliance and successful outcome. This finding holds across all therapy approaches studied (Castonguay, Constantino, & Holtforth, 2006; Horvath & Bedi, 2002; Krupnick, Sotsky, Simmens, Moyer, Elkin, Watkins, & Pilkonis, 1996; Martin, Garske, & Davis, 2000; Wampold, 2001).

There are at least 30 different definitions and measures of the alliance currently in use (Elvins & Green, 2008; Horvath, 2006; Horvath & Luborsky, 1993; Luborsky, 2000), but we can extract two fundamental facets of the alliance that are included in all of them. You will see that nearly everything we discuss in this chapter can be related to these two general characteristics.

First, the *personal bond* between client and therapist includes the kinds of characteristics that most people think of when they think of good relationships—personal warmth, empathy, and acceptance. This part of the alliance is fundamental throughout therapy, and it is probably most critical early in therapy when the client is establishing trust in the therapist. Eaton, Abeles, and Gutfreund (1988) concluded that the "strength of therapeutic alliance is established within the first three sessions of psychotherapy with little significant change over the course of therapy" (p. 536). This finding has enormous significance for how much attention we pay to forming a bond with a client from the first moment.

Second, in a good alliance, both the client and the therapist have a *collaborative commitment to the mutual work and goals of therapy* (Tryon & Winograd, 2002). This facet of the alliance is more task oriented. In general, the client and therapist are in agreement about where they are going, and both of them see their work together as a collaboration rather than something under the control of the therapist. The element of commitment is necessary for the client to be the active source of growth in therapy, and the therapist's commitment to the process is one of the most powerful ways the therapist demonstrates that the client is valued and accepted.

It is also important that what the therapist and client do in session makes sense to the client as a way to bring about healing. This is so important that you need to be ready to provide your clients with a rationale for why what you do is helpful. To repeat something I said in the previous chapter, when a client asks how therapy works, I often say, "Your job is to explore whatever is on your mind. It doesn't all have to fit together before you say it—just explore. And my job is to help you do that exploring. My experience has been that three things will happen as we do that exploring. We will discover things about you and your life that you didn't know before; as we talk, your feelings will change; and you will figure out new solutions."

Usually, a statement like this satisfies clients and gives them a way to get started; it tells them what their job is. Occasionally, a client still has questions about, "How does it help just to talk?" Or, "What causes the changes?" If it seems important to the client, I listen hard for the concerns behind the questions and answer them as well as I can and as thoroughly as the client seems to want (being careful not to "overanswer" the question just because it interests me). The process should at least seem plausible to the client.

In a study of 61 therapists seeing 201 clients in long-term therapy, the strongest predictor of having a poor therapeutic alliance was a cold/detached manner in the therapist (Hersoug, Høglend, Havik, von der Lippe, & Monsen, 2009) That's not surprising. They also found, however, that the amount of professional training—"years of formal postgraduate training in psychother-apy, including supervision, personal therapy and attendance at an institute for advanced psychotherapy training" (p. 103)—was negatively related to the strength of the alliance as perceived by clients, although "the therapist seems to be either unaware of this, or not influenced by it" (p. 107). The more formal the training, the worse the alliance, in clients' eyes. What are we to make of this? Should you quit school right now before you're completely wrecked? Probably not, but this finding should alert us to the fact that therapy is a human relationship far more than it is a technology or an intellectual process.

Hersoug et al. mentioned three possible explanations for their finding. First, prolonged training may have no causal impact on therapist characteris-tics; this is only a correlation, and other factors might be at play. Second, their therapists were mainly from the psychodynamic tradition and, "the dominant role model in postgraduate psychodynamic clinical training is the 'neutral and distant' therapist, while patients may view a more distanced atti-tude in the therapist as indifference" (p. 108). But this problem probably goes beyond just psychodynamic training. If your training is based on a model of "intellectual expertise" on the part of the therapist, who applies methods to clients, you may be at risk of having the good therapist trained out of you. The third possible explanation is that "therapists with more interpersonal problems may seek more training or stay longer in training" (p. 108). This third explanation should probably be stated more subtly than just referring to interpersonal problems; there are many therapists who love the intellect and are deeply uncomfortable with emotions. It may be that some therapists find safety in more detachment and more training.

■ Respect and Prizing

Many attempts have been made to describe what it is about the therapy relationship that helps the client. Rogers' early term was *unconditional positive regard* (1957), but it led to a lot of misunderstanding because many took it to mean some kind of impossibly tolerant permissiveness in which no limits were set. Rogers clearly did not mean that, but rather meant that the thera-pist's positive feelings were not conditional on the client's thinking, feeling, and talking in certain ways and not in other ways. He implies an acceptance of the person but sets limits on certain behaviors when he says:

> The effective therapist may feel acceptant of [antisocial] behavior of his cli-ent, not as desirable behavior, but as a *natural consequence* of the circum-stances, experiences and feelings of this client. Thus the therapist's acceptance may be based upon this kind of feeling. "If I had had the same background, the same circumstances, the same experiences, it would be inevitable in me, as it is in this client, that I would act in this fashion." In this respect he is like the good parent whose child, in a moment of fear and panic, has defecated in his clothing. The reaction of the loving parent includes both a caring for the child, and acceptance of the behavior as an

entirely natural event under the circumstances. This does not approve of such behavior in general. (Rogers, Gendlin, Kiesler, & Truax, 1967, p. 103)

Other phrases have included *nonpossessive warmth, prizing, dependable acceptance*, and *respect*. All of these imply that the therapist somehow communicates the message that the client is a worthwhile person, regardless of what he or she is experiencing. They all avoid words like "love" because the therapy relationship is a limited relationship, in some ways unlike any other, and the therapist cannot realistically offer love, in the usual reciprocal meaning of the word. He or she offers a chance to explore and think and feel in a context of acceptance and respect. Later we will discuss the notion that "you are not the solution," meaning that your job is to help your client live well and relate well in the world outside therapy. You will be dishonest and will hurt a lot of people if you implicitly promise your love as a solution—a promise that you can't fulfill for your clients.

So therapy is a limited relationship, but it is also a powerful one. Respect and dependable, nonjudgmental acceptance are incredibly helpful to the client (Farber & Lane, 2002). How can they be communicated?

Commitment and Effort to Understand

I said that evocative empathy is something different from acceptance, but your attempt to understand communicates powerfully that you value your client. You are saying with your behavior that he or she is worth intense effort on your part, that what he or she is experiencing is valuable enough to be worth a lot of work exploring, and that you are not afraid of that experiencing.

Certainly implicitly, and often explicitly, you say to your client, "I am in this with you until we find new ways for you to be and to live. I have a commitment to helping you." You follow through on that commitment by being dependably involved. The way that you really communicate your commitment is over the long run, by your behavior—you really do stay with the person.

Expressing Acceptance, Explicitly and Implicitly

What you do speaks more eloquently than what you say about how you feel toward your client—partly because saying, "I really care about you and value you," can be a cheap shot. Anybody can say such words; everybody knows that is what therapists are supposed to say; and besides, it's part of their job. Another problem with saying these words is that for many clients words like these may have meant betrayal and undependable acceptance and may have masked feelings of dislike and rejection. Words are easy; demonstrated respect is what counts.

This is not to say that you should never openly express respect and prizing for your clients, particularly when they ask for or seem to need to hear some acceptance. The problem comes from thinking that the words will have much power and from taking the focus of therapy away from the client's exploration of his or her own experiencing. If the client says, "I really feel that nobody cares anything about what happens to me or how I feel," and you say, "But I care," you are saying that the client's feeling is not a valid experience and he should not be feeling it. You are trying to use reassurance and talk your client out of a feeling, and it won't work. If you really have to express your caring here (to be honest, your need to do this is partly just that—*your* need), you might say, "That's a horribly lonely feeling . . . not to matter to someone . . . I want to say that *my* feeling is that you matter to me, but it really sounds like it doesn't feel that way to you . . . that you really are alone." In most instances, this response would have been more helpful without the explicit expression of caring. The client will likely appreciate the words to some extent, but you will also introduce a lot of other issues: "Maybe I shouldn't have said nobody cares, because she says she cares—how awful of me not to appreciate that; that's easy to say, but it's just the therapist's job; I meant nobody cares enough to love me, and that's not what she means, so she didn't understand; maybe that is what she meant, and she will be my source of love."

You absolutely must express your caring, but you do that most effectively with your intense effort to understand.

Belief in the Person

In chapter 5, I was pretty insistent that the client be the problem solver, sometimes to the frustration of our clients who come to us for advice and solutions. One subtle but important implication of this is that we really do believe in our clients. We trust their ability to solve problems—a trust that clearly implies immense respect. One woman, for whom independence and personal strength were central issues, said near the end of therapy, "You know, this really has been feminist therapy. You respected my ability to take care of myself. I remember when I came how desperately I wanted you to guide me . . . I felt like I was going to the doctor . . . and how angry it made me when you wouldn't. I know now that if you had tried, I wouldn't have done anything you told me to do and probably would have quit."

The client I mentioned earlier, who said at the end of therapy, "I did this myself," had knocked me down a peg or two earlier in therapy over this issue. We were well into therapy, and I think I had been pretty consistently letting him be the problem solver. But I made a clear error in judgment and behavior in therapy when he moved in with a new roommate. This roommate started verbally tearing at my client, trying every way he knew to make my client feel bad about himself. I directly suggested that the client move out of his new living arrangement and can still remember my foolish, protective worry that this creep was going to undo all the gains my client had made in therapy. My client nodded (he was quite surprised, although I couldn't see it at the time) and seemed to consider my advice thoughtfully. The next week he came in angry, saying, "You didn't trust me . . . I can take care of this." I had to agree, and we discussed this for some time, but what it drove home for me was how important it was to him that I trust him—trust his strength.

Dependable, Nonjudgmental Acceptance

It is important that the therapist be immune to shock and embarrassment. The client is afraid to face his or her own experience, which is hard enough to do alone, and is afraid of shocking the therapist and losing his or her respect and acceptance. Very often a client will have enormous difficulty saying something and may take several sessions to get around to it. "I want to tell you," she will say, "but I just can't . . . God knows what you'll think of me." Finally, she will get around to saying it, and you will feel, "That's *it*?" This is not to cheapen the client's pain at telling you, but what felt so disgusting and unacceptable to the client will be understandable and acceptable to you. The client then will be able to face this painful material and still feel acceptable, and the curse will be taken off whatever was so awful. If you flinch, however, and are shocked or embarrassed, you obviously will confirm your client's worst fears, and that part of her experiencing will be harder to look at.

This clearly requires that you be comfortable with a wide range of experience. This comfort will come partly with experience, as you hear and become used to more topics. It also can come from your own personal growth. If there are topics and behaviors that shock and discomfort you, you have some work to do, either in your own therapy or in discussions with friends or in thinking through what your own areas of discomfort are. If explicit sexual talk makes you blush or strong expressions of anger scare you, for example, you will have trouble helping your clients freely explore such issues. It is often said that clients can't go farther than their therapists can go. We have a compelling responsibility to do our own emotional work so that we don't hold our clients back, a topic we will discuss in chapter 14.

Privacy

Another way that you offer respect to the client is through the confidentiality you promise. You imply that what the client has to say is important and personal and worthy of being taken seriously. Confidentiality in therapy is almost never total, of course, and I will discuss this at length in chapter 11, but therapy does give a privacy in which the client can build enough trust to make him- or herself vulnerable.

■ Presence

One of the most powerful gifts the therapist brings to therapy is *presence*. It is also one of the most difficult aspects of therapy to describe. We often have some understanding of what we mean when we say something like, "You really know when she's in the room because she has so much presence." Putting that understanding into words, however, is not easy. In chapter 8, I will try harder to describe presence, but for now we can understand it as a focused concentration on the client. Therapy is probably the only place where two people are focused exclusively on one person's experiencing, and the client usually feels the therapist's presence as an undistracted interest in what the client is dealing with. There is an intensity to presence, but it is a quietly strong intensity, rather than a frenetic intensity.

■ Sharing Your Experiencing

Therapy centers on the client's process of exploration, but there are times when the therapist can appropriately say how he or she feels about things, when the therapist's experiencing is shared through self-disclosure.

Benefits and Dangers

It may seem unnecessary to say this, but the therapy session is for the benefit of the client. It is not a place for the therapist to work on his or her own needs—to get understanding and acceptance from the client, to impress the client, to satisfy needs for power and control, or any of a hundred other purposes for which the therapist might use the client (Audet & Everall, 2003; Peterson, 2002). Some therapists cloak their misuse of therapy in the disguise of "honest and open self-disclosure" and spend a lot of time talking about themselves and "expressing" their "here-and-now reactions." It can also be disguised by, "I know just how you feel . . . I've been through the same thing myself."

Self-disclosure can serve the positive purpose of being honest about your feelings in the relationship. It also can give the client some feedback on how other people feel when he or she says or does certain things or how other people react to particular situations. At least it can give this feedback about how one other person reacts, since when you share your feelings, that is exactly what you are sharing—your feelings. It is important that both you and the client know that this sharing is not sneaky advice about the way a person *should* react. You might say in response to a question about how you would feel in a particular situation, "Sure, I'll tell you how I think I would feel, but I want to be sure you know that it is just my feeling, and what might be right for you could be very different. I think I would be angry and a little self-righteous if someone told me that . . . but that's just me. It sounds like you would like to fight back somehow, but you immediately start doubting yourself and thinking 'Maybe he's right.'" You have answered the explicit question about your feeling but immediately put the focus back on the client's reactions.

Moderate Levels Are Best

Self-disclosure can have positive effects, especially in strengthening the therapy relationship, but it occurs relatively infrequently in good therapy (Hill & Knox, 2002, 2001). In orthodox psychoanalysis, the analyst is to remain a truly blank slate, to facilitate the patient's use of the analyst as a screen on which to project fantasies and transferences. This can be carried to extremes that deter the course of therapy; in one instance described by Greenson

(1974), for example, the patient came to the session with a large head bandage and obvious serious injuries. The analyst, strictly following tradition, made no personal reaction to the patient's plight and waited for the patient to bring the topic up. This absurd insensitivity left the patient unable to continue. But Malcolm (1980) quotes an anonymous analyst who says that Greenson's story is "heartrending and affecting" but completely misses the critical point. This analyst tells of an incident in which he profusely apologized to a patient for being late to a session. Looking back on it, he could now see that rushing his own feelings into the situation prevented the patient from reacting to the analyst's lateness. Greenson's point with the bandage story was to say that complete disengagement is destructive, and the anonymous analyst's response does not take away the truth of this. What it does do, though, is show a subtle (and therefore too common) way that "self-disclosure" hampers therapy by taking responsibility away from the client and by turning therapy to meet the therapist's needs. If you apologize profusely for being late, you almost cut off your client's freedom to be angry or hurt or confused by your behavior. You are protecting yourself from that at his or her expense.

You and the client are in an important human encounter, but one with an unusual one-way structure. You are there to serve the client's personal growth. In some cases, your disclosure of how you feel will serve that growth, but you should be quite clear about exactly how your self-disclosure is going to be helpful when you do share your own experience.

■ Genuineness

The "core conditions" of therapy discussed in chapter 1 included empathy, dependable respect, and genuineness. The last is the most difficult to define and to measure. Several phrases that capture some of its meaning are "authenticity," "being the person that you really are in the therapy relationship," and "being congruent with yourself in the relationship." None of these, however, is very helpful to the therapist struggling to know what to do in therapy to be genuine. It is easier to say what genuineness is not: it is not phony and not artificial; it is not playing a role, pretending to be an expert; it is not acting as though you feel something you don't. The idea is easier to grasp this way, although it doesn't sound nearly as marvelous as being "authentic." The word *congruent* (Rogers, 1957) captures part of this not being phony, because it means knowing how you really do feel in the relationship, being accurately in touch with your own experience, and acting in ways that are consistent with that.

There is evidence (Grafanaki & McLeod, 2002; Klein, Kolden, Michels, & Chisolm-Stockard, 2002; Schnellbacher & Leijssen, 2009) that genuineness/ congruence has positive effects in therapy, and some (Lietaer, 2001) argue that it is the most important of the core conditions. Near the end of his life, Rogers also seemed to feel that being genuine was more important than any techniques in therapy.

Actually, I've had many students who had a little epiphany that released them to do better therapy when they stopped worrying about following "rules" of good therapy and said something like, "I do a lot better when I'm just myself in session." They still really wanted to know their clients, and they were still present and empathic, but when you realize there are no rules—there are only principles of therapy—you will be freer to do therapy naturally, and it will help you connect with your clients.

Genuineness takes many forms, of course, but one quote from a client wonderfully illustrates how a client perceived her therapist's honest clarity.

> What I immensely appreciate in her is that she is clear about everything. Clear about the expectations I can have, clear in the way she works, clear in the progress. She regularly evaluates where we stand, what is still possible, what we will take on next. And also clear in arrangements; from the beginning it was really clear, when do you inform. . . . So she is very clear on every level, and that is something I find very important. (Anna, fragment 5) (Schnellbacher & Leijssen, 2009, p. 219)

Facilitative Genuineness—Not Just Self-Disclosure

Probably the most common misunderstanding of genuineness is that it involves a blurting out of whatever the therapist is feeling, rather than the therapist just being aware of what he or she is feeling and acting in ways consistent with those feelings. When self-disclosure is confused with the notion of genuineness, some therapists use it as an excuse to be "open and honest" in an attacking way. Carkhuff and Berenson note that "many destructive persons are in full contact with their experience; that is, they are destructive when they are genuine" (1977, p. 12). It is important to be open and honest and not be playing a role with your client, but it is also important to remember that the expression of your feelings is appropriate in therapy only if it facilitates the client's process.

I have talked about instances in which your expression of positive feelings could help but also could hinder therapy. The more obvious problem is with negative feelings you have toward your client. The expression of these feelings can quite obviously hinder therapy, since they usually carry a strong implication of judgment of the other person's worth and character. But the notion of judgment also gives a clue to when the expression of your negative feelings can be helpful in therapy. Your reactions can be an important lesson for the client in knowing how he or she affects other people with particular actions and words. If you can express your negative feelings without judgment of the client's character, your reaction can be helpful. This requires great sensitivity and skill, since negative reactions usually imply rejection and judgment in our everyday lives. But if you have a relationship in which your client trusts your acceptance as truly dependable, you could say, "I want to share my feelings when you keep saying 'That's *your* opinion.' I'm not sure why, but I get irritated . . . like you're slapping me down." Quite clearly this statement is not empathic, and in most contexts it would imply judgment and advice about what the person should be doing. If, and only if, you have laid a strong foundation in which the client knows you do not take over as the problem solver or judge his or her personal worth, then a comment like this could be a helpful piece of information for the client. These conditions tend to be met only later in therapy, and this kind of response would probably still be fairly rare.

An interesting problem that we will face more thoroughly below is that of your own distortions as they relate to "facilitative self-disclosure." You have to be pretty humble about the accuracy of your own experiencing. The feedback in the last paragraph was to help the client know how "That's *your* opinion" affects others. Who's to say that your reaction is typical and doesn't come primarily out of your own needs and blind spots? Something to think about.

Being Caught off Guard

One of the most severe tests of your genuineness will come when you are made uncomfortable by something you have said or done or by something the client says that catches you off guard. A common reaction is to want to cover up, acting as though nothing bothers you, trying to save face. You will have to be pretty smooth not to be seen through, and it is probably better just to comment on your own discomfort and lack of infallibility and be sensitive to the client's reactions to the incident. The importance of the incident is not in your reaction to it anyway. This situation is especially likely to plague you if you are hung up on the need to be seen as an expert. If you make a mistake, there is no need for a lengthy defense of yourself, but trying to avoid it will surely establish you as a phony.

■ Immediacy—Dealing with Your Relationship

In good therapy relationships, you will become very important to your clients; you will be a significant part of their lives. It is almost inevitable, then, that your relationship will become an issue that needs to be explored. There are important things that your client can learn from your relationship—trust, what it means to be listened to, how to listen, and that your acceptance makes self-acceptance easier. Your client will often try to talk about these issues and sometimes about more complex issues such as intense attachment to you, a very difficult problem. These relationship issues are about as "here and now" as you can get, and dealing with them is often called "immediacy" in therapy.

An Empathic Context

In one sense, talking about your relationship is no different from talking about any other topic that might come up in therapy. It is part of the client's life and experience and is involved in his or her problem solving. It should be dealt with in the same evocatively empathic way as any other issue. The focus is on the client's implied experiencing and attempts to understand and take action, and your job is still to hear what the client is trying to say about you and your relationship but can't quite say.

Your Troubles Hearing Immediacy Issues

That last paragraph was so easy to write, but talking about *you* in therapy is going to be a lot more difficult than talking about most other topics. It is here that your third ear will be most needed and most difficult to use, because the implicit message touches you. It can threaten you if there are negative feelings and even (or maybe especially) if there are positive feelings. If your client wonders just how qualified you are or how old you are or whether you're happily married or why you get so uncomfortable every time he mentions you-know-what, you will likely be reluctant to hear the message and even more reluctant to put the message into words in an evocative way.

It's easy to be afraid of getting egg on your face when you respond to what you think are the client's attempts to talk about your relationship. Imagine this situation: The client says, "I really like coming here and being close . . . to . . . well, sort of, I guess, things that mean so much." You respond, "It means a lot to you being able to be close to me, it sounds like, in a way that lets you talk easily," and the client draws back a bit in the chair with, "No, I didn't mean that. I meant get close to talking about how much my family means to me." Normally when you miss the message this way (or maybe you heard something accurately but went beyond what the client intended you to hear), you can just back off and correct yourself. This time it's different, however, because you and your feelings are involved. You will have to deal with your own awkwardness somehow, without getting defensive and ungenuine.

Successive Approximations

Issues that you are involved in will be more difficult to deal with, and so it is very likely that you will avoid them, consciously or unconsciously, unless you make a pointed effort to listen for them. They must be dealt with. It is easy to see that if you consistently avoided responding to some other issue in therapy, you would be communicating that this aspect of the client's experiencing was somehow taboo and unacceptable; it was too frightening to be dealt with. The same principle applies to immediacy issues. They must be dealt with if they are important to the client.

I probably can't help you very much in this book with the problem of being able to hear when the client is trying to talk about you and your relationship. You should deal with this issue by being supervised or by sharing your therapy experience with another therapist/friend who will help you explore the issues that give you trouble. But I can say some things about what you do with the message once you hear it.

In our unnerving example in the previous section, the poor therapist is probably imagining the client saying to someone, "My therapist is pretty hung up on himself. Everything I say makes him think I'm in love with him."

Almost certainly, the client wouldn't have reacted this strongly, but the experience might well have scared the therapist off from openly discussing immediacy issues in the future, to prevent more hoof-in-mouth disease. But these issues must be dealt with.

It is here that using successive approximations is an especially helpful way to respond. Be cautious but tenacious, sensitively wording your response so that the client will be able to react internally with, "Yes, that's what I meant," but at the same time don't let go of the issue easily. This may mean that you will make more statements than you might about some other topic, each statement conveying a more finely shaded meaning; take more but smaller steps to go the same distance.

Your client might say, "My brother fell in love with his therapist, and it really hurt him when she wouldn't have anything to do with him outside therapy." You quietly catch your balance and say, "That obviously meant a lot to him . . . and it sounds like you could really tell how strongly he was feeling." I think this is about as far as you can go with what the client has given you, without eliciting a threatened denial that the comment had anything to do with your relationship. We're pretty sure the client is trying to say something about being attached to you, but the actual statement made no mention of any of the client's feelings. In your response, you skillfully got ahead of the client, heard the implicit feelings that the client intended—how strongly he felt for his brother's strong feeling—and put that into words. You have acknowledged the importance of what was said for your client, and you have opened the door for further exploration. In fact, you have done more than just open the door; you have faced your client with his immediate experiencing in a way that virtually demands further exploration but demands just enough to be difficult and challenging without being threatening.

Now the client might say, "Yes, I do . . . in a way, that didn't seem right." You are still scrambling; you can't let the issue die, but you don't want to step right in the middle of something untoward. "It confused and hurt him," you say, "and I think it puzzles you too." (Notice that you have said the brother is "confused and hurt," words that the client probably wouldn't accept about himself; but you use your vocabulary of shadings to acknowledge and articulate similar feelings in your client with "puzzles you.") "Are you sort of asking, 'Why can't there be more in a relationship like this . . . if a person feels strongly?'"

You are "working your way toward the "truth" with successive approximations, just as you do with any difficult issue, but immediacy talk takes special sensitivity and skill.

A Place to Work Out Issues

One of the values of immediacy talk is that it can give clients a chance to come to terms with the way they relate to others in a nonthreatening atmosphere, where the consequences of mistakes aren't devastating and words can be taken back. Many psychoanalytic therapists would say that interpretations of the "transference relationship" are the foundation of therapy. Most other therapists seem to feel that such issues can be important, but helping clients deal with life outside therapy is more typical.

Anger between You

Anger and the fear and anxiety triggered by angry feelings are some of the commonest problems clients bring to therapy. In effective therapy, clients will often feel anger during the therapy session as they talk about people and situations in life outside therapy. Sometimes, though, they will be angry at you, and sometimes you will probably be angry at them. If you have any of the discomfort that most people feel when someone is angry with them, it will be difficult to listen accurately, but you obviously must do so. All the things I said about immediacy apply here, but there is also your need to know whether the anger was something you earned in some way you are unaware of or whether it is coming from the client's distortions and problems. It is easy to lay all this at the client's doorstep and presumptuously talk about his or her defensiveness and inappropriate reactions, but it is also a good idea to be as open to your own contribution as possible. A client who is quite angry with you is probably a good cue for you to consult with another therapist for another view of what you are doing in therapy.

The point I really want to get to is that some therapists advocate provoking the client's anger—with the best of intentions, but with some unintended results. They argue, quite correctly, that an important lesson for a person to learn is that anger does not mean the loss of the relationship or rejection— that anger is not to be feared. For many people, anger does mean loss of love, and the fear of this loss becomes so overwhelming that they avoid anger at all costs—costs such as failing ever to assert themselves, feeling helpless and depressed, and being devastated by fear of their own angry feelings.

The skillful therapist very often *evokes* anger, as the client tries to deal with experiences from real-life situations and relationships. In order to provoke anger as a technique, however, the therapist must be manipulative and dishonest and take on the role of the expert master of the treatment process. Therapists obviously can't tell the client why they are goading and attacking, or it won't work. A powerful and experienced therapist might well pull off such an encounter so that the client ends up feeling that he did survive an angry outburst and the therapist is still there, but this lesson has been won at a cost of putting the client in a subordinate role in therapy. The therapist becomes someone who does things to you, and the client is the recipient of treatment. The client must also, consciously or unconsciously, view the therapist with suspicion from now on; what clever tricks await in the name of therapy?

All the benefits of this provocative approach can be won without paying these costs. The point is that the person face his or her own anger, experience and think more accurately, and use the resulting new understanding in life outside therapy. The whole point of evocatively empathic therapy is to confront experiencing; your client will be facing a lot of anger, if that is part of the problem, and then finding ways to deal with that anger and express it constructively. This process may include anger at you, but if it does, the anger will grow honestly out of your interactions. If the client gets angry at you for some mistake you've made, then it's a real interaction, and you're still trustworthy—clumsy maybe, but trustworthy—and not cleverly manipulative. If he or she gets angry because of personal needs and distortions, then it's still a real interaction in which the anger will be explored.

This discussion of provoking anger points up sharply the more general issue of how the therapist's approach to therapy is very much a relationship issue. You will read and hear many ideas about therapy that are inconsistent with an evocatively empathic approach—ideas about giving clients paradoxical instructions and using therapeutic games or environmental interventions. There are times when some direct interventions are called for (see chapter 9), but these times are rare. You must be clear about what the goals of therapy are and sensitive to how the nature of the therapy relationship affects those goals. If you want your client to gain independence and to be honest in relationships and to be able to think clearly, you must relate in ways that facilitate these things, both directly and by your example.

Expressing Your Anger

Of course, the issue of your own anger at the client is also important here, and I discussed this earlier when I talked about self-disclosure. The expression of your feelings can be helpful under the special circumstances of a strong, trustworthy relationship.

What we haven't looked at is why you feel your anger. The first glib thing we think is that the client provoked it with inappropriate behavior, but it is important that you find someone to help you explore yourself through to an understanding of how your needs play into your interaction. In one way, it makes no sense for you to feel anger toward a client. You are in a one-way relationship in which you are not directly involved in the client's outside life, and so the client's behavior affects you only within the therapy session—a session in which blame has no place and where the client is expected to deal with inappropriate behavior. You understand the client's experiences and actions as the result of his or her life and don't see them as somehow based on evil intentions. Why are you so angry?

Of course I'm not saying that you should never feel anger; that would be imposing on you the same impossible demand to avoid anger that your client is trying to get free of. Just recognize that your anger comes partly from you, and it would be worth knowing yourself as well as possible by finding someone with whom to talk it through.

When you do express your anger in therapy (or in any relationship, for that matter), there are several principles to remember (Gordon, 1976; Trenholm & Jensen, 1996). A destructive expression of anger lays blame on the other person's character and motives: "You are so insensitive and don't care anything about me!" This confrontation is so general and laden with judgment that the other person almost has to defend against it with denial and returned blame and judgment. You can get the same point across without the judgment by including three elements (not necessarily in this order):

- Name your feeling or reaction.
- Name the other person's specific behavior (not motives or character) that makes you feel that way.
- Name the tangible connection between the behavior and your reaction.

Rather than say "You're insensitive and don't care," you might say, "I get annoyed when you read things while I'm talking because your not listening shuts me out." It will be a very rare occurrence in therapy that you will express your anger, but it is possible to do it in a way that the client can learn and benefit from it.

When You Disagree

The foundation of therapy is evocative empathy, in which you neither agree nor disagree with the client's statements; you nonjudgmentally facilitate the client's exploring. Perhaps it would be more accurate to say that you neither approve nor disapprove, since there will be things that you personally believe that your client will not. Usually, as you know by now, your opinion on these topics doesn't matter much in the therapy process. Sometimes, however, your client will ask your opinion, and one example of a useful response might be "I think I see this differently than you do, but I don't think my opinion is the important thing here. It seems to me that people in general are neither bad nor good inherently, but the important thing is that from your perspective, people should be and are basically good . . . that when they do hurtful things it's because they are hurting." You have not dodged the issue, but you have kept therapy focused where it needs to be—on the client.

■ Relationship Weakeners

You already know that the power of the therapy relationship comes from being nonjudgmental, and so the quickest way to weaken the relationship is to make judgments. But there are others.

False "Understanding"

Saying, "I understand" when you don't is risky because your client, who may sense your puzzlement, will often call on you to prove that you understand. Your words will become empty if this happens very often, and when you're puzzled, you're probably better off just saying so. "Keep talking . . . I don't really have all that yet . . . I'm puzzled right now because I'm not sure what you mean . . . help me get a handle on that . . . I thought I understood, right up to the last two sentences, and then I got lost" are all things you could say and still be expressing your empathic intent—your desire to understand and to explore with the client.

A friend of mine who is a counselor suffered a personal tragedy, and afterward said she was ready to write a book on "how not to be helpful." Things she had often said to people felt very different when she was on the receiving end, and at the top of her list was "I know just how you feel . . . I felt the same way when I lost my job [or whatever]." She had the strong feeling that the person didn't understand and was distorting what she was feeling to fit the listener's quite different experience. An empathic response would, of course, have demonstrated understanding by articulating her feeling. A high school student said that when she felt down and tried to find someone to talk to, the person usually started out, "I know just how you feel. I felt the same way when . . . ," and then the rest of the discussion centered on the other person.

Most Reassurance

One of the hardest things to grasp intuitively in therapy is that reassurance almost never works, and it often slows therapy down. Our faith in reassurance must have something to do with how often people in our lives use reassurance to deal with others' painful emotions; it becomes the only way we know to respond. When your friend feels worthless, you say, "Come on . . . you're a good person. Look on the bright side of things." When you feel worthless, and your friend says the same thing to you, it annoys you. How do you think your friend (or client) feels? I guess, more accurately, you appreciate your friend's concern and are glad he or she feels that way about you, but you also feel quite misunderstood, thinking, "That's easy for you to say because you don't really understand."

The principle is that reassurance implies that you are not supposed to be feeling the way you feel—that your experience is not acceptable or even a valid way to feel. Reassurance says that it doesn't make sense to feel the way you do, and so there is even some blame implicit in it. "Don't feel that way," reassurance says, as though persuasion could change your feelings.

Until you trust the therapy process, though, you will be overwhelmingly tempted to give reassurance, especially when you see your client hurting over things that seem to you so clearly not worth hurting over. Maybe you will be afraid that if you don't somehow pull your client out of the feeling, it will get worse. All you will do is cut off the therapy process and prevent the facing of experience. It is unnerving, though, not to give the reassurance that you so much want to give, unless you have something more effective and more powerful to do instead. It will take time and experience to fight against the intuition that you want to save the person, and to build your trust in the power of evocative empathy, but it will be worth the period of awkwardness.

Detachment

In the section on "presence" and elsewhere, I have used terms like *intense involvement* and *focused listening* and *effort to understand* and *respect* to describe the therapist in the relationship; this is hard work. The opposite of these qualities is found in the therapist who is just doing a job and going through the motions of technique. It is nearly impossible to be evocatively empathic and to remain detached, although it conceivably could happen, since empathy is theoretically only communication of understanding of the intended message. Involvement in the relationship is communicated by the intensity of the therapist's effort—by caring enough to be working hard. Later I will discuss a kind of distance the therapist keeps because of the limits of the therapy relationship, but that is quite different from an uncaring detachment.

Intellectualizing and Jargon

My past discussions of intellectualizing have been about honest attempts to understand that dampen therapy but don't necessarily weaken the relationship. Show-off intellectualizing, however, is a sure-fire relationship weakener. Playing the doctor, with marvelously impressive jargon, may wilt the client into acquiescence and "yes doctor" reactions, but it will do nothing to facilitate the client's experiencing and will almost certainly prevent the client from learning to trust you to hear. The use of jargon is a reliable indicator of a therapist who is meeting his or her own needs for admiration or who is covering up insecurity with self-deceptive pomposity.

Moralizing

There are limits to what the effective therapist will accept on moral grounds, but those limits recognize that there are thousands of ways to live effectively, and the therapist's way isn't the best way for everybody. The limits are wide, and if you are not comfortable with this, you are probably headed in the wrong direction by becoming a counselor or therapist. One trainee used to describe his clients as "wholesome" or "unwholesome" and spent considerable time in therapy discussing his client's experiences in moral tones—preaching, in a sense. There is a place for preaching and moral training but it is not in therapy. Quite obviously, the problem is that moralizing is judgmental in the strongest possible way.

Therapist Negative Characteristics

In a summary of research, Ackerman and Hilsenroth (2001) concluded:

> Therapists' personal attributes such as being rigid, uncertain, critical, distant, tense, and distracted were found to contribute negatively to the alliance. Moreover, therapist techniques such as over structuring the therapy, inappropriate self-disclosure, unyielding use of transference interpretation, and inappropriate use of silence were also found to contribute negatively to the alliance. (p. 171)

■ Dependency and Attachment

In one way, evocatively empathic therapy prevents dependency on the therapist. It tells the client that she or he must do the work and cannot depend on the therapist to guide the process. In other ways, however, the therapy relationship can lead to the client's dependency and attachment on the therapist. This is understandable, since the therapist is probably one of the few people ever really to listen to the client and also gives the incredibly rare experience of dependable acceptance. Therapy offers part of what a mature love relationship offers, but it is not a love relationship. It is a limited relationship, and these limits can set up some confusing tensions for the client.

I said at the beginning of this chapter that we were entering deep water, and it will probably be these relationship questions that will take you the longest to become comfortable with. This book can only get you started.

You Are Not the Solution

You will need to be clear for yourself exactly what the nature of the therapy relationship is, or you will become involved in ways that will startle and bother you, and you will promise your client things that you cannot and will not deliver. You can do a lot of damage this way. It is tempting to think that your love is curative—that you will give your client the relationship that he or she has missed out on. That is partly true, but only in a limited way, and unless those limits are clear to you and to the client, you may seem to be offering yourself as the solution to the person's problems. You cannot possibly follow through on this offer. You cannot be the solution, but you can help the person find solutions in life outside therapy. In purely practical terms, you cannot be the most significant person in very many people's lives, and if you try you will burn yourself out, damage your own relationships, and ultimately hurt your client when you pull out.

It seems paradoxical that the therapist is supposed to provide warmth, understanding, acceptance, and intense involvement—all parts of mature love—and at the same time maintain a distance that says: I am not part of your "real life." I am part of your life here in therapy and give you some very powerful and helpful things, as your therapist. But that's exactly what I am— your *therapist*. The resolution of this paradox and ways to deal with it become clearer when we think about the functions and setting of limits in therapy.

Limits of the Therapy Relationship

You provide your client with remarkably attentive listening, intensely worked-at understanding, unusually dependable respect and acceptance, and the freedom to deal with all kinds of thoughts and feelings. You provide these qualities at a level that you could not maintain continuously, and so you set limits that prevent behaviors and demands on you that would force you to pull back. At the extreme, if the therapy session might last anywhere from one hour to seven and the client were free to call you at any time to talk as long as he or she wanted to, you would have to pace yourself quite differently than if you know how much is going to be asked of you. Setting limits frees you to give more fully in the session.

There is no limit on what may be discussed in therapy, but, for example, the client is prohibited from harming you physically. This knowledge frees both the therapist and the client to deal openly with feelings and thoughts of hostility toward the therapist. Thus, although the primary function of limits is to permit the therapist to function more fully as a therapist, a second function is to provide the client with a similar reality-based structure. This structure frees him or her to deal more fully with thoughts and feelings, secure in the safety of knowing that both he or she and the therapist are prohibited from acting in certain ways on those thoughts and feelings.

Knowing what your own limits are and being able to set them clearly will be partly your own idiosyncratic responsibility. Partly, though, limits are implicit and explicit in such documents as "Ethical Principles of Psychologists" (American Psychological Association, 2002) and similar standards of professions that include psychotherapy. Therapists, for example, avoid "dual relationships" with their clients by not treating colleagues, close friends, and relatives. Clearly this limit permits the therapist to stay uninvolved in making judgments in a way that he or she couldn't otherwise. The statements, "Psychologists do not engage in sexual intimacies with current clients/patients. . . . Psychologists do not accept as therapy clients/patients persons with whom they have engaged in sexual intimacies. . . . Psychologists do not engage in sexual intimacies with a former therapy clients/patients for at least two years after cessation or termination of professional services . . . [and even then only under] the most unusual circumstances" (American Psychological Association, 2002, p. 15), set clear limits. You are unquestionably required to study and follow the ethical standards of your profession.

But it is the idiosyncratic nuances of limits that will require you to do some hard thinking. Surely if your best friend wants to talk to you, you will respond therapeutically—but somehow without becoming his or her therapist. Is it clear to you what you will do when a client invites you to dinner or to a party or asks you to teach him or her to swim? The principle is that you remain as the person's therapist; how you do that is a complex business. At the risk of looking a little naive, I might ask you exactly what "sexual intimacies" are. Do they include putting your arm around the client's shoulders supportively when he or she cries? "Of course not," you respond, "that's silly." But where is the limit for physical contact between you and your clients? Is it the same for all clients? Why or why not? More importantly, is the limit clear to you and to the client? If it is not, uncertainty floats between you about what will happen if the client says, "Sometimes I wish you would lie down with me here—not for anything sexual, just for the comfort and support of feeling you close to me." Not knowing where the limit is might well make it more difficult to talk about such feelings.

Some limits get set explicitly. For example, it may be standard practice at the clinic where you work for all client calls to be handled through a switchboard (rather than taken by you directly) and for sessions to last 50 minutes. Your client may assume from these explicit limits that many other limits exist, and they will never arise in therapy. Many other limits will be irrelevant to your relationship with particular clients. The problem is in setting limits of which the client is unsure, which matter to him or her, and which he or she only hints at wondering about. As with any other issue, you are listening for implicit messages about testing limits, and we might continue with our client from several pages ago who said, "My brother's therapist hurt him by not having a relationship with him outside therapy." You skillfully respond in increasingly complete ways until he finally says, "Yeah, I do think about you a lot. You've been good to me and helped me so much, and you're just the kind of person I've always wanted for a friend . . . could that . . . well . . . I wish. . . ." He's asking in a way that touches you and makes you want to reach out and help him, but you know that you are his therapist, not his friend. You combine limit setting with empathy by saying, "I guess you're asking me . . . in a way like your brother . . . and wanting to have a different kind of relationship with me . . . more than therapy . . . and it feels like that would mean a lot to you. I think you've told me this will hurt you some, but for me it is quite clear that our relationship has to be here in therapy. I say that largely because for me to be your therapist—or anyone's—I have to know what the boundaries are. And the boundary I'm comfortable with is that therapy not include other relationships." Now you've probably said enough and will tune in to hear the effect this has on your client, but you will likely return to this problem again. I hope that, in reading this, you can see how you have to have your feet under you to set limits without dropping a brick on your client. Only by thinking through ahead of time what your limits are will you be ready.

Transference

The term transference has taken on a great many meanings. Originally, it was Freud's characterization of the patient's irrational (that is, having no basis in the reality of the therapy relationship), intense attachment to the analyst. Since, he argued, he had done nothing to elicit this attachment, it must be feelings held toward other significant persons and transferred to the analyst. Negative transference was equally unearned hatred and anger felt toward the analyst. Many people now use transference to refer to virtually any feelings the client has toward the therapist, and the therapy relationship is, almost by definition, a transference relationship. Others react strongly against this denial of the therapy relationship as a real relationship, arguing that of course all relationships are based in part on past relationships, but it is avoiding the real human encounter of therapy to dismiss it as transference.

Whatever the merits of these arguments, Freud's original observation is worth understanding accurately. Most psychoanalysts argue that an irrational transference attachment is inevitable in therapy, and some argue that it is essential and that the only good interpretation is a transference interpretation. Most other therapists would say that transference attachments do happen in therapy sometimes but that they are neither inevitable nor essential. On the contrary, many clients will use therapy and the therapist to solve their problems outside therapy, appreciating and liking their therapists, but not out of proportion to the quite realistic positive feelings that grow from such a good relationship.

However, transference attachments do occur in nearly every therapist's experience, and you do need to be ready to deal with them openly and help-fully. The client will want you to break the limits and to be more than a thera-pist. Sometimes clients will drive past your house, feeling strong infatuation; sometimes they will phone you repeatedly, perhaps begging you for a more complete relationship. You have become part of the problem. Your response should include firm and consistent maintenance of your limits and empathi-cally helping your client work through the attachment feelings. Strong attach-ments take a long time to work through, and a new element in the problem is that now your client has a strong motive not to improve, because if he or she no longer needs therapy, he or she loses regular contact with you.

Your Own Distortions and Needs

Psychotherapy is a complex interchange, and your own blind spots and open nerves will interfere with it—unless you never distort anything, of course. The extreme expression of this is Freud's *countertransference*, the thera-pist's irrational attachment to or anger at the client. Fortunately, this extreme reaction is less common than transference, but it does happen, and you should be alert to the signs of it in yourself so that you will know when to find a trusted therapist/friend to help you figure out what's going on for you. More importantly, even if your reactions don't fit this definition of counter-transference, your own needs and problems *will* distort what you hear from clients. And sometimes your issues will prevent your clients from going places they need to go because you can't go there. You need to be as self-aware as you can be—an issue that is so important that we will return to it often.

We should clarify some terminology because people throw around the term "countertransference" with many different meanings. *Objective counter-transference* refers to situations when the therapist reacts to client behavior in much the same way that most people would react to this behavior (Hafken-scheid & Kiesler, 2007). However, we are most interested in *subjective counter-transference*, when a client evokes reactions based on the therapist's personal issues and distortions. Originally, Freud proposed countertransference as the therapist's irrational and intense reactions to a client, such as falling in love with or hating a client. Even though these reactions do occur occasionally, it is more useful to adopt a more moderate definition. "The moderate view defines countertransference as therapists' idiosyncratic reactions (broadly defined as sensory, affective, cognitive, and behavioral) to clients that are based primarily in therapists' own personal conflicts, biases, or difficulties (e.g., cognitive biases, personal narratives, or maladaptive interpersonal pat-terns)" (Fauth, 2006, p. 17). *Negative countertransference* refers to the therapist's unpleasant reactions and *positive countertransference* refers to positive or pleas-ant reactions to clients.

Unusually strong feelings toward a particular client are your most impor-tant clue to countertransference. You may feel that only you can really help this particular person or have powerful "rescue fantasies" that a relationship with you will change the client's life, or you may have frankly sexual feelings toward the client. Especially looking forward to or dreading sessions with particular clients is a sign that something may be wrong, or getting inexplicably sleepy during sessions can be cause to wonder.

Beyond the rare strong instances of countertransference, there is good evidence that nearly all interactions with clients are affected by the therapist's emotional involvement. My goal is to alert you to these influences and encourage you to think and talk about them. In one study, countertransference behavior among therapist trainees had a negative impact on treatment, especially with cases with poor to moderate treatment results (Hayes, Riker, & Ingram, 1997). Therapists and their supervisors agreed quite well on ratings of such therapist characteristics as "able to recognize boundaries between self and others . . . aware of own feelings elicited by clients . . . not overly anxious in the presence of most client problems . . . able to see things from client's point of view" (p. 147). They concluded that countertransference can be both harmful and useful. It usually causes problems in therapy, but it can be a source of insight and positive impact if managed and used well. Not surprisingly, negative countertransference is related to weaker therapeutic alliances and poorer outcome (Ligiero & Gelso, 2002), but even positive countertransference often interferes with good therapy (Gelso & Hayes, 2002). Strupp (1993) has observed that many therapists form a positive or negative attitude toward clients very quickly and that this attitude is very difficult to change. If you quickly form a positive or negative attitude, before you even know much about the client, you have to admit that your attitude must be largely based on your own needs and perceptions. Many therapists, for example, do poorly with clients who enter therapy with hostile, resistant, and negative interpersonal behaviors. They respond to these clients with "interpretations advanced in a subtly blaming manner or 'supportive' messages that simultaneously conveyed a criticism of the patient" (Strupp, 1993, p. 432).

A good summary of both clinical and empirical investigations of countertransference is presented by Singer and Luborsky (1977). They drew several conclusions from both the clinical literature and the research literature. Their conclusions from the clinical literature include these:

> Countertransference is a hindrance to effective treatment of the patient. . . . Countertransference hinders the treatment by preventing the therapist from properly identifying with the patient, a necessary part of the process of understanding. . . . One of the marks of the occurrence of countertransference is an inordinate intensity or inappropriateness of sexual or aggressive feelings toward the patient. . . . Avoiding countertransference problems can be aided by self-analysis or by discussion with a supervisor or colleague. (pp. 447–448)

Their conclusions based on research deal more with the general issue of how the therapist's emotions distort the therapy process, rather than the intense instances of countertransference. These research-based conclusions include the following:

Therapists are more inclined to avoid patients' feelings, especially anger, when they are directed against the therapist than when they are expressed toward someone else. . . . Therapists are much less accurate in reporting their own and their patients' behavior in psychotherapy when the issues are related to personality conflicts of their own—less accurate in terms of a greater discrepancy between their own report and a judge's report of what happened. . . . More experienced therapists tend to show fewer indications of countertransference in their work than do inexperienced therapists. . . . In response to client hostility (versus friendliness), counselors use more avoidance behavior such as suggestion, disapproval and information giving, and less interpretation, elaboration, and reflection. (p. 448)

These lists of conclusions are only a sampler, and you would be wise to read the whole article. What our sampler does is point out that you and your personality are deeply involved in what happens in therapy; and your involvement will often escape your conscious notice. Feedback from another therapist is essential to your continued growth as a therapist and diminishing of countertransference effects.

Therapy for the Therapist

I have repeatedly recommended that you explore your own experiencing with a therapist or friend (or both), and an important issue you should think about is whether therapy for yourself would be helpful. Hayes (2004) has studied five therapist characteristics that help to manage countertransference problems: empathy, self-insight, conceptual skills, self-integration, and anxiety management. Being effective in all these areas will require that you do your own emotional work. We will discuss this more in chapter 14, when we explore ways to take care of yourself.

Another of Singer and Luborsky's conclusions from the clinical literature was, "The therapist's emotional maturity is a deterrent to his potential countertransference needs which might interfere with the relationship, and psychotherapy or psychoanalysis is usually necessary to achieve this emotional maturity" (1977, p. 448). We all have anxiety-based problems and distortions, and we all could grow in a good therapy relationship. A therapist is especially called on to be clear and congruent with him- or herself, but there are other reasons for therapists to seek therapy.

Several other therapists and I have shared the feeling that it is a remarkable experience to be in the other chair, to feel what it is like to be deeply understood, to feel the release of saying things that have choked and haunted for years, to face the pain of looking at ourselves and feeling clearer and cleaner afterward. (See Appendix B: On Being a Client.) As a client, I have left sessions just sick about what I had said and then felt the pain transform— exactly the way it is supposed to. We tell clients about this transformation, but there is no way really to know what it means without having experienced it. Being a client can teach you a lot about doing therapy because it so strongly lets you get closer to the client's experience. In surveys of psychologists, psychiatrists, and clinical social workers, over 70 percent of the therapists report having had some therapy for themselves. Over 90 percent of them report that it had been helpful and that they learned a lot about therapy, especially about the impact of the therapy relationship (Norcross, Bike, & Evans, 2009; Norcross & Guy, 2007; Norcross, Strausser-Kirtland, & Missar, 1988).

Peebles (1980) reports evidence that the number of hours therapists had been in personal therapy significantly correlated with the level of empathy and genuineness they offered their clients, as rated by other professionals applying rating scales to tapes of therapy. In general, therapists report that they benefited professionally from having their own therapy, and other studies have found that personal therapy has a positive effect on therapists' empathy and acceptance (Macran & Shapiro, 1998). There seem to be no studies that link the therapist's personal therapy to improved outcome for clients, but that would be difficult research to conduct.

Whether it makes you a better therapist or not, you deserve to have a strong sense of your own worth, to feel stronger and more autonomous, to accurately experience yourself, and to be able to be intimate. Just be sure you get a good therapist.

Sexual Issues

Our culture is not exactly forthright and mature about sex, and so a lot of your clients will need to talk about it. For the same reason, you will probably have some discomfort hearing and articulating sexual messages. In one sense, sex is no different from any other difficult topic that you help your client "take the curse off" by your comfortably using language that explicitly says what your client implies. In another sense, though, sex has a special status because it so often intrudes on the therapy relationship in ways that other issues don't. This is especially clear when transference and countertransference develop, but we call these situations by special names only because they are so obvious. The same processes are operating to different degrees in all close relationships. It would take a lot of denial to think that warm, intimate relationships don't carry some implication of physical closeness, and whether our culture is forthright about this or not, you will need to be forthright about it in therapy.

You will need to make a special effort to hear your client talk about sex, and you will need to be sensitive to what you are communicating to your client. You will become very important to your client, and what you intend as a supportive physical gesture (let's assume you're not distorting your intentions) might well seem very different through the client's eyes.

■ Values and Expectancy Effects

There is some evidence that clients' values shift in the direction of their therapists' values over the course of therapy (Bergin, Payne, & Richards, 1996;

Beutler & Bergan, 1991; Rosenthal, 1955; Welkowitz, Cohen, & Ortmeyer, 1967). This may well be because therapists tend to have more mature values, and clients naturally move in their direction as they become more mature. It is also remarkable, though, that clients of Freudian therapists have Freudian dreams, clients of Jungians have Jungian dreams, and clients of Ellis turn out to have problems that fit his theory.

It's difficult not to think that therapists subtly influence the course of therapy, beyond the ways that they think they do. Work on expectancy effects, or self-fulfilling prophecies (Rosenthal, 1994, 2002), makes it clear that we often reinforce in others what we expect them to do. If they do things we don't expect, we tend to ignore it, even though we would deny having done so. Copeland and Snyder (1995) found that under some circumstances, peer counselors elicited extroverted behavior from clients whom the counselors believed to be extroverted. They called this the *behavioral confirmation* effect. This effect happened whether the clients were actually extroverted or not. The danger that this apparently inevitable process poses for evocatively empathic therapy is that we may be fooling both ourselves and our clients into thinking that we are permitting freedom and autonomy to grow, when in fact we are being quite controlling. In a sense, this is a countertransference issue because, although some such unintended directiveness is inevitable, the greater the therapist's distortions, the greater the danger. The (partial) solution is to build in the safeguards of getting feedback on your work, listening critically to your own therapy tapes, and knowing yourself as honestly as you can—perhaps through your own therapy.

■ Gender Roles and Therapy

Books like Chesler's (1972) *Women and Madness* raise one last relationship issue for you to think about. Chesler and many others (Brown, 2007; Enns, 1997) argue that psychotherapy is structured in the same way as the generally oppressive male-dominant culture that gave rise to therapy. These complaints are largely with psychoanalytic therapy, which does have considerable sexism in its theoretical base. But the general argument is that the expert male therapist tells the passive female client (in the usual arrangement) that her psychological health lies in accepting her role as a woman. Feminist therapists stress the importance of encouraging women not simply to adapt to cultural demands, which are themselves the source of many women's problems in living. Some (Brown, 2007) see Rogers' core conditions as helpful but incomplete because they pay insufficient attention to "issues of power and politics" (p. 257).

I like Maureen Walker's article, "How Therapy Helps When the Culture Hurts" (2008). She writes about our culture's "power-over paradigm" and examines the impact of the exercise of power on women's issues, sexual orientation, and race. She says that "conflict becomes a pathway to deeper connection when embraced with such processes as empathic attunement, authentic responsiveness, and mutuality" (p. 87). Done well, evocatively empathic therapy is quite clearly nonsexist. The goals are autonomy and self-esteem and accurate experiencing and good relationships—generally that the person find the life that's best for him or her—regardless of gender. I mentioned a client who said, "This is really feminist therapy." That was right for her, but I would rather think of it as nonsexist therapy (Enns, 1997). A female client can take charge of her life, and so can a male client; a male client can become more sensitive, and so can a female client. The therapist needs to be aware of the effects of power and politics, but our goal is to bring empowerment, connection, safety, and insight to all of our clients.

Getting Started

The only way to learn therapeutic skills is through practice. You must make yourself articulate responses, feeling all that initial awkwardness, until doing it becomes second nature. It is difficult, though, simply to read descriptions of what good therapy is and then start out doing it; you may find it helpful to begin with some pretty mechanical exercises. Jacobs (1981) showed that students could be taught, with an hour of instruction, to respond to written "client statements" in a way that would be rated as highly empathic on Guerney's (1977) Acceptance of Others Scale, a rating scale for empathic responding. One of Jacobs' points was that if it is this easy to get high empathy scores on such tests, it is amazing that the bulk of experiments on training report low empathy levels among their trainees. It is extremely likely that Jacobs trained his subjects to "beat the scale." They studied the scale, were given concrete examples to learn from, and were taught specific strategies, such as making plausible guesses at feelings. It is unlikely that his subjects were truly empathic in the sense that they could have made a client feel understood, but his training procedure does give you a way to get started.

■ Written Exercises

You can start out all alone in your room where nobody will know what you're doing. Transcripts of therapy sessions from which you can select client statements appear in Appendix A. Choose a few fairly long statements (so there will be more to respond to) and take your time formulating an empathic response. To be rated at the minimally facilitative level, Jacobs would tell you simply to paraphrase the content of the client's statement. This will probably feel inane to you, as it probably would to an outside observer. Surprisingly, though, such a paraphrase often has powerful effects on a client. Gendlin (1974) quotes a person in a training group as saying, "It feels so odd to repeat what someone said, but it feels so powerful when someone does it for me" (p. 220). I frequently hear from trainees, "People really are solving their problems, but I'm not doing anything. I'm just listening." *Just* listening! Learning to paraphrase is an important first step in your skill development, and it will help to compare your written paraphrases with a friend's.

Jacobs instructed his subjects that they could get a higher rating by making a *plausible guess* at something the talker was feeling. To get a higher rating, make a plausible guess at a feeling and at something the person is saying he or she wants, wishes, or hopes for. Plausible guesses at two feelings will earn this higher rating in lieu of wants or wishes. You can also raise your ratings by using introductory phrases such as "Sounds like . . ." and "It seems to me that you're saying. . . ." Jacobs was demonstrating some serious problems with rating scales for empathy, since his subjects could earn high scores with one hour's training and rigid following of a few rules, whether the trainees understood another person or not. You can use his procedure, however, to get started with written exercises, as long as you promise to remember that this is just a "training wheels" exercise.

■ Role-Playing and Practicing in Dyads

My experience has been that beginning therapists make their greatest strides in confidence and skill by role-playing therapy in groups of two or three with other students. One person plays the therapist, one plays the client, and the other sits as a silent observer until the end of a role-playing session, which may last from 5 to 20 minutes or so. The observer can then join in a discussion of the session from a different perspective than either of the direct participants. The advantages of role-playing are that threat is low (unless a teacher or supervisor drops in to observe), mistakes don't cost anybody anything, and you can sit as long as you want to formulate a response. At first, it's easier if the "client" plays some other person or some composite person with a problem. This makes the situation artificial, but it also lowers the difficulty. After a while, though, I hope you will be able to move beyond role-playing toward discussing real problems. These don't need to be deep personal problems, which might be quite inappropriate to discuss with other students, but to the extent that trust can be built, you will benefit more as the therapist and as a person who can experience the releasing power of being understood if real problems are at the root of the discussion.

■ The Value of Listening to and Watching Yourself and Others

I consider both audio and video recordings of therapy to be essential tools of training. They permit you to learn by listening to or observing others. In addition, when you listen to or view a recording of yourself, you get an accurate version of what you did, as opposed to only the well-filtered version that any therapist-observer gives of a session. However, when others watch or hear your recording they can provide feedback about your work. Although feedback can be threatening, it is essential.

Alvin Mahrer (1996) made three suggestions for a therapist who wants to take less than 40 years to learn to do therapy. His first bit of advice was,

"Study tapes of impressive sessions" (p. 139). He suggests observing therapists from a wide variety of orientations and especially trying to understand moments in which impressive changes take place. As a graduate student, I was lucky enough to have a job rating therapy recordings for a research project. That experience was one of the most powerful influences on me as a developing therapist.

One of the most instructive ways to learn from a supervisor is to have him or her listen to a recording of you doing therapy, stop the recording at the end of particular client responses, and have the supervisor give a hypothetical response. This will probably be a good experience for both of you, since many experienced therapists have become so comfortable with their style that they often give very helpful responses but can't say why. Having to explain a response to you may also help the supervisor to stay sharp and to improve.

Beginning Therapy
Reflections of a Novice Therapist
by Michael Stambrook

For me the process of beginning training in psychotherapy was one of the most demanding and eventually rewarding challenges I have encountered. What I hope to do here is to communicate and share my experience of being confronted by clients who have come to me for help.

The initial hurdle I needed to overcome was to become comfortable with my role of supposedly having expertise in the process of helping my clients find the solutions that work best in their own lives and resisting the pressure to provide what clearly would be gratuitous advice. This pressure, I believe, was due to my feelings of uncertainty and anxiety related to my new role as a neophyte therapist wanting to do the best possible job for his clients. I found it difficult and sometimes two-faced to communicate to my clients that they could trust me and the process so that in time, through a collaborative exploration, they would come to face what was most troublesome and work out the best possible solutions. Further, although sincerely acknowledging the distress and pain my clients felt, I was unwilling and unable to impose on them my unique solutions in the form of advice.

For me there was an additional and powerful source of uneasiness, which was due to my having to take on faith, and what seemed to me face validity, that the process that I was learning to use did work and would be very successful for me. Part of this was learning to trust that through my use of evocative empathy my clients would in time get to where they needed to go. It seemed sort of paradoxical that before I was able to have the implicit faith and trust in my clients' own resources to reach their own solutions, I had to see firsthand that such faith and trust were warranted. Bluntly, I had to learn to have such implicit trust and faith so that my clients could increasingly approach what they feared most through my reinforcing their approach attempts in an active but nondirective, nonthreatening manner.

In terms of actually learning to respond in an evocatively empathic mode, one of the most difficult aspects was attempting to get beyond the content of what was being presented, to what were the reactions to what was said. It was as if I had a task of attending to and responding to multichannel input, but I was so skilled in dealing with only one of the channels that at first it was almost all I heard.

Based on my academic training in psychotherapy, I was skilled in thinking and responding that was predominantly content-oriented. Initially I found it surprisingly difficult to keep these intellectualizing and analytic modes of thinking and reacting in check. While I had to stay very much in tune with the content of my clients' verbalizations, I somehow also had to keep track of all the verbal and nonverbal affective cues that gave the content its life. Because clients need to face the emotional impact of their experiencing, the goal for me as the therapist was to help them confront the experience fully without resorting to defensive avoidance maneuvers. The demanding and difficult task for me was to attend to these affective cues that were behind the explicit verbalizations and help my clients confront them immersed within the content of what was presented.

I have already identified one of the reasons it was hard to attend to the affective components of my clients' messages—that is, the need to break from that deeply ingrained and well-reinforced intellectual mode of reacting; but for me there was another reason, related to the fact that for the most part the emotions dealt with were very painful. It seemed at times that confronting clients with that which was implicit in their message, even though they had almost stated it, would hurt them more, and there was a tremendous urge to back off. *SPEAK TO THIS*

For me there were two parts to this desire to pull back, both of which are clearly countertherapeutic. First, although this urge not to further expose my clients to the distress they felt was due to my wanting to see them free from anguish, it would not have been respectful and would have demonstrated a lack of trust and confidence in their ability to face what troubles them most and be able to come through the experience intact. *YES CRYSTAL CLEAR*

The other part of not wanting to hurt my clients more by confronting them with their experience was self-protective. That is, to help a client get to where he or she had to go, I had to be willing to go there myself and be able to face with the client the full impact of the experience. Although for my part this sharing of the experience had an "as if" nature, I had to be willing to see and experience in myself similar painful emotions to be able to be useful. I felt that if I was not able to deal with issues of competency, dependency, intimacy, mortality, and so on, I would not be able to help my clients deal with such issues in themselves. That is, if I could not face in myself some issue my client was struggling with, I doubt I could help my clients confront the full impact of their experiencing, because it would be too threatening to me. In many instances during supervision sessions, I have needed to talk about my reactions to the experiences clients have presented, and it was always a shock to me for a therapy supervisor to point out issues that at first I was blind to, which later became glaringly obvious.

At present, I believe that the first part of not wanting to hurt clients further has been dealt with by my increased maturity and experience in that I have discovered that I can trust my clients to live through the worst of their experiences. I believe the second part, however, is something that will be in effect insidiously throughout my career practicing psychotherapy; effort and attention will always have to be given to preventing clients from building defenses based on my own defenses. To put this into the perspective of beginning psychotherapy training, these issues forced some rather intense and sometimes painful self-exploration in which I felt impelled to examine parts of myself that I had previously avoided. To this end I was lucky in having the opportunity to be in a "growth group" with fellow students who were also beginning therapy training: we could explore these issues and common concerns in a nonthreatening environment. It was extremely reassuring and supportive to learn that what I was experiencing was not unique to me but was shared by my colleagues.

Looking back now from the perspective of having three years of training and experience in psychotherapy with many kinds of clients it seems as if the issues that before felt so acute are no longer as troublesome. Although much remains a mystery, I feel confident in what I do in therapy and strongly believe that I have something valuable to offer my clients. I have found that writing this has been difficult because I have not been able to recapture, in all its vividness, the unique experience of beginning and taking the first steps as a therapist.

Through continual discussions with my fellow students and countless hours of intensive tape-work supervision sessions that involved role-playing and learning by shaping, I no longer feel that I have to consciously and strenuously force myself to attend to that which my clients are implying and can't quite face—somehow, although it is still an active process, it feels as if it comes more naturally.

Beyond Skills

I thought about calling this chapter "Beyond Skills: From Skillful Therapist to Artist." There is useful truth in this title, because the artist first starts with skills and then "forgets" about the skills when he or she is producing art. However, there is also a problem with drawing this analogy between being a therapist and being an artist. The artist is the virtuoso who produces the work of art. The therapist is, at most, the co-creator of the process that occurs in therapy. The client's growth is not the product of the therapist's virtuosity; the client is the primary producer of the growth. So, take only half of the analogy to the artist. You will need to become artistic in many ways in your therapy as you move beyond skills, but you will not become the producer of brilliant art.

■ What You Can't Learn from a Book

I also thought about calling this chapter "Beyond Skills: Things You Can't Learn from a Book." We are going to discuss qualities of the therapy process that are extremely difficult to put into words. I have repeatedly told you that we have started out focusing on skills, which is probably a necessary place to start for almost all of us. But if you depend on skills as the way you do therapy, you will never be more than a pretty good therapist. Actually, pretty good isn't bad, and you will be able to help many clients. But to be a great therapist, you will need to learn ways of being with your clients that are intuitive and experiential and full of presence.

I'll Never Know Anything for Sure, Probably

I think that I know more about doing therapy than I knew 10 or 15 years ago, but I'm amazed at how much less sure I am that I understand fundamental human nature or the basic nature of reality. Uncertainty is unnerving, but there also is comfort in the openness of knowing that our human understanding of reality is incomplete and probably always will be incomplete. Releasing the need to have logical, intellectual explanations for everything probably opens a person up more to experiential knowing.

Our task is to find enough certainty to offer our clients effective therapy while we remain humble and open enough to learn as much as we can, even from people who seem to disagree with each other. This learning almost always will involve *knowing* that cannot be expressed in words, that is, knowing that is ineffable. I believe strongly that therapy is a cognitive-experiential process. I also believe that learning to become a therapist and providing therapy require both cognitive and experiential learning. Cognitive learning alone would be superficial and incomplete and so would experiential learning alone. It is worth the effort to try to put the ineffable into words as much as possible.

Words may at least point the way.   My hope is that by describing some of the parts of therapy that are ineffable, I will help you recognize these experiences when you feel them at a gut level. In the next section we will be talking about the client's experiential knowing as an important part of therapeutic growth. Much of what happens for the therapist is also experiential knowing, and I wish for you many experiences that will give you the sensation of, "Ah, that's what presence means!" or, "Now I know what it means to sense the edges of another person's experiencing." You may even be trying to teach someone else how to do therapy and have that person ask you how you knew what your client was experiencing. You may know that you know but be unable to put it into words to explain it. There are many truths that a person can't understand until he or she feels the experiential knowing of those truths. If we try to come as close as possible to describing these experiences, however, it may prepare you to recognize and learn from them, even though our verbal descriptions are terribly inadequate and limiting.

Learning the rules. Unlearning the rules.   One therapist I know says that he thinks we all need to be taught a theoretical orientation in graduate school so that we have something to rebel against later. There is so much to know and so little solid knowledge that most of us have a kind of desperate need for structure, and we fervently adopt a structured position to give us the comfort of feeling that our knowledge is more solid than it really is. This need for structure makes it tempting to learn rules and strategies to which we adamantly commit ourselves. It is often said that beginners in a field learn and follow the rules, while the experts in that field seem to break many of those rules. It is not a bad thing that you want rules and techniques to guide your practice as a therapist, as long as you don't cling to those rules and techniques but rather use them to point you in a direction. As you gain experience, if you have committed yourself to move into uncharted territory in the direction your rules point, you have a chance to become good enough that you can "forget the rules" and become a deeply healing therapist.

Is there a sudden leap from technique to artistry?   It seems likely that most therapists develop and grow gradually and continuously, rather than in sudden epiphanies of insight. As a beginning therapist, you will probably resonate with much in this chapter, but you will also be overwhelmed and confused by some of it too. I will quote gifted, experienced therapists about some of their experiences, and some of these experiences can be intimidatingly difficult to understand. I hope that you will take what you can from this chapter and then come back to it again in a few years. I think that this chapter will then resonate with you.

It takes a very long time to become an effective evocatively empathic therapist, and I hope that your learning never stops. I have had many students re-read this book after two or three years of experience as a therapist and then have the reaction, "Now I see what it means!"

■ Experiential Knowing

In chapter 4, we mentioned the work of Gendlin (1962, 1969, 1974, 1978, 1991, 1997), who emphasized that much of what goes on in therapy (in all human functioning, actually) is experiential; it is a process of direct experiencing that is different from intellectual functioning. He says that, "direct experiencing is 'implicitly' rich in meanings, but is never equatable to words or concepts" (1974, p. 227). This isn't "just a feeling." The *felt sense* is a physical, bodily process that is full of meanings that are only inadequately expressed in words and concepts. "The felt sense is vague at first, sensed directly but not yet in explicit words or images. It is neither drowning in strong emotions nor is it just thinking. . . . When the felt sense is responded to little steps inwardly arise directly from the client's own process" (Hendricks, 2007, p. 41). When a client directly experiences his or her felt sense, there can be a noticeable sensation of resolution or falling-into-place that Gendlin calls a *felt shift*. This felt shift brings new experiential meanings, and it may result in a more complete conceptual or intellectual understanding, in addition to the enormous amount that has happened at the experiential level.

Experiential learning occurs in many places in human life. How do you keep from falling over when you ride a bike? A careful, logical analysis would reveal that you are constantly making tiny turns in the direction the bike is falling and this keeps you upright. However, this information is virtually useless to a person learning to ride a bike. You may not even have known it until I told you, but you ride bikes well. We learn to ride experientially, perhaps with another person gasping along beside us holding the seat until we "get it." Once we "get it," riding is easy, although we can't explain how we stay up.

Bohart (1993) argues that experiencing is "the basis of psychotherapy" (p. 51). All learning that results in meaningful change requires experiential learning, both within the person and in the environment. Hendricks says working with the bodily felt sense is the foundation of all orientations to therapy.

> It is the experiential use of any theory in any modality that brings the possibility to resume the implied but stopped (therapy) process. This explains why different schools are equally effective and it also shows how a therapist can use many theories with any one client. From within any orientation we can help the client to articulate implicit intricacy and thereby find the meaning and small steps of change that carry forward life. (Hendricks, 2008, p. 46)

Levels of Cognitive/Experiential Knowing

The process of extracting meaning from a felt sense can be understood in two general stages (Vanaerschot, 1997). At the level of the felt sense, meaning is a bodily experience. Second, as we focus on the felt sense, we can start to extract explicit meanings from it and express those meanings symbolically by making them cognitions. I have repeatedly said that therapy is a cognitive-experiential process. However, as we come to understand that direct experiencing is primary and cognitive knowing comes afterward, perhaps we should use the term "experiential-cognitive."

Bodily felt sense.   Bohart's (1993) description of experiential knowing is especially helpful. He says that experiencing is (1) immediate, (2) bodily, and (3) holistic. There is a suddenness in experiencing that feels different than the linear time of logic and reason. It is felt in the body and happens without thinking and conceptualizing. Experiential knowing occurs as an integrated whole. It sometimes is called "grounded cognition" (Barsalou, 2008), "embodied cognition," or "embodied emotion" (Niedenthal, 2007) because it is felt physically—as perceptual, visceral, and motoric. Felt knowing is different than emotional knowing and cognitive knowing.

Psychology usually describes human behavior as either cognition or emotion/affect. In psychotherapy, when people refer to experiencing, they often mean emotion, but it is important to understand that *felt knowing* is different than both cognition and affect. Bohart (1993) says, "How then does experiencing fit within the cognitive-affective dichotomy which typifies most psychological theorizing? It doesn't. The cognitive-affective dichotomy does not handle the phenomenon of experiencing very well" (p. 56). The *feelings* of experiencing differ from emotions in many cases. We can *feel* emotion such as anger, joy, and fear, of course. We also *feel* cold, tired, sick, and thirsty, none of which is an emotion. Most importantly for us, a "third class of feelings . . . consists of nonverbal or 'felt' apprehensions of meaning patterns" (p. 58). We *feel* that we understand a situation but can't put our understanding into words. You will hear clients say things like, "I know I'm a successful person, but I don't feel successful. I don't really believe it." Or, "I know perfectly well that it is irrational to worry about her leaving me, but I feel every morning like it will be the last." Or, "It makes sense now that I left home when I did. I really knew it was right when I did it, but I couldn't say why." You might even get frustrated with a client who feels unattractive and try to prove to her that she is physically attractive using pictures and talking about norms. You might become even more frustrated when the client says, "OK, I know with certainty that you are right, but I still feel ugly." Feeling ugly is not an emotion or a cognition. In fact, the client now has the cognition that she is attractive, but that contradicts how she feels experientially.

Forming explicit meanings from the felt sense: Cognition is essential too.   The term *cognition* has many meanings in psychology, but it is most commonly used to refer to the conceptual manipulation of symbols that is usually called thinking. These processes are, at least by implication, conscious and available to be put into words, while experiential knowing is primary and doesn't involve logical inferences.

The second stage of our experiential-cognitive process moves from a bodily felt sense to symbolization of our experiences (Vanaerschot, 1997). Cognition is essential in human functioning, and an important part of therapy is the process of forming explicit meanings from the implicit and preconceptual meanings of experiencing. Language is a limited medium for expressing meaning, and the felt sense is more complex and carries meanings that aren't and sometimes can't be put into words. On the other hand, the felt sense is often vague, sometimes distorted, and hard to "use" in everyday life. The structure of cognition and language help us to "tame" our experiencing and make it more useful to us.

Implicit and Explicit Problem Solving

Clients will surprise you sometimes by "just getting better" for reasons you can't figure out. Or one may say, "I'm not sure why, but I like myself better." Of course, it is good to understand and solve problems rationally, and the more we consciously understand, the more control we have over events in our lives. However, it also important to understand that much human functioning occurs at an experiential level, and this includes the resolution of problems. When we were interns, a friend of mine treated a boy who repeatedly rubbed open, bleeding sores on his arms. While others were healing, he reopened old lacerations and had no idea why he did this. He loved to talk about trains, so he and my friend did this for weeks. One day, the therapist impulsively said, "Why don't we switch chairs? You be the therapist and I'll be the client." They did, and shortly afterward the boy stopped his self-destructive behavior. The boy's parents thought my friend was a miracle worker, but he told us, "I'll never understand therapy until I understand what happened here." I don't think we'll ever know what happened, but I'm sure it involved a massive *felt shift* within the boy.

Entering Another Person's Experiential World

We have been discussing the process through which clients work at both an experiential and cognitive level. We also need to understand that one of the most important and difficult things a therapist must learn is how to be attuned to a client in an experiential way.

I once asked Bob Lee (whose session appears in Appendix A) how he knows what to respond to among the many things a client says and implies at any moment. He answered, "It just forms inside me." I was frustrated by his answer, because I wanted an explanation. (I was younger and more rigid then, of course.) Bob was entering into the client's experiencing in an experiential way, and he could sense what was happening for the client. As he resonated to the client's experience, his understanding "just formed inside" him in ways he could share with the client. Up until now in this book, we have talked about hearing the client's implicit message in a more conceptual way. We have talked more about drawing inferences—"figuring out" what the client was trying to say and was feeling. I even used language like, "Your job is to find some way to get as far ahead of the client as you can without losing what the client will recognize as part of the message." This is still good advice, but now we are seeing that entering another person's experiential world involves more than just making accurate inferences.

Sensing another person's experiencing.   Trying to explain how to *sense* another person's experiencing is probably the most important and most difficult part of writing this book. Therapists have to operate at two very different levels at the same time. They are logical and cognitive as they pick up the meaning of their clients' stories, and they are simultaneously *sensing, feeling, resonating to,* and *intuiting* their clients' internal experiences. I recently saw a client in a demonstration session in front of several therapists in training. Afterward, the client was trying to explain what the session felt like, and he said, "It was almost like he didn't hear the words I said, but he obviously did because he knew what I was feeling."

When I am supervising a therapist, I sometimes use phrases like, "What is going on inside your client right now? Can you tune in to what that feels like?" At first, most people try to think their way through to an answer to these questions, but that is only part of the answer. *Sensing* what is going on inside your client is very different from figuring out what is going on inside your client. One gifted therapist in training told me that when she felt most attuned to a particular client, she felt like she was "rotating in space." She had no other words for the experience, and she didn't talk to her client about rotating in space, but she was especially effective when she had that feeling. I wish I could explain this incident to you in rational terms, but I can't.

The words *attunement* and *resonance* might be helpful in understanding this process. A metaphor for this is two guitar strings tuned to the same note or perhaps an octave apart. When one string is plucked, the other vibrates in resonance. You attune yourself to the client and let his experiencing stimulate your experiencing. To the extent that you can do this, you will have a *felt apprehension* and *felt understanding* of your client.

Empathy as an attitude.   Rogers often expressed his dismay that his writings about empathy became distorted into techniques with names like "reflection of feelings" (1980). He and others (Bozarth, 1984, 1997) have a strong preference for thinking of empathy as an attitude rather than as skills or techniques. The therapist's intentions to be fully present and attuned with the client express this attitude.

Experiential Learning in Becoming a Therapist

Learning to be a therapist is much like learning other complex tasks. We usually start with intellectual understanding and then, as we gain experience, we learn how "it's really done." Gaining experience obviously means, in part, doing the task and learning from our mistakes and successes. There are also more subtle and complex ways that experiential learning can help you become a therapist.

The master knows more than can be said.   The primary reason that training in many professions requires some kind of apprenticeship is that much of the important knowledge in the profession is seldom or never put into words. It is learned experientially. There is an old saying, "The master knows more than he can say." The nuances of practice can be subtle and complex and sometimes "the master" even acts in ways that contradict what he or she says and consciously believes. Observing and working with a master may be the only way to learn some of what a therapist does. Near the end of his life, Carl Rogers told a group of us that he had given up trying to teach people how to do psychotherapy. He said, "All I can do is let people watch me work." All of this is one reason Mahrer (1996) so strongly recommends that we all "study tapes of impressive sessions" (p. 139). Even better would be the opportunity to observe experienced therapists doing therapy live, although the opportunity to do that is very rare.

Learning through experience as a client.   It is common to be drawn to *healing with what healed you.* We would all like to believe that our choice of therapy approach is based on a rational examination of the evidence and some kind of reasonable choice process. Like most human choices, however, this one almost certainly involves some unconscious, experiential, and accidental causes. I talked earlier about how many of us will acquire a theoretical and therapeutic approach in our graduate training and then later rebel against that training. Not everyone rebels like this, of course, and so a lot of why we choose one approach over another depends on the accident of where we were trained and who our mentors were. Another important factor in why we choose one approach over another is whatever we ourselves experience as healing. If a person has had a powerful healing experience as a client in therapy, it is very likely that that approach to therapy will have a compelling draw for the person (see Appendix B).

No book or teacher can ever explain to you what it feels like to have someone understand something that is terribly important to you emotionally but that you have difficulty grasping. I could describe the experience as a "rush, full of relief," but until you feel it, you won't know what it means. Having your own therapy will help you in many ways to feel better and live better, but it will also help you understand your clients' experiences in a way that nothing else can give you (see Appendix B).

The tendency to use "healing with what healed you" goes beyond our experiences in therapy, however. We bring to our choice of therapy personal characteristics and preferences that also influence us. To a highly intellectualized person, strongly cognitive approaches "just feel right." Experiential approaches might feel like "frustrating fluff" to such a person. To a highly experiential person emotion-based approaches "just feel right," and cognitive approaches might seem rigid and superficial.

As with many of the things we have discussed, healing with what healed you can be both damaging and helpful. The therapist who knows firsthand how life-changing a particular therapy approach can be will have a stronger commitment and probably a more intense presence in therapy because of that personal knowledge. The problem is that not everybody in the world is like you. The essence of therapy is still to be deeply known and accepted, but for some clients this experience will come from more focus on interpersonal relationships and for other clients it will come from an appreciation of independence and autonomy. An important part of being clear about yourself as a therapist is being able to hold your issues and wants and feelings in abeyance and to tune in to your clients' inevitably different experiences.

Evidence that Supports the Importance of Experiential Knowing

There are two kinds of evidence that support the importance of experiential knowing. The first is an extensive research literature on information processing that is precognitive or preconceptual, and the second consists of studies that look at experiencing in applied contexts, such as therapy.

In chapter 16 we will examine the first kind of evidence in more detail, but for our purposes in this chapter it is worth repeating the conclusions of three summaries of the research. Bargh and Chartrand (2005) summarize research on "automaticity" and social cognition and conclude that

> conscious, intentional control is actually quite limited, so that most of moment-to-moment psychological life must occur through nonconscious means if it is to occur at all. . . . Three major forms of automatic self-regulation are identified: An automatic effect of perception on action, automatic goal pursuit, and a continual automatic evaluation of one's experience. (p. 228)

Toth and Reingold (1996) conclude that there is "clear evidence that prior conceptual processing can unconsciously influence subsequent behaviour" (p. 71). Posner and Boies (1971) report from their review of selective attention, "Conscious awareness is itself rather late in the sequence of mental processing" (p. 407). An enormous amount happens in human functioning that is preconceptual, and this includes both emotional and informational processing.

Experiential knowing encompasses many kinds of preconceptual processing and is extremely difficult to study within psychotherapy. Although our research tools are not adequate to study something as complex and private as experiencing, Bohart and his associates (1996) reported several interesting studies. In one, university students were asked questions such as, "Has there been a time when you knew something to be true before you were able to intellectually verify to yourself that it was true?" (p. 202). Students' responses demonstrated that they clearly had such experiences and that they combined this kind of knowing with cognitive knowing to understand new experiences. In a second study, the researchers examined recordings of six expert therapists and found that they "experientialized" the therapy process, especially in contrast with a television talk-show therapist, who was more abstract and intellectual. Finally, four therapists met with 21 clients in a therapy analogue study. The clients talked about mild personal problems, and the therapists provided empathic feedback. Clients responded more quickly to empathic responses that captured the experiential flavor of what the client said than to similar empathic responses said in a more conceptual or abstract way. The investigators inferred that clients had to pause to think about the accuracy of the conceptual responses but immediately recognized the "rightness" of the experiential ones.

■ Many Ways to Communicate Empathy

We have talked a lot about how the therapist enters the client's experiential world, which is the first part of being empathic. An understanding of experiential knowing also applies to how we communicate our understanding. The absolute essence of evocative empathy is that the client feels deeply understood—deeply known. There are many ways to make this happen. It may even be that when the therapist's *intention* is to understand and accept the client, almost anything the therapist does will be perceived by the client as understanding (Bohart & Rosenbaum, 1995; Bozarth, 1984, 1997). In many ways, this is a relief for the therapist. If your intentions and attitudes are right, you have a great latitude in the actions that will help heal.

Most of the time, the form of evocative empathy we have been learning is the most effective way to make another person feel understood in a way that helps him or her grow. But sometimes sitting in silence for 20 minutes is the most empathic response possible. Think of the insensitive irony of a therapist who says, "I sense the sadness you want to hide. It seems like you don't want to be alone right now but you also don't want somebody talking to you about your sadness." This might have earned the therapist a high score on some scale of "empathic responding" but left the client silently feeling, "That's right, now shut up and stop talking about it." The most empathic thing might have been just to sit in silence. I once had a young client who felt most understood when we talked about the stock market. We need to be sensitive to what makes *this client* feel understood.

I worry that much of the training we provide therapists actually makes people more intellectualized and less empathic. This can happen when we focus on the intellectual and conceptual aspects of clinical practice, but it can also happen when we try to "teach empathy" or "teach basic skills." There are many people who connect easily with others and make others feel understood in their own idiosyncratic way. If we then teach such a person one rigid way that is the "right way" to express empathy, we can make him or her less effective in therapy. I hope you find from this section that there is much latitude in developing your own way to help your clients feel known and accepted.

Responding from within Your Empathic Resonance

When you are attuned to your client, your own internal reactions can guide your responding. We used both "attuned" and "resonate" to describe the therapist's experiential knowing of the client's world. As the therapist resonates to the client, the therapist's own reactions may help the client move forward. Bohart and Rosenbaum (1995) like the metaphor of two jazz musicians improvising together. Neither one copies the other, but what one plays grows out of what the other has just played and is in tune with it. It is a process of joint creation of something that continues to move forward.

The client might say, "I really liked the way our family did things together when I was a kid." If the therapist is immersed in the client's experiencing, she might say, "That was a great part of your life. As you said that, though, I got a sense of discouragement or sadness or something. Is that just my feeling?" Or she might say something very different. "I kind of felt a joyful longing when you said that." We don't know what the client meant because that can come only from being attuned to this particular client, but the sensitively attuned therapist can use his or her resonant response to move the process forward.

There is an obvious risk in responding from your own resonance. Every therapist in the world distorts what the client says to some extent, and we all perceive and experience through our own needs and issues. How can you know that you are resonating accurately with your client? It is helpful to check regularly with the client. The client is the final word on the accuracy of your understanding. The therapist in the previous paragraph, for example, asked, "Is that just my feeling?" She will listen carefully to the client's response to her offering of her own experience. She will not assume that if she's feeling it, it must be accurate.

Clients' Perceptions and "Received" Empathy

Bachelor (1988) asked clients to describe "a situation in which your therapist was empathic toward you (i.e., when you felt that he or she demonstrated the ability to put himself or herself in your place). Write in detail what happened and what you felt" (p. 229). Analyses of the clients' responses resulted in four different kinds of client-perceived empathy. *Therapist (facilitative) cognitive empathy* was reported by 44 percent of clients. This style of empathy most closely resembles evocative empathy as we have been discussing it. The therapist showed understanding, usually verbally, of the client's innermost experience. One instance, however, was completely nonverbal, in which the client said, "A great sadness and tears welled up but didn't let go. At that moment we were looking each other in the eyes. And I felt that she understood what had just happened. It was nonverbal but I am sure that she grasped what was going on inside of me" (p. 231). In *therapist affective empathy,* 30 percent of clients reported experiences in which the therapist personally experienced emotions that the client was experiencing. Eighteen percent of clients reported feeling understood through *therapist sharing empathy.* These experiences occurred when the therapist spontaneously shared personal opinions or personal experiences that related to what the client was saying. Finally, 7 percent of the clients responded to *therapist nurturant empathy.* These were instances of expressed, security-providing support and attention. This was relatively infrequently perceived as empathic.

Bachelor's results teach us an important lesson. Different clients respond to different styles of empathy. Most of the "received empathy" in her study was expressed verbally by the therapists, but some instances were entirely nonverbal. Most of the time, sensitive and evocative reformulations were most effective, but self-disclosure sometimes makes a client feel more understood. Sometimes even advice or an interpretation are perceived as deeply understanding by the client. We can't say that it doesn't matter what the therapist does, but there is great variety in what clients perceive as empathic.

■ Mindfulness

One of the newest areas of interest in therapy is also one of the oldest. Mindfulness practices have received a lot of attention and have been incorporated into many kinds of practice recently (Shapiro, 2009; Shapiro & Carlson, 2009), but the roots of these practices are found in the core teachings of the Buddha. Kabat-Zinn (2003) says that mindfulness is

> the awareness that emerges through paying attention on purpose, in the present moment, and nonjudgmentally to the unfolding of experience moment by moment. . . . And mindfulness, . . . being about attention, is also of necessity universal. [In that sense,] there is nothing particularly Buddhist about it. (p. 145)

Most people think of meditation as the practice of mindfulness; meditation is a powerful form of mindfulness, but mindfulness is much more than just meditation. You can brush your teeth, eat supper, drive to work, and kiss mindfully, although most of us usually don't; we live distractedly and automatically. Living mindfully improves life in many ways, including ways that matter to us as therapists. It can enhance peacefulness and improve your health, and it can also help you be more deeply empathic and more fully present with your clients. In chapter 14 we will discuss mindful ways to improve your life, but here we are especially interested in you as a mindful therapist.

Defining Mindfulness

On the surface, mindfulness seems simpler and easier to do than it actually is. Here are two definitions that may flesh out your understanding. Read them with the intent to understand how you might use them in being more mindful—more mindful in your life and especially more mindful when you are focused on your clients.

Shapiro points out that mindfulness is both a way of being and something you do.

> It is important to remember that mindfulness is both an outcome (mindful awareness) and a process (mindful practice): (1) Mindful awareness: an abiding presence or awareness, a deep knowing that manifests as freedom of mind (e.g., freedom from reflexive conditioning and delusion), and (2) Mindful practice: the systematic practice of intentionally attending in an open, caring, and discerning way, which involves both knowing and shaping the mind. (Shapiro, 2009, p. 556)

Dimidjian and Linehan (2003) identify three things you do when you're being mindful, "(1) observing, noticing, bringing awareness; (2) describing, labeling, noting; and (3) participating." (p. 166). You are alertly engaged. They also suggest ways to do these activities: "(1) nonjudgmentally, with acceptance, allowing; (2) in the present moment, with beginner's mind; and (3) effectively" (p. 166).

Standing in the Face of Your Experiences

The link between mindfulness and evocatively empathic therapy that means the most to me is found in the phrase, "Standing in the face of your experiences." Mindfulness means intentionally looking at what you are experiencing in the present moment fully and without judgment. You don't run from it or suppress it or decide if it's bad or good; you experience it fully. When we say that the therapist is a brave companion who will "walk through the fire" with the client, we are talking about being fully mindful of the client's experiencing in a way that helps her be more mindful also.

How does this help? Standing in the face of experiencing changes that experiencing in ways that avoidance, analysis, and distraction cannot. There are several possible explanations for why this happens, and we probably don't know enough yet to choose among them. Some that have been suggested include exposure (extinction), cognitive change, self-management, relaxation, acceptance (Baer, 2003), and cognitive defusion. Actually, they all probably have some truth to them. As a further possibility, a study of brain function that has been interpreted as supportive of mindfulness is Lieberman's clever experiment using functional MRI readings. Lieberman and colleagues (2007) demonstrated that the act of naming negative emotions actually reduces the brain arousal associated with them. Subjects were shown pictures of faces with intensely negative emotions such as anger and fear. The pictures caused increased arousal of the amygdala. In some cases, the subject named the emotion in the faces but at other times was distracted from the emotion by naming the gender of the person in the picture or making a decision about whether two pictures matched each other. After trials of naming the emotion, arousal in the amygdala calmed down, but when the subjects performed the avoidance tasks, arousal in the amygdala remained high, as other brain centers were activated.

Standing in the face of our emotion does transform that emotion. Distracting ourselves from it only appears to change the emotion by arousing competing brain processes that just mask the still-active emotion. A phrase that captures this and applies to how we do therapy is, "The only way through is through; going around gets you to a different place."

Mindfulness and the Effective Therapist

Evocative empathy involves attuning ourselves to our clients' experiencing; it involves presence, engagement, humility, and nonjudgment. It certainly sounds like being mindful should enhance our ability to connect empathically. Dimidjian and Linehan (2003) suggest that mindfulness can be expressed in the therapist's attitudes and behaviors, rather than as a method the therapist teaches to the client. They call for research to operationalize the qualities a mindful therapist would show and suggest "spontaneity, nonjudgment, moment-to-moment awareness, nonattachment to outcome, and compassion" (p. 169). They see the therapist having these qualities in order to model mindfulness for the client. But I would go beyond modeling and say that, in themselves, these are among the most healing qualities a therapist can have.

Several studies have found that therapists who meditate are more empathic (see Hick, 2008, for a summary). In an unusually well-done study, Grepmair and colleagues (2007a, 2007b) compared various measures of outcome for 124 patients being given therapy by 18 therapists in training. Nine of the therapists were randomly assigned to receive a meditation course. Remarkably, the patients of the therapists who meditated did better on both test results and behavioral measures such as symptom reduction and better assessments of their progress.

> Promoting the use of the "psychotherapist as an instrument" has long been neglected in favour of psychotherapeutic techniques and in training psychotherapists. Our study using PiTs [psychotherapists in training], who are completing their training program to be licensed as psychotherapists showed that the directed promotion of mindfulness could positively affect the therapeutic outcome. (Grepmair et al., 2007a, p. 337)

A Note on Mindfulness as a Therapy Approach

Many programs now teach mindfulness techniques to clients for stress reduction, usually as Mindfulness Based Stress Reduction (MBSR) (Kabat-Zinn, 2003). Sometimes therapists explicitly integrate mindfulness techniques into therapy, and this can be helpful, especially when it is offered as a tool that the client may choose to practice.

The evidence for the effectiveness of mindfulness practices with clients is promising and growing rapidly, but it is still in the beginning stages of establishing "demonstrable effectiveness." The evidence for physiological effects is strong, but more research has to be done on psychotherapy outcomes. A combination of attention meditation ("sessions focused on developing awareness of the breath, sounds, and bodily sensations with a stance of accepting whatever arises") and loving-kindness meditation (focused on "extending friendliness, compassion, joy, and peacefulness to the self and others") resulted in decreased anxiety and negative emotions as well as increases in

hope (Sears & Kraus, 2009, p. 564). Kabat-Zinn (2003) reports some remarkable outcomes of meditation practice. Skin clearing in psoriasis was four
times faster among patients who added meditation to medical treatment,
compared with patients who only received medical treatment. In another
study, participants in an eight-week Mindfulness Based Stress Reduction
(MBSR) program were compared with people who were on a wait-list for the
treatment. The participants showed EEG changes related to positive mood
and more active antibody production stimulated by an influenza vaccine.

In 2003, Dimidjian and Linehan reported that outcomes with mindfulness in 21 studies were positive and promising but not yet established enough
to claim demonstrable efficacy, although Baer (2003) calls the evidence
"probably efficacious." Lazar (2005) says:

> We have compelling evidence that volitional control of attention through
> meditation affects neurophysiology. We are not certain how these mecha-
> nisms affect mental and physical health. . . . Mindfulness meditation
> practices have begun to demonstrate their utility in benefiting the health
> of our patients. (p. 238)

■ Presence

Presence is another important but difficult-to-define characteristic of a
good therapist, and understanding mindfulness will help you understand
presence. Presence certainly involves profound concentration on the client. It
often includes a sense of connection that communicates, "I really want to
know you." At other times the essential part of presence has more to do with
a solid, open receptiveness. To repeat from chapter 6, therapy is probably the
only place where two people are focused on one person's experiencing, and
the client usually feels the therapist's presence as an undistracted interest in
what the client is dealing with. There is an intensity to presence, but it is a
quietly strong intensity, rather than a frenetic intensity.

I was talking about writing this chapter with a friend who said that she
recognized presence when she saw it and when she felt it in herself, but she
wished me luck in trying to explain what presence is in words. I did not
understand presence in psychotherapy until I observed two gifted therapists
doing therapy live. One of these therapists was Carl Rogers, whom I had
observed many times on film. My impression of him was that he was very
supportive and empathic but a bit passive. When I had the opportunity to
observe him demonstrating therapy in front of a group, though, I experienced
the intensity of his focus on the client as startlingly complete. I learned the
same lesson again several years later while watching Bob Lee demonstrate
therapy (see Appendix A).

Focus

Sometimes a therapist with presence seems intensely focused on nothing
but the client. At a concrete level, we can describe presence as involving

intense focus on the other person, a level of concentration in which nearly all other stimuli are ignored because the other person is such a clear center of our attention. Thus, *focus* is one aspect of presence. It is sometimes said that the client becomes the therapist's mantra. This draws a parallel to the practice of concentrative meditation in which the meditator focuses all of his or her attention on a word or a sound or an object, the mantra. This intensity of focus enables the person to be free of outside distractions.

The therapist disappears.   In some of the best moments in therapy, the therapist "disappears," not in the sense of fading away and being unimportant but in the sense of being so thoroughly interwoven in the client's process that we don't notice the therapist much. When the therapist is being clever and powerful, the client often has to stop and think about what the therapist has said—and maybe even to wonder at and admire the therapist. When the therapist disappears, whatever he or she says feels so *right* that the client recognizes instantly that "Yes, this is mine . . . That is exactly where I am going . . . And what's more, here's where I'm going next." When the therapist disappears in this way, change is most likely to occur from within the client. There is a kind of paradox here; the most powerful therapist is the one who gives up the most power. The therapist gives up as much control as possible to the client, but this is the most influential way the therapist has to help the client change.

I want to know your story.   One of my mentors gave us some very helpful advice about what to do when we were having trouble focusing on the client. It seems inevitable that the therapist's mind will at times wander and lose focus. She said that when this happened she found it helpful to focus her attention on wanting to know the client's story. Everybody has an interesting story to tell. If you can focus on the story, you are less likely to be distracted by your own thoughts and strategies, and you almost automatically become more present.

Energy

Another part of presence that we can put into words is the therapist's level of energy. It is difficult to be present when you're tired or worried or thinking about writing your next paper. Sometimes the energy to be present just seems to be there, and the therapist feels sharp and quietly intense. Other times, therapists have to work at being present by pulling themselves together and consciously concentrating. The quality of presence will be different, of course, in each case, but the point is that presence requires a lot of energy. Even though you might be "just sitting" for the therapy hour, you will often feel the physical drain of energy after an intense session. Fortunately, such sessions can also bring a sense of renewal of energy.

This is more than a job.   Once in supervision, the trainee I was working with was disarmingly candid when he said, "You're turning this into hard work. I decided to be a therapist because it looked like an easy way to make good money, just talking to people." He wasn't kidding. Doing therapy is rewarding in many ways for most therapists (as we will see in our discussion of "flow" later), but it is not easy. It is not just a job that can be done well by following a set of rules, because it requires an investment of emotional energy. Whether the therapist is making that investment is usually apparent in many ways, including tone of voice, body language, and clarity of understanding.

The therapist's emotional state.   At one time I was going through a discouraging time both professionally and personally. I felt that I was still doing a good job as a therapist, even though I often had to work at gathering my energy for therapy sessions. As I look back on that time, however, I realize that I was doing therapy that was only acceptable in form. It probably would have been perceived by observers as good therapy, but it had a mechanical, "absent" quality. Then, at a therapy workshop, I had a brief but powerful experience as a client, which dramatically changed my emotional state. The point of telling you this personal story is that after I returned from the workshop, I resumed my practice without much thought about the impact my recent experience might have on me as a therapist. One of my clients surprised me by commenting, "since you got back from your trip, you've been a lot more present." I was startled that she used the word "present" and that she perceived this difference in me as making a dramatic difference in the quality of our therapy together. One reason to stay as clear as possible about yourself is that your emotional state will affect your ability to be present, often in ways you're not aware of.

The Therapist as Brave Companion

Everything the therapist does says, "I really want to know you." This means knowing everything that the client wants to share with you. It means courageously facing with the client anything the client is trying to face, including things that feel painful and horrible. It helps to see the therapist as a brave companion who walks with the client and who is willing without timidity to stare down the client's demons with the client. The brave companion doesn't lead the journey but also never hangs back or recoils from whatever the client is exploring.

A phrase that I find meaningful and sometimes share with a client when we talk about the therapy process is that "I'm willing to walk through hell together" if that's where the client has to go. For the client, whatever he or she has to face often does feel hellish and frightening and never ending. The therapist is not offering to walk through hell *for* the client, but there is enormous comfort and strength in having someone who will go *with* him or her.

Another quality of the brave companion is a *staying with*. In the next section, you will read a client's note in which she uses this phrase. Many clients say that one of the most astonishing experiences in therapy is the tenacity with which the therapist stays with him or her.

The Client's Experience of Presence

It might help to approach an understanding of presence through the way it feels to a client. The client of a therapist with presence might say, "She is really with me when I am talking," or "He is very interested in me and what I'm going through." One client tried to describe the ineffable experience of therapy in the following note to her therapist. As an aside, this client also beautifully describes the experience of "knowing" new things before she was aware of them. In addition to describing what the therapist's presence felt like, she helps us understand what experiential knowing felt like.

A Note to Her Therapist

In order to better understand this "ineffable" experience, I will try to describe participating in it with you.

It is a "Staying with" experience. You "Stay" with me, wherever I have to go, and I never know where that might be. This kind of experiencing precedes or foretells "real life," or gives some other kind of "advanced knowing" about real life. So I cannot tell where you will have to go with me. It is as if some inner level of myself knows what the issues are long before my "cognitive self" has any awareness at all. But these are the issues that are getting in my way, on every level.

So, what *is* the "Staying with"? I can describe it only by analogy. It is as if I am a diver going into deep water. You are the life-line, the oxygen. That fits because as I am going through the experience, I often have trouble breathing. But you are not sitting in the boat on the surface; you are also swimming with me, at only arm's length. So, you are the oxygen *and* the presence! I *feel* your presence!

When these feelings (about my issues) come for me, they are *almost* overwhelming. Physically, they overcome my body, and, emotionally, they scare me in a way that I have never experienced before. It's an "Oh, my God!" feeling and it truly is gazing into the pit. My only life experience to which it compares is waking up from an anaesthetic, being totally out of control, visualizing all the existential horror all at once! But when you are there, you have, figuratively, a hand on my shoulder. It is not a light grip—it is a firm, solid clasp that says that I can go as far into the pit as I want and you will stand solidly there, with me, but also grounded in reality.

If I were to say what kind of "connectedness" this is between you and me, I would find this equally as hard to describe. If I were to line up all the different kinds of human "connectedness" on a continuum, this experience would lie right next to sexual connectedness. It is not sexual; I am not aroused. But the feelings are just as physical, just as powerful. It is a "physical" connection.

You do not speak during the "Staying with." If you did, it would divert my process (or stop it). So, if you do not speak, or touch me, how do I know you are there? Because I "feel" your presence! So, I have come full circle to conclude that this process is, indeed, "ineffable"!

Very Advanced Therapists' Experience of Presence

Few therapists have written extensively about presence. You will hear and read references to how important it is to be fully present for your clients, but these are usually passing mentions that assume you know what presence is. While I hope that our discussion of presence has been at a useful level for therapy as most of us practice it, it also would be useful to get what we can from the writing of some gifted therapists who have tried to describe their own experiences of presence. Some of what these therapists write is beyond my personal experience of therapeutic presence, and so I have as much to learn here as anyone.

One helpful attempt to describe presence is in the book *Therapeutic Presence*, in which Robbins (1998) wrote:

> As a fledgling psychotherapist, my notions of therapeutic presence were driven by a focused attention to my patient's communications and a concerted effort to make empathic contact. In many respects, this approach seemed appropriate to the everyday problems and issues that were presented by my patients. Yet, upon reflection, I wondered why I felt so tired at the end of a day and, in fact, emotionally burdened. I mused to myself that perhaps more personal psychotherapy was in order. (p. 9)

It may be a little discouraging to hear that focused attention and effort are not all that are required for therapeutic presence. When we are "fledgling therapists" we can understand focused attention and effort; all we have to do is work harder to achieve them. Robbins is telling us that therapeutic presence requires something more than just hard work.

> Therapeutic presence, best described as an ego state, has several specific qualities. First, it is a dual level of consciousness, of being one but yet separate with any given patient. Next, it manages linear and non-linear time, which exist simultaneously. In this state of therapeutic presence, both parties shape and reshape non-verbal and verbal expression. It is a state of emotional and cognitive presence. (p. 11)

> We must be comfortable with a holistic, intuitive and receptive orientation that is essentially spatial, while always being ready at any moment to shift to a more synthesizing mode in which the choice of words gives structure and definition to non-verbal flow. This ability to synthesize and articulate the multiplicity of levels in the patient-therapist dyad goes to the heart of what I describe as therapeutic presence. (p. 19)

Therapeutic presence, then, overlaps dramatically with mindful, experiential knowing of the client. The therapist freely enters into the client's experiencing (which often will defy explanation and logic) but is able just as freely to shift to the articulate and rational. This can hardly be called a skill; it is more like an ability or a way of being or, as Robbins said, an ego state.

Late in his life, Rogers wrote about a new discovery he had made within himself as a therapist. His description of his experience is even less structured than Robbins'. He talks of a powerful state in which presence alone seems healing. Such a state must be a powerful and rare gift.

> When I am at my best, as a group facilitator or a therapist, I discover another characteristic. I find that when I am closest to my inner, intuitive self, when I am somehow in touch with the unknown in me, when perhaps I am in a slightly altered state of consciousness in the relationship, then whatever I do seems to be full of healing. Then simply my *presence* is releasing and helpful. There is nothing I can do to force this experience, but when I can relax and be close to the transcendental core of me, then I may behave in strange and impulsive ways in the relationship, ways which I cannot justify rationally, which have nothing to do with my thought processes. But these strange behaviors turn out to be *right*, in some odd way. At those moments it seems that my inner spirit has reached out and touched the inner spirit of the other. Our relationship transcends itself and becomes a part of something larger. Profound growth and healing and energy are present. (Rogers, 1989, p. 137)

Finally, Breggin (1997) also writes of a "healing presence" that is the fundamental essence of how one person can be helpful to another.

> To create healing presence, we fine-tune our inner experience to the inner state of the other person. We transform ourselves in response to the basic needs of the person we are trying to heal and to help . . . to empower the other person. (p. 5)

> Healing presence is not magical. It is the product of ways of being in relation to each other. It expresses the reality that the very presence of a person can have a healing effect. At times I will speak of healing aura—the relationship or the atmosphere created by a healing presence. . . . Some people understandably reject the concept of an aura that invests a relationship or a place. I have accepted it simply because I occasionally experience it, always in a positive manner. The concept does not require a belief in mystical realities. It can be understood as the personal, subjective experience of a positive, joyful, or loving attitude toward other individuals and life. (p. 6)

> This idea of *being in a certain way* as the starting point of helping people has evolved over 30 years of clinical practice. It had become so much a part of my approach that it took me some time to recognize it. Like the proverbial fish in the water, I did not realize that I was swimming in something. . . . Nearly all of the progress I have made in my life as a psychiatrist, therapist, friend, father, or husband has involved learning . . . to find a way of *being*, rather than doing, that meets the psychological, social or spiritual needs of the people I am trying to help. (pp. 8–9)

Breggin's last comments about "being, rather than doing" highlight an important part of the writings of many gifted therapists. It is easier to talk about how to do something than it is to understand "just being" or "an ego state" or "being fully present." Even in this chapter, we have been talking about what we can *do* to experience these higher levels of therapist functioning, but ultimately we will have to understand experientially what it means to "just *be*" with our clients.

■ Flow (Being in the Zone)

Many therapists I know have told me that occasionally when they're doing therapy everything seems to fall into place almost without effort. They feel completely and effortlessly focused on the client and have an uncanny sense of understanding the client's experiencing. I also occasionally experience this in psychotherapy and think of it as being in a state of *flow.* Many therapists find their work intrinsically satisfying and engaging and report relatively frequent experiences of varying levels of flow (Parks, 1997; Whitmire, 1991). Although very intense experiences of flow may not be common, it is worth understanding flow because the experience will probably be associated with times when you feel you are doing your best therapy. Csikszentmihalyi (1990, 1996, 1997; Nakamura & Csikszentmihalyi, 2009) has studied the phenomenon of flow extensively and has some very helpful ways to describe flow as well as some advice about how to make it more likely to happen.

A state of flow can happen with almost any relatively complex activity. We hear it most often related to athletic events in which the athlete "gets into the zone." Athletes who describe being in the zone say that they stop thinking about what they're doing and "just do it." Musicians, rock climbers, surgeons, and dancers are a few of the groups who have been studied in Csikszentmihalyi's research, and they all report similar experiences at many levels of intensity. The more you can experience flow as a therapist, the better therapist you will be and the more satisfying you will find your life as a therapist.

What Flow Feels Like

You will notice considerable overlap between our description of what flow feels like and our discussion of both therapeutic presence and mindfulness. The therapist in a state of flow is almost inevitably attuned to the client in a concentrated way. In addition to providing the client with a more present therapist, the state of flow provides the therapist with a heightened sense of personal satisfaction. (The lead-ins in this section and the next are from Csikszentmihalyi, 1996.)

Action and awareness are merged (p. 111). In most of our activities, our attention usually wanders. Even when doing therapy most therapists are sometimes distracted by thoughts about what time it is, thoughts about how well they are doing as a therapist, and even concerns from their own life. In the state of flow, however, there is a one-pointedness of mind that is marked by clear concentration on the task.

Distractions are excluded from consciousness (p. 112). As a part of the one-pointed focus on the task, the person in flow is free from distractions. In our discussion of therapeutic presence, we spoke of the client as the therapist's "mantra." In the state of flow, there is a meditative quality of awareness of only the present moment. This lack of distraction obviously helps the therapist to be more focused on the client. It also frees the therapist from the worrisome distractions that usually follow us through the day.

There is no worry of failure (p. 112). One of the distractions from which the therapist is set free is the fear of not doing therapy well. Beginning therapists are especially vulnerable to this worry. Unfortunately, as we will see, beginning therapists are also less likely to experience the state of flow in therapy. Sometimes after a session marked by the feeling of flow, therapists report having felt very much in control. In the time of the session, however, being in control simply did not arise as an issue. If it had, that would have been an achievement/failure distraction.

Self-consciousness disappears (p. 112). Most of the time we are concerned about other people's perceptions of us. In therapy, this may be especially true when the therapist is receiving supervision. The self-conscious person is almost an observer of himself or herself, and the self-consciousness of a beginning therapist under supervision often includes an awareness of the supervisor "looking over the shoulder." In the state of flow, we are free of this burden.

In flow we are too involved in what we're doing to care about protecting the ego. Yet after an episode of flow is over, we generally emerge from it with a stronger self-concept; we know that we have succeeded in meeting a difficult challenge. We might even feel that we have stepped out of the boundaries of the ego and have become part, at least temporarily, of a larger entity. The musician feels at one with the harmony of the cosmos, the athlete moves as one with the team, the reader of a novel lives for a few hours in a different reality. Paradoxically, the self expands through acts of self-forgetfulness. (p. 112)

The sense of time becomes distorted (p. 113). In our discussion of experiential knowing and of presence we talked about both time and knowing being nonlinear. In a state of flow, "experienced time" is different than clock time. In therapy this usually means that the time seems to pass very quickly, even though paradoxically it may seem that an enormous amount has happened in a very short time.

The activity becomes autotelic (p. 113). Any activity that frequently results in a feeling of flow becomes autotelic—intrinsically motivating. Much of what we do is exotelic, motivated by external rewards. Some things we do, however, are autotelic. The only reason for doing them is that we like the experience. There are many rewarding things about being a therapist, but being a therapist also extracts a cost, especially an emotional cost. Obviously, there are external rewards, such as being paid for doing therapy, but one of the most important reasons that some people love doing therapy and others become disillusioned with it has to do with the frequency of the experience of flow.

Conditions that Promote Flow

There is a balance between challenges and skills (p. 111). Flow is most likely to occur when the person has a high level of skills and the challenge faced is high. In this case, the level of skill is well matched to the demands of the situation. It may seem discouraging to a beginning therapist, but the state of flow is almost inevitably linked to the therapist's level of development. Thus, the highly skilled person who is pushed to the edges of the limits of her skill is most likely to experience flow.

If the skill level is low and the challenge high, *anxiety* and frustration will occur. When both skill and challenge are low, *boredom* is most likely. If the person has a high level of skill but faces a low level of challenge, two reactions are possible. The original model of flow predicted that high skill and low challenges would result in boredom. More recently, evidence has suggested that the combination of high skill and low challenges leads to a sense of *relaxed readiness* (Csikszentmihalyi, cited in Parks, 1997). It seems likely that a person with high skills would feel competent and ready for the next challenge, but, if the lack of challenges is chronic and unchangeable, then boredom would result.

There are clear goals every step of the way (p. 111). Some activities provide clearer goals than doing psychotherapy. The surgeon has a definite procedure to follow, with little room for error. The dancer has his or her own ineffable, artistic qualities to deal with but also has procedures and models and choreography to follow. Step-by-step goals are less clear in therapy, but they do exist. The therapist intends for the client to feel understood, to explore experience, to solve problems, to talk, to attend sessions, and to do many other more or less complex things. As our understanding increases, more complex goals are at least implicit, such as making discoveries, experiencing a solid contact with the client, and changing in problematic behaviors. Flow is far more likely to happen when goals are clear, and our clarity of understanding what the goals are will increase with experience.

There is immediate feedback to one's actions (1996, p. 111). Without fairly clear and quick feedback on whether goals are being met, our experiences are usually diffuse and uncertain. Vague or delayed feedback make flow unlikely. The dancer knows immediately the effect of a movement; the rock climber has no doubt whether the last step was successful or not. The intensity of flow depends on immediacy. As with goals, immediacy of feedback in therapy is less well structured than in music, dancing, surgery, or rock climbing, but there are many cues that can give us feedback. These include the client's reactions, what the client says about the process and his or her own life, and many other sources of information.

Flow in Psychotherapy

"The most direct efforts to assist individuals in finding flow lie in the sphere of psychotherapy" (Nakamura & Csikszentmihalyi, 2009, p. 202). Flow has become an important part of the positive psychology movement, and there are many ways that clients can benefit from flow, but our interest here is in what flow can mean to the therapist. Both Parks (1997) and Whitmire (1991) found a direct relationship between a therapist's level of experience and the frequency of experiences of flow. Even among the novice therapists, however, Parks' subjects reported more experiences of flow than they did of anxiety or boredom. Therapy seems to be a relatively autotelic activity, in the sense that it is inherently meaningful. It is not surprising that Parks' novice therapists reported significantly more anxiety than other groups; they are the group most likely to face challenges beyond their skill level. It also seems likely that the intensity of experiences of flow increases as a therapist becomes more confident and experienced. Flow probably occurs at many different levels of intensity and can even reach the level of what feels like the "slightly altered state of consciousness" that Rogers reported in our discussion of presence. I wish for you many experiences of flow.

■ Mindfulness, Presence, and Flow

Mindfulness, presence and flow are all different, but they are also obviously intertwined with each other. You probably can't be present without being mindful, and the rare times when you're in a state of flow it's virtually certain that you will also be mindful and present. I think there is an exciting way of being that mindfulness, presence and flow all seem to point toward but that is very difficult to describe in words. I think of this way of being as a kind of living fully and in the moment. We probably can't be in this state much of the time, but it is exciting to me to think that there are ways to bring more of it into our lives. Having a meditation practice often helps. Approaching others with attention and focus probably makes it more likely to happen. Amazingly, practicing our craft makes it more likely to happen. A friend of mine says that doing therapy is such a powerfully meditative activity that it is a "path to awakening." I sometimes feel that when I am doing therapy well, I am doing my best mindfulness practice. It can be draining at times, but it is peacefully energizing when I have wholeheartedly shared another person's experiencing. It gives me an opportunity to be intensely mindful and intensely connected.

PART TWO

Other Issues in Practicing Therapy

9

Direct Interventions

The first eight chapters have described a therapy that gives the client control, trust, and independence to find his or her own solutions. It would be naive, though, to say that evocatively empathic therapy, done within an accepting relationship, is the answer to all human problems. There are times when other approaches are more appropriate, depending on the circumstances and the nature of the problems. I will try to specify some of those times in this chapter.

■ Behavior Modification

It may or may not surprise you to hear that I see great explanatory power in learning theory, especially in more cognitively oriented versions of it. I think that thinking and feeling are extremely complex behaviors that occur inside the skin and are the most important behaviors to understand if we want to understand human functioning in all its complexity.

I operate at two very different levels. In doing therapy, I seldom think in terms of learning principles; I am trying to be with my client, to understand deeply, to let the client know all that I hear, and to let her struggle toward becoming the unique person that she is. Outside the therapy session, if someone asks how and why therapy works, however, I shift gears and use many concepts and principles, including learning principles, for explanation. You will see this somewhat jarring shift in perspective when you read Part Three of this book, "Theory and Evidence."

Some of what I have to say in this chapter and in chapter 10 would make more sense if you first read the chapters on theory, but putting those chapters here would break the flow of the practical orientation of the book. You can decide whether to read them first or not.

Powerful Principles—Different Applications

Although I believe that the principles that underlie behavior therapy can also be used to explain one way that evocatively empathic therapy works, proponents of the two approaches usually view each other harshly. I once was on a panel at a behaviorally oriented convention, to discuss "the relationship" as an important part of behavioral interventions, and was introduced as a clinical psychologist. Before I said anything, someone shouted from the audience, "Don't reinforce that bullshit!" Checking the location of the nearest exit, I said I thought there was value in living like a humanist and thinking like a learning theorist. They did not find me charming. One panelist sarcastically referred to empathy as, "some kind of essence," and another totally ignored me, using his time to give a summary of other papers at the convention. On the other side, I have heard more traditional therapists refer to behavior therapists as rigid, compulsive mechanists who have no appreciation for human experience.

The principles are similar; the *application* of the principles is different in evocatively empathic therapy and behavior therapy. I will try to integrate the two and specify some of the times when each is appropriate.

Behavioral Methods

This book is not a manual on behavior therapy techniques. Books by other people present that material (for example, Martin & Pear, 2006; Spiegler & Guevremont, 2010) and a well-trained therapist should have a good grasp of these techniques. In general, the techniques can be divided into three approaches: (1) desensitization methods designed to reduce undesirable emotional reactions, such as fear and anxiety, through extinction (exposure to the feared stimulus with no aversive consequences) and/or counterconditioning (exposure to the feared stimulus along with positive consequences and responses that are incompatible with fear); (2) operant or positive reinforcement methods, which use reward to establish desirable behavior; and (3) aversive conditioning, which uses punishment to eliminate undesirable behaviors.

It seems to me that there is good evidence that the first two approaches are effective in the treatment of clearly definable behavioral problems. Aversive methods, however, are rarely used today and are effective only as a part of treatment that includes much positive reinforcement (Martin & Pear, 2006; Spiegler & Guevremont, 2010). Aversive methods sometimes make problems worse (Gomes-Schwartz, Hadley, & Strupp, 1978; Rachman & Teasdale, 1969) and usually lead to the development of "narrow and inflexible patterns of behavior with respect to many, many events, including many of the contents of our own conscious experience" (Wilson & Murrell, 2004, p. 129)

Within these three broad categories, it is difficult to specify a short list of particular techniques. Rather, the emphasis is on principles of learning, and specific techniques are limited only by the imaginative application of the principles to the complexities of individual cases.

When Behavior Modification Is Effective

Using this broad definition, one student argued that I was a behavior modifier, which, in a sense, is true, since I explain what I do at least partly in learning terms. Evocatively empathic therapy can be seen as a form of graduated extinction, graduated counterconditioning, or even systematic desensitization. What the client fears is his own thoughts and feelings—internal experiences (or covert behaviors, to use that language). Thus, the client doesn't think clearly—doesn't know himself or herself accurately. The therapist helps the client face those feared thoughts and feelings, and the fear extinguishes and is counterconditioned (by the therapist's acceptance). The principles are similar; the applications are different. In its common usage, however, *behavior therapy* does not include evocatively empathic therapy. What I hope to lead you toward is an eclectic appreciation that the distinctions between psychotherapy and behavior modification are needlessly exaggerated.

There are several circumstances in which explicitly behavioral treatment approaches are most appropriate. I will discuss a few of them. *Directly conditioned fears* result from experiences of pain in the presence of particular cues. If a person feared water as a result of nearly drowning, or long dark hallways after being trapped in a mine cave-in, or dogs after being bitten and scratched, or automobiles after being in an accident, direct reconditioning of the fear would probably be the most appropriate treatment. Much of this kind of "treatment" goes on in everyday life. We are often advised to face the things we fear (in small doses) and "face down the fear." There is a lot of experimental evidence that this explicit desensitization approach is effective with mild fears, such as fears of snakes and spiders. However, it is misleading to generalize from these analog studies to the treatment of clinical phobias. As we will see in chapter 16, the development of clinical phobias is vastly more complex than that of directly conditioned fears.

A large area that is commonly called *behavioral deficits* can be appropriate for explicitly behavioral approaches, although boundary lines between treatment and teaching become hard to establish. If the client lacks particular information or has missed the opportunity to learn particular skills, giving that information and teaching the skills can have an important beneficial effect. The problem here is in distinguishing a lack of information from an inability to use information that is available to the client but that the client is unable to use for anxiety-based reasons. The temptation to teach can be very strong in therapists, so there is a real danger that giving advice and solutions can masquerade as simply giving information and teaching the client skills. Both the therapist and the client may be fooled into thinking that the therapist has not taken over control of the process. So teach. But be sensitive that your teaching be limited to giving information that is not available to the client.

Clearly defined, limited goals often can best be achieved with behavioral approaches. Most surveys (Klein, Dittmann, Parloff, & Gill, 1969) and practicing therapists report that very few clients who find their way to therapy have well-defined problems that fit the phobia or specific-symptom pattern. The vast majority are deeply unhappy or can't understand why they can't stay in an intimate relationship or have unpredictable anxiety attacks or report other such complex and ambiguous problems. The process of evocatively empathic therapy both discovers the real complexities involved and relieves the problem. In those cases, however, with clearly specifiable problems and goals, a behavioral program can be helpful, and can be helpful in a relatively short time.

There is a real risk here, though. One client came to me with a fear of water and the information that he had almost drowned in a pond as a child. He wanted to pass a swimming test but panicked each time he got into the deep end. Piece of cake, I prematurely thought, cleverly planning a desensitization program in my head. Fortunately, I followed my usual procedure of doing a fair amount of empathic therapy and simply offering the behavioral approach to him as a tool for him to use. The more I listened, the clearer it became that I had better open up my ears (to say nothing of my mind). After the first session, virtually nothing was said about water as we discussed a complex situation in which he desperately feared the independence that he seemed so actively to be seeking. About six weeks later he said, "Oh, I forgot to tell you I passed my swimming test a couple weeks ago." Therapy went on for some time after that; the water fear had quite clearly been a side issue.

A year after this client terminated therapy, he phoned to say that he had had some recurrence of the water fear at a lake. We talked again, and when he asked me about the relevant learning principles, I explained about graduated extinction and step by step exposure to feared things. He took this principle, designed a behavioral program for himself, and phoned a week later to report that it had worked well. I tell this story to illustrate another area of useful application of explicitly behavioral methods, *self-defeating habits based on former conflicts*. Conceivably a self-defeating behavior pattern might develop because it helped avoid some complex internal anxiety. It would be rewarded so often and so strongly that it might become a strong habit. Even if the terrible anxiety were relieved by therapy, the behavior might persist as a habit. If it no longer served as a way to avoid anxiety, directly changing it should work well. The risk, obviously, is again that it is difficult to know that the real anxiety problem is relieved.

■ Combining Approaches

In chapter 1, I said that evocative empathy is the fundamental skill you need to learn. Behavioral methods are clearly among the other skills a well-trained therapist has. The flexible therapist should be attentive to the fact that behavioral approaches might be appropriate in therapy, under much the same conditions as those for the therapist filling the role of teacher. Many of the dangers of the teacher role also apply to the role of the therapist as behavior modifier, since much depends on the accuracy of the judgment that a particular problem is not based on internalized conflicts—that is, on fear of one's own internal experiencing. It is also possible that the therapist will take on the role of the expert healer rather than contributing to the client's ability to solve his or her own problems.

With these cautions in mind, a therapist might well incorporate behavioral techniques into interview therapy, without losing the perspective that the client is the problem solver. In fact, most behavior therapists would argue that good behavior therapy is always conducted in a collaborative manner, and some studies have found that behavior therapists can show higher levels of empathy than many psychotherapists (Sweet, 1984).

A Philosophical Conflict

In practice, the differences between empathy-oriented and behaviorally oriented therapists seem to center on the role of the therapist. The basic principle of evocatively empathic therapy is that the client is the problem solver who can be trusted to guide the course of therapy content. Behavior therapy traditionally casts the therapist as an expert who generally assumes that it is his or her responsibility to plan and direct the course of therapy, which should not be "left to the vagaries of clients" but should be "carefully regulated by psychotherapists" (Bandura, 1969, p. 484). In chapter 17 I will argue that it is perfectly respectable to be an empathic learning theorist and that a complex learning-based view of emotional problems indicates that clients' direction of therapy is not based on "vagaries" at all—that clients will try to talk about what they need to talk about.

Offering Tools

The resolution of this who-is-the-expert philosophical conflict that I find most helpful is to treat behavioral methods as information—as tools about which I know something and which I offer to the client to use or not, as he or she decides. As you know from the previous 8 chapters, I want to facilitate the client's own thinking, feeling, and taking action. If we therapists make ourselves the experts, we deprive clients of the experience of solving the problems independently, and we will inevitably make errors in choices of goals. We are experts on processes, not on individual persons. There is no reason, however, not to share our expertise on processes and principles with the client, as long as we honestly offer them as tools and not as (subtle?) manipulation. As we noted in chapter 8, such an offering of tools can be received by the client as a deeply empathic gesture.

A Growing Rapprochement

As early as 1970, Naar reported the "peaceful coexistence" of empathy-based therapy and behavior therapy and presented an illustrative case study. D'Alessio (1968) described his attempts to combine behavior modification techniques with a general psychoanalytic approach, and Strupp (1979) wrote an article called "A Psychodynamicist Looks at Modern Behavior Therapy," in which he found many commonalities. Egan (2004) and others oriented toward empathy-based therapy have explicitly incorporated learning principles into their thinking. The "psychotherapy integration" movement (Norcross & Goldfried, 2005) has been growing for over 20 years, and Ablon, Levy, & Katzenstein, (2006) argue that we need to go "beyond brand names" in psychotherapy and research whatever processes work.

I want to repeat, with continuing hope and some optimism, something I said years ago (Martin, 1972).

> Polemics and hostility between more traditional psychotherapists and behavior modifiers have been elicited and emitted by both sides, and the resultant split has hampered communication among therapists. Both groups have distorted the other's positions, and we must hope that we will move toward integration and winnowing of ideas, rather than toward the kind of rigidification of "schools" that has marked psychotherapy in the past. (p. 136)

■ Direct Environmental Interventions

It is clearly inconsistent with evocatively empathic therapy to view the therapist's role as taking direct action in changing the client's life circumstances as a therapeutic tool. There are social roles in which this is considered appropriate, but therapy is generally not one of them. Even highly directive therapists usually exert their influence through the client's action on the environment, as prescribed by the therapist.

Emergencies

Life-threatening circumstances sometimes demand intervention by a therapist. Short of this obvious situation, however, there are occasional situations that will call for very difficult decisions about your role in a client's life—decisions that will trouble you no matter which way you decide to act. These situations will be ones in which your client will be about to take action, or fail to take action, with serious long-term consequences.

Judgment Calls and the Price You Pay

There will be no clear guidelines on which to base your decision to intervene directly by giving advice, admonitions, and taking some action that affects your client's life. Once the evocatively empathic therapist decides to intervene directly, the price she or he pays is that the direction of therapy changes hands—to the extent that the therapist took over direction. This is a high price to pay, but sometimes it is worth it. Sometimes the therapist needs to intervene. A client once phoned me on the weekend, somewhat drunk, and said, "David, I'm gonna take my babies out into the bush. They're never going to take them away from me." He went on like this for some time. I knew reasonably well that nobody was really going to take his children from him and thought that he was distorting the situation. I also was afraid that if he did run off into the wilderness with the children, someone might consider that reason to take the children away. I listened and responded and hoped he would "come down" if we talked long enough. Eventually I felt I had to try to persuade him to change his plan. I did, and I'm glad, but a couple of weeks later I mentioned that he could call me about a particular situation if he needed to, and he said, "No, I don't think I will; you talk me out of things too much." I paid the price, but I think I would do the same thing again.

Other incidents trouble me. In chapter 6 I told you of advising a client to move out of his apartment to escape a destructive roommate. The next week he said, "You didn't trust me," and he was right. I had made an incorrect judgment that intervention was called for. Similarly, a colleague told me he had phoned a university dean because a client had said he definitely was going to beat up his roommate. This therapist felt he needed to prevent the fight and made a judgment that seemed to me to be both a clearly unwarranted intervention in therapy and a betrayal of the client's confidence. My colleague disagreed. What if the client had quite convincingly threatened to kill someone? Even here, though, the issue isn't all that clear. Of course, a therapist would prevent a killing, but many clients talk about wanting to kill someone. In most settings it is seldom obvious that a therapist must intervene.

Many therapists would have made judgment calls different than mine; these gray areas are very difficult to work in. The most helpful approach is to find your therapist/friend for a consultation in these fortunately rare situations, but that's not always practical. I couldn't very well hang up on my client so that I could consult somebody. Experience will teach you a lot, and it will help to share experiences with other therapists. The more of this preparatory work you do, the readier you will be to make your judgment calls under fire.

Potential Suicides

Nearly all therapists with whom I have discussed suicide find it one of the most difficult issues they have to deal with. David Rudd (2005) specializes in treating suicide, but he includes himself when he says, "Suicide is one of the few topics that almost uniformly trigger anxiety and apprehension in clinicians, whether novice students or seasoned practitioners" (p. 157). The end of life is so overwhelming in its finality; chances for change end; and it is very common to feel guilt over the death of someone close. When the therapist has been involved in the very issues of emotional distress that contribute to suicide, thoughts over what might have been done that wasn't are very difficult to resolve. I suspect, too, that a client's suicide feels like a failure as no other therapeutic failure, including psychotic breaks, can. Therapists' trouble in dealing with suicide makes this a special area of deafness in hearing clients. Intuitively, it often seems to the therapist that talking about suicide might make the risk greater, and so clues are missed or intentionally avoided. The client might say, "I'm not sure it's all worth it—but at least I know there's one way to find peace." Since this statement may or may not refer to suicide, you don't want to suggest that in a way that might be frightening to the client. He or she might have been talking about moving away or getting drunk or even coming to therapy as a way to find peace. You can't ignore the possibility that she is talking about suicide, either, and so you could firmly but gently get ahead of the client without using the word *suicide*. "I'm not sure of all you mean there, but sometimes you'd like to give up—to stop this pain by escap-

ing it somehow—how? . . . just by stopping everything?" The therapist is trying to be forthright—not at all timid about grasping the issue and staying
with it—but not scaring the client off.

> **C:** Yeah, stopping everything is right . . . everything.
>
> **T:** When you say it that way, it sounds like you mean dying.
>
> **C:** "Mm-hm."
>
> **T:** So suicide feels attractive, even peaceful, at those times when you
> feel like giving up.

As soon as the therapist was sure of what the client was hinting at, he or
she used the explicit words to give the client freedom to discuss the real issue.
It is frightening to talk so openly about suicide, but you really have no choice.
Ignoring the issue won't make suicide not seem peaceful. It is very unlikely
that you can argue or persuade the person out of the feelings. You can explore
the feelings together. In the process of this exploring, you might express some
of your own feelings and reactions, saying something like, "You probably
know this, but I want to say that it matters to me that you live." If done sensitively, this would be only an expression of concern and caring, not a judgmental guilt message that the client shouldn't feel the way he or she does.

Suicide talk should always be taken seriously and dealt with openly. It is
sometimes used manipulatively by clients, especially when dependency is a
central issue, and so you will have to walk the narrow line between refusing
to deal with the issue and being upset and overly responsive to the implicit
threat that if you don't give more, you'll have the client's life on your con-
science. It is more obvious here than anywhere that you must be as clear as
you can be about what the limits of therapy are. You are not the solution to
the person's problems. Will you accept calls in the middle of the night and
subsequent long talks? How often? I would say to my clients that I am available for such emergency calls, but only occasionally and within the limits of
real emergencies. Beyond these limits, there are agencies and hospitals
designed to handle emergency needs. I can't serve that function regularly and
live my own life.

If a client calls in a suicidal crisis, the therapist must take it seriously and
do what is necessary to see that care is provided without making the incident
an integral part of the therapy relationship. Depending on circumstances, you
might suggest that the client phone an emergency service (whose number you
should memorize) or even phone the police for help getting to a hospital. In
the process of talking with the client, you might make the judgment that the
effects of an overdose are too advanced for the client to take such action and
call such an agency yourself. You might even take the action of transporting
the client to the hospital yourself, but this has a lot of consequences, and you
should have a colleague accompany you—both to protect yourself and to
make it clear that the quality of your involvement is very different from your
involvement in therapy.

Two issues that will confront you when dealing with potential suicides are: (1) making no-suicide contracts with clients, and (2) assessing the level of suicide risk. These issues are too complicated to deal with in detail here, but they are so central to doing therapy that I want to introduce you to two articles that I think you will find helpful.

Rudd, Mandrusiak, and Joiner (2005) argue persuasively that the long-established practice of making "no-suicide contracts" with clients has many problems and is not supported by evidence. They propose the use of a "commitment to treatment" statement.

> It is defined as an agreement between the patient and clinician in which the patient agrees to make a commitment to the treatment process and living by (1) identifying the roles, obligations, and expectations of both the clinician and the patient in treatment; (2) communicating openly and honestly about all aspects of treatment including suicide; and (3) accessing identified emergency services during periods of crisis that might threaten the patient's ability to honor the agreement. (p. 247)

The commitment to treatment statement is not a binding prohibition against suicide; it is a commitment to living that is more likely to promote the therapeutic process.

When you suspect the potential for suicide, you must assess your client's level of risk. This assessment will guide much of what you do. In its simplest form, this assessment will consider (1) level of intent, (2) the explicitness with which the client has a plan of how to commit suicide, and (3) how much opportunity the client has to carry out a suicide. Bryan and Rudd (2005) urge clinicians to assess whether the risk is acute or chronic. They also provide a nice balance of practical advice about what to look for in a risk assessment and empirical evidence about risk assessment.

Finally, you should consult your supervisor or a colleague when suicide is an issue, and you should carefully document your ongoing risk assessment in your clinical notes. Your main concern will be your client's welfare, but you also need to protect yourself from criticism or liability if a client does attempt or commit suicide.

Assessment

The two extreme positions on the role of assessment in therapy are, on one hand, that assessment is totally inappropriate, misleading, and detrimental to therapy and, on the other, that we need to diagnose and categorize clients in order to plan their treatment more carefully. In this chapter I will take a middle line, leaning somewhat toward the first position. With regard to treatment, the two functions that assessment serves are (1) the selection of particular clients to be assigned to particular kinds of treatments and (2) the ongoing planning and execution of treatment as a function of ongoing assessment.

Personally, I use formally identified assessment with clients only rarely and reluctantly, primarily because it so heavily places the therapist in the expert role, implying that the therapist diagnoses and fixes people, once he or she has gathered enough information. It often means to clients that the therapist has secret methods for getting things out of the client and making judgments based on this information.

In *The Gift of Therapy*, the psychiatrist Irvin Yalom (2002) wrote a brief chapter called "Avoid Diagnosis (Except for Insurance Companies)" as part of his "open letter to a new generation of therapists and their patients." (You would find his book helpful.) He says:

> Managed-care administrators demand that therapists arrive quickly at a precise diagnosis and then proceed upon a course of brief, focused therapy that matches that particular diagnosis. Sounds good. Sounds logical and efficient. But it has precious little to do with reality. It represents instead an illusory attempt to legislate scientific precision into being when it is neither possible nor desirable. (p. 4)

Yalom is careful to say that diagnosis is absolutely essential for many severe disorders that have a strong biological component, such as schizophrenia, major affective disorders, organically based disorders, and bipolar disorder, and I agree with him. But "diagnosis is often *counterproductive* in the everyday psychotherapy of less severely impaired patients" (p. 4).

Yalom's and my concerns would be troubling enough if we had reliable and valid assessment methods and diagnostic systems. Extensive reliability and validity data are not fully established for *the Diagnostic and Statistical Man-*

ual, fourth edition, text revision (DSM-IV-TR) (American Psychiatric Association, 2000), and many critics argue that recent versions of DSM have actually decreased validity of diagnoses, often because of attempts to increase the reliability (Barron, 1998; Beutler & Malik, 2002; Hsieh & Kirk, 2004; Kirk & Kutchins, 1994). In addition, previous evidence on the reliability and validity of diagnostic methods should make us extremely cautious (Boy, 1989; Garfield, 1986). Temerlin (1970) reports a distressing study in which psychiatrists, psychologists, graduate students in psychology, law students, and undergraduates listened to a taped interview with a man who said he had read a book on psychotherapy and wanted to discuss it. He was actually an actor who played an essentially healthy person—happily married, confident without being arrogant, and generally reporting none of the traditional "symptoms" of emotional disturbance. Professionals who were told ahead of time that this was an employment interview or who were told nothing rated the man as mentally healthy in most cases, although about one-third called him neurotic. If there had been a prior suggestion that the man was emotionally healthy, all the professionals rated him as healthy. The shocking results came among those raters who heard a respected person say, "I know the man being interviewed today. He's a very interesting man because he looks neurotic but actually is quite psychotic." Fifteen psychiatrists called the man psychotic, 10 said he was neurotic, and none said he was mentally healthy. Among the other groups, the bulk said neurotic, a few said psychotic, and a few said healthy.

Garfield (1986) made an observation that most practicing clinicians will recognize as true.

> Anyone who has worked in a large clinical setting has probably noticed that there is no unanimity among the staff in diagnostic conferences. I have participated in staff conferences in which the final decision (on a patient's diagnosis) was conclusively settled by an eight to seven vote of the staff members present. (p. 101)

There is some evidence (Kring, Johnson, Davison, & Neale, 2009) that diagnostic judgments can be made fairly reliably within large groupings, such as schizophrenia, panic disorder, and antisocial personality disorder, although even these levels of reliability are only just acceptable. The validity of such judgments is difficult to establish, however, since most criterion measures also involve diagnostic judgments. Our current system of diagnosis (DSM-IV-TR) is extremely widely used, but it includes serious problems (Watson & Clark, 2006). It "is primarily descriptive and relatively atheoretical . . . extraordinarily complex. . . . [In it] comorbidity (i.e., the empirical co-occurrence of different disorders) is a pervasive phenomenon . . . [and] significant heterogeneity exists within many of the current DSM disorders" (pp. 210–211).

These observations lead into a discussion of the first application of assessment to the practice of therapy—can we assign different clients to different treatments?

■ What Treatment for Whom?

Kiesler (1966) discussed "the uniformity myth" in psychotherapy. He argued that it is misleading to speak of "clients" who receive "therapy" as though such terms told us anything about who receives what. Because there are many kinds of therapy and many kinds of clients and problems, questions like "Does psychotherapy work?" are nearly meaningless. Many others have echoed this idea (Roth & Fonagy, 1996; Seligman, 1990).

The notion of specifying treatments for disorders is a popular idea that seems sensible in principle. In application, however, such a practice would require us to make diagnostic judgments that we are not equipped to make (Shoham-Salomon, 1991; Stubbs & Bozarth, 1994; Wampold, 2006). This has been called a "perhaps unattainable goal" (Groth-Marnat, Roberts, & Beutler, 2001, p. 115) and has "precious little to do with reality," as Yalom said earlier in this chapter. The evidence seems to be that we can only make moderately reliable judgments of the three major groupings: neurotic, psychotic, and antisocial personality disorder.

As I understand these three kinds of problems at present, I am willing to say only that evocatively empathic therapy works with anxiety-based disorders (neurotic disorders, to use the old terminology). I suspect that it would make some kinds of antisocial behavior worse (from society's perspective) by lowering anxiety in persons who already have few feelings of remorse for such acts as hurting others. The psychological treatment of psychosis is a puzzle to me (and to most other therapists I know). It seems clear that medication is often called for as part of treatment. Karon and Vanden Bos (1972) reported suggestive evidence that two very experienced therapists were more effective than medications in treating patients with schizophrenia, and Karon (2003) argues passionately that psychotherapy should be part of the treatment of schizophrenia. Those who advocate psychotherapy for schizophrenia stress the issue of supportive trust and that of focusing on reality rather than on inner conflicts. Purely expressive kinds of therapy may be damaging in treating schizophrenia (Roth & Fonagy, 1996).

These last observations make it clear that some assessment decisions need to be made in the practice of psychotherapy. My purpose here is not to detail assessment methods. I assume you will either learn such methods elsewhere or seek consultation about them when decisions are needed. I will discuss some of the practical implications of assessment decisions for therapists.

Anxiety-Based Problems

Unless you work in a hospital, the bulk of the clients you will see will have anxiety-based problems in living. (The term *neurosis* is dying a slow but well-deserved death.) These are the problems that I think I understand and for which evocatively empathic therapy is effective. In chapters 16 and 17 I will give a detailed description and explanation of such problems.

In practice, I nearly always start therapy being as empathic and accepting as I can, assuming that external assessment is not going to be needed. If I become concerned about possible antisocial or psychotic problems, I slow down (become more intellectually structured and less evocative, less leadingly empathic).

In a very important sense, I do match treatment to particular emotional problems. I will follow the same general principles, but each client's content of therapy and solutions are unique to that client. I am objecting to the contention that evocatively empathic therapy treats everybody the same way; it treats everybody differently because there is no prescribed personality pattern and no best solutions that grow out of a particular theory.

Antisocial Behavior

The older terms *psychopathic* and *sociopathic* are being dropped in favor of *antisocial personality disorder* in DSM-IV-TR. The labels describe behavior that seems relatively devoid of feelings for others, of appreciation for future consequences, and of the ability to enter into interpersonal relationships—behavior that centers on immediate gratification. This focus on immediate gratification often seems extreme and often results in horrible consequences for the person and for others in his or her life. Just as no one is "a neurotic," no one is "a psychopath." These problems in living are on a continuum with "normal," and there are no sharp dividing lines between them. Some people, however, do seem to be in trouble a lot and do not seem to respond well to the experiences that guide most people to appreciate the interpersonal consequences of what they do.

Attempts to treat such problems with relationship-based therapy have been notoriously unsuccessful, and devoting your career to such therapy will probably trigger a very early midlife crisis for you (see Ruegg, Haynes, & Frances, 1997, for an overview of assessment and treatment issues).

I don't think I should be treating such "sociopathic" problems. I am not comfortable with the powerfully controlling role that seems required, and what I am comfortable doing seems to make some people behave more destructively. I am, however, comfortable treating some people who show antisocial behavior. The enormous difficulty comes in validly deciding whether a particular person's antisocial behavior results from impulsive immediate gratification or from anxiety-based problems. In addition, some antisocial behavior is not even a treatment issue; it's a cultural issue. If everyone you know fights a lot, and you have always been rewarded for what other groups call criminal, in a sense it's normal to act antisocially. This last source of antisocial behavior is seldom an issue in therapy, however.

The real problem is knowing whether your client's acting out is somehow related to anxiety. Perhaps the client seeks continual stimulation as a distraction from internal conflicts; maybe there is a partly conscious guilt that is relieved only by being punished, and acting out brings the punishment; possibly fears of sexual inadequacy can be avoided only by being so harsh and violent that no one will become intimate with the person. The possibilities are endless. The principle is that if the anxiety were relieved, the person would no longer behave so destructively, and so evocatively empathic therapy is entirely appropriate.

Because I do feel obliged to be careful that I not contribute to "sociopathic" antisocial behavior, I am sometimes caught in the bind of making internal judgments about the occasional client who displays this behavior. Such thoughts are destructive to the therapy process with a person with anxiety-based problems, and so we have a very real problem. In practice, this dilemma makes me go slowly in therapy at first, knowing that I am being judgmental in a sense, but trying to make up my mind as soon as possible on whether I should continue seeing the person. I want either to commit myself to therapy or to refer the person as soon as I can.

This particular judgment will face you only rarely unless you work primarily in the correctional system or receive many forced referrals, in which clients come to you under some kind of external pressure. In fact, the path by which the client comes to therapy is one sign that alerts me to think about this issue. You should be familiar with the description of antisocial personality disorder in DSM-IV-TR and with Cleckley's (1976) classic list of characteristics of "sociopaths." The Minnesota Multiphasic Personality Inventory (MMPI) can also be used as a source of data for making a decision about antisocial personality, but I would use such a formal assessment procedure reluctantly because of the effect it has on the therapy process.

Psychotic Problems

It also makes me cautious in therapy when the client frequently makes very loose associations that seem to reflect grossly illogical thinking. Again, this book is not able to teach you details of recognizing different kinds of problems; this is just a general alerting you to issues. If you have any concerns along these lines, you should either be well trained in psychopathology or freely consult with someone who is.

No one really knows what the effects of evocatively empathic therapy are with people who have trouble with psychotic thinking. My experience and the writing of people like Fromm-Reichmann (1950) and Sullivan (1962)—both rare therapists with reputations for success treating schizophrenia—suggest that reality-based structuring and focusing are needed rather than evocative arousal and facing of internal conflicts. Roth and Fonagy (1996) say, "Whereas supportive individual therapy may be helpful for schizophrenic patients, expressive psychotherapy is unlikely to be of value" (p. 195). In a sense, defenses need to be strengthened, rather than faced and got through. If I am concerned about grossly illogical thinking, I still respond empathically but more cautiously. In other words, I become more cognitive and rational, in a supportive and empathic way (Dickerson & Lehman, 2006).

Again, the difficulty is telling what is loose association that results from a thought disorder and what is metaphorical and meaningful experiencing. The latter can be an important part of evocatively empathic therapy.

The Intake Interview

Many counseling and therapy jobs require the professional to do intake interviews to decide whether the potential client is appropriate to the agency and to guide assignment to a particular therapist or treatment format. This interview is serving two purposes that sometimes conflict. First, information has to be gathered on which to base a decision. Second, however, it is important that the client have a positive experience in his or her first contact with the agency and with therapy. A difficulty is that the intake interviewer often does not become the person's therapist, so that it would be inappropriate to begin therapy, but if the intake interview is done in the Chief Inquisitor style of evidence gathering and judgment making, a powerful set can be created in which the client expects therapy to be a question-and-answer session, with the expert therapist treating the client.

A useful approach is often to start the intake interview with a brief description of its purpose and with the information that the interviewer likely won't be the person's therapist. If the interviewer then responds empathically, helping the client feel comfortable and understood, it is probable that far more information will be offered than if the interviewer starts digging for it. The interviewer might ask minor questions to fill in the client's story, and near the end of the interview he or she will have some idea of information still missing that is necessary for the decisions that have to be made. Asking for it now will be less jarring, and both purposes of the intake can be served.

■ Assessment within Therapy

A large difference exists between therapists who see external formal assessment as essential to treatment and those who see therapy as a process of mutual search in which the client is the problem solver. As you know, I think that our assessment methods and our diagnostic schemes are so crude and unreliable that they can't possibly form the basis for treatment planning. More important, they are not needed for effective treatment because well-done evocatively empathic therapy helps the therapist and client discover together the unique nuances of the client's problems and solutions.

Therapy as Continuing Mutual Assessment

One student suggested that I call this book *How to Get Your Client to Tell You What's Wrong with Him*. He had a strong commitment to behavioral treatment but was willing to grant some validity to evocative empathy if the problem was difficult to specify. Another title he suggested was *Evocative Empathy: A Behavioral Approach to Nonspecific Anxiety Disorders*. A section of chapter 5 was called "The Hierarchy Emerges," making the point that the client's problems are complex and, to some extent, unknown to both the client and the therapist, but you can trust the process. In therapy, steadily more accurate understanding emerges as the client becomes more able to think fully thoughts that previously were so anxiety arousing that they were avoided.

In this sense, therapy is a process of continuous assessment—but not assessment imposed by the expert therapist. The assessment is an integral part of therapy, carried out as a mutual search. The goal is for the client to discover the essential information and to use it to solve problems effectively.

Tests

I have already mentioned the use of tests to make decisions about the appropriateness of evocatively empathic therapy and have said that the implications of doing this are often deleterious to the kind of therapy I have been discussing. Tests, however, can have a useful function in therapy if they are offered as tools for the client and therapist to use together. Vocational interest tests can form the basis for helpful discussions; intelligence tests can help the client know his or her own strengths and limitations; responses to projective test stimuli can form the basis of discussions, much as you might discuss dreams in therapy. Two important principles to remember are that all the tests we have are of limited validity and must be interpreted cautiously and that, to be useful, the tests should be used nonjudgmentally. I assume that you will not use tests unless you are well trained with them and know their limitations, and therefore the first principle is not of great concern. The second principle is more difficult to follow because tests traditionally carry a strong implication of judgment. If their use clearly grows out of the client's interest and if the therapist is very candid about the limitations of the tests and about the uses to which he or she will put them, they can help.

Behavioral Assessment

The principle that makes tests useful is that they be used as a shared tool. The same principle applies to explicit methods of behavioral assessment. I am talking, of course, of the use of behavioral assessment as a part of treatment and not of its other uses, such as in research and in making judgments about people in the more traditional sense of assessment. Behavioral assessment, like most assessment procedures, is traditionally seen as imposed by the professional on the client. This is clearly not essential to its use, and like so many other skills and tools the therapist has, it can be offered as one more way available to the client and therapist for mutual problem solving.

11

Ethical Issues

As a practicing counselor or therapist, you will almost certainly be associated with an organization with an established set of ethical standards. These guidelines cover many aspects of professional activity. Although I will only touch on some principles that apply to your treatment of clients, it is your responsibility to be familiar with all the standards. I assume that your training program includes formal exposure to ethical issues and an opportunity to examine and discuss the complexities of actual incidents. An excellent overview of ethical issues is Ogloff's chapter, "Navigating the Quagmire: Legal and Ethical Guidelines" (Ogloff, 1995).

In chapter 6, I discussed several examples of ethical dilemmas that can arise in the therapeutic relationship. This chapter will center on more general issues.

■ In Whose Best Interest?

It is easy enough to state the general principle that therapy is designed to serve the best interests of the client. In nearly all instances of conflict of interest, thinking of this principle will resolve the issue. Occasionally, though, you will face difficult decisions that make it obvious that therapy does not occur in glorious isolation from the rest of the world, all of whose members claim that their best interests count for something too.

Therapist Needs and Client Needs

First we can say that, within therapy, the therapist's needs are secondary. One of the functions of putting limits on therapy is to enable the therapist to set aside his or her best interests for a limited period of time. In therapy, whether or not the therapist expresses feelings or talks or is accepting is determined by what is best for the client. It is a very real problem that some therapists and counselors use the therapy hour for their own gratification— perhaps by eliciting admiration from the client or perhaps by inducing the client to continue therapy needlessly for the therapist's financial gain.

Outside the limits of therapy, different principles apply. Clearly the therapist cannot make his or her own interests secondary to the client's, although there still is the obligation to do everything possible to be helpful to the client, within the limits that the therapist is willing to accept.

Social Needs and Individual Needs

The issue becomes more clouded when the client's best interests are weighed against the needs of others in the society. Here we face some of those difficult judgment calls discussed in chapter 10. Then we were concerned with the client doing something that would be severely damaging to his or her own best interests. Occasions also arise in which your client will talk about doing things harmful to others. In most cases your responsibility will still be to your client, with intervention called for only in extreme circumstances. If, because of his emotional conflicts, your client is yelling at his wife a lot in ways that seem to you to be doing her emotional damage, it would almost certainly be useless and would damage therapy for you to intervene in some direct way. Your most effective intervention is to do the powerful things you can do to facilitate his resolving his emotional conflicts. It is possible that you might express the distress you feel, but it is likely that whatever restraining effect that would have on him would be offset by his withdrawal from the therapy process. But, to move along the continuum, what if he said he felt like cheating his wife by transferring their savings and then leaving her? What if he said he felt like killing her? What if he said he was going to kill her? Clearly somewhere along this continuum we passed the point at which direct intervention was called for—or did we? What if you don't think he really means what he says because he has said it many times before?

The APA ethical principles say that psychologists reveal information obtained from a client "with the appropriate consent of the . . . client . . . (or) only as mandated by law, or where permitted by law for a valid purpose" (American Psychological Association, 2002, p. 8). The general guideline this offers is that society's interests must be considered, but it is a rare instance in which they take precedence over the client's. The principles go on to say that information from counseling or therapy is shared with colleagues "only to the extent necessary to achieve the purposes of the consultation" (p. 8) and only with the consent of the client, unless the disclosure cannot be avoided. I frequently advise you to seek consultation with another professional. In these consultations you should protect the identity of your client whenever possible. I hope this doesn't sound like an evasion that lets me escape dealing with difficult issues here. It is the best and most responsible advice I can give you about these gray-area decisions.

■ Role Conflicts

So far, our discussion has assumed that you will be operating in a setting such as private practice, in which you have only one fairly well-defined and understood role. You may, however, have conflicting roles, especially if you work for an agency. I sometimes teach counseling skills to probation and parole workers, to school counselors, to therapists in large hospitals, to counselors hired by firms to help their employees, and to those in settings in which their administrative superiors are insistent on meeting agency needs.

Whose Agent?

It is most comfortable to be able to say that you are the client's agent, with only the rare problem arising over the fact that you also have some responsibility to society. Conflicts of interest are nearly inevitable in some settings, however, and they nearly always have a dampening effect on therapy. It will be necessary to be honest with yourself and with your client about the limits these role conflicts place on therapy. Your evocatively empathic skills will still be useful, and your client can gain meaningful help from your counseling, but the process will be different.

The two biggest problems are confidentiality and making judgments. The power of the therapy relationship lies in its being nonjudgmental. Many counseling and therapy roles ask you both to give counseling and to make a judgment about the person; the two are incompatible because in one instance the client's best interests are served by being open about weaknesses, and in the other they are not. Some schools, for example, require that counselors report any drug use or use of contraceptives that students discuss. Such a requirement would, in my opinion, make therapy nearly impossible. If I were under a constraint like this, I would tell the client exactly what the limits of the relationship were and say that he or she was free to withhold any information, but we would do what we could within those limits.

As it is, I do tell clients that I don't have privileged communication and can be subpoenaed by a court, so that they should consider that in what they say. Even trying to maintain clear guidelines, however, can fail. Once a parole service asked me to see a potential parolee and his wife, apparently at the man's request (it turned out later that it had been implied to him that counseling was a condition for his receiving parole). I went to great lengths to make it clear to the clients and the agency that I couldn't operate as a therapist if I was ever to be called on to make judgments, that it would then serve the clients not to be honest with me. Everyone agreed that this was wise, but several months later both the parole service and the clients said that if I would only give my approval the man could get a day parole to be with his family. The day parole did seem like a good idea. The couple practically pleaded with me. The parole service said they were sorry, but they felt I was the only person in a position to make such a judgment, and so they would not grant the parole unless I said so. I still don't know whether I did the right thing. I wrote a letter approving the parole, but in retrospect that clearly changed therapy. Now I was useful to the couple in manipulating the environment, and so they needed to hide some things from me.

A colleague once consulted me on whether he should act as a counselor for a friend's family that was breaking up, since he might be called on to testify at a child custody trial. The answer was clearly no, although that was not clear to the counselor—I suspect because of his personal involvement in the case. (He clearly did the right thing in seeking consultation over his uncertainty.) First, one definitely does not attempt therapy with clients with whom one has other relationships—exactly because of the personal involvement. The more subtle issue here, though, is one you will probably face numerous times in your career. If the family involved saw the counselor with the knowledge that he might soon be testifying about each of the parents' competence to care for the children, there are many things that neither the mother nor the father would honestly say in counseling.

Almost all jurisdictions require that persons with knowledge of child abuse are required to report it. You must inform all of your clients that this is a limit on the confidentiality of your relationship.

Judgmental roles conflict with therapeutic roles. Therapists and counselors almost inevitably face this conflict at times, and so you must clearly think through your position in each such case. When possible, I try to be as absolutely clear with the client as I can about such conflicts. Sometimes I have told clients about whom I might have to testify, for example, that this probably means there are things they shouldn't tell me. Usually, after the need for my other role disappears, therapy changes toward a more complete and useful process, although the prior sessions were not wasted. They might even have been quite productive, within the limits demanded by my role conflict.

Involuntary Clients

I usually avoid seeing clients who have been forced into therapy. Many people and agencies act as though psychotherapy were a kind of magical treatment that could be imposed on people, but it is just a human relationship with certain special structures and limitations. The client enters therapy to improve his or her life by making personal changes. The motivation to do this comes most effectively out of the person's dissatisfaction with the way he or she is living life. Therapy done for other motives may not be impossible, but it surely is difficult.

If I do see an involuntary client, perhaps an adolescent whose "parents said I should come," I acknowledge the reluctance, respond as empathically as I can, say what the limits of our relationship are, and suggest that we talk "at least this one time, since you're here, to see if there's any way I might help you be happier or figure things out or whatever you decide you want." In a sense, now my goal is to make the process attractive enough that the person will want to continue out of his or her own desire. If the person decides not to continue, I accept that decision (Martin, 2003).

■ Confidentiality

An issue implicit in all of our discussion of role conflicts is confidentiality. The APA standards say, "Psychologists have a primary obligation and take reasonable precautions to protect confidential information obtained through or stored in any medium, recognizing that the extent and limits of confidentiality may be regulated by law or established by institutional rules or professional or scientific relationship." (American Psychological Association, 2002, p. 7). The promise of confidentiality is fundamental to counseling and therapy. It frees the client to face thoughts and feelings that he or she couldn't otherwise face, because the client comes to trust the therapist's acceptance. The client doesn't have to worry about who else might hear these things and judge them. One of the most indefensible violations of this principle occurs when counselors and therapists use confidential information in a gossipy way, even when discussing therapy with another counselor. By this I mean discussing clients with the implication of, "Boy, have I got something interesting to tell you!"

Confidentiality does have limits. Professional considerations will require you to consult with another therapist about the course of therapy or about concerns you have at times. In training you will be discussing therapy with your supervisor and perhaps a few other trainees. The "clear danger" rule will apply in very rare instances. The law limits your confidentiality, and the structure of your job may have the role conflicts discussed earlier. An article by Younggren and Harris (2008) is a good guide to how to deal with the gray areas and possible legal problems with confidentiality. The legitimate limits of confidentiality will be different for each counselor, and you should be very clear what those limits are.

Having Clear Ground Rules

One reason that you must be clear about the limits of confidentiality is that you will need to make those limits absolutely clear to your client. Most clients assume that therapy is confidential and are not highly concerned with confidentiality (some are, of course), and so I usually look for an opening early in therapy—a time when I will not interrupt the therapy process—to state my view of confidentiality. I say that confidentiality is total except that I can be subpoenaed; that I must report child abuse; that I must act if the client is an imminent danger to him- or herself or to another person; that I sometimes consult with one or two other therapists about my sessions, mostly to help me stay clear about what I am doing; and that any other sharing of information will be done only with the client's permission. You may need to say something different, but it is essential that you be explicit and clear.

Legal Testimony

The legal requirement that therapists testify under oath if subpoenaed is, in my experience, a formidable-looking but rarely encountered limit on confidentiality. It does create a conflict over the completeness of records it is wise to keep. Ethical standards require record keeping about client contacts, but detailed reports can be subpoenaed and are easily misunderstood. The condensed notes that you might write for your own reminders can mean quite different things if read in court or by some other agency. A compromise solution is to keep only brief records that are carefully worded to avoid misunderstanding. You should also keep in mind that in most jurisdictions, clients have a right to obtain copies of their files.

Parents and Young Clients

An awkward confidentiality problem often arises when parents want to know what their child or adolescent is talking about in therapy. The parent has legal responsibility for the child and can remove the child from treatment, but if you can't promise the child confidentiality, therapy will be difficult or impossible. More subtly, and probably more likely to happen to you, the parent can phone and say, "Don't tell John that I've called because it would hurt him, but there is something that you just have to know to be able to help him, and I don't think he'll tell you." Even more insidiously, the parent might say there is something that even John doesn't know but that you should know to understand him.

You might be quite clear that you are not going to betray the client's confidences but be caught very off balance by this intrusion. As soon as you enter into this secret agreement with the parent, however, you are compromised and in danger of losing the client's trust. Now the parent is in a position to destroy that trust by revealing to the client, maybe weeks later, that he or she talked with you. There is no perfect way to handle such a situation, but you might say to the parent, as soon as you realize what the drift of the phone call is, "Can I stop you for a minute? It's important that I explain something to you about the way I work. I'm sure you can understand that it's important that John be able to trust me for therapy to help. What I always say to a person who talks to me about someone I'm seeing is that I have to be able to share with my client anything that is said to me. I know that makes it difficult for something like what you want to talk about, but I find that I can't work otherwise." Now you are free to share with your client whatever is said. If the parent insists, you could say that you would rather work without the information but be just as insistent about your ground rule.

■ Therapist Competence

Finally, you are required to work within the limits of your competence. "Psychologists provide services, teach, and conduct research with populations and in areas only within the boundaries of their competence, based on their education, training, supervised experience, consultation, study, or professional experience" (American Psychological Association, 2002, p. 4).

You might be registered or licensed as a school psychologist or clinical psychologist or psychiatric social worker or social worker or mental health worker or psychiatrist someday and be permitted by law to perform a wide range of services for a wide range of clients. Operating within the letter of the law, however, will not necessarily meet ethical standards. Well-trained professionals know that there are procedures with which they have too little experience to offer the service independently to clients. There will be clients whose problems personally bother you intensely or feel beyond your depth. In such cases it is important either to refer to another therapist or to seek consultation. If experienced therapists have to seek consultation and further training, it is obvious that therapists in training must be sure that they don't get in over their heads, that they be closely supervised, and that they not try to operate independently "on the side."

12

Beginning and Ending

It's been a long time, but I still remember my first real therapy interview as a practicum student—not the interview actually, but the nervous waiting before, half hoping (maybe three-fourths) that the client wouldn't show up, wishing that I had a better idea of how to start the session, and being afraid I would get stuck with nothing to say to a client with nothing to say. I muddled through, but I hope you will do better. I hope this book might help you have some confidence that there are skills you will take into your sessions.

■ Arrangements

Many details of physical arrangements and making appointments will depend on the setting in which you work. I can share with you some of my experiences.

Making Appointments

When working in an agency, the therapist typically does not make the first contact with a client. A receptionist might explain something of agency procedure and schedule an intake interview. Subsequently, the client is assigned to a therapist, who then contacts the client to arrange an appointment. During this contact, the client will be forming some impression of the therapist, and so it helps to be friendly and quietly confident on the phone but to limit the conversation to arranging the time. Clients will usually be uneasy about discussing any aspect of their problem in such a contact, but if one does start talking about the problem it is a good idea to gently suggest that you wait until the first appointment to get into those things. If the client's desire to talk seems to grow out of an urgent distress, you might ask whether it would help to have the appointment be earlier than scheduled and to try to accommodate that. In the rare instance that the client persists in talking, it is important to him or her that you listen and respond supportively and move toward making an early appointment as soon as the client is comfortable.

In private practice, the therapist typically makes the first contact with the client. It will take some skill to assess quickly whether an appointment with you is appropriate, whether you should refer the person elsewhere, or whether he or she just wants information. Again, the potential client is being affected by this first contact with you and your manner and in this case will not have had the buffer of an intake interview. Clients seldom want to say much in such a conversation, so I usually get some feel for the general area of the problem and how they have come to call me and suggest that we "get together for an hour to see if I'm the right person to help you." This phrase permits both the client and me to treat the first interview as a trial session, without a commitment to longer therapy. You would give practical information about the location of therapy, fees, and length of sessions at this time.

During this first phone contact, it is important to be sensitive to the intensity of the person's distress. When I suggest a time for us to meet, I listen carefully to the quality of the response. If I sense any dismay, I ask, "How does that feel, waiting that long to talk?" This gives the client an opportunity to express any felt urgency, which leads me to try to work in an earlier appointment. If the client seems to want the earlier appointment but refuses so as not to impose, you can leave the door open by saying, "OK, we'll leave it for Tuesday at 3, and if something comes up that you want to talk sooner, give me a call."

Physical Environment

The most comfortable room arrangement is to have two or three (for seeing couples) chairs of about equal size and comfort arranged facing each other, perhaps with a low coffee table between them or off to the side to hold a box of tissues—be sure that a wastebasket is within easy reach for disposal of soggy tissues. This arrangement implies that therapy is a face-to-face mutual process and avoids the initial awkwardness of who gets the big chair or the most comfortable chair. Some offices imply that the therapist is the aloof expert, mainly by putting a desk between client and counselor, an arrangement that I have always suspected is designed to protect the therapist somehow. A friend of mine got a good deal on a matched set of chairs for his office, but it turned out that one was slightly higher and better padded than the other—apparently the "daddy chair." He kept the chairs, but a lot of people comment on the difference, and clients, especially couples, often stumble for a moment deciding who is going to sit where.

Recording and Note Taking

Most training settings require that sessions be recorded or videotaped for supervision, and I have repeatedly said that listening to yourself on a recording is one of the most effective ways to improve as a therapist. Even if you take extensive notes immediately after a session, you will filter and distort what happened in the session when you consult with a colleague or supervisor. The recording is a faithful history. It also can be used for research and teaching, if informed consent has been obtained from the client.

The presence of a tape recorder or camera does seem to have an inhibiting effect on some clients but not most. It is a good idea, if you record sessions, to present it to the client as standard procedure with assurances of confidentiality and to place the recorder in an unobtrusive but not hidden location. Read the client's reactions sensitively so that if there is hesitation you can say, "Well, let's try it, and if you find it interferes too much, let me know. I use the recording only for my own growth as a therapist, so I can listen to myself and occasionally to consult with the one or two other therapists that I told you about here at the clinic." Another helpful phrasing can be, "I much prefer to record because it helps me improve as a therapist and be sure I'm hearing you accurately, but if we cover some material that you want erased, just tell me, and I'll erase it right away." This takes away some of the threat, since the client has control of the recording after the fact.

Recording is also threatening to the therapist. Trainees sometimes say they feel as though someone were watching them. I still feel that way sometimes, unless I record all my sessions. If I record only a few, I can feel myself sometimes trying to "work harder" and do therapy "by the book" in those sessions, which distorts what I do by making me "techniquey." It's probably better just to get used to recording and do it regularly. One problem I have with this is that I am reluctant to record private clients, who are paying fairly substantial amounts for therapy. In a training or free clinic, the client (and therapist) may perceive recording as a price the client "pays" for service. My experience has been that few therapists in private practice do much recording, and so others may share this reluctance.

Note taking is a different matter; it usually interferes with the process between the therapist and client, since it is nearly impossible to write notes at the same time that you are engaged in an intense listening and responding to the client. Note taking also strongly implies that therapy is an evidence-gathering process rather than a mutual search. Any notes that you need can be written in a few minutes immediately after your session. In fact, many therapists schedule clients for the traditional 50-minute hour so that they have a few minutes to record some notes while the session is still fresh in memory. If you do keep notes, be clear about the purpose they are to serve. A therapist who is seeing many clients will probably need some reminders of details to keep things straight. Therapy, however, is an ever-changing process that goes in unpredictable directions, and so notes probably won't be useful to "pick up where we left off last week," because the client is nowhere near where he was last week. You should also remember that, in most jurisdictions, the client has a right to obtain a copy of your notes and records.

Money and Time

In a clinic setting, the issue of fees will probably be out of the therapist's hands and is less likely to enter therapy as an issue, since the client will tend to perceive the fees as imposed by the agency. Most clinics charge on some kind of sliding scale according to ability to pay, so that the client ends up paying some amount that is a real cost but not a debilitating one.

In private practice, the issue is more salient because it is the therapist who is personally charging the fee, although this can be complicated by insurance coverage. There is a lot of discussion of whether paying a fee makes clients work harder in therapy and appreciate it more or whether fees distort therapy by inducing clients to work toward short-term goals or whether charging fees keeps clients from inappropriately extending therapy. No one knows the answers to these questions. Whatever the effect on therapy, the main function of fees is that the therapist must be compensated for his or her time. Fees are not based on benefit received; they are based on time devoted, and so ultimately they will be set according to the level of compensation that sufficiently rewards therapists for doing therapy.

From the client's perspective, fees introduce considerations of trade-offs into therapy. Is the benefit received—the relief of problems in living—worth the financial sacrifice? To some clients, $5 a session is as personally costly as $50 or $180 would be to some other clients. Considerations of simple justice would suggest that all clients should be seen on a sliding scale, but then many therapists would be unable to afford to continue working. Most therapists I know work out some kind of compromise in which they do some work through an agency where therapy is subsidized and in their private work charge a standard fee consistent with general professional fees in their community, occasionally reducing a fee if it is burdensome. Be prepared, though, for fee setting to be an issue to be discussed as a relationship problem.

Most therapists see clients for slightly less than an hour, once a week, leaving a small break between appointments. Some clinics, especially free community clinics, normally see clients every other week, primarily so that more people can be served. Occasionally a client will be seen twice a week, especially at particularly stressful times, but more frequent sessions than this seem to suffer from diminishing returns. The client has to live life in between sessions too. Some clients seem to use a longer session more productively, but it is best to anticipate this with an individual by scheduling a one-and-a-half or two-hour session ahead of time. Setting flexible ending times for sessions can create problems, even if you can tolerate the uncertainty and unused therapy time. The ending time of a session is not absolute and inviolate, but you're asking for trouble if, near the end of a session, you are always deciding whether a continuation of the hour is justified. It can happen that the client has to "earn" a time extension by saving the painful material till the end, or stopping at an hour could mean that you didn't think the session was all that good.

I find it helpful to say, as I sense the end of the hour, "I'm going to have to stop in a few minutes." This gives the client time to bring the session to some closure, makes it clear that your time is limited and you do have other things that you want to and have to do, but does not have the abrupt and uncaring feeling of "Time's up." Many therapists arrange the room so that a clock is easily visible because frequent checking of your watch can be disruptive.

I break all these rules at times, of course, but try to be clear about why.

■ The Initial Interview

So your client really has shown up for the first appointment. If this is your first appointment, you're pretty uneasy and are hoping that the client won't recoil and say, "But you're so young!" or, "Are you sure there's no mistake?"

Introductions

Using the client's name as you approach expresses your interest and involvement. I prefer to use his or her first name and to introduce myself by first and last name in most cases. This helps create an atmosphere of mutuality and diminish the doctor/patient nature of therapy. I said "in most cases" because there are awkward instances, particularly with older clients, when using the client's first name feels overly familiar. This is all related to cultural training, of course, and so you should follow your impulses, keeping in mind the principle that you are trying to establish a mutual exploring set. I must also admit that when I was an intern I frequently wished I had finished the dissertation, so I could be "Dr. Martin" and impress my clients. That way they would have known they were getting good therapy, see?

Openers

Your client will probably sit down with a what-do-we-do-now look, and you can get therapy started with, "Let me tell you everything I know about you, and we can go from there." Some therapists want extensive background information on a client before the first session, but I feel quite strongly that this creates powerful and inaccurate expectations about the client. The background material can be useful, and I certainly do go over it after I have a connection with the client, but much of this information will emerge in the session, and you will be getting it straight from the client's perspective. Any information you receive ahead of time is already well filtered through the selective perception and memory of the person who provides the information. It will inevitably include distortions. I much prefer to know very little about the client in the first session, both to avoid these expectations that will cloud my perceptions and to be able to say to the client words that imply, "I don't have the drop on you here. I don't work that way. I can quite openly tell you everything I know about you. What really matters to me is your problem solving and experiencing."

After saying something like, "So I know that something's got you pretty unhappy and scared," I would help the client start talking with an open-ended, "Why not just tell me what's on your mind and let me get to know you?" If I don't know anything about a client, I might start with a phrase like this or, "How can I help you?" or, "What brings you in?"

Creating a Mutual-Exploration Set

Once the client starts talking, you should be very attentive, listen very hard, and start responding to what the client is implying. Your client has come in with some expectations and a lot of apprehension about therapy, and so these first minutes are showing him or her what therapy is. The client will probably fear not having anything to say and will expect you to ask a lot of questions. If, however, you respond evocatively empathically, he or she will keep getting the feeling of being understood and will find it easier and easier to talk. You will be teaching by example that mutual exploration is the nature of therapy.

Teaching about Therapy

In chapter 5, I discussed ways to teach the process and rationale of therapy, and so I'll only briefly mention the principle again here. Usually, the process will just get going if you respond empathically. Occasionally, the client will ask, "What should I do?" or, "How is it going to help just to talk about it?" The principle is that you are an expert on a process but not on this particular client. You can teach the process, using some of the phrases from chapter 5.

Starting Subsequent Sessions

Since the client is in charge of the process, the best way to start most sessions is simply by remaining silent until the client starts or by making some general opening invitation like, "Hi" or, "How are you?" or, "What's on your mind?" For the therapist, there is a continuity between the previous session and the current one, and so it is sometimes tempting to try to start up "where we left off last time." So much has happened in the client's experiencing since last time, however, that this will almost inevitably distort the exploration process. The client is at a much different place from the ending of the previous interview. Sometimes there will be issues that the therapist needs to deal with or hopes the client will deal with, and sometimes this is legitimate. It is more helpful to hold these issues back and wait for an opening. This opening can take the form of the client's trying to talk about the issue, and the therapist's having waited will have helpfully left control in the client's hands. There is a risk that the therapist will "hear" the client deal with the therapist's issues when he or she really isn't doing so, and it is therefore important to be careful not to fulfill your own prophecies. If the client doesn't bring up something that you need to discuss, it will be more honest just to create an opening by waiting for a pause in the client's process and saying, "There's something I need for us to talk about. . . ."

■ Termination

One of the most gratifying and most difficult aspects of counseling and therapy is ending a relationship, particularly a long one. Successful therapy is obviously rewarding to the client, but the therapist also gains satisfaction at having contributed to another person's emotional growth. Unsatisfying terminations can feel like personal failures to the counselor, in addition to the concern they cause about the client. Knowing when and how to terminate a therapy relationship takes sensitivity and skill.

A Mutual Decision (Who Is the Problem Solver?)

My experience has been that the most common route to termination is also the most satisfying one. When the client has made progress toward relief of the problems that brought him or her to therapy and feels stronger, the client starts feeling less need for therapy. There will be hints and implications of this in many things the client says, and, as with any issue, the therapist's job is to hear these tentative approaches to the idea of quitting therapy. The therapist can articulate what he or she thinks the client is implying, being tentative and leaving control in the client's hands. There is some risk that if the therapist says, "When you talk about how well things are going, I wonder if part of what you mean is you're thinking about trying it without therapy," the client might hear this as the therapist's urging termination—if this isn't what the client was implying. This therapist statement is tentative enough, though, that the client probably wouldn't take that meaning. It is a message that clients often fear, and so you should be sensitive to their hearing it.

When the evocatively empathic therapist makes the client the problem solver, part of the control that is given to the client is that of deciding when treatment is over. There is some cost to the client of being in therapy, and there are meaningful advantages to being independent once he or she is strong enough, so that usually the client will want to terminate therapy at a time that is good for him or her.

I always try to make it clear, long before termination is an issue, that deciding to quit therapy is not an all-or-none decision. Virtually any format—tapering off, quitting and then starting up, or stopping with the understanding that the client can call to resume therapy if he or she chooses—is acceptable to me. This knowledge makes it easier for the client to consider termination because it is not such a momentous decision.

When Just the Client Wants to Terminate

Termination as a mutual decision is the most common ending to evocatively empathic therapy, but it would be naive not to think about the less satisfactory ways it happens. One of these is when the client wants to terminate or just stops coming, but the therapist feels that there is much work yet to be done or that the client's decision is impulsive and unwise. Between a third and a half of terminations are premature in this way (Vasquez, Bingham & Barnett, 2008). The temptation is to argue the client out of his or her decision, but this strategy is almost doomed to be useless. To win the argument is to take over the course of therapy and treat a reluctant client who may well feel betrayed by your insistence. To argue and to lose anyway will make it very difficult for the client to return to therapy later because of the loss of face.

It would be within the spirit of therapy to say, "That surprises me some, and I'm not completely comfortable stopping now. But I really believe that ultimately you're the one who knows best for you. What I would like to say very clearly is that my door is open, and if you'd like to talk again, I'd certainly see you. It could turn out that a break right now would be helpful or that it really is time for you to do without therapy." I would try to hear, too, whether the client wanted to continue therapy with another therapist, to be as accepting of this as I could, and to help find that other therapist.

I know that I would seek out my therapist/friend to explore my discomfort (which might well just be my problem) and possible reasons for the early termination.

When Just the Therapist Wants to Terminate

An even rarer (fortunately, because it's also more complicated) problem is when a client wants to continue, but the therapist wants to terminate. Legitimate reasons may be that the client has achieved reasonable goals and just comes in to chat, using the therapist in a friend role, or that other demands and limits on the therapist make it very difficult for him or her to continue. It may also be, however, that the therapist is responding to countertransference needs. The therapist may be bored or discouraged or threatened by what the client is dealing with. Most insidiously, the therapist may be threatened by a client's growing dependency and attachment. Without being aware of what's happening, the therapist might run from therapy, rationalizing that termination is somehow in the client's best interest. This could contribute to the client's problems by rejecting him or her in the middle of the kind of dependency problem the client may need to deal with. Probably the biggest potential problem with therapist-initiated terminations is that the client may feel abandoned (Vasquez, Bingham & Barnett, 2008). Abandonment can have serious consequences, and Vasquez, Bingham, and Barnett give good advice on how to lessen its effects. In any case, the therapist's independent decision to terminate has to be made very carefully and certainly with consultation.

When the therapist does terminate the sessions, the reasons must be specified to the client and effort made to remove implications of personal rejection. The process can be accomplished more gently with an "open door" statement like, "I know you're not comfortable with stopping now, but it seems important to me because . . . [whatever the reasons are]. How about trying it for a while, like a break and then you call me in a couple of months if you want to get together to talk about how things are going." There is no getting around that this violates the perspective that the client is the problem solver, but it may be necessary at rare times.

Forced Terminations

Because many training settings operate on the school year, it looks as if clients tend to get well in May and June. These artificial limits often interfere with the most productive course that therapy might take, but they can be handled in a nondestructive way. Several months before circumstances require the therapist to leave (or even go on vacation, by the way), it should be made absolutely clear to the client that this will occur. This "several months" guideline is very important, because clients need a long time to get ready emotionally for termination; many therapists are so afraid of "giving bad news" that they stall and rationalize and ultimately hurt their clients by not giving them enough warning. The information should be repeated a few times, and effort should be made to read the client's reactions to and understanding of what this means. The advantage is that termination is imposed from the outside and does not reflect rejection from the therapist. Similarly, when the client's life circumstances force a termination, therapy can be productive and not end unsatisfactorily. In fact, the impending time limit can sometimes accelerate progress in therapy. An interesting study reported by Shlien, Mosak, and Dreikurs (1962) showed that clients reported as much improvement in self-esteem in 20 sessions of time-limited therapy (client-centered and Adlerian therapy) as did clients in unlimited therapy after an average of 37 sessions. I was in a practicum with Shlien at that time, though, and he mentioned the impression of therapists in the study that clients felt some rejection at the therapist-imposed time limit—rejection that did not seem to occur when similar time limits were forced by outside circumstances.

13

Other Formats
Building on the Foundation

This book focuses on individual therapy, but the skills I have been discussing are also the foundation of what you will need for many kinds of therapy and for virtually all of the helping professions. Evocative empathy is far from the only thing a therapist does and often is not the most appropriate thing to do in therapy. For all these other things to work, though, you first need to make your client feel understood. You have no coercive power over clients; your constructive influence exists because it is rewarding to your clients to be influenced by you. This chapter will extend your skills to formats in which there is more than one client, and we will look at the important issue of cultural diversity. I told you therapy is hard work in which you have to scramble. Group, family, and couple therapy is even harder work because there are so many permutations of relationships. Working with clients from cultures other than your own will require "empathy on steroids," because you will be trying not to be biased by your own worldview.

Making two persons feel understood at the same time is not easy, especially if they strongly disagree with each other. What saves you is that empathy is not agreement or sympathy but simply understanding. You can say, "As I hear it, John, when she comes home late, you feel worried—in two ways, I guess—worried she might be hurt and worried she might be with someone else. But, Mary, to you that's hard to understand because you feel you've clearly said you wouldn't do that—but that you need some freedom." Both persons will feel understood and will be facing not only what they said but also what the other person said. This skill will be useful when doing group therapy, as well as couple and family therapy.

It is beyond the scope of this book to give you an adequate introduction to cultural diversity or to group, couple, and family therapy. Each is an area of study in itself. I will mention some ways that evocatively empathic therapy applies and can be adapted to these areas, and I will point you toward other resources. I will also discuss how the principles we have been learning can be "woven into" work in other helping professions.

■ Groups

The most typical format for group therapy seems to be that one therapist meets with about 6 to 10 clients for at least an hour and a half, once a week. There are significant advantages to having two therapists working with a group, but this arrangement usually occurs in training settings or in agencies where the economics of having two therapists aren't so restricting. Group therapy is sometimes thought of as a cheap substitute for individual therapy, but each format has benefits and limitations that the other doesn't. A discussion of these advantages and disadvantages will make more sense if we first look at what Yalom and Leszcz (2005) have called the "curative factors" in group therapy. Yalom and Leszcz's book, by the way, is one of the best introductions to group therapy.

Curative Factors in Groups

Yalom and Leszcz (2005, pp. 1–2) say:

> From my viewpoint, natural lines of cleavage divide the curative factors into eleven primary categories:
>
>   1. Instillation of hope
>   2. Universality
>   3. Imparting of information
>   4. Altruism
>   5. The corrective recapitulation of the primary family group
>   6. Development of socializing techniques
>   7. Imitative behavior
>   8. Interpersonal learning
>   9. Group cohesiveness
>   10. Catharsis
>   11. Existential factors

Some of these factors are available in both group and individual therapy, but some of them require group membership to occur. *The instillation of hope* can come solely from the therapist's confidence and acceptance, but only in a group can the client see others make progress and hear them tell of gains made in problems similar to the client's. *Universality* refers to the discovery that one is not unique in having threatening thoughts and debilitating problems, a discovery that is more likely to be made in a group. *Imparting of information* simply refers to teaching about coping techniques, the dynamics of emotional adjustment, and the like. It can be part of the teaching aspect of either individual or group therapy, although in a group, other clients probably can add information not available to the therapist. *Altruism* is an experience that the group member can have through helping another client grapple with problems. In a good group, the members learn to become therapeutic toward each other, often giving empathy, caring, and honesty in a much more powerful way than the therapist can.

Only a group offers the possibility of reliving the complex kinds of relationships that exist in families, and Yalom and Leszcz (2005) feel that this *reliving of family issues* is often an important part of group therapy. Clients are often assigned to group therapy after an intake procedure if a lack of *social skills* is an important part of their problems. The group offers a chance to learn to talk to several other persons and to be in a more reciprocal relationship than individual therapy usually is. *Imitative learning* is extremely powerful and occurs in both group and individual therapy. In a group, though, the client has several persons to imitate and, probably more importantly, has the opportunity to see and learn from the therapist's interactions with other clients. It has been my experience that clients steadily become more empathic with each other as group therapy progresses. The first few sessions are usually filled with advice giving, since each member is sure that the others could solve their problems if they would just try some fairly simple solutions. Later, however, clients come to show an appreciation for and communicated understanding of the other clients. I would hope that they are learning to be therapeutic, partly by imitation.

Interpersonal learning and relating can take place more in a group than in individual therapy, whose limits usually make it a one-way relationship. *Group cohesiveness* refers to a remarkable experience that develops in a successful group—a feeling of belonging to a group that is really important and trusting. This feeling is qualitatively different from having a good relationship with a therapist. They are both powerful but in different ways. "Our group" often becomes a very important part of the person's life with many benefits.

> For example, interpersonal elements of cohesion can be found in a group member's sense of belonging and acceptance and a personal commitment and allegiance to the group. Intragroup elements include attractiveness and compatibility felt among the group; mutual liking and trust; support, caring, and mutual stimulation that creates learning; and collective commitment to the "work" of the group. (Burlingame, Fuhriman, & Johnson, 2002, p. 71)

Research on group therapy identifies group cohesiveness as the strongest predictor of successful outcome in group therapy (Burlingame, Fuhriman, & Johnson, 2002).

Yalom and Leszcz use *catharsis* to refer to the emotional relief that follows talking out painful material, a process that also happens in individual therapy. Finally, *existential factors* center on realizing and accepting personal responsibility and the ultimate impermanence of life.

Advantages and Disadvantages

With this long list of advantages available in group therapy, you might wonder why one would do individual therapy at all, but there are clear advantages to individual therapy, too. In fact, my personal preference is to do individual (and couple) therapy, both because the logistics of organizing and running a group are very difficult and because some therapeutic processes seem more likely to occur in individual therapy. (I have friends, however, who strongly prefer doing group therapy.) Acceptance and understanding from six persons are surely more powerful than from one, but they are also less likely to occur. One problem with groups is that trust is very difficult to build in even one other person, so that clients frequently hold back in group therapy material they would have talked about in individual therapy—often for good reasons. Some therapists do damage, primarily those who are "open and honest" in an attacking way (Ackerman & Hilsenroth, 2001; Lambert, Bergin, & Collins, 1977; Mohr, 1995; Yalom & Lieberman, 1971), and the group therapist often has to deal with similar interactions between group members. In fact, Roback (2000) has documented negative effects of some group therapy; clients were made worse. In individual therapy, if the client perceives the therapist as empathic, accepting, and honest, a successful outcome is much more likely (Gurman, 1977; Lambert & Barley, 2002; Lambert & Simon, 2008). But Gurman says that what little evidence exists for group therapy suggests that this finding is much weaker in this treatment format. He speculates that group members' perceptions of each other as empathic, accepting, and honest will, if we ever have the data, turn out to be more important. Gurman's prediction is largely borne out by the evidence that, in group therapy, the most powerful factor in good outcome is the relationship among group members—the sense of cohesion in the group (Burlingame, Fuhriman, & Johnson, 2002).

A format that many clients find helpful, when it is feasible, is to combine individual therapy with group therapy. This gives the opportunity for group interaction and dealing with material too sensitive for the group. The obvious disadvantage, especially when another therapist does the individual work, is that the individual therapy becomes the "real therapy" at the expense of full involvement in the group. It also can be very destructive to the group process when the group therapist sees some of the group members in individual therapy, because of the secrets and implications of special status that result.

Changes in the Therapist's Role

In group therapy the therapist has a special role but still is only one of several persons with whom the clients interact. The relationships are much more complex. The clients can be together against other clients, for example, and the therapist often is a member of the group in a more personally involving way than in individual therapy. In addition, a group process is occurring at all times, and the therapist's job is often to comment on and intervene in this process. The clients are still the primary problem solvers. The therapist (and group members) still needs to be evocatively empathic, accepting, and honest. But much more is involved.

■ Couples and Families

One dissatisfaction that is often voiced with individual therapy is that it is removed from the person's life, especially when he or she is involved in significant relationships—that the person can't really change except in relation to those significant others. The most obvious instance of this is in married and cohabiting couples and in families, but even "network therapy" is sometimes tried, in which many people in a client's life are brought together as a group. It's not unheard of to see a client, spouse, and lover together, although skills in addition to evocative empathy, acceptance, and genuineness might be handy to have.

You're Dealing with a System

The fundamental principle that guides and justifies family and couple therapy is that these persons who live together are an interacting system, and changes in one part of a system cannot occur without changes in another part. Bell (1963) tells of his having to switch from the perspective that the client was a problem to the insight that "the family is the problem!" (p. 3). From this basic principle, family therapists argue that treatment should occur within the context of the entire family—within the system that maintains the problem. Franklin and Jordan (1999, 2002) present an overview of theory and technique in family therapy.

The Relationship Is the Client

A common risk in couple and family therapy is that one person will become singled out as the *identified patient*. Usually, the initial contact made for therapy does center on the problems of one person, and so one task of the therapist is to take the perspective, and help the clients take the perspective, that no one is the patient. The relationship is the focus of treatment. Often one spouse will be "willing to come in if it will help" the other spouse. Sometimes therapists let a statement like this pass, as a means of engaging the reluctant family member, but the perspective should be shifted to the relationship as soon as possible without driving anyone from therapy.

Make Them Feel Understood

This won't come as a big surprise, but your first and most fundamental task is to make each member of the family feel understood—both because that will facilitate his or her problem solving as it does in individual therapy and because you have no coercive power to make a person engage in what is inevitably a difficult process. One family therapist I know talks about various techniques and interventions she uses but says that she does none of these things until she has "won the family." The therapeutic alliance is just as important here as it is in individual therapy. You can be brilliant and have a hundred therapeutic tools, but nothing will work until you have won the family. Rait (2000) says, "[V]irtually every prominent clinical theorist has addressed the importance of establishing and maintaining a positive thera-peutic relationship with the family" (p. 211). Establishing a good alliance is essential, but it is also difficult. "The alliance in couples and family treatment differs from the alliance in individual psychotherapy in that the couples and family therapist must establish and maintain multiple alliances" (Rait, 2000, p. 211). You really have to be alert and fully present.

More Direction of the Process

Family therapy is communication-based, and its effectiveness comes pri-marily from changing destructive patterns of communication between the members of the couple or family. As with group therapy, the therapist's job is often to comment on the nature of the process and to directly change it. With a couple, I often empathically respond to one person and turn to the other to ask, "How did you hear that?" Or sometimes I will simply ask one of them to tell me what the other has said. You will often be startled at how helpless this leaves the person, who, it turns out, wasn't listening to a thing. Usually I don't let the person stew and get threatened (like all rules, this one gets bro-ken sometimes) too long before I say what I thought I heard the other person say. Gradually, the clients start to be able to articulate what the others are say-ing, although they may do so grudgingly. In a sense, I am forcing empathic listening between the individuals.

Fading Out as a Communication Channel

The goal is that the couple or family be each others' therapists, in the sense that they are understanding and accepting of each other. You can think of the therapist as one point of a triangle with a couple (or as the hub of a wheel with a family). At first, the communication flows from each individual through the therapist, who is listening to everybody. Later in therapy, the goal is that the communication occur between the clients, as the therapist gradu-ally fades out and becomes unnecessary. You won't be able to force this change simply by ordering it. The clients will start listening to each other and risking communication with each other only as it becomes safe and reward-ing to do so. You teach by your example of listening and by keeping the pro-cess going in positive ways.

Emotion Matters Here Too

Family and couple therapy almost always involves intense emotion. There will be lots of emotion—both positive and negative—between the clients, and each individual will also be dealing with internal emotions. Bischoff (2008) says, "Whatever theoretical perspective we bring to bear when conducting cou-ple therapy, the research evidence to date is so convincing that it would be irre-sponsible to not consider and address the role of emotions in therapy" (p. 363). Emotion has to be dealt with sensitively, and the evidence Bischoff cites says that the therapist needs to be sure that positive emotion predominates as much as possible. Family and couple therapy needs to be focused on problem solving, of course, and this inevitably means some negative emotion will emerge. But it is a mistake to encourage a process of "getting it all out" through expression of lots of negative emotion. Your job is to create a place where the family or couple feel safe to self-disclose and to be empathic without fearing that showing each other understanding will make the empathic person vulnerable to attack. Interestingly, it is especially important that male partners be able to self-disclose and be empathic; this has a very strong impact on therapy, probably because self-disclosure and empathy are usually less common among male partners.

One approach to couples therapy that is supported by a growing body of research is Emotionally Focused Therapy (EFT) with couples. Johnson (2007) describes it this way:

> A focus on emotional processing in the present moment, on process factors and on a genuine empathic connection with both clients is at the heart of this model. The creation of new patterns of emotional responses results in the creation of key new interactional responses. EFT is empirically validated on several levels: on the level of treatment outcome, and on the levels of the relational theory in which it is based and key moments and factors in the change process. (p. 47)

EFT combines experiential and cognitive processes in therapy with couples, using the principles we have been studying for individual therapy.

Goals—Explicit and Implicit

Setting goals in individual therapy is a complex enough process. In couple and family therapy, several individuals' best interests are involved, and these interests often conflict. Even the format in which clients are seen implies certain goals. Ideally, I say to all involved that my goal is that they all find the most satisfying solutions they can. But even before therapy starts, there is sometimes a decision about whether a separated couple should be seen together or each separately or whether only one person will be seen in therapy. Seeing them together carries more implication that reconciliation is a goal than seeing them separately. How will you make this decision? If a couple with children asks for help with their marriage, will you include the children in the sessions? One person in a couple might be quite decided that the relationship is over but afraid to tell the other person, who is still quite hopeful that they can work things out. This situation would probably call for couple sessions to clarify the situation but could quickly change to individual sessions. The point is that family and couple therapy nearly always involves complex and different specific goals. As with individual therapy, goals will emerge and change in the process of therapy, but it is an issue to which you will have to be very alert.

Cotherapy

In doing sex therapy, Masters and Johnson (1980; see also Masters, Johnson, & Kolodny, 1992) recommend the use of male/female therapist teams so that each client will have a "friend in court" to facilitate the feeling of being understood. This often is an advantage of cotherapy. Another advantage is that, especially with families, the interpersonal dynamics are so complex and so often involve the therapist that it is easy to lose perspective on the process and feel overwhelmed. Having a partner often permits one therapist to hang back, be less involved, and bring a different perspective to the process. In addition, it is often a rewarding shared experience for the cotherapists to be working together. Particularly with families, having a cotherapist helps, whether the therapists are of different genders or not. The biggest problem seems to be economics. When seeing therapists who are in private practice, few families or couples can afford two therapists at once, and the caseloads of many agencies are so large that cotherapy is not practical. This is an unfortunate reality, and so if you have a chance to do cotherapy in training, grab it.

Combining Multiple-Client and Individual Sessions

One serious problem with couple and family therapy is that, for all the advantages of seeing people together, there are a lot of things people just won't say in the presence of other family members, especially early in treatment. There are issues of mistrust and unwillingness to become vulnerable by giving the other person ammunition. There is no easy solution to this problem, and my experience has been that the most productive approach is different for couples than for families. With families, as with group therapy, there are so many permutations of relationships that individual sessions with one person (or some persons) in the family help make that person the "identified patient" and set up a special status that breeds mistrust of the therapist in other members of the family. The therapist could try to see each family member equally in individual sessions, but that is seldom practical, and so it is usually best to settle for a role in concentrating on changing family processes.

With couples it is a more manageable (but still complicated) matter to say that the main work of therapy is in couple sessions. You need to communicate that the relationship is the client, that the goal is to establish solutions as a couple, but that you will occasionally see each of them individually. If there are cotherapists, it is important that each therapist see each client, so that neither therapist becomes identified as "on the side" of one person. Masters and Johnson (1980; see also Masters, Johnson, & Kolodny, 1992) report considerable success with this format, but the ground rules are tricky and therefore must be made absolutely clear. I usually say, "The purpose of these sessions is that sometimes there are things that are hard to say in front of the other person, especially at first. If either of you wants things kept private from the individual sessions, you can say so, and I will respect that. Whether we deal with those things eventually in couple sessions will be up to you." This requires a good memory in the therapist and carries some clear risks, but my experience has been that such sessions are especially helpful early in therapy and that they actually facilitate the couple's dealing with threatening issues more quickly. The issues often would never come up just in couple sessions, but trying them out in individual sessions helps make them more manageable.

Individual versus Couple or Family Therapy

Proponents of family therapy sometimes seem to be saying that a person in a relationship should always be treated with the others involved in that relationship. In my opinion, this is clearly an overstatement. Individual therapy is often called for with individuals in families and couples, but it is also often destructive to the extent that it ignores the effect it has on other relationships. There is a place for both approaches, but deciding when each is appropriate is difficult.

The ideal principle is that problems that result mainly from internal conflicts (see chapters 16 and 17) are best suited to individual therapy, and those that result from poor communication patterns are best handled with multiple client approaches. In practice, though, there are elements of both in nearly all problems. You will need to be flexible enough to feel free to consider both general approaches, depending on the demands of particular circumstances. To do this you will need training in family and couple therapy. Abraham Maslow is often quoted as saying, in another context, "I suppose it is tempting, if the only tool you have is a hammer, to treat everything as if it were a nail" (1966, pp. 15–16). Try to have as many tools as possible.

■ Cultural Diversity and Therapy*

The fields of counseling and therapy have a long and unfortunate history of ignoring and underserving ethnic minority clients. There are powerful reasons for this to change, and professional groups are focusing increasing attention on the problem (American Psychological Association, 2003). "Minority clients underutilize psychotherapy services and have high rates of dropping out of treatment" (Vasquez, 2007, p. 878). There are disproportionately few psychologists who are members of ethnic minorities. The services that are available tend to be of low quality (Fouad & Arredondo, 2007). There are many reasons for this neglect—political, professional, and personal; the therapeutic alliance is essential in therapy, but ethnic minority clients might have a harder time experiencing it; misunderstandings between therapists and clients are probably more likely when they're from different backgrounds; the general context of therapy is based on several unacknowledged assumptions; cultural biases influence practitioners. But there are obviously many reasons to do what we can to become culturally competent therapists. Ethnic minorities are a large and growing population who face intense stressors and who need far more mental health services than are available.

This chapter will give you only an overview of how to be a culturally competent therapist, and you would enjoy other more complete books on the subject, such as *Counseling the Culturally Diverse: Theory and Practice, 4th edition* (Sue & Sue, 2003). Fouad and Arredondo (2007) have written *Becoming Culturally Oriented: Practical Advice for Psychologists and Educators,* and *Culture, Psy-*

---

*I thank Dr. Rob Santos for his help with this section.

chotherapy and Counseling (Hoshmand, 2006) is a collection of papers that you would probably find helpful. *Inclusive Cultural Empathy* (Pedersen, Crethar, & Carlson, 2008) is a comprehensive text that combines theoretical understanding, information about cultures, and practical advice.

Cultural Competence

Whatever your own culture is, you will almost certainly be working with clients from other cultures at some point; our field is rapidly moving toward more inclusive practice. Becoming a culturally competent therapist has more to do with perspective and attitudes than it does with learning new techniques. I will make some suggestions about methods to use and will certainly talk about being empathic and forming a good relationship, but we also need to look at you as a flexible, open person. "Cultural competence is not a technique but a way of construing the therapeutic encounter" (Sue, 2003, p. 968).

Many attempts have been made to define cultural competence, and they generally include three major elements. Cultural competence is a function of the therapist's (1) cultural awareness and beliefs, (2) cultural knowledge, and (3) cultural skills (American Psychological Association, 2003; Sue, 2006; Sue, Zane, Hall, & Berger, 2009).

Knowing Yourself: Cultural Awareness and Beliefs

"The provider is sensitive to her or his personal values and biases and how these may influence perceptions of the client, the client's problem, and the counseling relationship" (Sue, Zane, Hall, & Berger, 2009, p. 529). Therapy is already complex when you're treating clients with whom you share a language and general cultural background. It isn't easy to enter another person's experiential life with deep understanding and acceptance, and doing so with a person from a culture different than yours requires a high level of self-awareness. You especially need to be aware of your biases and your assumptions about the nature of reality—your worldview.

Self-awareness: Your worldview is like the air you breathe. Your advice, empathic understanding, judgments, interpretations, and opinions are all filtered through your cultural biases—many of which are not shared by other cultures and many of which you are only partially aware of. Sue (2006) urges therapists to know their own stimulus value. "Counselor know thy cultural self" (p. 240). The more clearly and accurately you know your own values, prejudices, defenses, and blind spots, the more comfortable you can be in forming relationships with clients and the more likely you are not to confuse your views with universal truths. You can more easily see things through the client's perspective.

All of us have biases that interfere with how well we hear our clients, and these biases operate largely without our awareness. Our *confirmation bias* makes us more likely to perceive events and information that are consistent with what we already believe and to fail to perceive disconfirming evidence.

The *actor/observer bias* leads us to attribute our own bad behavior to the pressures of circumstances and other people's similar bad behavior to flaws in their character. Social psychologists have identified many more biases like these, and they all should make us worry and be humble about the accuracy of our beliefs. They also should motivate us to seek consultation, get good therapy, and be as self-aware as possible.

Working cross-culturally adds another level of bias that we seldom think about. Your culture has taught you a worldview—a set of beliefs and perceptions that are so much part of your functioning that they just seem obviously self-evident. Is it best that marriage should be based on love? The answer "yes" seems painfully obvious to most people from North America, but the majority of cultures in the world don't believe this, and North Americans believe it much more strongly now than they did even 50 years ago (Miller & Perlman, 2009). Is it human nature to want to excel? People from many cultures would be ashamed to be singled out for praise; it would violate the good of the group. Do you believe that everything that happens has a cause? Are humans free to make choices? These last two seem self-evident to most Westerners, but we don't even notice that these two beliefs are logically inconsistent with each other. These few examples are meant to alert you to the unconscious but powerful hold your worldview has on you and to motivate you to examine your assumptions. The other thing they should do is to make you humbly receptive when you see a client from another culture.

Cultural biases.   There is often subtle condescension in our cultural biases; without much awareness, it is easy to see people who are different from us as simpler than we are. Vasquez (2007) worries about the impact of *microaggressions,* in which a person with privilege or power subtly communicates attitudes of superiority and denigration in cross-cultural communications. Her unsettling observation is, "Microaggressions are often perpetrated by well-meaning people who hold egalitarian beliefs but who have not become aware of their negative attitudes and stereotypes about people of color and/or who have not had sufficient contact with people different from themselves" (p. 880–881; also see Fouad & Arredondo, 2007) Most of us are *well-meaning people who hold egalitarian beliefs,* and so we need to be humble and vigilant about our self-awareness. Pedersen, Crethar, and Carlson (2008) claim, "Counselors are all vulnerable to cultural encapsulation. . . . A culturally encapsulated counselor sees the world through a cultural lens without recognizing that many of her or his perceptions may in fact be biased and thus damaging to clients" (pp. 93–94), but, for example, with regard to racial biases, "not all racism is intentional. . . . [R]acism commonly emerges as an unintentional action of well-meaning people" (p. 80). These writers seem to be ganging up on us well-meaning people, but their point matters. Our cultural biases are powerful and must be taken seriously if we hope to overcome them.

Cultural biases inherent in therapy in our culture.   Bias doesn't just occur in us as individuals; the very structure of our profession hides some unspoken assumptions. The goals and processes of counseling and therapy are often subtle and more culturally biased than we realize (Hoshmand, 2006; McClure & Teyber, 1996). As I describe these assumptions of therapy, in some cases you probably will think, "But what's wrong with believing that?" I'm not judging these characteristics as good or bad; the point is that these are all commonly accepted assumptions in Western culture, but they are rejected by some other cultures:

- Implicitly, most therapy approaches encourage individuation and individual empowerment, often at the expense of being securely attached to others; empowerment sounds good; dependency sounds bad. More broadly, the individual good is emphasized over the good of the group or the system.
- We value and emphasize the psychological over the social.
- Therapy often promotes prescriptions about how men and women should think, feel and act.
- Western psychotherapy often values cognitive functioning over emotional functioning.
- Therapy is usually described as "intervention," a word that strongly implies that professionals do things to clients rather than with clients.
- Therapy is seen as a commodity that is exchanged for remuneration.
- We avoid language that implies morality or love as part of therapy, and we avoid the spiritual or metaphysical—or at most we accept only a limited number of spiritual views. Pedersen, Crethar, and Carlson, (2008) say:

> [T]here appears to be a lack of connection between the perspectives of clients and the perspectives of psychologists when it comes to religion and spirituality. If religion and spirituality are important to our clients' worldviews, then they should also be important to us as culturally inclusive counselors. (p. 105)

Self-awareness and professional awareness are dauntingly large achievements that will require a serious commitment.

Cultural Knowledge

> The counselor has knowledge of the client's culture, worldview, and expectations for the counseling relationship. (Sue, Zane, Hall, & Berger, 2009, p. 529)

Learning culture-specific information.   Learning as much as you can about your clients' culture is a way of showing respect, and it helps you understand better. It can build your credibility with clients as long as you demonstrate humble interest and don't try to show off how knowledgeable you are. Through reading, you can acquire intellectual knowledge about the key identity issues related to at least one or two other cultures. It isn't possible, obviously, to learn a great deal about many cultures, and it is likely that the cross-cultural therapy you do will be with clients from just one or a few cultures. Key identity issues include race, gender, language, religion, education, family structure, education, intergenerational patterns, religion/spirituality, and political history (especially if it includes oppression or traumatization). Having intellectual knowledge will help you connect with clients, but you should also arrange to have some experiential knowledge. There is value in having your client educate you about his or her culture, and it will help you form a better alliance if you have also participated in an event particular to your client's culture, such as attending a religious ceremony or a wedding, participating in a sweat lodge, attending a soccer match, or going to a culture-specific concert.

Specific cultural knowledge will also help you with what Sue (2006) calls "dynamic sizing," which consists of

> skills in knowing when to generalize and be inclusive and when to individualize and be exclusive in working with clients. That is, the therapist can flexibly generalize in a valid manner. The skills are quite important because one of the major dilemmas facing individuals is how to appreciate culture without stereotyping. Often, when the cultural values or characteristics of various groups are discussed, there is a stereotypic quality to the discussion. Statements such as, "Asians are collective rather than individualistic in orientation," "Native Americans appreciate nature in contrast to Americans who try to master nature," and "For African Americans, the Church and spirituality are important," can be viewed as accurate cultural portrayals or overgeneralizations and stereotypes. On the one hand, the statements may reveal important cultural characteristics of groups. Those who are skilled in dynamic sizing are able to avoid stereotypes of members of a group while still appreciating the importance of culture. (p. 239)

Dangers of a little knowledge. Dynamic sizing is an important skill to develop, but it is deceptively difficult to master. Learning culture-specific information is helpful, but it also carries the significant danger of encouraging generalizing and stereotyping. There probably is no way to become really familiar with another culture unless you live in the culture for a long time. The nuances of meaning and language are enormously complicated. "Culture is complex and not simple" (Pedersen, Crethar, & Carlson 2008, p. 70). In our wish to honor and understand the worldview of clients from other cultures we sometimes develop shallow knowledge. Our intentions are good, but it's easy to cling to generalizations that give us the illusion of more understanding than we really have. Even worse, if you know many therapists who work with another culture, chances are good that you know at least one who has a false pride in being expert on that culture.

Often we learn some generalizations that have some truth to them and our little bits of knowledge are both a blessing and a curse. "We are both similar and different at the same time," (Pedersen, Crethar, & Carlson, 2008, p.

62). Our similarities and our culture-specific knowledge can help us understand more quickly, but they can also blind us to exceptions. These bits of
knowledge comfort us as something we "know," but for every such observation there are thousands of people for whom it's not true, and some of them
will be your clients. The message of this whole section is that absolutely every
client you will ever see is different, and your job is to know this particular client. If you are open, you will never have a client who doesn't surprise you.

Cultural Skills

> The counselor has the ability to intervene in a manner that is culturally
> sensitive and relevant. (Sue, Zane, Hall, & Berger, 2009, p. 529)

Culture and the alliance. There is overwhelming research evidence that
the therapeutic alliance is the strongest predictor of successful therapy, but
very little of that research has been done specifically about cross-cultural
counseling. Cross-cultural research is increasing for some ethnic groups but
not others, and there does seem to be enough evidence to conclude that therapy is effective with ethnic minority clients (Miranda, Bernal, Lau, Kohn,
Hwang, LaFromboise, 2005). Still, we don't have much evidence about the
role of the alliance. In spite of this, virtually all writers in the cross-cultural
field assume that the relationship between successful outcome and the alliance holds for ethnic minority clients too, and the real problem is determin-
ing whether minority clients have a fair chance to experience a good
therapeutic alliance.

> Attention to the therapeutic relationship and the working alliance with cli-
> ents/patients of color may require special considerations. What are the
> unique issues that may interfere with the therapeutic alliance of clients dif-
> ferent from psychotherapists? . . . One issue is that [because of uncon-
> scious biases] psychologists may not always be aware of when the
> potential for developing an effective therapeutic alliance may be compro-
> mised. . . . Although there is mixed evidence, most clients of color are
> more comfortably matched with therapists similar to them. More specifi-
> cally, clients working with clinicians of similar ethnic backgrounds and
> languages tend to remain in treatment longer than do clients whose thera-
> pists are not ethnically or linguistically matched. (Vasquez, 2007, p. 880;
> see also Farsimadan, Draghi-Lorenz, & Ellis, 2007)

Culture and empathy. The essence of therapy is in making clients feel
deeply known as they really are and deeply accepted as they really are. Being
empathic with a person from another culture is extremely important and
extremely complex. It is in the service of becoming more empathic that we
have spent so much time on your awareness of your worldview. "This awareness of the subjective nature of their own worldview seems to make effective
counselors willing to suspend their worldview more readily and enter more
fully into the subjective experience of others" (McClure & Teyber, 1996, p.
12). Temporarily suspending your worldview takes focus and awareness, and

it usually causes the therapist some discomfort; it is inevitably somewhat threatening to consider the possibility that what seems obvious to you about reality might not be the whole story. This discomfort arose in college students in an experiment by Nelson and Baumgarte (2004). When students were asked to make judgments about people demonstrating unfamiliar cultural norms, they were less empathic and assigned more blame to the target person. For example, in one scenario a manager's efforts resulted in his receiving an award. The manager, John, then was "mortified by the individual attention and wondered why the division as a whole was not recognized for their success. The incident left John feeling depressed and dissatisfied at work" (p. 395). No mention was made to the students who were giving their opinions about this scenario of cultural differences. The students were aware only of John's anxiety over what was to them the cultural norm of taking pride in winning an award. John's reaction caused the students to be less empathic, and judge negatively.

We can see from the example above how easy it is for us to judge, unconsciously, because we are not starting with a clean slate; we are operating from what is embedded in us. Therefore, we must work hard to suspend our worldview and acquire as much new knowledge as we can so that we can "understand clients' perspectives" (Sue, 2006, p. 243).

Empathy on steroids.   Cross-cultural empathy is not much different from the empathy we have been learning together in previous chapters. It is just harder to do because there are barriers of language, knowledge, and worldview. I know—I've already asked you to be fully present, to be mindful, to be in the zone at times, to enter the client's experiential world, to cognitively make sense out of that experiential world, and to help the client feel known and accepted. What more could we want? Nothing, really, except that you do empathy on steroids; understanding a person from another culture requires new work from you and a heightened alertness to the barriers you have to overcome.

> Even though studies have shown that ethnic similarity between the counselor and the client create obvious advantages and increase the probability of a positive therapeutic outcome, ethnic similarity is not a prerequisite to achieving cultural empathy. The display of culturally sensitive responses and attitudes by the counselor is more important than an ethnic match. (Chung & Bemak, 2002, p. 156)

Empathic communication may not even require much shared language. This was demonstrated by Bill Coulson's session, transcribed in Appendix A of this book. He saw a Japanese woman for a session, and, even though they struggled linguistically, they seemed to connect in a helpful way. Alberta and Wood (2009) use a broad definition of "empathic communication" in cross-cultural therapy "because, while language represents an important aspect of cultural competence, it is often an overrated one; . . . communication goes beyond language" (p. 567). Sometimes just sitting in pensive silence is deeply connecting. The fundamental issue is: does your client feel that you "get" him or her?

Some special methods of a culturally competent therapist.   Stanley Sue is one of the most prolific researchers and writers on cultural competence in therapy, and he has outlined several aspects of treatment that are unique to cross-cultural counseling (Sue, 2006, pp. 240–244).

Assessment of client.   It is important to assess two major issues about an ethnic minority client. First, you need to consider the degree to which a client is acculturated into the dominant culture. There is huge variability within ethnic groups in the degree to which individuals have adopted the culture of mainstream North America. Clients who are not very acculturated will retain the values and behaviors of their country of origin and probably would work better with a counselor who is ethnically and culturally matched. The second area of assessment is to determine how important minority-group experiences have been in the person's life. If a client has been the victim of intense discrimination and racism, consideration should be given to finding a therapist whose race or social position won't make it difficult to for a relationship to form.

Pretherapy intervention.   People from other cultures are often not familiar with Western psychotherapy, how it is structured, and how it can help with problems. There is evidence that a kind of psychoeducational presentation (about what to expect in therapy, the nature of confidentiality, the roles that therapists and clients play, and other similar information) seems to increase both participation in and success of therapy.

Hypothesizing and testing hypotheses.   Sue suggests forming and testing hypotheses about the client, especially when the therapist is not sure if the client's behaviors, attitudes, and situations are the result of the client's internal issues or are being influenced by culture. Some of his suggestions for testing these hypotheses include gathering evidence from others in the client's life. I have concern about the impact this might have on the relationship with and trust of the therapist, however.

Attending to credibility and giving.   *Ascribed credibility* is the trust attributed to a therapist by cultural beliefs and values. *Achieved credibility* is trust earned by the individual therapist. When working with Western clients, therapists generally start out with some ascribed credibility, partly because most people who make it into therapy have a general idea of what therapy is and that it has professional status. Clients from other cultures may have little idea of what therapy is and why they should trust the therapist. In fact, many cultural values would interfere with credibility, values such as "only the weak seek help" or "only older people have wisdom" or "women defer to men." The therapist should be especially aware of the credibility issue and take special measures to earn achieved credibility. One strategy that can help is the pretherapy intervention described above. Once therapy has started, it often helps to build credibility to give the client a "gift" of a direct benefit from treatment, in the first session if possible. Possibilities might include a specific tension reliever such as progressive muscle relaxation, a gentle focusing session if the person seems amenable, or specific advice or useful information. These "gifts" can be given within the context of building a relationship and generally being empathic—that is, doing the things in therapy that will be helpful in the long term, along with a quick credibility builder.

Understanding the nature of discomfort and resistance.   Therapists should be ready for their own frustration, discomfort, and resistance when working with clients whose values and expectations are not what the therapist is used to. Clients might be more likely to question the value of therapy or respond belligerently or, the opposite, respond unusually passively. In both cases, the therapist might be caught off guard in new territory. Sue says to expect more of your own discomfort and use that discomfort to explore and understand your own issues. In a sense, if you feel discomfort, frustration, and resistance in therapy, it's a counterransference issue. Therapy is about the client; why are you so bothered by what is happening? It is an opportunity to learn, especially if you can consult a colleague about your reactions.

Strategizing or planning for intervention.   By this, Sue does not mean that you make plans for the client. He is recommending that you think carefully about what approach you are going to take. Your plan might be to take a very unstructured approach, for example. The point is that you must be alert and aware of why you are doing what you're doing. This might seem an obvious requirement, but you can often develop a rhythm and usual way of doing things in therapy; cross-cultural therapy requires more conscious awareness of that rhythm and knowing that it may need to be altered or abandoned.

Assessing the session.   After every session you should ask yourself how well the session went—kind of a mini outcome evaluation in which you consider issues like your level of credibility, the strength of your alliance, opportunities for giving the client "gifts" of concrete benefits, and what would be helpful in the next session.

Having the willingness to consult.   Finally, it is important to consult with colleagues about treatment and to consult with sources of culturally-specific information that might inform your treatment.

■ Culturally Competent Therapy Looks a Lot like Competent Therapy

Wampold (2007) makes a strong case that "the essential aspect of psychotherapy is that a new, more adaptive explanation is acquired by the patient" (p. 862) and that this explanation of the presenting problem "must be different from presently held explanations for a patient's troubles but not sufficiently discrepant from the patient's intuitive notions of mental functioning as to be rejected. A corollary is that the explanation . . . must be consonant with the cultural context of the healing practice" (p. 864) and is highly dependent on the therapeutic relationship. This is a general description of the basic change that occurs in all effective approaches to therapy. It says that the change must always take the client's culture into account, whether the therapist is from the same culture or not. It also says that the "new, more adaptive explanation" emerges from the human connection. The fundamental principles are the same ones we've been talking about for 12 chapters.

I don't want to dilute the importance of understanding cultural competence with ethnic minority clients, but if culturally competent therapy looks a lot like competent therapy, we do need to know that good therapy is based on the same principles with virtually all of our clients. In a way, all of your clients will be from a "different culture," unless they are exactly like you, which they never will be. When I see a female client, I will have special difficulty understanding her because there are so many important ways that a woman's experience is different from anything I can know directly. In fact, some writers argue that gender issues are a cultural diversity issue (Becker, 2006; Gere, 2006). When a Canadian therapist sees a client born and raised in California there clearly are cultural differences, even if both people are middle-class females of the same race. There can be miscommunications built into conversations between clients and therapists from different social classes. Being from different ethnic backgrounds is obviously an important issue, but it's just more difficult than some other situations. It's also less difficult than some other situations. No one can ever fully understand another person; but we try, we come close sometimes, and some ways of being come closer than others. Most importantly, coming close really helps.

■ Weaving the Principles into Other Jobs and into Your Life

Many of you will work in helping professions that deliver services in settings other than counseling and therapy. The skills we are discussing still will be the foundation of your work. Unless you have coercive power over clients, your best hope of having an influence will still lie in your relationship with them. If you are doing work training or occupational therapy, arranging housing, taking abused children into care, nursing a patient back to health, or doing any other job that includes human contact, making the other person feel understood will powerfully enhance your effectiveness. You still go about the methods of your profession, but you constantly are guided by attuning yourself to the other person and hearing his or her intended message. This attunement is relatively rare, and, partly because it is rare, your clients will respond to it with a hunger to interact with you. You seamlessly weave listening into all of your ways of operating, and this empowers your clients or students or children or partners. There is an almost Zen-like paradox here; the more direct control I give up, the more influence I have.

This even applies to business and sales. I once attended a local "Sportsman's Show" and ran into one of our graduate students who was there selling windsurfers. He called me over and said enthusiastically, "I just took a sales course, and it's all evocative empathy!" I replied, "Yeah, it's powerful, and it can be used to manipulate people, I guess." His boss (who, by coincidence, had taken an undergraduate course from me) overheard us and said, "We don't manipulate people. We just help them know what they want." This was just bantering, but it revealed a fundamental truth about influence. Watch how the best salespeople make you feel like they "really get you" and make you comfortable with them.

Finally, and maybe most importantly for your life, your close relationships must include good listening to have any chance of flourishing. This topic is way beyond this book, of course, but I strongly recommend *Getting the Love You Want* (Hendrix, 2008) as a practical and insightful guide to enhancing intimacy in your life.

Taking Care of Yourself

By Caelin White and David Martin

> *. . . I promise you this:*
> *I will tend to my own healing*
> *so we do not stumble over my pain.*
>
> —Ginn Buzzell, in Remen (1991, p. 22)

■ The Importance of Self-Care

Of the many elements that contribute to good therapy, the least obvious may be the therapist's self-care. It is the job of the therapist to manage the therapeutic process (Kurtz, 2005), so the therapist must be stable, resilient, and able to provide a "container" within which the client's unfolding process can take place. We want this chapter to encourage you to take good care of yourself—both for your sake and for the sake of your clients. You need to live well and to have the resources to keep the client as the focus of therapy, rather than having you abandon the client for any reason (such as stress or distraction) or holding your clients back (because of places you can't go in therapy).

In *Self-nurture: Learning to Care for Yourself as Effectively as You Care for Everyone Else,* Domar and Dreher (2000) say that there are four reasons the therapist needs to be well taken care of—to be "resourced."

First, if the therapist isn't resourced, he or she cannot be in an emotionally supportive role for the client. The inability of many therapists to cope with sensitive or painful information presented by clients often results from the inability to self-nurture. Everybody struggles, and your struggles can potentially interfere with your ability to support, empathize, and develop a meaningful connection with your clients. You will always be struggling and growing, but with self-care—with being well resourced—you can reduce the amount your own issues interfere with therapy.

The second reason is that we have a professional and moral obligation to be well resourced. When a client arrives for a session he or she expects the therapist to be both prepared and eager to go wherever the client needs to go in that session. The therapist must provide emotional "substance" with which the client can connect. Any distractions or issues occurring in the therapist's life prior to and during a session should be acknowledged and somehow resolved by the therapist (even if only temporarily) in order to provide as good an experience as possible for the client. You need to leave your issues at the therapy room door, at least during the session. This issue may seem similar to the first point, but it is different; beyond our wanting to provide the optimal experience for the client, we are morally required to do so. Norcross and Guy (2005) call therapist self-care an "ethical imperative" (p. 5).

The third reason is that being well resourced will improve your own health and well-being. It would be ironic if we didn't practice what we preached, and as professional practitioners in the mental health field we know that it is important to care for both our internal and external environments; we know how important self-care is.

Fourth, we need to model resources for our clients. We need to "walk the talk" and model self-care, even if we don't directly teach clients our own specific life solutions. If we don't provide ourselves with self-care it is like a "sin of omission," if we expect the client to do otherwise.

We will discuss a number of ways for you to take care of yourself and hope that this will both help you along the path and give you permission to make self-care a high priority in your life. Many therapists suffer from an exaggerated need to be helpful—maybe even an exaggerated need to rescue others. Being helpful is a wonderful thing, but, without self-care, it can lead to burnout. Burnout in a therapist is an ugly thing; the therapist starts to run out of resources and starts (mostly without awareness) to push clients away with unexpected coldness or rejection. Or the therapist might "find reasons" to terminate therapy prematurely or become inappropriately controlling. None of this comes from malice; it is the burned out therapist's way of surviving by escaping stress.

Taking care of oneself as a therapist is significantly different than taking care of oneself in many other professions; it involves more than simply getting eight hours of sleep each night and eating your vegetables. Providing effective psychotherapy requires a large stash of emotional energy and clarity about your own issues. The sooner the beginning therapist starts developing the resources to manage his or her energy the less likely he or she will be to burn out. Loehr and Schwartz (2003) refer to burning out, or the failure to effectively manage personal energy, as being "wired up, but melting down." Conversely, effective energy management

> allows one to bounce back from disappointment and frustration, to sustain focus and concentration over time, to move between rational and intuitive, and embrace multiple points of view . . . [and] increase tolerance for values and beliefs that are different from one's own. (p. 11)

There are many reasons to "do your own work." Your life will be better, and you will be better equipped to be your clients' brave companion with the strength, flexibility, and resilience to "go into the pit" or "walk through the fire" with your clients as they stand in the face of their own experiencing.

■ Getting Centered: Being Present, Grounded, Contained, and Boundaried

The quality of the therapeutic relationship is the best predictor of success in therapy, and the person of the therapist is an essential part of that relationship. It is also important to know that the therapeutic relationship is reciprocal—not in the sense that the therapist shares the focus of therapy, but rather that what the therapist says and does affects the client, and what the client says and does affects the therapist (Taylor, 1995). Being mindful of your own experience and internal state during a session is essential to the process of therapy.

Many events in a session can interfere with the therapist providing an effective therapeutic experience; you can be thrown off your stride. For example, the client has said something you strongly disagree with or that you find offensive. If you are not centered within yourself, your reaction could easily take you away from providing the client acceptance and empathy. As another example of becoming distracted, during a session you suddenly realize you forgot to lock the front door when you left the house. This time, the client isn't the source of the distraction, but you still might "leave the room" mentally and break the flow of therapy.

These kinds of distractions will occur at times, but there are ways to center yourself that soften your reactions. In order to stay centered, the therapist needs to be resourced in four specific ways: being (1) present, (2) grounded, (3) contained, and (4) boundaried.

Being Present

We discussed the role of presence in chapter 8 and learned there is a "quiet intensity" in being present. The client is a kind of "mantra" or object of meditative focus for the therapist. The therapist disappears, in the sense that only the client's experiencing matters in this moment. Without the therapist being fully present, his or her reflection of the client's experience will likely be inarticulate, vague, and off-target.

In this chapter we are still interested in being present with the client, but we also need to think of presence in more general terms, such as being "tuned in" to your environment at the same time you are aware of your internal experiencing. Do you live with mindful presence, or do you live distractedly?

Living with presence is an awareness of each moment as a single, holistic experience comprised both of perceptions of the outside world and of sensations within the body; it is being mindful. As psychiatrist R. D. Laing writes:

> The range of what we think and do
> Is limited by what we fail to notice
> And because we fail to notice

There is little we can do
To change
Until we notice
How failing to notice
Shapes our thoughts and deeds. (quoted in Clarke, Mackaness, Ball, & Horita, 2003, p. 15)

Presence is a way of noticing, through which we are able to learn about ourselves and our clients and the unique characteristics of their therapeutic process. There are hundreds of ways to grow in mindfulness, and we will discuss a few of them later in this chapter.

Being Grounded and Contained

Though being "grounded" and being "contained" are different concepts, they are related, and so we will discuss them together. Being grounded is the sensation of being rooted or solid. Physically, you feel firmly and heavily planted in your chair, without agitation. There is a sturdy stability to your body and a peaceful, undistracted readiness in your movements. Containment is the ability to have a sense of well-being and other emotions without a drive to talk excessively or without being distracted by wandering thoughts (Rosenberg & Rand, 1991). If we are distractible and uncontained we are likely to lose our focus on the client, and there is a danger that the client will also become less contained. Being contained is not about suppression of emotions, but rather it is about managing emotions (such as excitement, anxiety, fear, pleasure, etc.) in a way that they do not become unhelpful or lead to too much talking, laughing, or movement. It is also the ability to contain the sense of well-being (Rosenberg & Rand, 1991).

Being Boundaried

People often think of boundaries as just "saying no" or setting limits, but this view is overly simplistic. Rosenberg and Rand (1991) define being boundaried as "the sense of experience of Self that is separate from the world yet exists in harmonious relationship within it" (p. 175). Being boundaried means being clear about who you are and what is your legitimate responsibility; you have a right to your inner life, and you are responsible for your own behavior and your inner life. It is also about respecting that you do not have a right to or a responsibility for your client's behavior and inner life. In general, it is when you think that you are responsible for what goes on inside the other's self that you have violated his or her boundaries, and the therapeutic aspect of therapy is lost. A well-boundaried therapist knows to ask permission when he or she wants to explore aspects of the client's inner life, and especially the more sensitive aspects of it.

■ Specific Strategies for Self-Care

When we are present, grounded, contained, and boundaried, we are better able to provide support regardless of where the client goes in therapy. To have these resources available in a therapy session, we need to have built them ahead of time. As a resourceful therapist you need to be able to access these tools automatically, without hesitation, and this requires practice and integration of learnable skills into the therapist's daily life. As Lutz, Dunne, and Davidson (2007) argue, "Many of our core mental processes such as awareness, and attention, and emotion regulation, including our very capacity for happiness and compassion, should best be conceptualized as trainable skills" (p. 545).

There are many "trainable skills" that can help you grow as a person and as a therapist. This process of skill acquisition may sound like a lot of work for a payoff that is hard to measure, but you have much to gain personally by doing this work. There are many benefits of practicing self-care techniques beyond simply improving one's skill as a therapist; three of these are especially important. First, by integrating these tools into your daily life you will reduce your level of stress. Stress is unavoidable, and it will serve you well to have some techniques you can call on to reduce its negative impact on your life.

Second, you will also engage more fully in your life. Being energized, mindful, sensitive, and perceptive of your surroundings are just a few of the positive results of applying these tools. In turn, these results will enable you to better develop meaningful relationships with others, eat mindfully (as in avoiding the temptation to eat too much or the wrong kinds of foods and eating with intention, and/or pleasure), improve the quality of your work, exercise healthfully, and even avoid accidents.

Third, you can lessen debilitating physical symptoms. Illnesses and physical problems are often caused by stress, and it is well-established in psychoneuroimmunology that stress can result in a wide variety of suppressed functions within the immune system (McEwen, 1998; Schneiderman, Ironson, & Siegel, 2005; Selye, 1973; Solomon, Kemeny, & Temoshok, 1991; Solomon, Temoshok, O'Leary & Zich, 1997; Solomon et al., 1968). Whatever unique pattern of stress-related physical problems you develop can be reduced with self-care.

There are many self-care techniques, and we can introduce you to only a few of them. What works for you will be as personal as your fingerprint, and not all techniques will be appropriate in all circumstances; it is not always possible to engage in a 30-minute meditation between sessions. Some techniques will be more effective for longer periods of time or in more private locations, while other techniques can be used anytime and anywhere. The shared theme among effective techniques is the integration of the mind and body; the goal is to become as mindful of your whole self as possible so you can eventually manage your physiological and psychological state. We will briefly describe some of these techniques, and we will suggest some sources of more in-depth descriptions and discussions.

Breathing

The aim of mindful breathing is to connect the mind with the body by activating the autonomic nervous system. Without consciously intervening in breathing, we typically take in only enough oxygen to keep our hearts beating, organs functioning, blood flowing, and neurons firing, or, in other words, to stay alive. While this kind of "survival breathing" probably evolved because it is incredibly efficient physiologically, it is far from efficient for enhancing presence. To be present you're going to have to break the deeply entrenched habit of breathing to survive and relearn how to breathe to be mindful. One effective way is to practice "abdominal breathing" in which you direct oxygen into areas in your lower body. To ensure you are breathing this way you can hold a finger on your belly button and then breathe in slowly and deeply through your nose while pushing your belly out against your finger; this is the target area for your breathing. After you take your breath in, pause momentarily, and then slowly exhale through your mouth. A good indication that you are breathing too high (chest breathing) is if you begin to feel anxious or if you feel your shoulders or chest rise up as you inhale. Abdominal breathing is very relaxing.

However, if you are feeling tired or lethargic you may want to breathe into your upper chest as a means of increasing your level of presence. You can place your finger on the middle of your sternum and breathe into where you feel your finger. The rule of thumb is to "breathe high" for energy and "breathe low" for presence, relaxation, groundedness, and containment. If you require both energy and presence you may want to try breathing into both areas in a circular fashion; breathe the first half of your breath into your chest and the second half into your abdomen. Then exhale slowly from both areas simultaneously. As you continue to practice your breathing you will learn what works best for you—in what situations certain types of breathing help you to stay present. There is no rule about exactly where to breathe; the goal is to breathe more deeply, as a means of enhancing presence and mindfulness.

One of the best ways to maintain presence is the "square breathing" technique. The term "square" is used because it involves four steps, each taking four seconds. First, inhale slowly and deeply through your nose for four seconds, then hold for four seconds, slowly exhale through your mouth for four seconds, and again, hold for four seconds. Repeat the cycle as often as you feel the need to maintain presence. Again, the key for identifying whether you need to get present will be to recognize early symptoms such as distractibility, lack of groundedness, or need for containment.

In addition to presence, breathing helps with staying grounded because becoming ungrounded often involves the stimulation of areas higher up in the body; reversing this effect requires you to direct your focus to the foundational areas of the body, such as your legs and feet. The breathing technique for grounding also involves abdominal breathing, or breathing into the lower belly. Other techniques for grounding include feeling the "pelvic floor," legs, or feet by standing or squatting to give them more involvement, shifting weight onto the feet, and/or placing your feet flat on the floor (Aposhyan, 2004).

Meditation

One of the most powerful methods for increasing mindfulness is meditation, but it is not as straightforward as one might think; being proficient at meditation is quite challenging. The meditator is mindful of his or her internal experience, but "without thinking." There are many ways to meditate; one very helpful way is "concentrative meditation." Proper breathing is important, as is the selection of a focus word, sound, or phrase (your mantra) for oneself. When choosing your word, consider that the purpose of this word is to assist you in "letting go" of control in order to just "be" with yourself and your thoughts. The traditional sound used is "om" or "aum," which in Buddhism represents the voice of the original Buddha or the sound of the universe (depending on the source). But the choice of what works best for you is entirely yours. Some people prefer a word like "one" or "love" or another word that feels right.

To begin meditation, first find a comfortable place to sit. Once you are seated, begin by taking several slow, deep breaths. Then close your eyes and slowly count down from 10. Take a deep breath in with each number and exhale slowly between numbers. After you reach zero, continue to breathe in the same pattern and begin to repeat your focus word slowly with each breath. Effective meditation involves not judging yourself as you meditate. If you begin to experience certain thoughts or sensations simply make note of them and continue to repeat your focus word. Allow your mind to passively wander (in other words, this wandering should not be intentional). By focusing on your breathing and your focus word, you should be able to simultaneously "observe" your own thoughts, but this is meant to be a passive process. If distracting thoughts occur, just notice them as though they were bubbles drifting through your awareness and return to your breathing and mantra. You can continue to meditate as long as you find it helpful (10 to 20 minutes is a typical length of time for meditation). Once you feel you are ready to return from your meditation, gradually begin to take note of your surroundings such as the smells, sights, and sounds. Take a few moments to breathe while looking down toward the ground, and when you are ready, get up slowly.

There are also many recordings of guided meditations that are often a good way to start meditating, or you can find a group to help you learn.

Mindfulness

You already know that mindfulness is essential to therapeutic presence and is often used in therapy. In this chapter we want to focus on what it can mean to you in your self-care. It is not possible to discuss mindfulness without mentioning the professional work of Jon Kabat-Zinn (1990, 2003), who has devoted his professional life to bringing mindfulness into the mainstream of modern medicine. As Kabat-Zinn defines it, mindfulness is "the awareness that emerges through paying attention on purpose, in the present moment, and non-judgmentally to the unfolding of experience moment by moment" (2003, p. 145). Thus, mindfulness is related to presence but is much more than that; it is being present and, furthermore, devoting intentional attention to what that presence reveals to us. It involves a directed focus toward the experience of one's internal and external worlds with the deliberate intention to attend to the experience itself. Theoretically, one can do or experience anything mindfully—even eating an apple. Mindfulness is similar to meditation in that one of the goals is to observe and note your experiences without judgment—to be mindful, but not controlling. However, it differs from meditation in that you don't necessarily need to be at rest or directing your focus inward. There are mindfulness meditations that combine the concepts of both inward and outward attention, but here we will briefly describe some of the important aspects of inward mindfulness.

Begin by taking a few deep breaths as a means of first "checking in" with your body (it may help to close your eyes while you are doing this). Focus on the feeling of the air entering and exiting your lungs. Are you feeling tense or anxious? Tired or relaxed? Take note of whether there are specific sensations in some areas of your body but not in others. Simply be aware of what is happening for you at this moment. Are you thinking or stressing about anything? Take note of what it is and how that stress feels in your body. What sorts of objects are in your surrounding environment? Pick one and note its textures, colors, and contours. You may want to visually follow along the edge of the object. What kinds of smells are in the air? Again feel the air entering your lungs. Take your time with any one experience. If you become distracted by a thought or feeling, do not judge yourself; simply note this has happened and continue to focus on your surroundings. Anchor yourself in each moment. When you feel you are ready to return from your mindfulness experience, you can slowly bring your experience back to your regular pace.

There are now many books with mindfulness exercises that will help you become more mindful; one that is especially helpful for all the healing professions is *Heal Thy Self: Lessons on Mindfulness in Medicine* (Santorelli, 2000). It is an artful combination of practical advice and inner guidance.

Progressive Muscle Relaxation (PMR)

The first goal of PMR is to increase awareness of tension in the body by highlighting the physical cues associated with muscle tension. This makes sense, since it is nearly impossible to know whether tension is present if you don't know what tension feels like, and so PMR works to enhance this awareness. The second goal of PMR is to help the individual relax through the systematic tightening and relaxing of muscles in a "progressive" top-down, head-to-toe sequence.

To begin, you need to find a place to lie down comfortably (while this is not critical, it is most effective) where you won't be interrupted. The process typically begins by focusing on your breathing; take several breaths before you begin. When you are ready, tighten the muscles in your forehead; make them as tight as you can. After a count of five, slowly relax those muscles as you take a deep breath in. Be aware of what the relaxation feels like; this awareness will help you learn how to have more control over intentional muscle relaxation. After a few moments, repeat the process once more for the same muscles. Proceed with this same process for the muscles around your eyes, mouth and jaw, neck, shoulder, upper arm, forearm, hand (do one side first, then the other), back, chest, abdomen, pelvis and buttocks, upper leg, lower leg, foot (do one side first, then the other), and finally the entire body all at once. Do a full check of your body. Do you notice any areas that are still tense? If so, repeat the process for those areas. It is important to not rush this process; try to ensure you have relaxed all the muscles in your body.

There is a good chance you will fall asleep during this process, and some people use a variation of it for that purpose. If you do just the relaxation part, without the prior tightening of the muscles, it becomes a "body scan," which can also be a mindfulness exercise.

Guided Imagery

This strategy for self-care involves the mental exploration of an imaged place that has a personal, relaxing quality to you. It is a combination of conscious exploration of an imagined place and the passive acceptance of whatever thoughts and feelings arise from "being" in that place. There are many benefits to engaging in guided imagery, such as boosting immune function, managing pain (Domar & Dreher, 2000), and enhancing the relaxation response. These benefits may be due to the brain's tendency to respond in similar ways to both imagined and real imagery (Pinker, 2007).

The process of guided imagery requires a bit of consideration prior to starting, as you need to first think of a place that is relaxing for you. Because this place is imagined, your having been to this place physically is not required, but it helps to choose a setting that you are familiar with enough to "explore." This place could be a beach, a spot near a lake, an alpine meadow, or anywhere at all. With the process of guided imagery, follow the same process as a mindfulness meditation but first "take yourself" to your relaxing place and then create and mindfully explore whatever you might find there.

Other Strategies

As indicated previously, there is no single technique that works for everyone. Beyond those listed above there are many options for self-care. If you've tried the four approaches above and decided they aren't for you, there are literally hundreds of books on self-care strategies in libraries and bookstores, as well as on DVDs and CDs. There are authors who address these strategies more generally, such as Domar and Dreher (2000) and Hanley and Deville (2001), as well as those who specialize in specific strategies, such as the body scan and mindful meditation. (Kabat-Zinn, 1990, 2003).

■ Therapy for the Therapist

You would probably benefit from finding a good therapist for yourself. First, it will likely make your life better in general. Second, it will help you be more confident and effective as a therapist.

It is surprising how little research has been done on the effect of therapists' receiving therapy—especially surprising because it is so common among therapists. In a survey of psychologists in the Psychotherapy Division of the American Psychological Association, 96% reported having had some individual therapy (Geller, Norcross, & Orlinsky, 2005). The large majority reported that the experience was moderately to very helpful, but about 2% found it harmful, and 15% said it was only somewhat helpful or there was no change. Bike, Norcross, and Schatz (2009) found that more than 90% of therapists reported positive outcomes of their own treatment. Although most therapists seek therapy for themselves, Norcross, Bike, Evans, and Schatz (2008) studied 119 American psychologists, counselors, and clinical social workers who had never been in therapy as a client and compared them with professionals who had sought therapy. There were no differences in the proportion of each profession (or each sex) that chose therapy, but academics and cognitive-behavioral therapists were less likely to do so.

In previous chapters, you have been urged to do your own personal work but to choose your therapist carefully. When therapists choose a therapist for themselves, the qualities they look for most are competence, warmth, experience, openness, and reputation (Norcross, Bike, & Evans, 2009), and the therapists they choose are much more likely to describe themselves as "warm" than are therapists who seldom treat other therapists (Geller, Norcross, & Orlinsky, 2005). When therapists were asked what positive features of their own treatment had the most influence on how they dealt with their own clients, their answers all had to do with the cultivation of the therapeutic relationship (Norcross, Bike, & Evans, 2009). You will learn a lot about what clients feel, and you will probably know fairly early in your own therapy whether you have a connection with the therapist. Gold and Hilsenroth (2009) studied the effect of having personal therapy among graduate clinicians, and this might be the most convincing evidence for you as a beginning therapist. The student therapists who had had personal therapy felt more confident as therapists, reported that their clients were more committed to and confident in therapy, and reported more agreement with their clients over the goals and tasks of therapy. Clients of both groups of therapists reported very good therapeutic alliances, but the clients of therapists who had had personal therapy stayed in treatment twice as long. Being a client yourself gives you a depth of understanding that you probably can't get any other way, so it's no surprise that therapists who have had therapy tend to be more empathic (Norcross & Guy, 2007).

The most compelling reason that therapy will make you a better therapist is that your own issues and blind spots will interfere with your ability to hear some of your clients. It is often said that clients can't go farther in therapy than their therapists can go. There may be exceptions to this rule, but it is almost inevitable that we at least slow down our clients when they start exploring issues that bother us. We don't do this intentionally, of course, but there are hundreds of subtle ways for a therapist to avoid a topic. Or more likely, the therapist may explore the painful topic but do so in more intellectualized ways or by dampening the client's emotion. The clearer you are about yourself and the more of your own "fire" you've walked through, the more you can allow—and even welcome—your clients' painful exploring.

■ You Need a Life:
Other Important Aspects of Self-Care

Some parts of this section will probably strike you as the kind of obvious "good advice" people give others freely, but you do need to have a life—for yourself and for your clients' sakes. Norcross and Guy recommend "healthy escapes" for therapists (2007, pp. 131–152). The demands of being in school often make this difficult, and we want to give you permission to remember your own fundamental needs.

McEwen (1998) describes two major factors that contribute, for all of us, to our vulnerability to "allostatic load" (the physiological cost of the stress response). First, unhealthy habits—poor diet, lack of exercise, and overuse of products such as tobacco, alcohol, and caffeine—all play a role in how stress impacts our overall well-being. Second, psychological factors such as the perception of stress can increase our allostatic load. Both our bodies and our minds play a major part in how well we are able to keep it together during times of stress. Here are some final things to consider as a means of maintaining a healthy balance in your life.

Form and Maintain Healthy Connections with Others

We are hard-wired to connect (Crowley & Lodge, 2004). When we are under stress or trying to manage a heavy workload we can lose sight of the importance of our relationships. Humans are innately social animals and need relationships to function well. Take the time and energy to meet regularly with friends and/or family for the simple sake of social connection. Maybe share a conversation with the grocery cashier, smile at strangers—interact. These kinds of exchanges will not only feel good at the moment but will also increase your social network and social support in general, which is correlated with self-rated well-being (House, Landis, & Umberson, 1988; Wills, 1998). Clarke, Murdock, and Koetting (2009) asked counseling graduate students what helped to buffer the effects of stress on burnout and career choice satisfaction. The most important factor mentioned was a specific form of social support—having a psychological sense of community: "a feeling that members have of belonging and being important to each other, and a shared faith that members' needs will be met by their commitment to be together" (McMillan, 1976, p. 11, cited in Clarke et al., 2009). Do you have a community? Does your life include people who nourish and accept you? It is difficult to function in isolation. Sometimes, of course, your strength, recharging, and recentering will mean having alone time, especially if you are more introverted. The trick seems to be finding a balance that respects and honors who you are as an individual and gives you a sense of connection.

Diet

Diet is as much about the food you eat as it is about how you eat it. First, as a result of long periods of cyclical famine throughout our evolutionary history, we have developed a strong preference for salt, fats, and sugars, a preference that does increasing amounts of damage. For most of us, famine is no longer an issue, but salt, fat, and sugar still have a powerful hold on us. Kessler (2009) outlines the evidence for how powerful and complicated this hold is. For most people it affects brain centers in ways much like addictions do, and Kessler suggests that we need "food rehab" to deal with it. Our diet is a huge issue in our culture, and we can't begin to give you specific advice about your eating. But we do want to alert you to the importance of the issue and urge you to take it seriously.

Second, whatever you eat, it is healthier to eat mindfully. You can do anything mindfully, but eating mindfully has both physical and psychological impact. The first part of mindful eating is to eat slowly. In today's rushed lifestyle, many of us zip through meals as we are running out the door or thinking of the next task to be completed. It is important to allow the body time to digest and metabolize food while you are still eating, so it can signal you when to stop. Mindful eating increases the enjoyment of eating and helps prevent digestive upset.

Exercise Regularly

It is easy to forget that maintaining a healthy caloric intake is only half the picture; we also have to train our bodies to use those calories efficiently. When we are inactive, our bodies have evolved to interpret this as evidence of famine or impending winter and shift toward fat storage to help us survive. When we're active, the body reacts as though it is a time of plenty, of hunting and moving, and shifts toward burning calories for energy (Crowley & Lodge, 2004). Of course, this description is oversimplified, but the bottom line is clear. In addition to the fact that exercising regularly helps our bodies use calories efficiently, it also decreases depression (Martinsen & Morgan, 1997) and anxiety (Raglin, 1997); lowers cholesterol and blood pressure; and increases adrenaline, well-being (Hanley & Deville, 2001), and self-esteem (Sonstroem, 1984, 1997).

Get Regular Sleep

If you've ever held a job involving shift-work or experienced jet lag you should be easily sold on this idea. There are individual differences in the amount of sleep each of us requires, but consistency in the sleep-wake cycle is crucial to the health of all people. If we don't sleep within the same range of hours each night, the body's natural hormone cycles (which are governed by those stubborn circadian rhythms) are quickly thrown into dysregulation

(Taub & Berger, 1973). We are quite resilient at recovering from short-term sleep disturbance (Mullaney, Johnson, Naitoh, Friedman, & Globus, 1977); thus acute sleep deprivation is not as much a concern as is chronic deprivation or a consistently inconsistent sleep-wake cycle. And beyond affecting future nights' sleeps, these chronic and inconsistent disturbances significantly influence mood, appetite, attention, and perception (Leproult et al., 1997; Maas, 1998; Taub & Berger, 1973).

Have Fun

Enjoying your work is a necessary part of well-being, but remember you have a life outside of work too. Plan to engage in activities that you find enjoyable as much as possible. If you are short on time, you might include exercise and other people in your activities. Perhaps take on a new hobby or low-impact sport such as swimming or rollerblading. And include laughter and humor, as there is support for its role in well-being and, more specifically, reducing negative feelings (Kuiper & Martin, 1998).

Connect Spiritually and Have a Sense of Mission

Having a spiritual connection can be done in many different ways—listening to music, reading a book, listening to an inspirational speaker, or simply walking in nature; connecting with yourself and your surrounding world is an important part of well-being. Spiritual renewal sometimes involves taking part in an activity that involves connection while not demanding a lot of energy. Spiritual practice (such as worship, meditation, or yoga), on the other hand, incorporates an element of spiritual connection while simultaneously providing the opportunity for mental and emotional recovery. When we spoke previously about having an inner life, we meant honoring your own meaningful experiential life. An important part of this is having a sense of mission or purpose—of making a difference in a way that matters to you (Norcross & Guy, 2007). Some of you are lucky enough to have a sense of "calling" to be a therapist; you've known for years that this is what you've wanted to do. Most of us, though, will need to evolve our sense of mission; we need to explore and develop what makes our work meaningful.

■ Further Reading on Self-Care

We have covered the usefulness of being resourced, and the core components of being present, grounded, contained, and boundaried. We have explored some of the fundamental techniques you can use to increase your resources and well-being. But this is just a start; you will need to continue to take good care of yourself through both education and integration. The more you know about wellness and self-care techniques the happier, healthier, and better resourced you'll be both as a person and as a therapist. The Dalai Lama writes, "There isn't anything that isn't made easier through constant familiarity and training. Through training we can change; we can transform ourselves" (Dalai Lama & Cutler, 1998, p. 43). The path to becoming a mindful, resourced therapist involves not only practice and integration (familiarity) but also education (training). To assist you with this information component of your transformation we've included the following list of readings to get you started. So explore, learn, have fun, and don't forget to breathe.

Aposhyan, S. (2004). *Body-mind psychotherapy; Principles, techniques, and practical applications.* New York: W. W. Norton.

Benson, H. (1984). *Beyond the relaxation response.* New York: Times Books.

Benson, H. (1996). *Timeless healing: The power and biology of belief.* New York: Scribner.

Benson, H., & Klipper, M. (1976). *Relaxation response.* New York: Avon.

Domar, A. D., & Dreher, H. (2000). *Self-nurture: Learning to care for yourself as effectively as you care for everyone else.* New York: Penguin.

Hanley, J. L., & Deville, N. (2001). *Tired of being tired.* New York: G. P. Putnam's Sons.

Kabat-Zinn, J. (1990). *Full catastrophe living: Using the wisdom of your body and mind to face stress, pain and illness.* New York: Scribner.

Norcross, J. C., & Guy, Jr., J. D. (2007). *Leaving it at the office: A guide to psychotherapist self-care.* New York: Guilford Press.

Taylor, K. (1995). *The ethics of caring* (2nd ed.). Santa Cruz, CA: Hanford Mead.

Santorelli, S. (2000). *Heal thy self: Lessons on mindfulness in medicine.* Toronto: Random House.

Theory
and Evidence

Why Theory and Evidence?

This chapter serves as a launching pad for chapters 16 and 17. Chapter 16 has a definite focus on the nature of emotional problems, while chapter 17 tries to make some sense out of why evocative empathy works, in theoretical terms. Both chapters present an original theory of therapy that explains, in the language of cognitive behavior theory, why evocative empathy should work. Chapter 18 will review the research evidence, which supports the effectiveness of evocative empathy within a good therapeutic relationship. Throughout the previous chapters, I have made brief reference to explanations of why a particular component of the therapeutic process would be effective at a specific point, but now it is time to organize these explanations into an internally consistent theoretical position.

The concern so far has been with being helpful to another human being, and I have focused on integrating experiencing and thinking. Now the gears shift from the personal and subjective to the structured and intellectual. I have been beating on you to stop intellectualizing, and you have done so well that your reward is four chapters of pedantry.

■ By the Seat of Your Pants, or Off the Top of Your Head Isn't Enough

My personal dilemma in writing these chapters is that I don't think any theory can possibly be entirely correct at this stage of our knowledge of psychology, but it seems irresponsible and even dangerous for therapists to be saying that they reject theory and go with what feels right at the moment. There is good evidence (Ackerman & Hilsenroth, 2001; Bergin, 1963; Lambert, Bergin, & Collins, 1977; Mohr, 1995) that some therapists do damage, and I talked about destructive "genuineness" in chapter 6. Doing what "feels right at the moment" depends enormously on the therapist's own freedom from distortions and destructive personal needs.

Thus, we need to make as much sense as we can of how therapy works, remembering that our thinking is only a successive approximation of the truth. Getting as close as we can to an accurate understanding, however, can serve us well if we humbly let it guide our practice.

The field of psychotherapy is full of "schools" of theory, each with adamant, quasi-religious commitment. While this commitment may contribute to the effectiveness of therapy at times, when our knowledge is so limited and therapy depends so on the client's hope and the therapist's confidence, it also has made therapists rigidly dismiss others' ideas with scorn—usually because the therapists distort the other theories. However, years ago, Strupp and Bergin (1969) asserted, "The barriers separating the major schools of psychotherapy are gradually being eroded, and the predominant direction of research is toward a nonschool approach" (p. 24). They seem to have been partly right. Many current writers are discussing *psychotherapy integration* and trying to distill the factors that are common to different approaches to psychotherapy (Asay & Lambert, 1999; Goldfried, 1995; Goldfried & Castonguay, 1992; Kelly, 1997; Patterson, 1989; Norcross & Goldfried, 2005). Nevertheless, Norcross, Prochaska, & Farber (1993) reported that the percentage of practicing psychologists who described themselves as "eclectic/integrative" when asked to describe their primary theoretical orientation remained stable at about 30% between the beginning and end of the 1980s. By 2001, 36% chose the "eclectic/integrative" label (Norcross, Hedges, & Castle, 2002). There was relatively little change in the percentage of therapists who adhered to specific schools of therapy. It is distressing to hear therapists ask each other what schools they belong to, because as soon as they have labels for each other, misunderstanding begins. The alternative to school labels is probably to say what one does in therapy.

At the risk, then, of being misunderstood, I'll say that what follows in chapters 16 and 17 is an attempt to explain how evocatively empathic therapy works, from a general cognitive learning-theory perspective, with elements of information processing, experiential knowing, and unconscious processes such as repression. There! Now let's see you put me in a category.

What follows in the next two chapters makes sense to me; you may or may not find it helpful. The evidence in chapter 18, however, suggests that even if you can't accept the theory, you can comfortably do evocatively empathic therapy, because it is effective with anxiety-based problems. It is possible to argue that all theorizing is premature, but I suspect that theory, evidence, and experience continuously interact to develop new knowledge and techniques. We need to keep rebuilding our systems, drawing from established therapies, restating different ideas that may only seem different, and integrating ideas in the light of new knowledge. The practicing therapist must be open to change—and even seek it—but at the same time trust what she or he does enough to offer services honestly to clients. The therapist must be a loyal revisionist believer, firmly committed to a tentative position.

■ The Key Question— Why Can You Trust the Client?

The following chapters will try to answer many questions about how therapy works, but the most important one is the question that implies that evocatively empathic therapy is naive. In chapter 5, I argued strongly that the basic principle is that the client is the problem solver, but the critic can answer: "That sounds very nice, but the client has come to therapy confused and unable to solve problems, distorting the truth and not sophisticated in psychological matters. The therapist knows more about behavior and, we hope, has a clearer perception of reality. It is irresponsible to let the client wallow around, not knowing where to go, when you could give helpful direction. Empathy is very nice and supportive and probably even a necessary precondition for therapy, but it is not enough. *How do you know the client will talk about the things he or she needs to talk about?"* This critic clearly misunderstands evocative empathy as a passive process, but I will try to answer his or her question in these chapters.

■ All of Our Theories Are Simplified "Line Drawings" of Different Parts of Reality

After he read the theoretical model in chapters 16 and 17, one graduate student said that he found it very helpful but that it was like a line drawing of reality. Reality is three-dimensional, in full color, in constant motion and terribly complex. A line drawing can never capture all of that, but it can be useful for understanding part of reality. Every theory is like a line drawing in this sense, useful but incomplete. We are all like the blind men and the elephant in the familiar story. One felt the leg and said an elephant is like a tree. Another felt the trunk and proclaimed the first man wrong; an elephant is like a hose. A third felt the tail and proclaimed both other men terribly misguided; an elephant is like a brush. They were all wrong, and they were all right from their own limited perspectives. Our theories of therapy are all like that. We need to look for what we can learn from each limited theory.

■ Being Eclectic

My theoretical understanding is different now than it was 10 years ago and, I hope, different than it will be 10 years from now. Yours will be different from any of these, of course, but our challenge is to find enough internally consistent structure to guide our thinking, practice, and development of new ideas, while we stay open to new ideas. We all want to be "eclectic," of course, but this could mean just about anything.

I hope that my own current "eclectic" view is apparent from this chapter and chapters 16 and 17. My practice has been influenced most strongly by some humanists, but my understanding of inner conflict draws from learning theory, particularly when internal behaviors are considered. This understanding has affected my practice of therapy and helped me understand and appreciate some phenomena associated with psychoanalytic theory. Theories of information processing and of experiential knowing are also useful to me. I understand each of these theories as describing the same reality from different perspectives.

It is an interesting sidelight that developing a theoretical model helped me see that I misunderstood empathy as fairly passive and forced me to change my therapeutic style to a more experiential and leadingly empathic one. It also became clear that many therapists seem to be doing similar things but are describing their actions in different words. A lot of the disagreement among therapists of different "schools" is unnecessary misunderstanding.

I suppose that I had two reasons why I needed the theoretical model presented in chapters 16 and 17. I had to have an explanation that made sense to me, and I needed to persuade the learning theorists I know (especially the cognitive learning theorists) that evocatively empathic therapy is effective. The next two chapters discuss the integration of empathy-based therapy and cognitive-behavioral theory. I hope you find the theory useful and that you will see it as a complement to many other perspectives on explaining how therapy works.

CHAPTER 16

The Nature of Emotional Problems

Understanding how therapy works requires an understanding of the causes of the problems we are trying to treat. Essentially, these are problems caused by (1) painful emotions, such as fear, anxiety, guilt, grief, and depression; (2) distortions of thinking and feeling caused by these painful emotions; and (3) self-defeating behaviors that help the person avoid the painful emotions, but at great cost—in other words, problems in living based on painful emotion. The older term for these problems, neurosis, is falling into disuse, largely because it was so misleading. It implied that these problems were some kind of illness, rather than the same kinds of problems that we all have. The term *neurotic/normal continuum* refers to this principle. We all have problems that would be called neurotic if they caused enough trouble for us and/ or those around us. The point at which "enough trouble" begins is arbitrary and is based on individual circumstances and even cultural norms. In this chapter I will use the term *neurosis* occasionally but will do so on the understanding that it refers to problems in living, not to illnesses. I may even use the term *neurotic symptom* but only on the understanding that it refers to *severely self-defeating behaviors that help a person avoid emotional pain*.

■ Principles of Painful Emotion

Sometimes, to simplify the discussion a little, I will use the words "painful emotion" and "anxiety" when I am talking about aversive emotions in general, including fear, anxiety, guilt, shame, grief, depression, hopelessness, and other aversive feelings.

Before discussing complex problems like painful emotion, I need to review a few of the simple principles of how aversive emotions like fear develop. I hope this review doesn't put you off with its simple-mindedness or with its seeming irrelevance to therapy. Trust me; things will get more complicated very soon. If you are not familiar with these principles, I'd suggest you read a basic learning principles text.

221

The baby is born fearing nothing that is not physically discomforting (although some fears do seem to be more easily learned than others). Through conditioning experiences based on the pairing of physical discomfort (pain, usually) with objects or even his or her own behaviors that were originally emotionally neutral, the baby develops fears of those objects or behaviors. Once the child learns the powerful lesson of imitation, fears can also be acquired vicariously from the fearful reactions of significant others. Although the process here is more complex than with simple fears, the principles are still the same. Painful emotions are fundamentally learned from association with physical discomfort.

Complex Fears

These simple principles can account directly for only the most obviously acquired fears, however, and most adult painful emotion, anxiety, guilt, and depression do not easily fit the model of directly conditioned fear based on painful experiences. You will treat a lot of people for fear of elevators before you find one who has been hurt or trapped in an elevator to a degree that would logically explain the fear. Understanding these complexities is the purpose of this chapter.

To Weaken a Painful Emotion You Must Feel It

One implication of the observation that all painful emotions are learned is that, in principle, they can all be unlearned. It is a well-established principle in the learning literature that the *only* way to weaken a conditioned response is to perform the response in the absence of reinforcement—in other words, to extinguish it.

■ Why Extinction Is Important

It is very important that you understand the components of extinction, because they will help you understand why therapy must be both experiential and cognitive. The three components of extinction are (1) exposure to the conditioned stimulus (in the case of fear, you must face the thing you fear), (2) performance of the conditioned response (you must feel the fear), and (3) absence of the unconditioned stimulus (nothing bad happens).

The person must feel the fear to get rid of it. In slightly less mechanical terms, one must face painful emotion and experience painful experiences to change them. To be most effective, this should occur in steps small enough that the painful response aroused is not strong enough to produce secondary conditioning of fear of the new situation or to cause the person to escape the situation before extinction can start. The term *graduated extinction* describes this process.

We also need to understand the process of *counterconditioning*, because it is often used to treat fears but works very differently from extinction. The general process is to present the feared cue in the presence of some positive stimulation so that the cue is now conditioned to arouse positive or pleasant responses. In other words, the new conditioning *counters* the old conditioning. The new conditioning does not weaken the old fear response—only extinction can do that. The new conditioning competes with and suppresses the old fear response, which can disappear from view but can later emerge again under the right conditions.

Counterconditioning has many valuable uses and often occurs along with extinction. But, by itself, counterconditioning is only a "band-aid" solution. The bottom line here is that emotional change requires experiencing of the emotions being changed.

The Persistence of Painful Emotions

There are at least four factors that make painful emotions last so long. Time, they say, heals all wounds, but that is not true of painful conditioned responses. As you just learned, the only way to weaken a painful emotion is to face it, feel the painful emotion, and have nothing bad happen. First, unfortunately (or probably fortunately for survival of the species), painful emotions just extinguish more slowly than other conditioned responses. A second, related factor is that humans quite understandably avoid the things they fear, and this prevents extinction from taking place. In fact, avoidance behavior is often strongly established and under conscious control, while the emotional reactions themselves take a few seconds to get started. Thus, we can avoid feared situations so quickly and efficiently that our painful emotions never extinguish unless circumstances force us into contact with the sources of our fears. The third factor is that avoidance behavior becomes extremely strong because every time we avoid something feared, we feel better. The experience of fear-reduction is a very powerful reinforcer, and the avoidance behavior becomes difficult to change. Fourth, the experiences that cause painful emotion are usually unpredictable. This kind of partial reinforcement results in reactions that are very resistant to extinction. The unpredictability comes from both the inconsistency of the persons doing the punishing and because we occasionally fail to avoid the real source of the painful emotion—the unconditioned source of pain that is so punishing. These occasional failures to avoid are unpredictable and establish the painful emotion and the avoidance behavior even more strongly.

Emotional Pain Cued by Your Own Thoughts and Feelings

An important principle for understanding anxiety is that your own acts can become cues for painful emotion. If one is severely punished for each head scratch, the act of scratching the head will subsequently arouse painful emotion. Similarly, if a person is punished each time she thinks a particular thought, the act of thinking that thought can become a cue for painful emotion.

I suspect that you have had the experience of being alone, thinking some particular thought or memory, and feeling awful or embarrassed or frightened. You must have been aroused by your own "painful thought." Any internal process, such as a feeling or thought, can become frightening, given the right learning experiences.

Punishment Works through Inhibition

One last simple principle is that punishment works, in general, by suppressing the punished behavior, not by eliminating it. The punished behavior seems to disappear, but in fact what has happened is that a new behavior has been learned—that of stopping the punished behavior. In the words of Campbell and Church, "Punishment puts down a response by force and tends to conceal it from public view" (1969, p. 111). This goes against our intuitions, but it is important for our understanding of anxiety-based problems. The punished behavior (including thoughts and memories) is not weakened in strength at all, and so if the inhibiting behavior is somehow lessened, the punished behavior that seemed to disappear will reappear in the same strength as if it had never been punished (Walters & Grusec, 1977).

■ Conflict and Anxiety

But we're not all that interested in simple behaviors. The experience we want to understand is the haunting, helpless feeling of apprehension or even dread that comes with anxiety. If someone asks, "What are you so afraid of?" the person answers, "I don't know. I don't know, but it's awful, and it just sneaks up on me and without warning. I'm so scared I have to run, but I can't run, and I can't think . . . it has to stop!" Or maybe it's quieter than this, with the person saying, "I do things that just don't make sense, but I don't really care anyway because you can't trust people who say they like you and then leave you." The person's confusion and anxiety touch us, and we want to help. After some time in which we are evocatively empathic, the person says, "I'm amazed, really, how much I felt trapped by my relationship with him and how angry I am at the way he puts me down . . . I don't know why I couldn't see that before, but now I see what I have to do." With a quiet sense of discovery, the person might say, "I really do care, and I'm so lonely. People have hurt me a lot, but I see now that sometimes it was me almost wanting them to hurt me so I didn't have to love them." Or perhaps the person has an "aha" insight experience with, "Of course! I just remembered how it was . . . she *didn't* love and support me all those times. She said she did, but now I can remember how fierce she looked and how worried she was about what the neighbors would think every time I did anything," although these smashing insights are relatively rare in therapy.

This is a remarkable process. Something hidden from awareness was still having a dramatic effect on the person, and a certain kind of talking made the person aware of it and somehow lessened its effect. Our problem is understanding this process without using concepts like "the unconscious mind" or "blocking and displacement of psychic energy"—to understand it in general cognitive-learning terms.

To do this, we must first understand conflict.

Principles of Conflict

Phillips has gone so far as to say that, "there is no psychopathology without conflict" (1956, p. 127). This is probably an overstatement but it seems safe to say that without conflict there would be no emotion-based problems. In general, conflict is *the tendency to perform two or more incompatible responses at the same time.* We are built so that we can be doing completely opposite actions simultaneously. A clear example of this is when we "freeze" with fear. We look like we're just standing there, but our bodies are trying to do so many different actions at the same time, they cancel each other out. The same principle applies to feelings; we frequently fear and want a particular thing at the same moment. Dollard and Miller (1950) described four kinds of conflict, arguing that, "an intense emotional conflict is the necessary basis for neurotic behavior" (p. 129).

Approach-approach conflict is the situation in which the person wants two things, but getting one means losing the other. You might want an intimate relationship but have two equally attractive persons to choose from in circumstances in which you can't have both without risking total exhaustion. In *avoidance-avoidance conflict* you fear and want to avoid two things, but avoiding one means that you must approach the other. You are late filing your income tax return and face punitive action when you do file it, but if you wait, the punishment will be greater. The immediate aversiveness of filing now feels just as awful as the worse consequences in the distant future.

Both of these situations are painful, but they usually get resolved because something tips the balance one way or the other or you escape the situation. But *approach-avoidance conflict* is devastating. Some people find this counterintuitive, but it is our nature that we can both want and fear something at the same time. A simple example of this is that, if you were strongly conditioned to fear and avoid red lights and to enjoy and approach yellow lights, we could throw you into conflict by suddenly showing you an orange light. You would freeze in a moment of conflict. You would actually both fear and like orange lights, which are a combination of red and yellow. It may seem weird, but if you were unexpectedly exposed to an orange light, your body would simultaneously be trying to move away and to move toward it. A young man might desperately want to be involved with a woman but at the same time desperately fear her, fear intimacy, and fear sex. He wants her too much to say, "Forget it, who needs her?" He can't just get involved, because he's too scared. What does he do? He suffers.

The fourth kind of conflict, *double approach-avoidance conflict*, is just an elaboration of approach-avoidance conflict in which there are two or more goals that are both desired and feared. Approaching one of the desired (and feared) goals means sacrificing the other desired (and feared) goal. In real life, conflicts are very complicated. Someone might want to graduate from the university but not want to because of the uncertainty of being alone, but if he doesn't graduate, parents will be hurt, and the person will feel guilty but also satisfied at hurting the parents, whom he both loves and hates, and so on.

Conflict is essential to an understanding of anxiety because simple fears are not much problem for the person. As Ohman and Ursin say, "Once [avoidance] behavior is established, the fear is quite efficiently coped with, and there is little need for further worry. It is only when the coping strategy is undermined by some approach contingencies that maladaptivity results" (1979, p. 180). Only when there is conflict does the person suffer, because otherwise feared things will simply be avoided. Thus, you know that if a person is suffering, he or she must be in conflict.

The figure below illustrates the way approach-avoidance conflict works, and will help us understand anxiety. The diagram addresses four important principles (Dollard & Miller, 1950). (1) First, the line depicting the "approach gradient" illustrates that as you get closer to something you want, your desire for it—your tendency to approach it—gets stronger. (2) Second, the "avoidance gradient" illustrates that as you get closer to something you fear, the more you fear it—the stronger is your tendency to avoid it. "Get closer" can mean get closer in actual physical distance, in time, or through a dimension of similarity (for example, if you fear a red light, you will also fear dark pink, but less than red, and light pink, but less than dark pink).

Note that an approach-avoidance conflict occurs when the person has both approach and avoidance tendencies toward the "feared goal." (3) It is at this point that the gradients illustrate the third principle—as the person approaches something both feared and desired, both the fear and the desire are increasing, but the fear is increasing faster. This means that if the person is far from the feared goal in this conflict situation, the approach tendency is stronger than the avoidance tendency, and so he or she will move toward the feared goal. Our young man is sitting in his room lonely and wanting to phone a particular woman. "I'm going to do it! I really want to talk to her, and there is just no reason I can't just go phone her right now." But he also fears her, and so as he walks toward the phone, his desire to talk to her is increasing (he's getting closer psychologically), but so is his fear, and the fear is increasing faster. He dials the phone as his mouth dries out and his heart starts to pound—the fear, the tendency to avoid, has almost caught up with the approach tendency. She answers in her warm and friendly voice, and now he is so close that his fear is stronger than his desire. He breathes heavily into the phone in panic and hangs up. She thinks she got an obscene phone call, and he returns to his room, mad at himself because now he wants her again. He is trapped in the "conflict region," in which his behavior will vacillate.

A fourth principle—(4) that the approach and avoidance tendencies can be strengthened or weakened, thus raising or lowering the gradients of approach and avoidance, provides four ways we can help the young man resolve his conflict. We can (a) weaken his fear; (b) strengthen his fear; (c) weaken his desire; (d) strengthen his desire. If he has some positive experiences with women or somehow lessens his fear, his desire for the woman will be the same as before, but the avoidance gradient might be lowered so that it never quite catches up with the approach gradient. Although he may get ner-

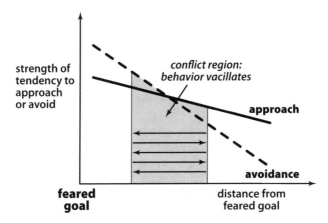

From *Personality and Psychotherapy: An Analysis in Terms of Learning, Thinking and Culture,* by J. Dollard and N. E. Miller. Copyright ©1950 by McGraw-Hill, Inc. Reprinted by permission of The McGraw-Hill Companies.

Figure 1
Diagram of approach-avoidance conflict showing the conflict area, in which behavior will vacillate between approach and avoidance.

vous, he will carry through with his approach and not be in conflict. On the other hand, he could try to phone her again, and before he can hang up, she screams into the phone, "Is that you, Charlie, you disgusting creep!" Now he will become a monk. If his fear of women is strong enough, it may at all times be higher than his desire, so he won't be in conflict. He will simply avoid women and not suffer and vacillate. If something could decrease or increase his desire for her, the conflict could also be resolved because the gradients would never be in balance with each other. Of these four ways to resolve conflict, decreasing the fear is the one that is most within the power of therapists to bring about. (The principles of conflict are currently used in a wide range of research on topics such as social anxiety [Kashdan, 2007], shyness [Schmidt, 1999], arousal and anxiety [McNaughton & Gray, 2000], and social relationships [Robinson & Wilkowski, 2006, 2008]. See Crowne [1979] for a good summary of the early research on conflict.)

You Must Understand *Internal* Conflict to Understand Anxiety

We still don't understand anxiety, though, until we apply all these principles to *internal* conflict. Essentially, in anxiety, the person fears his or her own internal processes—thoughts, feelings, memories, and desires. But if you just fear particular thoughts and feelings, there is no problem; you simply avoid thinking and feeling those particular ways. The problem arises when feared thoughts and feelings are also motivated. Now you are in approach-avoidance conflict over processes inside your skin.

Internal conflicts develop in two steps:

1. Thoughts and feelings become fear cues because they have been punished. "Punished" can mean obvious physical punishment such as spanking a child for masturbating; the overt behavior is being punished, but so are the concomitant thoughts and feelings. "Punished" more likely means subtler processes such as guilt inducement and love withdrawal. The child might have been rejected and called evil and sinful whenever she expressed anger at a parent. Now, even when the parents aren't around, the act of feeling anger is frightening—an internal process has become a cue for painful emotion. This painful emotion, of course, could take many different forms, like fear, shame, guilt, or depression.

2. If the thoughts and feelings are somehow motivated, a conflict will develop. This motivation can be either (a) biological or (b) a result of learning experiences. An example of biologically motivated conflict is that children who are punished for masturbating likely will seem to lose interest in sex at about eight years of age. They will not be in conflict about it until puberty starts and the strength of the approach, the desire, increases so much that it is about equal to the fear of sexual feelings. They will suffer—guilt or anxiety or some other painful emotions, as they strongly need to feel sexual feelings and strongly need to avoid them at the same time. An example of internal conflict based on learned motivations is that children who are punished for anger will be in conflict if they have also learned to have feelings of aggression toward the parents—if they learn to feel aggressively, as seems nearly inevitable. Another example of internal conflict based on learned motivation might involve dependency feelings, which are strongly rewarded, especially through early childhood, and at other times strongly punished, especially among males. It is very likely that an individual might feel dependent and at the same time be "ashamed" of feeling this way. In our theoretical terms, he or she is being aversively aroused by his or her own strongly learned impulse. The most likely explanation of what has been called free-floating anxiety is that many different things cue the feelings, so that the cues are frequently encountered or, more likely, cued by internal processes that are always potentially with the victim. The anxious person fears his or her own thoughts and feelings.

People in conflict are constantly and painfully vacillating. They must think and feel the motivated thoughts and feelings, and they must avoid them. They suffer.

The Power of Anxiety, Guilt, Depression, Shame, and Grief

It is difficult to find words strong enough now to make the jump from these simple principles of conflict and anxiety to what the human experience of anxiety, guilt, depression, shame, and grief is really like. It can vary in strength, and we all experience it to some degree, but we can have a helpless, sick feeling of guilt; a frantic, desperate shaking with no way to grasp the demons that seem to threaten; a confusion that prevents thinking about even simple things; or any of hundreds of experiences. One of the worst things about the experience is that we often can't name what is bothering us; we just feel horrible.

The principles are simple; the actual experience is powerfully painful and complex. It is so powerful that it underlies one of the most important principles for understanding self-defeating behavior. *Anxiety reduction is an extremely powerful reinforcer.* This principle will help us understand behavior in others and ourselves that otherwise would make no sense.

■ Repression and Cognitive Distortions

Before we see how anxiety can cause people to do such self-defeating and odd-seeming things, though, we need to understand how one can have painful emotion about something without awareness—or, more accurately, with partial awareness. I have mentioned unconscious influences; we all have painful emotion about things without being able to name them, but explaining this process is remarkably difficult. We say things like, "I was lying to myself about that," but we can't really mean we are two persons, one of whom, "I," lies (consciously?) to "myself." The basic process underlying these cognitive distortions is repression, the unintentional forgetting of well-learned aversive memories. Repression is usually associated with Freudian ideas like "pushing thoughts into the unconscious mind," but we will try to understand the process in learning terms that assume only that we are dealing with brain processes, not a mind with different "places" in it.

Defining Awareness

Learning theorists have tended to avoid anything to do with terms like consciousness and awareness, wanting to reject their almost mystical-seeming meanings, but it is pretty obvious to most of us that ignoring a phenomenon that feels so important to virtually everybody will not make it go away. It is possible, though, to understand awareness in terms that don't imply mystical mental energy. The basic principle is that there is an enormous amount going on inside the brain, and only some of these processes include symbolic expression. These symbolic processes include the use of words, gestures, and pictures—anything that stands for something else—and we learn to call these particular brain processes "awareness."

Only some of what goes on in the brain qualifies as thinking. When driving a new car one frequently tries to put the key in the ignition where it was in the old car "without thinking." Hebb has pointed out that it is possible to read out loud for some time (perhaps to a child) and then to realize that, "I . . . have no notion at all of what the heroine had been up to" (1972, p. 31). Obviously, much complex brain behavior was involved "without thinking."

It would be difficult to imagine, however, that reading out loud does not involve some of what we call "awareness," and this points to a second critical aspect of our definition. *Awareness is on a continuum.* One can be partly aware, to the extent that one could symbolize if called on to do so. Thus, it is inaccurate to speak of a person as either aware or unaware. Hebb was partly aware of more than one thing at a time. There is no difficulty with understanding that a person can be aware of several things at once, if awareness is seen as symbolizing brain processes that can occur at many different degrees of completeness.

Now the groundwork is laid for understanding anxiety; you can be frightened by thoughts (brain processes) that are fear arousing but are only partly conscious—partly symbolized. You avoid them quickly to reduce the anxiety, but this prevents facing the painful thoughts—prevents your getting over the fear. We are getting ahead of the story, but therapy helps the person face those thoughts both by articulating them more completely and by experiencing them in nonverbal ways.

A Learning View of Repression

Repression is one primary way we avoid those painful thoughts, and the spooky thing is that it sometimes happens "automatically," without our knowledge or plan. (The term *suppression* is used to refer to conscious strategies to avoid painful thoughts. The person can intentionally think of other things or engage in distracting activities. It may be that habitually suppressing painful thoughts also inhibits them, with the same consequences as repression.) Remember that punishment works by inhibition and that thinking is symbolizing brain behavior. If a particular thought is punished, the act of thinking that thought will become punishing. The inhibiting behavior of stopping that thought will be rewarded by escape from the discomfort it arouses. Thus, repression is an instance of inhibition.

If thoughts are behaviors, they operate by the same principles as any other behaviors. If you punish me for scratching my head, that behavior will be inhibited. Now, where are all my unused head scratches? That's silly, of course; we all know they're in my unconscious hand. Actually, they're not anywhere. Head scratches are events, not things that can go somewhere. My arm and nervous system are still capable of performing head scratches and are still trying to do so, but the opposing behavior of stopping that is more powerful. Thoughts, similarly, don't go somewhere; they are symbolizing behavior that gets inhibited to some degree in repression.

Thoughts that have become fear cues will be followed by emotional pain when they occur and thus are likely to be inhibited. The degree to which they will be inhibited will depend on the balance of forces among (1) the strength of the punishment, (2) the strength of the motivation of the thoughts, and (3) the strength of environmental cues that are reminders of the particular thoughts. Remember that the punished and inhibited behaviors (thoughts in this case) are not weakened in strength in the least. They are only inhibited.

This description of repression is a general explanation for the phenomenon of the failure to think accurately because of selective inhibition of aversive brain processes. The general phenomenon could also include self-deception, denial, and the other traditional defense mechanisms. Anderson's (2006; Bower 2004) cognitive neuroscience approach to repression discusses the role of inhibitory mechanisms in repression.

Freud and even Rogers (1959) readily accept some version of repression, but learning and cognitive theorists have tended to reject it (Holmes, 1990, 1974). Recently, though, unconscious influences have been recognized more, and there is good experimental evidence for this view of repression that you may want to examine for yourself (Anderson, 2006; Bower 2004; Brewin, 1997; Gleaves, 1996; Glucksberg & King, 1967; Glucksberg & Ornstein, 1969; Martin, Hawryluk, Berish, & Dushenko, 1984; Martin, Verman, & Miles, 1984; Ross, Homan, & Buck, 1994; Waldinger & VanStrien, 1995; Weiner & Higgins, 1969).

When Repression Is Costly

Repression is a normal process that serves an important adaptive function. If you constantly remembered all the disgusting things you've ever done or thought, you would be a mess. Up to a point, repression is adaptive. There are at least two general ways, though, that repression can cause trouble.

First, the person can fail to learn from experience, remembering events inaccurately. Second, and more painfully, repression is often only partial, since awareness is on a continuum and repression may inhibit only parts of thoughts. The thoughts (and other internal processes, such as memories, feelings, and urges) can still be active enough to arouse anxiety without being complete enough for the person to be able to symbolize them. This, clearly, is the general explanation of anxiety, the remarkable process in which we are frightened of things we can't name. If an aversive memory were totally repressed, it wouldn't bother the person. Total repression probably does occur, but it is partial repression that causes anxiety.

Anxiety Cues That Have Never Been Articulated

Repression involves the inhibition of brain processes that were conscious at one time. Our understanding of anxiety as cued by partially symbolized internal processes is incomplete, however, if we consider only repression. We often see the effects of repression being relieved when a client says, "It's amazing that I didn't remember those awful things. They've obviously been bothering me for a long time." But it is at least as common to hear something like, "No wonder I'm always yelling at my wife. It never occurred to me that I was trying to prove to her that I'm strong. That's obviously ridiculous. I never thought of it this way." Here the client was being affected by threatening thoughts and feelings that were only incompletely symbolized, not because of repression but because they were never fully symbolized. This is an example of what is often called "learning without awareness." Of course, it would be more accurate to call it "learning with partial awareness." We are most interested in the fears that are learned without full awareness, but the process also applies to other kinds of experiences, including joy, liking, and the whole range of human experience. I want to be clear that I am not saying awareness doesn't count for much; it obviously is very important. In fact, a major goal of therapy is to enhance awareness to help the person get over fears and gain control of life. The point is that there is a lot of experiencing that occurs without awareness, and it is this experiencing that is often the important focus of therapy.

I hope that it is obvious to you that this is just another way to talk about the *experiential knowing* that we discussed in chapter 8.

Evidence for Processing without Awareness

The research literature on "preconceptual information processing" is so huge that I can only point you toward it briefly. The reason I want to point you there is to convince you that experiential knowing is real and it's important. As you know from chapter 8, conscious cognitive functioning is important, but experiential functioning seems to precede conscious understanding. For many people, this is counterintuitive and almost insulting. We need to think of ourselves as in charge of our lives, and the notion of unconscious influences is unsettling. But we end up with more control of our behavior and our problems if we accurately understand human functioning.

As Posner and Boies (1971) conclude from their review of selective attention, "Conscious awareness is itself rather late in the sequence of mental processing" (p. 407). Toth and Reingold (1996) conclude that there is "clear evidence that prior conceptual processing can unconsciously influence subsequent behaviour" (p. 71). Bargh and Chartrand (2005) summarize research on "automaticity" and social cognition and conclude that

> conscious, intentional control is actually quite limited, so that most of moment-to-moment psychological life must occur through nonconscious means if it is to occur at all. . . . Three major forms of automatic self-regulation are identified: An automatic effect of perception on action, automatic goal pursuit, and a continual automatic evaluation of one's experience. (p. 228)

Gladwell (2005) has written a fascinating popularized book on the evidence called *Blink: The Power of Thinking Without Thinking*.

Skinner's (1969) analysis of awareness is especially useful here. He argues for two kinds of learning—contingency learning and rule learning. Thinking, feeling, and overt behavior are consistently affected by various contingencies (reinforcement and punishment, as examples), and only sometimes does the person formulate (become aware of) the rules governing these contingencies. "Learning without awareness is simply a special case of behaving without awareness, and the latter is common" (Skinner, 1969, p. 246).

Reviews and research evidence can be found for perception without awareness (Bornstein & Pittman, 1992; Dretske, 2006), implicit learning

(Eitam, Hassin, & Schul, 2008; Stadler & Frensch, 1998), unconscious mental events, (Hassin, Uleman, Bargh, 2005; Reisberg, 1997), and for implicit cognition (Cleeremans & Dienes, 2008; Underwood, 1996). This evidence is especially important in supporting our discussion of experiential learning as different from intellectual or cognitive learning. Some especially relevant evidence can be found in studies of emotional processing without awareness (Balconi & Lucchiari, 2007; Christianson, Saeisae, & Silfvenius, 1996; Fox, 1996; Hermans, De-Houwer, & Eelen, 1995; Ohman, Carlsson, Lundqvist, & Ingvar, 2007; Seeburger, 1992; White, 1996; Winkielman, Zajonc, & Schwarz, 1997; Zajonc, 1980), subliminal stimulation (Balconi, 2006; Erdelyi, 1980; Hunt, Keogh, & French, 2006; Stambrook & Martin, 1983), operant learning without awareness (Hefferline & Keenan, 1963), and conditioning without awareness (Asli, Kulvedrosten, Solbakken, & Flaten, 2009; Both, Spiering, Laan, Belcome, van den Heuvel, & Everaerd, 2008; Corteen & Wood, 1974; Esteves, Dimberg, & Oehman, 1995; Forster & Govier, 1978; Martin, Stambrook, Tataryn, & Beihl, 1984; Von Wright, Anderson, & Stenman, 1975).

As a sidelight, it is also possible that anxiety results from fears of objects and situations in the environment of which the person is only partially aware. Likely both fear of external and internal cues are involved, but fundamental to both is understanding partial awareness. It is also interesting that both repression and fears learned with incomplete awareness have parallels in Freudian theory. Freud's "neurotic anxiety" can be fear of both repressed material and of "id impulses" that have never been conscious. A learning explanation of these phenomena is very different, of course, but we are probably trying to explain the same human experiences.

How Does Experiential Knowing Fit in Here?

In chapter 8, we saw how important experiential knowing is to psychotherapy, and we should briefly tie that discussion to this evidence. The implication of all this theory and evidence on processing outside of awareness also supports the notion that much of what happens in therapy is experiential. It is entirely possible for a person to learn and "know" life-changing new things without being able to put them into words—or, in Gladwell's words, "thinking without thinking."

Forming "Schemes"

None of us perceives reality accurately; in fact, the term *perception* means the interpretation of the direct sensations of our senses. We develop organized expectations of our world, and to some extent we perceive what we expect to perceive—what fits these "templates" to which we fit reality (Searleman & Herrmann, 1994). The language of information-processing theory can be applied to understanding therapy for anxiety-based problems (Rice, 1974): People develop "schemes" to facilitate the processing of new information. Elaborate and organized sets of information help us organize and select new information more effectively than if we had to start from scratch making sense out of each new situation. In addition to this useful function, how-ever, "schemes" can prevent the accurate processing of novel experiences that don't fit our expectations. The person can encounter a situation, quickly fit it to a familiar "scheme," and stop processing novel information prema-turely, distorting the experience. Information theorists would generally say that this process does not require such notions as repression, but the two views are not incompatible; they are just different ways that distortions enter thinking. Habit may stop the thinking process too early, without anxiety being an important factor, and anxiety can also inhibit aversive thoughts from being accurately thought. It is even possible that information that vio-lates our "schemes" is threatening just because it's unexpected and is there-fore inhibited.

In any case, the implications for therapy are the same—the person must be helped to "stay with" experiences to process them in new ways.

Impaired Problem Solving

The second characteristic of emotional problems mentioned at the begin-ning of this chapter was "distortions of thinking and feeling" caused by pain-ful emotions. Painful emotion makes people unwise. Dollard and Miller (1950) coined the phrase *neurotic stupidity* to describe some of the foolish binds that people get themselves into, when the rest of us can see so clearly what "should be obvious" to the other person. Of course we do the same thing, to different degrees, forgetting or failing to consider threatening aspects of situations. Sometimes we later think, "How could I not have seen that? Of course I can just [whatever the "obvious" solution is]."

One goal of therapy is to reduce these distortions—to help the person experience more accurately—in two ways. First, therapy reduces anxiety about particular issues, and second, the person becomes an independent thinker who tends to consider issues more completely.

■ Maladaptive Behavior ("Symptom") Development

An interesting term is the *neurotic paradox*. If people do what they are rein-forced for doing, why do some of them constantly lie and alienate people when they are desperate for friends; obsessively think about the death of a child in a way that brings great distress; scratch their arms until they bleed, for no appar-ent reason; fail to study until just before the exam, or do any of the thousands of self-defeating acts that people do? These behaviors are often called "neurotic symptoms," but this older term implies that neurosis is an illness. It is more accurate to think of them as *self-defeating behaviors that are usually established and maintained by anxiety reduction*. Anxiety reduction is an extremely powerful rein-forcer, especially when the anxiety reduction comes immediately and the nega-tive consequences of the reinforced behavior are delayed.

The Basic Process

The way in which anxiety reduction behaviors develop is complicated. The basic principle is that through trial-and-error learning some behaviors become effective in reducing anxiety and avoiding conflicts. Remember that "behaviors" include internal processes, and a lot of this learning goes on with incomplete awareness. Accordingly, any behavior that is followed by anxiety reduction is strongly reinforced and therefore potentially a "symptom." It will be called a neurotic symptom only if it seems self-defeating.

Anything Can Be a "Symptom"

Trying to decide what *self-defeating* means, however, is a swamp of complex issues. Some anxiety-reducing behaviors are absolutely necessary for effective living, of course. When I feel anxious, I sometimes talk to my wife, who listens until I figure out what's wrong, face the painful thoughts, and feel better. This is anxiety-reducing behavior; is it neurotic? "How sweet," you say; "of course it's not neurotic." What if I add that I do this about five hours a day, following her around talking about my anxiety? Now it's neurotic, right? It is exactly the same behavior, but now you tell me that it's "too much," meaning that it has become self-defeating. I will ask you at what point talking to my wife became "too much"—four hours, two hours, one hour and 12 minutes? I may be perfectly happy with the five-hour arrangement, but she may be miserable. Is my behavior self-defeating? That depends partly on what she does, of course.

The whole point is that calling a particular behavior a "neurotic symptom" is an arbitrary judgment based on social norms, personal wishes, others' demands and needs, and even shifting historical trends. Some years ago, if you asked another person not to smoke in public, you were considered weird. Now you might just be thought rude, but it is possible that in a few years smoking will be thought of as neurotic and smoking in public will be thought of the way spitting on the floor is now. The answer to "What's neurotic?" must always be "That depends. . . ."

If any behavior can, under the right circumstances, be considered a "neurotic symptom," it may seem foolish to try to discuss specific "symptom syndromes," but some patterns of anxiety-reducing behaviors have attracted special attention and are worth considering as illustrations of the basic process.

Phobias

Phobias have recently received a great deal of attention, but they are widely misunderstood. A phobia is a morbid dread of something or a fear disproportionate to the actual threat represented by an object or situation. A useful distinction can be made, however, between strong, directly conditioned fears and fears that develop as a result of other anxiety problems (what we might call "true phobias").

If a man were trapped in a mine explosion that nearly smothered him and then had a fear of long, dimly lit hallways, we would call his fear disproportionate to the actual threat involved, but we could understand the cause of the fear. This would illustrate a strong directly conditioned fear. However, some people fear long, dimly lit hallways even though they have never had any traumatic experiences associated with them.

The general principle is that some fears, although they may cause real emotional pain, help the person avoid a much worse pain of anxiety. Remember that anxiety results from incredibly complex internal processes and intense fears of one's own thoughts and feelings. I can think of dozens of ways a person could develop a fear of hallways. Perhaps a 28-year-old teacher has strong feelings of responsibility for her aging parents, who she fears will die of accidental injuries if left alone but toward whom she also feels intense resentment for the guilt-based limits they have put on her life. She has some desire to be rid of them but would be sick with guilt if she fully thought such ideas. I could go on for some time complicating her situation, but even this oversimplified picture of internal conflicts helps us understand how she might one day enter her school, feel panic and fear for no apparent reason, and return home, unable to face the "fear of the long hallway" that she felt. She doesn't know what causes her fear, but she does know that the panic swept over her as she entered the hallway. Other circumstances could have led to an anxiety attack in her car, in a restaurant, or in any other place related to her absence from home, leading her to attribute it to something other than hallways. Fear is a response, and the enormous relief she felt as she returned home strongly reinforced that fear. As long as she is afraid of hallways, she has to stay home, where her thoughts of the accident in her absence don't plague her. Her phobia is an anxiety-reducing fear, although that sounds paradoxical if you don't understand the principles. What she really fears is her own thoughts and feelings.

This is not to diminish the importance of directly conditioned fears. They do occur and sometimes need treatment, but at least with adult clients, the more complex fears are vastly more common.

Physical Symptoms

Hysteria is the classic term for physical symptoms with no physiological basis, and such symptoms were the basis of Freud's earliest work. Physical symptoms, although truly painful and debilitating, can develop through anxiety reduction without the victim's awareness. Pain is a response, and our teacher could have developed a headache, had to stay home and experienced anxiety reduction, strongly reinforcing the pain. Here the "underlying causes" are exactly the same, but the "symptom" is entirely different from the phobia, illustrating the difference between an illness model of symptoms and a learning model.

Acting Out

In chapter 10, I said that some antisocial behavior probably cannot be treated effectively with evocative empathy—namely, antisocial behavior that is usually called "sociopathic" and is marked by impulsive immediate gratification without apparent remorse for the sometimes horrible consequences to self and others. To repeat, however, antisocial behavior can look very much like sociopathic behavior but really be an anxiety-based problem. I once had a client who repeatedly got involved with a woman, moved in with her, and eventually beat her, ending the relationship. He then went through the same pattern with another woman and then another. This could have resulted from thoughtless impulse gratification, seeking a sexual relationship and then hitting the woman just because he felt like it at a particular time whenever he was angry. Picture for a moment, however, the graph illustrating approach-avoidance conflict and imagine the behavior of a man who (to oversimplify) both wants and strongly fears intimacy, needs to prove his virility to himself by impregnating a woman (which has never happened in spite of his never using contraception), and feels both great longing and great anger and hurt over the death of his mother. All these factors combine to make him deeply ambivalent over being close to a woman. When he is not in a relationship, his desire is strong. As he becomes more and more involved with an individual woman, his conflicts will intensify until he can go no further, but he is not aware of what is happening to him. All he knows is that he is miserable. Many things could happen to relieve his conflicts, but one of them, the one that developed for him, was to hit the woman and end the relationship. Once therapy reduced his conflicts, however, he was able to enter a marriage that was satisfying. Had his behavior been based on impulse gratification and not on anxiety reduction, therapy quite possibly would have just made him more comfortable with his violent behavior.

It is often a difficult decision whether to treat a person with antisocial behavior, an issue we discussed as an assessment problem in chapter 10.

Obsessions and Compulsions

Intuitively, one of the most difficult problems to understand is obsessive thinking, because the victim suffers so intensely that it is hard to see how the obsessive thoughts could be anxiety reducing. We might imagine a father who constantly worried and brooded over the possible death of a child, to the point where he couldn't function normally. The principles are the same as with other problems, however. It is quite possible that the father feels some hostility toward the baby, a fairly common feeling that most parents find totally unacceptable in themselves, and may even want to be rid of it—as well as loving and wanting it. Like our teacher's wishing her parents would die (as well as loving them and wanting them to live), these thoughts are so horrifying that when they are even thought in very incomplete form, the person suffers intense anxiety that must be reduced somehow. Frantically thinking about and caring for the baby every moment is not only unconscious proof against the unacceptable feelings, it is also so very distracting that the real anxiety can be avoided. Painful as the obsessive thoughts are, they are preferable to the internal conflicts they help avoid. Instead of developing a hall phobia or headaches, the teacher could have spent all her time worrying about her parents, protecting herself from her other thoughts.

Compulsive behavior can serve the same anxiety-reducing functions. Constant hand washing, elaborate rituals, and extreme orderliness can be both "proof" of correct behavior and a strong distracter from other, terribly painful thoughts.

■ Problems in Living

These examples of "neurotic" problems are offered only to illustrate the general principles involved in anxiety-based problems. All of us obsess too much sometimes and have some unreasonable painful emotions and lie sometimes because we're scared and even have physical symptoms that avoid anxiety. These are all problems in living that can be understood according to the learning principles that affect all of us. When they become extreme enough, the help we call therapy is needed, but it also operates according to the principles through which we all deal with life problems.

The Vicious Circle of Avoidance

Most of us are solving most of our problems most of the time. We face thoughts and situations that we fear, often because circumstances force us to, and we get over our painful emotions and correct many of our distortions. We talk with friends, and that helps sometimes. Sometimes, however, the painful emotions are strong enough or the circumstances are wrong enough that we get trapped so quickly and thoroughly in the vicious circle of avoiding the situations, things, and thoughts that bother us that the problems don't get solved. Then a special kind of structure is needed to help us face what we can't name but that must be faced, and we call that special structure psychotherapy.

Human Complexity

I need to say very strongly that the principles outlined in this chapter are grossly oversimplified. As far as they go, they are accurate and helpful, but the human problems they try to explain are incredibly complex—so much so that if you lose sight of the unique complexity of each of your clients, you will categorize and distort their experiences to fit your "schemes." Remember that I've never had a client who didn't surprise me, and I think the same has to be true for you, if you are open to your clients' complexity.

A Theoretical Understanding of Therapy

This chapter assumes that you have a good grasp of what an evocatively empathic therapist does, including an understanding not only of evocative empathy but also of specificity of language, of relationship issues, of the experiential and self-confronting nature of therapy, and of all the other issues discussed in the first eight chapters. I will now use your theoretical understanding of emotional problems to explain, in theory, how this approach to therapy seems to work. For clarity, I will often use the term "anxiety-based" to refer to the variety of emotional problems we discussed in Chapter 16 that included emotions like depression, shame, fear, hopelessness, and guilt.

■ Answering the Basic Question: Trusting Your Client

The fundamental theoretical question that must be answered is: "Why do you trust your clients to talk about the things they need to talk about?" In answering this question I will be using theoretical language, but remember that my ultimate goal is to explain why I really do trust my clients to solve their own problems, to take responsibility for their lives, and to leave therapy as autonomous, self-accepting, open-to-experience, and caring persons.

There are a lot of general reasons that people are problem solvers. There is evidence that humans are naturally stimulus seeking (Butler & Rice, 1963, apply this to empathic therapy); they have the capacity to learn and are constantly being rewarded for learning; and even their discomfort can motivate them to do something to create change. These reasons are important, but none of them really faces the issue of knowing that the client will talk about and experience the specific thoughts and feelings that she or he needs to in order to be a problem solver.

The logic of the answer to the question is quite straightforward, and one student, when he heard it, said, "That's it? That's too simple to be true."

If there is an anxiety-based problem, there must be conflict. If there is no conflict, then there is no problem, since the person will simply avoid the feared
objects, situations, thoughts, memories, urges, and feelings.

*If there is conflict, there must be some motive to approach the feared thoughts,
memories, urges, feelings, situations, and objects.* We won't know what those
motives are in any one case, but we know they must be active, or the person
would not be in conflict. The most important point for therapy is that this
principle especially applies to internal conflict. The client must have some
motive to approach painful internal processes such as thoughts, memories,
feelings, and urges.

Thus, the person is continually approaching and retreating from the
things that cause his or her anxiety, getting as close as he or she can stand to
get to the thoughts and feelings and then "backing off" through repression,
self-defeating behavior, and other kinds of avoidance behavior. Even "well-
defended" people are continuously getting as close as they can stand to get,
before escaping through defenses—otherwise there would be no problem.
These people vacillate, suffering, but do not advance enough to face the
source of pain before retreating.

The client will approach the elements of his or her conflicts. The therapist's job
is to hear this attempt, which the client will be too frightened to articulate
fully, and to put into words what the client is trying to say but can't quite say.
If you are working with anxiety-based problems, you can trust your clients to
try to talk about the things they need to talk about.

■ Relieving Conflicts—in Theory

Referring back to the principles of conflict and to the conflict diagram
presented in chapter 16 (see page 227), we can see that the way therapy
relieves (mostly internal) conflicts is by lowering the fear of the feared
thoughts and feelings. The client will vacillate in the "conflict region," trying
to say difficult things and backing off in the face of the pain. The therapist
hears the approach attempt (the leading edge of what the client implies) and
helps the client not retreat by articulating the implied, slightly frightening
thoughts and feelings. Now the person is in the presence of mildly anxiety-
arousing cues and feels the discomfort; nothing bad happens, and some of the
fear of the cues (the thoughts and feelings) extinguishes. This extinction is the
primary process that "takes the curse off" the painful thoughts and feelings,
but there probably is also some counterconditioning happening too; the person feels the discomfort, not only without something bad happening, but also
in the context of the therapist's acceptance of the client as a worthwhile person. The strong therapy relationship acts as a counterconditioning agent.
Thus, both extinction and counterconditioning help the client feel better, but
it is important to remember that it is the extinction that actually weakens the
emotional pain. The counterconditioning does help with feeling better, but
only by suppressing the emotional pain, not by weakening it.

■ Step-by-Step Progress

Think of the "distance from the feared goal" dimension (see again the diagram on page 227) as going from "partial experiencing of particular thoughts and feelings" on the right to "accurate experiencing" on the left. The person is constantly approaching accurate experiencing of the feared thoughts and feelings; that is, the feared thoughts and feelings are being experienced more and more completely. The person then backs off in fear when the thoughts and feelings are being experienced completely enough to be in the "conflict region." Now the fear is stronger than the approach, and the client would normally retreat at this point. When the therapist articulates the leading edge of the message, those thoughts become less fear-arousing and easier to talk about because of extinction and the counterconditioning effect of the therapist's acceptance. Because the fear of the "goal" and related thoughts is now somewhat less, the avoidance gradient will be lowered, and the "conflict region" is closer to the goal. Thoughts that used to be too painful to think can now be hinted at—implied—because they are less painful. Thoughts that used to be painful enough that they could only be implied can now be fully articulated because they are harmless. Step by step you approach more accurate, complete experiencing together. The client can now think more clearly, plan more wisely, and take more effective action.

Reinforcing the Client's Approach Responses

In addition to the client's becoming clearer about specific issues, another incredibly important experience is also happening. It is possible that another kind of therapist might cleverly guide the client to the correct feared thoughts and feelings, expose the person to them, and extinguish (and countercondition) the fears. But it is not just the "truth" that makes the client free; it is also the process of finding the truth that makes the client strong and independent.

In evocatively empathic therapy, the client makes an approach response (tries to experience painful things accurately), is held at the leading edge by the therapist, and feels some discomfort. Then the discomfort drops; the enormous power of anxiety reduction reinforces the last thing the client did—bravely approach the painful experience. Thousands of times in therapy, the client goes through the experience of exploring, of thinking hard thoughts, of getting closer to feelings, of being a problem solver, and being rewarded for it. If the therapist engineers the facing of painful thoughts (expertly interprets, for example), it is the therapist's expertise and strength that lead to relief. Paradoxically, the client is being reinforced for depending on others.

■ Relieving Conflicts—in Practice

Since the first eight chapters were devoted to the practice of therapy, we needn't dwell on it here. For the sake of continuity in this chapter, I'll just say that the therapist listens for the intended message—what the client is trying to say and can't quite say—and then articulates that message in an evocative way that brings the experience to life, especially the emotional part of the experience.

The beauty of understanding the term "the intended message" is that it gives you a handle on knowing where the leading edge is. Clients are automatically pacing themselves because of the dynamics of conflict. They are getting as close to the issues as they can stand to get by implying—intending for you to hear—as much as they can handle. *Your goal is to get as far ahead of the client as you can but have the client recognize what you say as part of what he or she meant. You do this by attuning yourself to the client's experiential world.*

■ Breaking Old Schemes

We can also return to the language of information-processing theory to explain what happens when the client is held in the presence of his or her experiencing. Rice (1974) has used information-processing concepts to understand therapy without depending "on the concepts of unconscious motivation or defense mechanisms" (p. 293). Rice seems to be rejecting Freudian explanations that I would also reject, and her language is entirely compatible with my more learning-oriented talk. We seem to be describing similar processes at different levels of abstraction and from different perspectives. She says:

> The basic assumption is that for any person there are some classes of experience that have never been adequately processed, and for some people, there are many such classes. . . . [A] more or less enduring construction or set of constructions is formed, which filters one's experience and guides one's behavior whenever situations of that general class are encountered . . . [the] problem for therapy, then, is to find a method by which the client can reprocess an important experience from such a problem class in a way that is relatively undistorted. It is this new, full, undistorted experience that is precisely what is needed to force reorganization of the old schemes. . . . [T]he client can fully explore his reactions to one such situation and become aware of the elements in a more accurate and balanced form, that is, can reprocess the situation, [and] the effect will be to force reorganization of all the relevant schemes. (1974, pp. 293–294)

The only difference between this information-processing view and mine is that I would stress the role of anxiety in causing the distortions.

Therapy both permits and forces the breaking of old "schemes," giving the client the chance to reprocess or process more completely "schemes" (experiences) that normally would have been only glimpsed and prematurely abandoned.

■ The Effects of Therapy

I can summarize the effects of therapy briefly—in theory—by considering the three general characteristics of anxiety-based problems and the general goals for effective living discussed in chapter 5. Keep in mind that these are just brief theoretical statements that assume you understand all the previous material.

Reducing Painful Emotions

If anxiety is the result of internal conflicts—fearing one's own motivated thoughts, memories, urges, and feelings—then resolving the specific conflicts will relieve the anxiety. The client accurately faces the frightening thoughts and feelings, being more completely exposed to them so that the fear of them extinguishes and/or is counterconditioned. The client entered therapy saying, "I feel awful and I don't know why." Therapy relieves the specific conflicts that led to these feelings.

Improving Problem Solving

The distortions and "neurotic stupidity" that plagued the client resulted from anxiety-based distortions about particular memories, feelings, and current thoughts. Therapy "makes the unconscious conscious" through step-by-step exposure of more and more complete experiencing of the client's thoughts and feelings. Now the client can think and act more wisely because he or she has more accurate information.

In addition, the client has become a better problem solver in general— beyond the solution of specific problems. He or she has been repeatedly reinforced for thinking and facing feelings and strongly seeking out experiences and solutions. The client no longer needs therapy to solve new problems that will inevitably arise.

Reducing Maladaptive Behavior ("Symptom Reduction")

Maladaptive behavior can be reflected in the inability to take effective action as well as in the self-defeating behaviors that often get called "symptoms." In the previous section I touched on the effective action that follows accurate self-knowledge. "Symptom" reduction follows from effective therapy because the anxiety that maintained the self-defeating behavior is reduced.

People do self-defeating things because they somehow lead to immediate anxiety reduction. The "symptoms" are by definition punishing, self-defeating behaviors (or they wouldn't be called "symptoms"), but they are preferable to the anxiety they help avoid. If the anxiety is reduced, the "symptoms" will no longer be reinforced and in nearly all cases will disappear because of the pain they cause naturally in the person's life. This pain is now able to naturally punish the self-defeating behaviors away because the behaviors no longer serve an anxiety-reducing function.

Symptom Substitution

A sometimes unfriendly debate has been going on between psychoanalysts and behavior therapists over the question of symptom substitution.

Remove the symptom, say the behavior therapists, and you have cured the neurosis. No, reply the analysts, the symptom is only an anxiety substitute, and if you remove the symptom, you only create a need for a new symptom, which you will get. My response is that both sides are partly correct, depending on the nature of a particular problem. I certainly reject the psychic-illness model, but a complex learning model using internal conflicts predicts that sometimes you will get symptom substitution if you take away a symptom directly and sometimes you won't.

In the instance of a directly conditioned fear (see chapter 16), such as with the miner afraid of dark hallways, direct treatment of the fear symptom would settle the issue without symptom substitution. If the "symptom" is based on internal conflict, however, the answer is still "maybe" to whether the person will develop a new symptom. If we directly treat the conflicted teacher's fear of hallways, she will still be in intense conflict over her relationship with her parents and will find some way to deal with it, to reduce the anxiety. If the way she finds is somehow self-defeating we will say she has a new "symptom," but she might well be driven to talk with a friend and develop a relationship that helps her contain her anxiety—not a new symptom, just because it's not self-defeating. Or she could do anything in between, such as throwing herself into graduate study to the exclusion of everything else and "succeeding" in a way that we would be hard put to judge as either self-defeating or adaptive.

Additional Personal Gains

More positively, we can say how therapy contributes to high self-esteem; personal autonomy; open, full experiencing; and rewarding intimate relationships. Again, I will be using brief and too-mechanistic language, but my purpose is to articulate theoretical connections. I am assuming that you will add the human complexity I intend from other chapters.

Feeling personal worth. One of the most common and most gratifying changes to hear in clients is when they say something like, "I'm not sure why, but I just like myself better now" or "I guess I am a more selfish person than I would let myself know before, but that's OK, really. I mean, I'm OK as a person." Theoretically, what happens is that clients come to therapy repelled by some of their own thoughts and feelings. At this stage, what these clients "are" feels bad and unworthy. As therapy progresses, those thoughts and feelings come to feel good, acceptable, and even worthy. Clients come to feel personal worth.

Autonomy and competence. I spoke earlier of improved problem solving that results from the client's doing the work in therapy. Beyond this, the client gains a sense of personal strength, a sense of control and independence that comes from facing a difficult challenge and winning—the "I did this myself" feeling.

Accurate self-experiencing. Also beyond "improved problem solving" that results from more complete information, the person has sought experiencing and become comfortable with it. He or she is not afraid to feel new feelings and seek new experiences and is congruent with him- or herself.

Ability to be intimate. The effects of therapy listed previously can be understood as direct outcomes of evocatively empathic therapy; they follow directly from its nature. It is not so clear that this kind of conflict relief leads as directly to the ability to be in a close relationship, but this is one of the important goals of therapy. We can say, of course, that being in a good therapy relationship helps the person feel comfortable and acceptable with another person. It is also likely that the client learns to be empathic from the therapist's example and that one of the important areas of understanding and action that the client will deal with in therapy is relationship issues. A consequence of this problem solving will be improvement of the client's relationships outside therapy. As with the chapter on relationship issues, though, the effects of therapy on the client's ability to be close are so complex that they are difficult to state succinctly.

■ The Consequences of Ineffective Therapy

Therapy is most effective when the therapist can be at the "leading edge" of the client's experiencing, bringing to life what the client is trying to say and can't quite say. Our conflict-relief model predicts that both working "behind" the client and working "ahead of" the client's intended message will be ineffective.

Working Behind the Conflict Region

Being "behind" the client means giving largely responses in which the therapist tries to reflect understanding but either exactly restates what the client said or dampens the meaning and feeling of the client's remarks. The therapist might respond to a feelingful comment with cognitive talk about feelings or might try to draw some general principle about what the client said, moving the client away from current experiencing. This exemplifies the common and incorrect stereotype of the client-centered therapist who is supportive but passive. In theoretical terms, this kind of functioning should be totally ineffective. Since the therapist never articulates anything but the material that the client can already explicitly face, or even draws the client back from this, the anxiety cues would never be faced. The therapist would be participating in the avoidance of the feared experiences, working at the point of retreat rather than approach. Actually, this passive therapist probably would make some progress, but very slowly. Since clients often explicitly verbalize conflict material, the therapist who responds only to explicit material will occasionally help the client face experiencing. Usually, however, progress will be painfully slow, both the therapist and the client may perceive the therapist as inanely repetitive, and therapy will frequently be stuck on dead center.

The therapist's role is an *active* role. Doing therapy is hard work, not a job that involves passive listening. Instead, it requires *actively* listening for the client's attempts to deal with conflictual material, or have I already said this somewhere before?

Working Ahead of the Conflict Region

Most therapists agree that passive reflection is an inappropriate approach to psychotherapy, but many will disagree when I say that working ahead of or out of the conflict region is also undesirable. I suspect that working behind the conflict region does its damage by frustrating the client and leading to failure experiences in therapy. I suspect that working ahead of the conflict region does its damage much more directly.

By using the conflict model (see the diagram on page 227), we can specify ways that a therapist could do some good by working ahead of the conflict region in ways that expose clients to painful thoughts and feelings in the presence of a supportive therapist whose acceptance helps the person face those feelings. These benefits, although real, are won at a price—a price that need not be paid if the therapist is functioning maximally as evocatively empathic. In addition, there are risks growing out of therapist error about what thoughts and feelings need to be faced.

First, let's consider the therapist whose personal strength and great acceptance and reassurance help the client face thoughts and feelings that the therapist has directed the client toward, through suggestions, interpretations, and therapist-initiated confrontations. Such an approach might result in anxiety reduction and in the person's trying solutions the therapist has suggested, perhaps even breaking some vicious circles in the person's life. This directive approach, however, lacks the element of reinforcing the client's approach responses—of making the client strong and independent. In fact, I would argue quite strongly that although this approach might result in the solution of particular problems (assuming the therapist is very wise), it will reinforce dependency on outside help in the client. In the long run, this may be a far greater disservice than the solutions are a short-term help.

Another way that working ahead of the conflict region discourages independence and autonomy is by subtly punishing the client's own approach responses—attempts to think and face experiencing. In evocatively empathic therapy, the client is continually making approach responses, feeling mildly anxious, and then having the anxiety drop. If, after the client tries to take a step, the therapist arouses intense anxiety, the relief does not follow the client's attempt. It follows, when it comes, the therapist's expert guidance. Just as strength and autonomy come from thousands of small experiences of facing pain and then feeling better, a powerful therapist can build dependency.

In addition, changes in self-esteem occur in subtly different ways in these two different approaches to therapy. Low self-esteem is the result of being made anxious by one's own thoughts and feelings, and if the anxiety responses to those inner processes can be changed, an increase in self-esteem should result, regardless of the therapy approach used. An important difference, however, is that the empathy-oriented therapist responds to the thoughts and feelings *as emitted by and originating with the client*. It is quite possible that the therapist can elicit the thoughts and feelings and extinguish and countercondition the fears aroused. If, however, the "curse is taken off" after the client emits the thoughts and feelings, it is he or she who is responsible for, and takes the emotional "credit" for, becoming a worthy person.

A further risk in working outside the conflict region is the arousal of intense anxiety that makes the client need defenses against the therapist and the therapy process. In learning terms, rather than the desired extinction, there will be higher-order conditioning of the therapist and therapy situation as anxiety cues. Not only is the therapist consistently being paired with powerful anxiety cues, she or he is seen as the source of these cues. The sometimes subtle effect that then escapes the therapist's notice is that therapy is slowed down as the client directly and indirectly engages in defensive avoidance. Do you remember the therapist who said, "I don't have the patience to shape clients"? He believed that direct attacks were quicker, but I think this apparent quickness was an illusion—the same illusion that makes so many people use punishment with children and subordinates. It seems to work quickly because there is short-term compliance. This is an illusion because there is also long-term resistance and defense.

Establishing the therapist as a source of threat, however subtle, sets the stage for a new conflict in which the client may fear therapy but be unable to leave it—because of the therapist's subtle pressures, society's pressures, and perhaps a desperate need for help. The therapist can create a conflict situation that itself calls for subtle and complicated kinds of defenses. The therapist's job is to take away the need for defenses in the therapy session. If the therapist creates a conflict situation, he or she is likely to meet therapeutic impasses, resistance, and perhaps most dangerously, "flights into health." What better way to get rid of your therapist than to "get better" suddenly?

A dangerous consequence of flights into health is that they give aggressive therapists false feedback about the effectiveness of what they do. Many therapists insist that they do their interpreting and manipulating because they have seen them work. We all want to believe that we are effective, and it is difficult to face one's therapeutic failures. It is easier to remember the successes, and clients who "get well" quickly may be additionally reinforcing some destructive therapist behavior. As an aside, all of us therapists are vulnerable to selective perception of our effectiveness, and so each of us is obligated to know the research evidence, to be able to say why we do what we do, and to get frank feedback from another therapist who can observe our work.

One last consequence of working outside the conflict region—that is, from the therapist's frame of reference rather than the client's—is that the therapist is just going to be wrong a lot of the time about the best course of action or what the client is "really" feeling. The comments made so far have all assumed that the therapist was exactly correct in his or her interpretation or advice but helped the client see it too early. You and I are not that smart; people are too complex, and it is almost irrationally arrogant to think that one can tell another how to live and to experience. Even the most self-assured therapist would have to admit to some errors in judgment and inter-pretation. When the therapist does make the inevitable errors, he or she pays a price by making the client feel less understood, by punishing the client for approach responses, and by providing misleading and even dangerously wrong "answers" that the client may have trouble rejecting. Therapists can do damage.

CHAPTER 100

Research Evidence

One of my professors in graduate school, after years of doing therapy research, told a group of us that if we ever wanted to do such research, we should have ourselves hospitalized until the urge passed. The problems are enormous in doing well-controlled research on such a complex process as psychotherapy, and it is easy to spend a lot of time with little or no payoff. Studies of actual therapy (as opposed to laboratory analogues to therapy) are vulnerable to many methodological problems: too few points were sampled; the therapists knew the purpose of the study; outcome ratings were not strictly independent of client perceptions; and so forth. We can't sit around waiting for perfectly controlled research, however. We have to use all possible sources of knowledge to offer honestly effective treatment and to improve treatment. Personal experience and the experience of others are certainly two such sources of knowledge, but as the Yiddish proverb says, "For example is no proof." It is sometimes said of the treatment of obesity that everything works and nothing works. There are patients who lose weight in virtually any program, but none of the programs are effective for large groups of people. There probably also are therapy clients who will benefit from nearly any kind of treatment, so that we constantly hear of marvelous new therapies (like the infamous tickling therapy of 30 years ago) whose founders regale us with case histories of their successes.

Experience is valid but needs the corrective influence of research. Imperfect as our evidence is, we need to learn from it what we can. There is sufficient evidence to make several conclusions that apply to the issues raised in this book. There are other valuable conclusions to be drawn, but I have selected ones that apply directly to us as therapists. For us the critical issue is whether we can honestly offer evocative empathy, acceptance, and genuineness within a good therapeutic relationship, as the foundation of therapy.

Several general conclusions are justified by the evidence. Some of them bear directly on the skills I have been discussing, and I will therefore elaborate on them, referring you to more complete sources on the others so you can examine them if you wish.

The Psychotherapy Division of the American Psychological Association established a Taskforce on Empirically Supported Therapy Relationships.

From their survey of the research literature, they said: "[from] hundreds of studies across 60 years . . . we can reliably conclude:

1. Psychotherapy is successful in general, and the average treated client is better off than 80% of untreated subjects.

2. Comparative studies of psychotherapy techniques consistently report the relative equivalence of therapies in promoting client change.

3. Measures of therapeutic relationship variables consistently correlate more highly with client outcome than specialized therapy techniques. Associations between the therapeutic relationship and client outcome are strongest when measured by client ratings of both constructs.

4. Some therapists are better than others at contributing to positive client outcome. Clients characterize such therapists as more understanding and accepting, empathic, warm, and supportive. They engage in fewer negative behaviors such as blaming, ignoring or rejecting" (Lambert & Barley, 2002, p. 26).

I think it is important to add a further conclusion to this list:

5. Some therapists do damage.

■ Therapy Works

"Psychotherapy is successful in general, and the average treated client is better off than 80% of untreated subjects" (Lambert & Barley, 2002, p. 26).

In the 1950s and 60s there was considerable debate over whether receiving therapy was any more effective than just being on a waiting list or receiving no treatment at all. Eysenck (1952, 1969) challenged the effectiveness of therapy and set the stage for decades of research on whether therapy works. However, by today, "the efficacy of psychotherapy has now been firmly established and is no longer a subject of debate" (Wampold, 2001, p. 59). "[T]he average effect associated with psychological treatment approaches one standard deviation unit" (Lambert & Bergin, 1994, p. 147). These statements are based on a huge body of data that I won't belabor more; the articles I've cited can give you excellent summaries of the research.

■ The Major "Schools" of Therapy Demonstrate Roughly Equal Positive Outcomes

"Comparative studies of psychotherapy techniques consistently report the relative equivalence of therapies in promoting client change" (Lambert & Barley, 2002, p. 26). This is an upsetting conclusion for people who have a fervent investment in one particular approach to therapy, but it is well established.

When the "all bona fide approaches are equally effective" idea first became popular, critics tried to ridicule it by calling it the Dodo Bird Effect, after the confused dodo bird in *Alice in Wonderland*, who judged a race as, "All have won and all must have prizes." But as evidence accumulated for the Dodo Bird Effect, proponents adopted the term with enthusiasm. "Indeed the 'Dodo Bird Verdict' was perhaps the most robust finding in psychotherapy research during the 20th century" (Nietzel, Bernstein, Kramer, & Milich, 2003, p. 314). "The Dodo Bird Verdict Is Alive and Well—Mostly," is a large meta-analysis of 17 meta-analyses that compared active treatments with each other found "small and nonsignificant (differences)" (Luborsky, Rosenthal, Diguer, Andrusyna, Berman, Levitt, Seligman, & Krause, 2002, p. 2). Messer and Wampold (2002) say, "Study after study, meta-analysis after meta-analysis, and Luborsky et al.'s meta-meta-analysis have produced the same small or nonexistent difference among therapies" (p. 23).

One school of treatment is not demonstrably superior to another when therapists are simply grouped by school or techniques used (Benish, Imel, & Wampold, 2007; Bergin & Garfield, 1994; Lipsey & Wilson, 1993; Luborsky, Singer, & Luborsky, 1975; Messer & Wampold, 2002; Seligman, 1995; Shapiro & Shapiro, 1982; Smith, Glass, & Miller, 1980; Wampold, 2001, 2006; Wampold, Minam, Baskin, & Tierney, 2002; Wampold, Mondin, Moody, & Ahn, 1997; Wampold, Mondin, Moody, Stich, Benson, & Ahn, 1997; Watson & Geller, 2005). Some writers have challenged the idea that there are no differences in efficacy among the major approaches to therapy (Beutler, 2002; Chambless, 2002; Crits-Christoph, 1997; Howard, Krause, Saunders, & Kopta, 1997), but the evidence seems overwhelming that if there are any differences among various techniques or schools of therapy, those differences are very small.

■ The Best Predictor of Outcome

"Measures of therapeutic relationship variables consistently correlate more highly with client outcome than specialized therapy techniques. Associations between the therapeutic relationship and client outcome are strongest when measured by client ratings of both constructs" (Lambert & Barley, 2002, p. 26).

If "schools" of therapy don't differentially predict success in therapy, what does? Across all approaches to therapy, the therapeutic relationship is the strongest and most consistent correlate of outcome. In reflecting on his long and productive career as a psychotherapy researcher and practitioner, Strupp recalled, "[I]t also began to dawn on me that 'therapeutic techniques' in the usual sense may have relatively little to do with outcome. I began to speculate that the greater weight was borne by the quality of the emerging patient-therapist relationship" (1996, p. 136). Strupp's insights are supported by the large majority of research findings (Lambert & Simon, 2008; Najavits & Strupp, 1994). Whiston and Sexton (1993) reviewed research on therapy outcome and said, "More than any other element to date, the therapeutic relationship is significantly related to positive client outcome" (p. 45).

As I have said many places in this book, the relationship is primary; techniques and skill are important, but they are secondary. Strupp (1996) concludes:

> Although the practice of psychotherapy demands skills—both personal and technical—in the final analysis we should be training *persons, not technicians*, and we should never forget—despite managed care and the technocracy of our age—that psychotherapy in the ideal sense seeks to effect healing and personality growth through an interpersonal relationship. Hence the contemporary emphasis on the *therapeutic alliance* is altogether appropriate. (p. 138)

Strupp's mention of the therapeutic alliance nicely leads into some further conclusions by the Taskforce on Empirically Supported Therapy Relationships. As we've seen, they concluded that relationship measures correlate with successful outcome more than any techniques. They refined this statement by identifying four "demonstrably effective relationship elements" that contribute to the therapeutic relationship and are supported by research (Lambert & Barley, 2002; Norcross, 2002).

1. The therapeutic alliance

2. Empathy

3. Goal consensus and collaboration

4. Cohesion in group therapy

The Therapeutic Alliance

We discussed the therapeutic alliance in chapter 6 and saw that the term has a number of definitions, and so it is not surprising that it has been measured by several different scales (Elvins & Green, 2008; Horvath, 2006; Horvath & Greenberg, 1994; Luborsky, 1993, 2000). All of the scales include some version of two fundamental facets of the alliance. The first facet includes the (1) *personal bond* between client and therapist. This bond is made up of such characteristics as empathic understanding, acceptance, supportiveness, and warmth. The second facet can best be described as a (2) *collaborative commitment to the mutual work and goals of therapy.* Studies of the alliance consistently demonstrate a strong relationship between a good therapeutic alliance and positive outcome in therapy. In general, this holds true when the alliance is rated by clients, by therapists, and by outside observers, but the client's perceptions are the best predictor of successful outcome, especially when measures are taken early in therapy. (Krupnick, Elkin, Collins, Simmens, Sotsky, Pilkonis, & Watkins, 1994). There is considerable evidence that the client's perception of a good alliance as early as the third interview is a strong predictor of eventual outcome. In fact, Eaton, Abeles, and Gutfreund (1988) say that "strength of therapeutic alliance is established within the first three sessions of psychotherapy with little significant change over the course of therapy" (p. 536). The therapist characteristics and techniques that promote the alliance include the ability to instill confidence and trust; dependability, benevolence, and responsiveness; empathy; and the responsive and collaborative application of techniques (Ackerman & Hilsentroth, 2001).

Well over a hundred studies and meta-analyses find a significant, consistent relationship between the therapeutic alliance and successful outcome. This finding holds across all therapy approaches studied (Blatt, Zuroff, Quinlan, & Pilkonis, 1996; Gaston, 1990; Gaston, Thompson, Gallagher, Cournoyer, & Gagnon, 1998; Horvath & Bedi, 2002; Horvath & Symonds, 1991; Krupnick et al., 1996; Martin, Garske, & Davis, 2000; Wampold, 2001).

> After an exhaustive literature review, the data from 79 studies (58 published, 21 unpublished) were aggregated using meta-analytic procedures. The results . . . indicate that the overall relation of therapeutic alliance with outcome is moderate, but consistent, regardless of many of the variables that have been posited to influence this relationship. . . . [such as] the type of outcome measure used in the study, the type of outcome rater, the time of alliance assessment, the type of alliance rater, the type of treatment provided, or the publication status of the study. (Martin, Garske, & Davis, 2000, p. 438)

Empathy

The component of the therapeutic alliance that has received the most attention and been studied most in research is empathy. Not surprisingly, measures of the whole alliance tend to predict outcome better than measures of just empathy. There is strong evidence that empathy is related to successful outcome, and this is especially true of empathy as perceived by the client. Hundreds of studies have found a moderate and consistent relationship between empathy and outcome (Bohart, Elliott, Greenberg, & Watson, 2002; Burns & Nolen-Hoeksema, 1991, 1992; Cain, 2007; Clark, 2007; Lafferty, Beutler, & Crago, 1991; Orlinsky, Grawe, & Parks, 1994; Sexton, Schofield, & Whiston, 1997). This includes studies with many different approaches. For example, Burns & Nolen-Hoeksema (1991, 1992) report strong effects for empathy with cognitive behavior therapy. "This study demonstrated that therapeutic empathy has a moderate-to-large causal effect on recovery from depression in a group of 186 patients treated with cognitive-behavioral therapy (CBT)" (1992, p. 441). "The causal effects of therapeutic empathy on recovery appear to be large" (Burns & Auerbach, 1996, p. 161). Research studies on all major therapy approaches have consistently found correlations between empathy and outcome. The single best summary correlation is .32, which for correlations is a medium effect size (Bohart, Elliott, Greenberg, & Watson, 2002, p. 96). The correlations between empathy and outcome range from .18 (for psychodynamic therapy) to .25 (for experiential/humanistic therapy) to .30 (for "other/unspecified") to .49 (for cognitive-behavioral therapy) (Bohart, Elliott, Greenberg, & Watson, 2002, p. 96).

Client perceptions of therapist empathy.   As you know from our previous chapters, the key is that the client feels known and understood. There are many ways for a therapist to be empathic (Greenberg & Elliott, 1997; chapter

8 of this book). It is most important that the client perceives the therapist as an empathic person.

As discussed in chapter 2, there are three steps in empathic responding: the therapist must hear the message; the therapist must convey his or her understanding to the client; and the client must perceive the understanding. Barrett-Lennard (1993) points out that the process can break down at any of these steps and that the critical element is the third one. It is conceivable that a therapist might articulate an understanding without the client's perception of the message as accurate—for whatever reason—so that an observer would call the therapist empathic, but the expected impact on the client would not occur. Thus, it is not surprising that the client's perceptions offer the strongest support for evocative-empathy-oriented therapy.

Gurman (1977) summarizes the results of 25 studies, 22 of which were of actual therapy conducted by therapists of different orientations—psychoanalytic, behavioral, client-centered, and eclectic. Of the 22 therapy studies, 21 showed a significant effect of client perceived therapeutic "core conditions," and Gurman concludes that "there exists substantial, if not overwhelming, evidence in support of the hypothesized relationship between patient-perceived therapeutic conditions and outcome in individual psychotherapy and counseling" (p. 523).

The most commonly used instrument to measure client perceptions is Barrett-Lennard's Relationship Inventory (RI) (1978, 1993). For our purposes, the RI also has some implications for training, and you might find it useful to obtain a copy (Barrett-Lennard, 1978) just to read the items that reflect the critical client perceptions—to see what you hope your clients will feel. Half the items are worded in a positive way and half in a negative way, so that the empathy scale includes items like, "He realizes what I mean even when I have difficulty in saying it" and, "Sometimes she thinks that I feel a certain way, because that's the way she feels."

Lafferty, Beutler, and Crago (1991) used the RI and several other measures to compare two groups of therapists in training. The therapists were divided into "more effective" and "less effective" groups, depending on how much their clients had improved. Their study "supports the significance of the therapist's empathy in effective psychotherapy. Patients of less-effective therapists felt less understood by their therapists than did patients of more-effective therapists." (p. 79).

One understandable but distressing finding that Gurman (1977) reports is that there is "very little agreement" between clients' perceptions of their therapists and therapists' perceptions of themselves. This results from therapists' rating themselves consistently positively, so that there of course is little or no relation between successful outcome and what therapists, as a group, perceive themselves doing. That is scary.

Raters' perceptions of empathy and the core conditions.   Although client perceptions are theoretically the most important measure of empathy and the other core conditions, most of the early research on them centered on data from trained judges using the rating scales developed by Truax and Carkhuff (1967) and others (Rogers, et al., 1967).

Rogers' pioneering work (Rogers, et al., 1967; Rogers & Dymond, 1954) is generally seen as the start of systematic research on psychotherapy, and his influence on theory, practice, and research has led to an enormous research literature. Earlier summaries of this literature (Truax & Carkhuff, 1967; Truax & Mitchell, 1971) were consistently enthusiastic about the findings from judgments of tape recordings of therapy and led many writers (including me [Martin, 1972], unfortunately) to accept uncritically the data as conclusive. It now appears that some of Truax's data "were presented somewhat selectively and did not convey the full findings that were available" (Gurman, 1977, p. 505).

✱ It has also become clearer that there are many methodological problems with tape-based judgments that would make it very difficult to find even a strong phenomenon that might actually exist in therapy. For example, tape sampling uses only a few minutes of therapy, sometimes from among many hours, and this would inevitably reduce the validity of the measure. Tape ratings, client perceptions, and therapist perceptions do not correlate strongly with each other. Audiotape eliminates all the visual nonverbal cues. The sex of rater may interact with the sex of therapist. There are some indications that the ratings may reflect some general dimension or "halo effect." The scales seem to measure therapeutic conditions as delivered by client-centered therapists more validly than therapists of other orientations even though the other therapists might well be perceived by clients as empathic, accepting, and genuine. (See Lambert, DeJulio, & Stein, 1978, for a critical discussion of these issues.)

Mitchell, Bozarth, and Krauft (1977) have forcefully discussed the most difficult methodological issue. In a great many of the published studies, therapists are compared as *higher* or *lower* on empathy, for example, rather than as high in absolute terms—that is, above the minimally facilitative level (3.0 on the rating scales discussed in chapter 1). In many of the studies for which Mitchell and his colleagues could reconstruct data, the "high empathy" therapists actually averaged less than the minimally facilitative level. Mitchell and colleagues conclude that the core-conditions hypothesis has not been tested adequately by these studies. It is clear that a study in which the best therapists averaged less than 3.0 on the rating scales would in no way be a test of evocative empathy.

That's the bad news. Although Mitchell, Bozarth, and Krauft (1977) say that the relation between outcome and rated core conditions is far more complicated than the early summaries implied, they also say, "In some respects it is surprising that higher interpersonal skills levels were found to be related to positive outcomes as often as they were, given such problems as the low levels of most psychotherapists' functioning, marginally rigorous measurement criteria, the difficulties inherent in training raters, etc." (p. 486). They report some studies, some of which support the core-conditions hypothesis and some of which do not. Lambert and colleagues (1978) are generally critical of this literature (focusing mainly on tape-rating evidence) and say that "generally well designed and executed studies . . . present only modest evidence in favor of the hypothesis that such factors as accurate empathy, warmth and genuineness relate to measures of outcome" (p. 472). In view of the difficulties with gathering valid data from tape ratings, that which does exist offers some support for the core conditions.

Throughout this book, I have stressed that the goal of evocative empathy is to make the client feel deeply understood. There are many ways to do this, and virtually any rating scale that only looks at therapist behavior will be doomed to limited validity. The convincing evidence is largely based on client perceptions of empathy and the core conditions.

Goal Consensus and Collaboration

The client's and therapist's agreement on goals and on a sense of shared responsibility for therapy is one of the major elements of the therapeutic alliance, but these two elements have also been researched separately. "There is general support for a positive relationship between goal consensus and psychotherapy outcome, [and stronger support for] collaborative involvement" (Tryon & Winograd, 2002, p. 119). Goal consensus and collaboration are both demonstrably effective parts of the therapeutic relationship.

Cohesion in Group Therapy

The fourth demonstrably effective relationship variable is one we discussed in chapter 13. Consistent with the finding that the relationship is the most important factor in individual therapy, group cohesion correlates with positive outcome more strongly than any other variable (Burlingame, Fuhriman, & Johnson, 2002). For group members, cohesion usually involves a sense of personal ownership and place. Here I want to reemphasize what was stated in chapter 13:

> For example, *interpersonal* elements of cohesion can be found in a group member's sense of belonging and acceptance and a personal commitment and allegiance to the group. *Intragroup* elements include attractiveness and compatibility felt among the group; mutual liking and trust; support, caring, and mutual stimulation that creates learning; and collective commitment to the "work" of the group. (Burlingame, Fuhriman, & Johnson, 2002, p. 71)

■ The Person of the Therapist Matters— Some Are Just Better

"Some therapists are better than others at contributing to positive client outcome. Clients characterize such therapists as more understanding and accepting, empathic, warm, and supportive. They engage in fewer negative behaviors such as blaming, ignoring or rejecting" (Lambert & Barley, 2002, p. 26).

This might seem an obvious conclusion, since in every human activity some people are better than others. But this conclusion goes deeper than that. It reveals something about why therapy is primarily a relationship matter. No matter which of the major techniques a group of therapists subscribes to, some of the therapists will have excellent outcomes, most will have good outcomes, some will have little effect, and a few will do damage. The therapist's personal characteristics such as indifference and detachment strongly influence the alliance (Hersoug, Høglend, Havik, von der Lippe, Monsen, 2009). "The essence of therapy is embodied in the therapist . . . [T]herapists within a given treatment account for a large proportion of the variance. Clearly, the person of the therapist is a critical factor in the success of therapy" (Wampold, 2001, p. 202).

"[T]herapists' effects generally overshadowed any differences between different forms of treatment" (Luborsky, Crits-Christoph, McLellan, Woody, Piper, Liberman, Imber, & Pilkonis, 1986, p. 509). A review of 15 studies that used 27 different treatments found that therapists accounted for about 9% of the total variance. (This is a significant amount of variance, roughly equal to an effect size of .50–.60) (Crits-Christoph, Baranackie, Kurcias, Carroll, Luborsky, McLellan, Woody, Thompson, Gallagher, & Zitrin, 1991).

Norcross (2002) says, "Although efficacy research has gone to considerable lengths to eliminate the individual therapist as a variable that might account for patient improvement, the inescapable fact is that the therapist as a person is a central agent of change" (p. 4). Some research has tried to standardize different treatments and compare them by using treatment manuals, intensive and highly structured training, and close monitoring. However, "although there were few outcome differences among the treatments, over 6% of the outcome variance (1%–12% range) was due to therapists. Despite impressive attempts to experimentally render individual practitioners as controlled variables, it is simply not possible to mask the person and the contribution of the therapist" (Norcross, 2002, p. 5). Aveline (2005) argues, "The character of the therapist is a vital component in effective psychotherapy, especially ambitious, relationship-focused, long-term work" (p. 155).

■ Some Therapists Do Damage

Finally, I will end on a note that is both disturbing and indirectly confirmatory of the value of the therapeutic conditions we have been discussing. Bergin (1963, 1966) coined the term *deterioration effect* to refer to the finding that groups of clients had higher variability of adjustment after treatment than before and higher variability than various control groups. This suggested that simply looking at findings of average improvement was masking the fact that some clients were getting better in therapy and some were actually getting worse. Bergin's thinking received its first impetus from an observation of patients in the Wisconsin Project (Rogers et al., 1967) on therapy with schizophrenic problems.

As a group, treated patients fared no better than nontreated patients. Some, however, had improved and some actually got worse; outcome was related to therapists' levels of empathy, acceptance, and genuineness. Subsequently, Bergin expanded his observations to a wide range of evidence and argued that many of the "negative effects" reported in the therapy literature resulted from lumping both positive and damaging therapy into group averages. Braucht (1970) criticized Bergin's position, but Bergin's response (1970) and a review by Lambert, Bergin, and Collins (1977) establish the deterioration effect as a frightening reality. Mays and Franks (1980; Franks & Mays, 1980) say that the "jury should still be out" on whether deterioration effects are the result of therapy. Bergin (1980) responds that, "the empirical case for therapist-induced deterioration is compelling" (p. 93) and that although the term *jury* isn't entirely appropriate, it is interesting that 90% of professionals surveyed (Strupp, Hadley, & Gomes-Schwartz, 1977), "agreed to the existence of the phenomenon" (Bergin, 1980, p. 98).

The critical issue is to determine what therapist variables and what client variables contribute to client deterioration. Mohr (1995) reviewed 46 studies that dealt with negative outcomes among nonpsychotic clients. He concluded that negative outcomes do occur in some psychotherapy, and he summarized some tentative conclusions about client and therapist variables associated with deterioration. Clients at risk for negative outcomes include those with borderline personality disorders and those with obsessive-compulsive disorders and severe problems with interpersonal relationships. Clients who expect therapy to be painless also are at risk.

Our more compelling interest, however, is in how therapists contribute to client deterioration and what we can do about it (Nolan, Strassle, Roback, & Binder, 2004). None of Mohr's conclusions will surprise you, after reading this book. He cites lack of empathy, high concentrations of transference interpretations, negative countertransference, and arguing with clients about therapy as therapist factors associated with negative outcomes. In some cases, it was also damaging when therapists underestimated the seriousness of clients' problems.

Low levels of empathy and acceptance certainly seem to be related to client deterioration but are not the whole answer. "Therapeutic encounters which are characterized by low levels [of empathy, warmth, and genuineness] can be expected to sustain a higher casualty rate" (Lambert, Bergin, & Collins, 1977, p. 464), but simply having low levels seems related to ineffectual rather than detrimental therapy. Important clues come from Yalom and Lieberman's (1971) study of "psychiatric casualties" in encounter groups. Of seven kinds of group leaders, the one that was most likely to do damage was the "aggressive stimulator," who was described as "intrusive, confrontive, challenging, caring, . . . self-revealing . . . charismatic, authoritarian, and as focusing on the individual" (Lambert et al., 1977, p. 471). A similar clue can be found in R. Mitchell's dissertation (1971, summarized in Mitchell et al.,

1977). Mitchell was interested in immediacy, the tendency to focus on the therapist–client relationship. She divided the therapists in her study into four groups: high facilitative conditions and high immediacy; high facilitative conditions and low immediacy; low facilitative conditions and high immediacy; and low on both measures. None of her analyses predicted success very well, but group three—low empathy, warmth, and genuineness combined with a high tendency to focus on the therapist–client relationship (high immediacy)—showed significant client deterioration over the course of treatment and was the only group to do so. This finding is probably consistent with Mohr's conclusion about the negative effects of high concentrations of transference interpretations.

Mitchell and colleagues caution us not to make too much of one study but say that these findings have great intuitive appeal. I agree. Much of the damage that I have seen done by therapy has been related to inappropriate and conflicting messages through which some therapists trap clients in dependency conflicts while being insensitive to their experiences. Authoritarian intrusiveness combined with the failure to establish appropriate limits on the therapy relationship seems especially dangerous. This may be the same issue, but Lambert et al. (1977) also discuss therapist exploitation of the client—by therapists who "consciously or unconsciously utilize dependent individuals (in this case their clients) to satisfy the therapist's own personal needs" (p. 469). Mohr (1995) says that expressive-experiential therapies tend to produce more instances of deterioration than other approaches. This is consistent with the evidence on "aggressive stimulators" and therapists who focus on the therapy relationship in a context of low empathy and acceptance. In many ways, this book presents an experiential/cognitive approach but always within a strong relationship. Experiential therapy is remarkably powerful in a beneficial way, but that power also carries with it a risk for abuse by aggressive therapists.

To summarize, the factors that seem to contribute to the deterioration effect include (Horvath & Bedi, 2002; Mohr, 1995):

- Therapist's "take charge" attitude early in therapy
- Insight or interpretations offered prematurely
- High concentrations of transference interpretations
- Arguing with clients
- "Aggressive stimulator" style: intrusive, confrontational, challenging, caring, self-revealing, charismatic, authoritarian, focusing on the individual
- High focus on the client-therapist relationship, combined with low empathy, genuineness, and warmth
- "Cold" therapists
- Therapist irritability
- Lack of empathy
- Negative countertransference

I guess this is as good a way as any to finish this book—with a sharp reminder that therapy is a complex relationship process. Part of what makes therapy interesting and challenging and rewarding is that it is complex and personal. That also carries with it a big responsibility to be as skillful and as clear about yourself as a person as you can be.

Appendix A
Observing Others

This appendix presents written transcripts of therapy sessions, along with comments by the therapists and one of the clients involved. This is one way to expose you to the work of others. You can also use the typed transcripts as a sort of programmed text by moving a piece of paper down the page, stopping at the end of each client response, and formulating a response you might have made. Doing this with a friend or in a group will be a sobering experience, as you will become aware of the various kinds of messages other people perceive, and it will be good feedback on the accuracy of your own perceptions. You can also compare your response with what the therapist actually said—which may or may not have been the best possible response.

■ Observing Bob Lee—Multi-Cultural Counseling and Consulting Center, San Diego, California

This therapy session was conducted as a demonstration in front of a group of other therapists and counselors at a workshop on therapy. The session itself interestingly illustrates therapy, and the discussion that follows gives a fascinating glimpse into what the session felt like both to Bob, as the therapist, and to the client. At the time, Bob and the client did not know that the session might be used as part of a book, but the evening after the interview, the client had written down her reactions, and some of her comments follow the transcript of the session.

The Interview

CLIENT: My nervousness is mostly related to the group, I think. Sometimes I have a . . . a hesitancy to volunteer because I . . . I always want to jump into things all the time. And sometimes I talk too much, and it . . . uh . . . don't let other people have a chance. That's why I've been waiting [Mm-hm]. . . .

THERAPIST: It's like there's some kind of . . . uh . . . enthusiasm or excitement to kind of get in there and get involved, but it's also a conflicting thing because part of you says, "Hey, let's let some other people have the . . . have some time."

C: I have been told a lot, even as a facilitator, I step in too much . . . and, um, . . . I want . . . I'm trying very hard not to do that . . . I'm getting better at it, but I'm hesitant. Also, something that's coming up—that I realized when I was sitting there was . . . the problem that I have . . . I can almost start crying about it right away because . . . but I don't want to do that.

T: Maybe right now you're doing some of that . . . like you're coming on a little too fast for your own self . . . and you're saying, "I want to step back a little from this and . . ."

C: Well, it's something that I . . . I've dealt with with many therapists and I've gone through it a lot [voice breaks] and, uh, being in a therapeutic setting with people who are doing it, I start to think about my problem. Whereas, you know, normally I can go through the day and not think about it [Mm-hm] and, uh, being around so many people who I know are good counselors, part of me wants to talk to 'em about it, and . . . and part of me says, "I'm sick of talking about it." [Mm-hm] It's, uh, well, I want to tell you what it is, so you won't just be responding to this vague problem and it . . . the label for it was originally called "anorexia nervosa." And I don't know if you know what this is. [Mm- hm] . . . I think the label upsets me. . . .

T: It's like you're having to live with some label. . . .

C: [crying] Sort of . . . I don't think other people label me that anymore, but it . . . on the outside it looks like it's gone, but it's not . . . on the inside of me it's always still there [Mm-hm] and, uh, I feel like it's . . . You know what that is, don't you? [Mm-hm] I don't know if we should . . .

T: Do you want to say more about that? Maybe we . . . it would be better if you just said something about it . . .

C: Well, uh . . . it's something that happens to you that you don't realize is happening to you in the beginning and, um, it started with me a long time ago when I was in college [voice breaking], and I just . . . went on a diet, like a lot of other people go on diets, but I . . . just, for some reason I couldn't stop doing it . . . I . . . It was almost like I had to have complete control . . . but anyway, I didn't realize what I was doing, and I had some doctor, my doctor, you know, say to me, gave me this book to read about it, and I said, "Naw, that's not me," and eventually I realized it was me, but I still couldn't stop it . . . and now, even though I've gained the weight back, I'm terrified by the idea every day . . . It's, um, it seems like there was another person inside of me, always talking to me [Mm-hm], and I want to get rid of it so bad . . . and I've talked to so many people, and I wasn't going to talk to anybody here because I've decided I can only get rid of it myself . . . but I guess every little discussion about it makes it get a little better, so . . . I volunteered . . .

T: Like there's still something compelling in you to tell somebody else about it, and hopefully this time maybe . . .

C: Somebody else who might . . . who might be able to help me understand it a little better because I could go around and talk about it sometimes. Sometimes I can talk about it very . . . like, therapist. And I've been asked to work with people who've had it, and . . . and, and I can't do it because what happens is I get jealous of the patient . . . [crying] That's hard for me to admit. [Mm-hm]

T: It's like that's something you don't like about yourself that you do that . . .

C: That I get jealous?

T: Jealous of the patient.

C: Yeah, I think, it's crazy . . . but on the other hand, if I see someone who's really thin or working with someone, and I think, "How come I can't do that?" . . . and I used to have so much control, and I used to be able to not eat, and I used to be able to turn down certain things and stuff, and now I don't have that anymore, and I get jealous of them, and I . . . feel a little crazy . . . now I can go around and have a normal life and no one would guess, there's a former anorexic walking the street, but it's . . . it's still there, it causes a lot of problems in relationships . . .

T: Like you can disguise that from most of the world most of the time pretty effectively, but inside you know that it's still there . . .

C: I can't seem to exactly turn it off, my, uh, my behaviors are changed—I'll sit down at the table and eat, but almost the entire time, I'm . . . someone's talking to me, . . . it's like, "You shouldn't eat that, you should eat that, this has that many calories, you can't eat the whole day if you eat that," and I just want it, just, "Shut up" . . . I guess . . .

T: "Shut up, leave me alone," those voices just keep hounding you.

C: I mean, sometimes it's from the minute I wake up . . . and sometimes it's . . . it's not this bad . . . as bad, I mean . . .

T: Like when you come into therapy, you talk again about the problem, why, then it . . .

C: Yeah, yeah, exactly . . .

T: . . . then it's exaggerated . . .

C: In this kind of setting, when you talk about people's problems and helping people and stuff like that, I start thinking about it, and it gets . . . builds up more and more and more . . . and, well, you know, the bottom line is that what I think is that nobody else can do anything about it. Uh, I don't know . . . uh . . . I'm reluctant . . . uh . . . I been wanting to seek therapy again for it . . . because it's not just the anorexic thing, I think you get that from a lot of other reasons—being insecure or whatever—but when I start being in therapy, I start talking to someone about it, I become more aware, like, after this session, when I go to the cafeteria to eat, number one, I'm going to be a lot more aware of it, and number two, everybody else who's in here is, I feel like they're gonna watch and see if I eat! [Laughter]

T: Yeah. Which is just going to make you more aware of it. It's like a vicious circle.

C: [Long pause, sighs] And sometimes I . . . sometimes I'm even a little embarrassed because I'm almost . . . a little proud of the fact that I was one . . . I was one [Mm-hm]

T: Like, I was something, I was this . . .

C: Uh-huh . . . That's exactly it. It's, at the time you think in a strange way that you're special. That you have something that nobody else has . . . And people talk to you about it . . . In the beginning, "Oh, you're so thin, how did you get so thin?" and then it becomes, "My God, you are thin," and then . . . but it's still . . . something special . . . [Mm-hm] and I think . . . I don't want to lose that . . .

T: Yeah, and it's really hard to let go of that. . . . On the one hand, you want to let go of it, because it's very tormenting . . .

C: It's not healthy . . .

T: Should do this, should do that, wake up in the morning with it . . . and on the other hand, there's something special . . . [Mmhm] like in some weird way it's an old friend, been with you a long time . . .

C: I think everybody wants to think they have something special, you know, about them [Mm-hm] . . . but . . . So then, there's another thing that comes in, you know, that, do I really want to talk about it, you know, because did I just get up here because I want everyone to know that I once was one . . . or do I really want help . . . you know, sometimes I can't decide, I don't even know what I want, you know . . . I'm not sure exactly why I came up here, I would hope to think it's because I really thought maybe I'd get something out of this . . . but there's another little part of me that says, "Oh, you just want to tell . . ."—that you were once one . . .

T: It's like, on the one hand, you're just compelled to do what you're doing . . . and then when you stop and look at it, you say, "Well, what did I do that for . . . what am I doing those things for?" . . . and sometimes maybe you have some answers, and at other times it's just like, "I have no idea . . . but there I am again . . . there I go again . . ."

C: Yeah, and also it's a good excuse in a sense, because, you know, nobody else volunteered, so that made it a little easier for me . . . [Mm-hm].

T: Yeah . . . It's like maybe some others could wait longer, but it's like whatever that compelling thing in you—

C: I was almost crying sitting down there [Mm-hm], and I was afraid to get up because I thought, "As soon as I hit that chair, I'm gonna cry . . ."

T: Yeah. Yeah. Like something takes over and it just starts working itself automatically.

C: I don't know . . . I wonder if things like that ever leave, you know. I wonder if they're always old friends that stay around, and maybe I just have to accept it as an old friend . . . I don't know . . . Maybe if I accepted it more as an old friend instead of trying to fight it . . . then I would be better off [Mm-hm] . . . like . . . that feels good to me, that thing about being an old friend, because, like when it comes knocking on your door, even though they may have done a lot of bad things to you, you let 'em in.

T: Yeah, like it has a home in me, maybe if I could just become friends with it . . .

C: I always let him in . . . I'm worried about my health . . . and, um, doesn't seem to me to be a healthy friend to have.

T: "It's hard to welcome it as an old friend and to really start maybe embracing that part when maybe it's really injurious to my health. . . . That could be a mistake, I wouldn't wanna do that . . . So it throws me into another quandary about what I should do, try to keep it, let it go . . . [Mm-hm]"

C: Yeah . . . it's interesting 'cause sometimes I do want to keep it, and sometimes I just . . . [Mm-hm] . . . What I almost just said is, "I want somebody to take it away" . . . that's what I almost just said, and that's like what I really do want . . . because I don't seem to be able to say, "Get out of here" myself . . . I wish someone would just come take it away. . . .

T: I guess you were asking me earlier, "Bob, could you take it away?" and then sometime later you said, "I don't think you can . . ." Maybe even you would give me a fight . . . 'cause it's special in some way. . . .

C: Yeah, I gave a lot of therapists a lot of fight, yeah . . . I mean, in one of the first this, this, God, this Freudian analyst I saw, after the very first session, offered me a Coke . . . and I was so pissed off at him. I thought he was trying to get me, you know . . . and I'd lie to them . . . say I ate when I didn't. Even though I kept going to therapy, you know, I kept going 'cause I wanted to be cured, but I lied . . . That was stupid . . .

T: I'm hearing you say, "Bob, on one hand, I want you to take it away, but on the other hand, I don't . . . I'm going to have to let go of this myself, and yet I'm not sure I can do it . . ."

C: Well . . . well . . . that's not exactly it. What it exactly is is that I want you to take it away, but I don't want to know when you're coming to do it. And I just want to quit . . . because if I know you're coming to do it, I'll fight you . . .

T: Yeah, yeah . . . okay . . . yeah . . .

C: Y'know, and I know, being a counselor, know that's not possible. I know, like I would say that, you know, if the situation were reversed and I was trying to help you, I would say that I would be doing the kind of things to try to help you help yourself. But being in this seat now, I don't want to do that, I don't want to help myself, I want someone to take it away. It wasn't as scary then as it is now, looking back at it . . . you know, I look at pictures of myself and I cannot believe I did that to myself . . . I . . . It . . . It feels like the same person, but . . . but when I get the image in my mind of who I was back then, and I think of myself back then, it feels like the same person— when I see a picture, it's not the same person. [Mm-hm] But the . . . the competitiveness, or the compulsion I have to do certain things, is almost exactly the same, but it's channeled in other ways. It's not channeled in food anymore; that one I've pretty much conquered—I won't want to eat it, but I will—that kind of stuff, but it channels out in other areas . . .

T: "So I've found ways to channel this away from food but I still feel that strong compulsion, that competitiveness, in . . ."

C: Yeah . . . yeah . . . See, I don't see that it's gone . . . a doctor can see that it's gone because I'm not, you know . . . 83 pounds or whatever . . . And I don't really see that it's gone. I just . . . I put it off into other places. One of the things I started doing was, when I started eating, I decided well what I have to do is exercise . . . So, you know, I was so compulsive about it, uh, well, I just, you know, I kept injuring myself . . . I'd hurt myself and not want to stop . . . I'd say, "Oh, you big baby," and I'd keep going . . . I was working with weights, and I'd say, "Oh, you know, don't be a baby just keep going," and I'd keep going and ended up on crutches . . . And I've done those things a few times . . . And I can't stand it anymore . . .

T: It's like there are two people in there, and one is like a baby and the other is older than that baby and kinda chides that baby, kinda harasses that baby. . . "Oh, you big baby, come on, you can do that" . . . And the baby kinda goes ahead and until it gets hurt . . . and then it can stop.

C: [crying] You know, people . . .

T: It's like you'd like to not have to go so far that you get hurt.

C: Uh-huh, uh-huh . . . I'm learning it, I'm getting better at it . . . But it's still there . . . I . . . You know, people tell you all the time . . . I said this to some-body here and we were joking about it and they didn't know the seriousness of it; now they're probably thinking about that, but I said: "You know, when you go into a spa, they always have signs up that say, 'No Pain, No Gain,'" so in my mind I always think, well, it's supposed to hurt . . . I'm afraid if I stop too early that I'm not being good enough . . . I'm not doing it the best . . .

T: Well, like that voice says, like, you're not good enough, you're not doing the best, come on, you can do it . . .

C: Uh-huh . . . Oh, I always have thought that I can do it, if I ever really want to do something, I can do it . . . And so I push myself to do the best, and I'm afraid to stop, because I'm afraid I haven't really given it my best shot. [Mm-hm].

T: "Like, just one more push, one more try, and I'll get there . . . if I stop, I'll never get there . . ."

C: Yeah, yeah . . .

T: "I'll be right there where I was . . ."

C: It'll be a waste . . .

T: It'll be a waste . . .

C: I won't ever grow . . . [yeah] . . . so I've been searching for a lot of people, like, it's almost like I have to have a doctor tell me, "OK, you can't run. You can't run for a month," and it's almost like they have to tell me that, and sometimes I go in there, and I want to say, "Please tell me I can't run." You know, because if you don't tell me, I'm going to do it. I'll run on my knee and hurt it again. And . . . the problem is . . . you know, I feel like I'm a pretty intelligent woman, and in my life and in my work, you know, people look up to me and stuff like that, and I can't understand why I keep doing this. It doesn't make . . . it's not . . . it doesn't seem like me.

T: "It's like it's not me that keeps doing this. There's something in here that's just doing this . . . going on and it's not me . . . and yet 'me' goes with that . . . "me" doesn't have any choice not to go with that."

C: . . . Rationally I know that it's me, but I can hear it . . . talking to me . . . Sounds pretty weird, but I hear it saying things like, y'know, "Oh, you baby" or, "Don't eat that."

T: It's like it's on a tape or something . . . like it's recorded in here . . . and once in a while somehow the tape gets thrown on. Says that to you . . . and the you that's like this little girl . . . this little child starts obeying, starts fol-lowing its commands. And like there's another you that's standing and saying, "I don't want to do this, and" . . . but it's like that part is lifeless. It has a voice, but it doesn't have any power to stop this kind of . . .

C: It doesn't have enough. Um . . . I think it's afraid to be by itself . . . the other part, the part that doesn't have any power. I think it . . . well it goes back to that being special. I'm afraid without it, I'll just be this normal person walking ar . . . like everybody else is.

T: Yeah, "I like being special" . . . that's a part of it.

C: Yeah. I mean too bad it had to come out in that way. [Yeah] No, I . . . people I'm really close to tell me, "Oh, you're special anyway. You don't have to have that . . . I liked you when you weighed 150 or when you weigh what you do."

T: "They tell me that, and I hear it, and I even know that many of them are sincere in that, but boy it's sure hard for me to . . . [Yeah] to let that make much difference to . . . to that part of me . . . just goes on."

C: I, uh . . . it is hard for me to believe. It's hard for me to believe when someone tells me now that I look nice or I look thin. I don't . . . and I don't think they're lying to me. I just don't see it . . . I want to see that. I think that . . . what I have said to other people is that once you look in the mirror and you weigh 83 pounds and you like yourself, then anything else over that is going to be gaining weight . . . being big, you know, so I constantly, when I look at myself, I berate myself all the time. Why can't you lose weight . . . and . . .

T: Why can't you be that 83-pound beautiful woman again?

C: Well, it's more not why can't I be that. Why can't I . . . It's not to get there. I don't think about being 83 pounds, because I don't want to be. What I think about is why can't I have the control I used to have then . . . why . . . sometimes I feel like I've lost a certain amount of willpower or control I had then. I mean I could . . . You know, people couldn't understand how I could do it. I had sort of a pride in that. Like people who fast, you know.

T: "It's like that's something I could do for myself. Like there was a me that could do that for myself. I did it for myself . . . not the little girl . . ."

C: Yes, exactly . . . I did it. No one else had anything to do with it.

T: "I was the power, and yet there's this other where this little girl was told do th- . . . you know, keep going, push some more."

C: It's like no . . . you know, that something you do all by yourself. No one else is going to starve you . . . well, maybe, but, you know in a sense . . . And I didn't feel like I was starving then, I really didn't feel like that. What I felt like was that—we don't need to eat as much as we do . . . these people are . . . look at all this shit that they eat, and I don't need to do that. That was basically it. I never thought about being 83 pounds. I never wanted to be. I even hid the fact.

T: Yeah. You were sort of telling them, "I don't need to do that. Look, I'll show you I don't need to do that." And then you showed yourself—I don't need to do that.

C: I was afraid . . . and I'm still afraid of . . . if I let go of a certain amount of control, that everything is just going to go all haywire . . . and it hasn't, . . . but each step of the way, the progression I made, it . . . everything hasn't gone all haywire, but I still maintain that in my mind that it's going to. I think . . . of everything that we've said, that the specialness part sticks out the most.

T: That "I'm somebody special." That "she" inside is somebody special. It's very hard to let her go—to say goodbye to her. It's like she's in control in a way—like she was in control—not so sure now, maybe, but she really knew she was, and that's sort of where the locus of the control is still. And it's like you don't want me or anyone else to do anything to take that away, 'cause that's like taking away that control . . . You're saying you need help for you to kind of sneak up and get it, because I don't know if I can let it go now. Like I've done such a . . . good thing of being in control that—like I'm a master at that—boy, hey, world, if you want a master on that subject, come to me, but the other side of it secretly is, like we're sharing here is that, will somebody please come and take this away.

C: And that exact thing happens in other areas . . . you know of my life— that secretly I don't want to be in such control all the time. I don't want to have to be . . . I don't . . .

T: It's a real burden [Yeah] . . . I thought you said too, [client's name], that it kind of scares you to let it go, and it's almost like having gotten so much control now, it's kind of scary to let it go. [Uh-huh] That will go, and then "I could lose . . . then I could lose control [Uh-huh] I could just . . . God, who knows how nutty I could be or wild or whatever would happen."

C: Yeah. It's interesting 'cause in a, in fact I've actually said both, you know. I want someone to take the control away, so I don't have to be in control, and in other words, I don't want to lose control. I didn't even notice I did that, but that's exactly what the problem is, because I don't . . . you know, there's a thin line that you walk in a lot of things, like when you're being a therapist and you're dealing with somebody. How much control do you want to have in that situation and how much do you want to back off? And I don't . . . what I feel like is I don't really have, many times, the internal mechanism that is able to decide [Yeah] . . . Like when I'm starting to injure myself. I don't know when pushing is pushing for the good of me and when pushing is going to hurt me. And, God, I don't know why I can't decide that. I mean that seems like a decision that you learn over experience. And I always err on the pushing-to-hurt-me side. I always err . . . I always go a little too far, rather than back off a little bit. It was the same way in school with grades, you know. I would study so hard that sometimes I would lose sight of the general feel of the class. Like if it was sociology class or something, I'd study everything in such complete detail that I would know it so well . . . and I always lost something that . . . and I'd say, "I'm not going to do that next time," and I'd do it next time. I'd be afraid . . . if I was studying for a test, I'd study so hard that I knew everything. Then I'd take the test and there would be so much extra stuff I studied, and I'd say, "I'm not going to do that again." But when I go again, I'm afraid if I leave off one little part, that's exactly what they're going to ask, and I'm going to look stupid . . .

T: "Yeah, like I have to cover it all, and then maybe they won't ask, and I won't have to look stupid, but boy, is that a lot of work."

C: Yeah. Constant work. I feel that every day I'm constantly working. I can't . . . it's hard to relax. I always feel I should be doing something. You know, if I go down to the beach, I should take a book down to the beach, you know. I hate that . . . If I have a break, you know, I should do something during the break . . . God!

T: Like, I think you're saying, "Please, whoever you are in there who keeps demanding these things of me, let me relax."

C: It's funny. I want to keep telling you how much better I'm feeling. I almost said it again, because to me right now, it sounds a lot worse than I feel that it usually is. Heightened—really heightened at this point. [Yeah, yeah] But it's always there to some degree.

T: "So I'm getting better in a lot of ways. There are a lot of ways I'm doing a lot better than I did those years ago. But there's still some more work . . . you know, there's still some more work. And it's only here in this kind of situation that it gets so exaggerated. It gets so magnified."

C: Uh-huh. And it's been a long time since I really talked to anybody extensively about it. 'Cause some of my friends knew I had it . . . you know . . . It's old to them and everything, but it isn't to me. It's constant to me. [The interview continued for a few more minutes.]

Discussing the Session

After a brief rest, Bob, the client, and those observing discussed the session. An edited version of that discussion follows.

GROUP MEMBER: Bob, I've known you over the past year [in a study group], and it was really good to see you work. And I saw, more than I ever have, your ability to help another person appreciate . . . recognize . . . the edge of ambiguity. Like, rather than getting out of a double bind, or trying to . . . structure your life so you never get in them, it's like that . . . to help a person really see that they feel this way and that way . . . And I don't think I've ever seen quite as skillful an appreciation of that "edge." Boy, I recognize it in myself, and I think you really helped [client's name]— I don't know how to describe it—embrace that or see that it's there and accept it more and more . . . I also appreciated the way you identified with [client's name] by actually using the first person often. You didn't always use it. The first person, saying, "Well, I really feel . . ." as if you were actually a mirror. Those were the two main things I noticed . . . very helpful demonstration.

THERAPIST: Let me say the question here was what was helpful to [client's name].

CLIENT: I have never been . . . I realized right now as it opened up . . . I have never been to a client-centered person about this, and I never was able to talk so much. I never was able to . . . you said a few—like the "old friend" thing. I was trying to figure out what that was; the "old friend" thing just really fit. And I guess I said that somehow, but I didn't know that I had said it to you . . . There were a couple times when you had said something back that I didn't feel was exactly right, but I really felt free and easy to say, "Naw . . . that's not exactly it," whereas before, I remember a couple of times before in therapy when they told me something, and I . . . I didn't tell them . . it didn't feel right, but I let them go on for a while on that thing. A great one was that I was embarrassed about having sexuality, like having breasts, and so I was not eating to hide that. And that didn't fit at all, but I said, "Oh, well . . . that may be . . ." I went on for a long time thinking about that. I really felt like you were a friend, and I could say, "Naw . . . [After some discussion from the group, she continues] To see client-centered therapy being done is a lot different from all of a sudden feeling it. As soon as we started talking, I wasn't aware of you as a therapist trying to "technique" me . . . but watching other people here, I was trying to figure out the client-centered technique. So it's totally different once you sit down in a chair and start doing it. I learned so much more just now, even about the technique, by having it done to me.

GM: It seems to me that one of the differences is that when I am a client in client-centered, I feel I have no obligation to understand anybody but myself. And somehow, in other kinds, I feel I have an obligation to understand the therapist.

C: Yeah, if they say something to you that you don't understand, you want to sit there and try to get it.

GM: Bob, can you say what's in your head as you're doing that? What your experience is like?

T: Sure . . . Somehow, over the years, I've really come to . . . it's been a process of what I have to say doesn't matter, when I'm in this kind of setting. It's just so clear to me it doesn't matter. And also, going with that, I really want to know you.

GM: One thing I noticed was that ambiguity seems to be at the core—both of the problem as well as of the session itself. And I wondered whether that was the technique.

T: Yes, and one thing I'm helping [client's name] learn—and everybody learn—to pick up on the earlier comment too, is ambiguity—to live with ambiguity. That's one of the critical things to me about client-centered therapy. Where in the world do people help you learn to live with ambiguity, and life is just full of ambiguity. I don't know of any other place. Other therapists get involved in their own way—and you learn other things. I want to say that too. I did. I've been in Gestalt and all that. But nobody got out of the way and just let me stay in an ambiguous state and work through it.

C: Uh-huh . . . just having someone let you . . . actually, it was almost like I felt you felt what that feels like . . . When you said it, I almost felt like, he knows what that feeling's like. You know when you said, "It just seems like . . ." and I think you even hit your knees one time, and I felt like that was me saying that—like, you know what that's like. Whereas before it was more like they were saying, "You're *saying* . . ." I felt like they were telling me what I was feeling, but they didn't really know.

GM: I first started listening, and I'd hear all these clues as to what the problem was, and I'd wonder "Gee, why doesn't he get into that?" And I realized that the simple thing is that it's her thing and what you're trying to do is help her get into it. And she jumped a lot . . . and she kept jumping back to the same things, but you didn't try to push her into it. She needs to do that, and if she wants to jump then that's where she is . . . And I really appreciate the word *ambiguity* that started this off, because it helped me see how simple it is.

T: There were times in this session I had the very same thoughts you did. So you'll have those thoughts. I just let them go. But I do have those thoughts—that's something I know is going on inside me . . .

C: You mean the thought that . . .

T: That I know what this is . . . that I can get her to the place . . .

C: I can see now that I was jumping around a lot . . . but as long as you understood what I said when I jumped, then when I thought about it for a minute, I remembered the biggest thing I felt, and I went back to it. But if you hadn't understood what I meant when I jumped, I would have gone on and tried to make you understand and maybe been lost . . .

GM: There was one statement she made that I wrote down . . . and your answer . . . she said, "I don't want to be in control. I don't want to have to be in control." And you said, "Yeah, it's a real burden." At that point, I would have been real tempted to say, "Yes, I don't want to be in control, but I'm afraid if I give up my control, I won't be special. I won't feel special." And I'm wondering why you didn't . . . if you had that choice, would you have said that? Did you just not think about it?

T: Yes, and other times I think I did say that. So the answer is yes, and if at that very moment, that were there, I would have said it. There are a lot of responses we could give at any one time. It would be fascinating if we all wrote down and compared our different thoughts . . . and they all have a validity, and the checkout is [client's name]. She would say, "Nope, that's not it." or, "That's close," like sometimes you said, "Well, that's like it but not quite." One of the keys of the process is that I relinquish that to the client. "Boy, forget about what I said; let's go with what you're saying."

GM: To offer a friendly criticism, it seemed to me that you were doing something in the way of cognitive structuring by going along with this idea that there are various "parts" [to the client]. You picked up on that and even extended it. So then there was this notion that there was one part doing this and one part doing that. . . . To what extent do you go along with the way people present themselves as, "I have this part and that part."? Really, do we have these parts? Or it's a way that I interpret myself or it's a way that I construct myself. The therapist might even respond in a way that makes it more ambiguous, but really, what do we know?

T: Well, I *don't* know. And I could have been way off, and she would have said, "Gee, what are those parts you're talking about?" And I would have said right then . . . I wouldn't have defended that or said—say, as in Transactional Analysis, there's a Parent, Adult, and Child [in each person]. I would have just said, "OK, well, help me with that. I'm not clear about what you said."

Same GM: I'd like to make another point, which is a paradoxical thing. In a situation in which there is a . . . a struggle . . . an issue around control and self-control—that clearly kept coming up again and again—who's in control? Who's in control of me being in control, and so on? I would imagine that if this client felt that the therapist was very invested in taking away the symptom, then the only course you would have would be to resist . . . You know, it's an attack against the self . . . it's not a symptom [to the client]. Paradoxically, the structure of client-centered therapy is perfect for that. You immediately begin to pick up that he wasn't interested in taking away your symptom.

C: That's true. It's a friend.

Same GM: Yeah, it was you [Bob] who suggested the metaphor of the old friend, and you [the client] loved that. "Oh! He's not mad at me that I like to diet," or whatever, and that seemed to me to be very, very helpful, and a way of avoiding a lot of that, uh, [power struggle].

GM: I want to ask a question about staying with the client and about reflection. There was some point that I might have been tempted to say, "You're concerned in a very serious way about losing control, and it looks like right now you're kind of trying to reassure yourself. You know, kind of calming down; pulling away from it a little bit, reassuring yourself that things aren't so bad. Things are OK. I really do have control." Well, that's not reflecting what the client has said, but it is aiming at what you're experiencing right now, and I wonder if you have some general feeling about how free you feel to make remarks like that.

T: I feel very free to, and you said a key word there for me. It's *aiming at*. I always remember that I'm pointing towards or aiming at [the client's experience]. That's all. Then she says, "That's it, jackpot" or, "Boy, you hit the mark."

C: . . . It's interesting . . . how much do you reflect just the words that they say or the body posture . . . that's kind of reflecting . . . not what I've said, but what I'm doing.

GM: What I've heard a lot of people speaking about seems to me to be the difference between reflecting and interpreting. There seem to be slight differences in degree that can or cannot be incorporated into client-centered therapy, depending upon the personality of the particular therapist.

T: But there's a "spirit" here. It's an attitude—that's a better word— that's the core. And then I have a style, and I have a personality, and all that comes into play, but I'm really loyal to that attitude . . . I'm having trouble saying what the attitude is . . .

Same GM: Well, I assume it varies at points in time, too.

T: Yeah, and yet there's some kind of a core that I don't want to be wishy-washy about. I want to be stubborn about it.

Same GM: My interpretation was that you stopped just short of an interpretation.

T: Yeah, and I have those inside of me, as I said earlier.

GM: Does your loyalty to client-centered therapy allow you to incorporate some of the other approaches that you use—with the same attitude, the same respect for the client?

T: Yeah. As long as I maintain that attitude.

Later Bob wrote about this attitude:

Two thoughts immediately pop into my mind about this core attitude. First, I *truly* want to know and understand my client. I believe that everything [client's name] said and did is pointing to her exquisite *meaning*. What is primary, i.e. focal, for me is to "catch" her meaning and give it back to her. Sometimes with a client I am very dramatic/demonstrative (my style/way of being) in describing to her or encouraging her to describe for herself what is her meaning. Secondly, I do not pursue helping the person. Rather, I am more like a discoverer/explorer passionately pursuing hidden truths in the service of, and with, my client. A *by-product* of following the core attitude is that the person feels "helped." By attentively straining my senses to know and understand what the client means, what ensues is the awareness of being deeply and personally known and understood, and this is sensed as being significantly helpful.

A Client's Reactions

I found myself reluctant yet wanting to be the client today at the Client-Centered Therapy Workshop. My problem, "anorexia," has been with me for a long time and not much light has been shed on it for a long time. But there were breakthroughs today. I didn't come to some new, clearer understanding of the problem. I certainly wasn't cured nor did I feel that I was partially cured. What I did feel was better. I felt better. Isn't that what therapy is all about? We want to feel better, be happier, live fuller.

Well, today after a session of client-centered therapy I realized I had never had that in *any* other of the therapies I've had. Other psychologists would give their possible explanation and I would entertain the notion for a while—trying to—even hoping that it was the answer, the reason— thus one closer step to being "cured," but I never felt better. Sometimes I felt worse; I wasn't sure if it was right, and I wanted to know, how could I know.

Other counselors tried to give me advice on how to stop my anorexic behavior, thus ending the immediate problem with perhaps exploring reasons afterward. I tried to do what they suggested. I never felt better; in fact, I felt worse. My anorexia felt better, so I preferred it to their therapy and their suggestions. Others asked and asked and asked me questions, to which if I knew the answer I wouldn't have been there, aside from the fact that even for those I could answer it didn't make me feel better.

Well, I felt better today. I was able to talk about my problem and truly feel understood, cared for, empathized with. I perhaps saw some things I hadn't clearly seen or understood before but mainly I left changed. I didn't go home upset, confused, worried, frustrated, wondering. I left feeling a little lighter, a little clearer, a lot happier. *Better.*

It just has struck me now, this evening as I think about the experience, that therapy is really just that. We can't go looking for cures or remedies. The looking is the cure and I get a little medicine each time I get this kind of experience. It's not as if the doctor had to wait and search until he found out all the reasons for my broken leg or my cold or my brain tumor before giving me medicine or treatment or surgery. And this is just what many therapists or counselors do.

(The client later said that this point marked a break in her writing. Later she was concerned that what she said was incomplete, and so she returned to add a less personal discussion of the following issue.)

I understand as I'm writing this that it is very limited (just a part), but I think definitely one aspect of therapy. For example, one would hope that therapy would not *merely* be a means for helping a client feel better about all the things he or she does, whether bad or good (from a cultural or even legal point of view). . . . Eventually the long-range goal includes much more than this—perhaps a better understanding for the client, ease of feelings, or even some solution of a particular problem being found—and also importantly clients learning the tools or "senses" to help themselves outside the therapy session. But all these often are overplayed or rushed into—even concentrated on—to the point where the acceptance, warmth, empathy, and thus the client's "feeling better" are neglected or lost.

■ Observing David Martin—The University of Manitoba, Winnipeg, Manitoba

Introductory Comments

Three of the interviews in this appendix are from early sessions, so I wanted to give an example of therapy after the client and I had been working for a while. This is the eighth interview with a 30-year-old professional woman. This excerpt begins somewhere into the session, so you will need to read a few lines to get into the flow of what we are exploring together. I like the word *exploring* to describe the mutual search that the client and I are engaged in. I hope that is made clear by what I do as the therapist. Some students who have listened to this session commented that at times they didn't know where my responses were coming from, although the client generally picks up on them as though they were accurate. I suppose that this happens partly because she and I have a shared store of knowledge from past sessions. I think, too, that by this time she knows that my intentions are empathic, that I will not try to take over the control of therapy, so I can take more chances; she knows that what I say is tentative and can be rejected. Similarly, I notice that I say, "Right" a lot, where others might say, "I understand" or, "Uh-huh." I'm pretty sure that my client knows how I mean this, but it is something that can be misunderstood as, "That is correct." I promise to try to stop saying, "Right" so much.

You will notice that I use facetious humor a couple of times in this interview. That is partly just part of my personal style, and I am comfortable with it, as long as the client and I are sharing a little joke. I don't really plan it as a way to "provide relief" or "regulate the tension level" or anything like that. I must say, however, that the only thing I'm really unhappy with in this session is the place where I do a kind of "interpret the defenses" move and comment on how the client uses humor in the hour. I don't know why I did this, but it certainly broke the flow of therapy temporarily. This is the kind of simple-minded therapist "cleverness" I have been warning you against for 18 chapters. Oh, well.

The Interview

> THERAPIST: . . . there is something distorted in here . . . Something's affecting your life that you don't understand . . .
>
> CLIENT: Yeah . . . like . . . well . . . It's certainly around this whole thing with [material omitted] . . . Is our time up yet? [laughs] . . . I don't like this . . . That's awful, isn't it? What a horrible feeling.

T: It's about ten to one . . . Time flies when you're having fun, doesn't it? [Mm-hm] Make you uncomfortable when I look at you? [Mh?] Does it make you uncomfortable?

C: Well, no . . . not really . . . I . . .

T: What makes you uncomfortable is . . . you're cornered, in a way.

C: Well, yeah . . . I feel very much like I'm cornered. 'Cause I think that I'm going to find out something about myself I don't like. Something I'm not facing. [right] Y'know, like I want to avoid a whole bunch of things, I think, around that . . . and what that says about me . . . something that isn't going to fit together very well, that I'm going to be some . . . I want . . . that I'm trying to be somebody that I'm not, or something . . .

T: Mm-hm . . . and that is frightening . . . yeah.

C: Like I keep feeling underneath all this that maybe this is . . . maybe I really want to be dependent on somebody . . . y'know like I am in a lot of ways . . . but I don't really . . . y'know like [right] . . . like I feel that maybe that's what's happening . . . some dependency that maybe feels all right but that I don't really want . . . uh . . . oh, I don't know what I'm saying.

T: That's pretty clear, I think [yeah . . . I . . .] . . . If I ask you what do you want, you say, "I want to be an independent, successful, strong person. That's what I want.' . . . And it's almost like part of you says, "No, I want to be taken care of." [Mm-hm] "I really want to be taken care of."

C: It's all too much for me, y'know, like . . .

T: Uh-huh . . . just somebody to hold me and take . . .

C: . . . nurture me . . .

T: . . . and if that's true, that part of you, you don't want to look at.

C: The part that wants to be taken care of [yeah] the part that wants to be dependent on somebody . . . yeah . . .

T: It's going to be a jolt to look at that part of yourself.

C: I guess . . . I know it exists, and I know intellectually that's fine because everybody has those parts, y'know.

T: But you don't accept it in yourself? . . . or at least . . .

C: I don't like it. I don't like to need . . . to need that or to have to let someone have that much power over me or to be that vulnerable to someone else . . .

T: And the you that you know well almost couldn't respect a person like that. Like the you that you know is the independent.

C: The "you" that I think I want to be [Uh-huh] . . . or like best about myself . . . and then . . . and then I think that I almost feel that I have to be dependent or let people control me to have people . . . to . . . there's that part there, y'know. I've got to do what he wants or they want or . . . a friend wants to be accepted and cared about and wanted, y'know . . . [Right] The conflict is really difficult. If there's any struggle, I'd give in to have the person, rather to have me, y'know?

T: Because you have to have the person. You . . . if . . . You're dependent. That means you have to let yourself be in trouble . . . 'cause you need the person so much.

C: Yeah. If the need to have that person . . . yeah . . . is that strong . . . then I would, eh? Like I . . .

T: Mhm. You wouldn't take the chance of losing him. You couldn't afford to take the chance of losing him.

C: I'd lose me.

T: So you'd lose something that you have to have . . . Pretty needy?

C: Am I? Well, I guess I must be . . .

T: Kind of hard to say this . . . [Mhm] . . . to say . . . You're almost saying . . . "I'm a dependent person."

C: And I need people always telling me, y'know, you're doing OK, and [Mm-hm] that this is right and that . . .

T: You can't just live on your own approval of yourself. You can't say, "I know I'm valuable and good." You need people to . . .

C: . . . need it to be said to me all the time.

T: . . . reassure you . . . I was just going to say to, "feed" you . . . (mhm) . . . occurred to me after, that's a double entendre . . .

C: Mhm . . . so what's that say about me? . . . Too insecure?

T: Oh, I see what you mean . . . too insecure . . .

C: Like everybody needs people, but why do I do it to the point of losing myself? Y'know . . . what is it that makes me need them so much that I won't, uh, that I can't say no, or I can't, uh, . . . like even last night when [material omitted] I didn't want her to come, because I wanted it to be people that had worked with this guy in the same unit, and we've had a lot of fun together, and . . . but I said, "Sure, you can come." I wanted to say, "No, I'd rather it be just a unit thing." I needed her to be there and give me all this support, and I didn't say no.

T: And you needed her not to be angry at you . . . [material omitted] uh, . . . you would have been the same with the department wimp too. If . . . it would have been very hard for you to say, even with somebody very passive, [yeah] . . . they'd say, "Can I come along?" . . . "Oh, all right."

C: Like that must affect me every day, eh? That must affect me all the time.

T: Sure does . . . I mean it must.

C: What do I think is going to happen?

T: Something awful. [Yeah, really] . . . really awful.

C: It's no wonder I'm always feeling irritable and pissed off . . . most things I really want to do, or . . . yeah . . . or rationalizing everything because I've got to do it to get, y'know, people to be involved with me . . . That's awful [Mhm] . . . but that's what I do.

T: [Inaudible] You sort of said something like this a couple times ago. Why can't I stand up for myself? Why can't I say no . . . take good care of myself. [Mm-hm] Now this makes it clearer, in some ways, because you're so scared . . . of losing a person, I guess . . . of the person being irritated at you.

C: Because that person is the only reflection of me that I've got. Like they, y'know [yeah].

T: I'm not quite sure how you mean that. I think it's like this . . . it's you don't have a "core."

C: I'm only OK if you say I'm OK.

T: Exactly . . . [Yeah] . . . you don't walk around knowing you're OK.

C: Yeah, I need someone to . . .

T: Autonomous [Yeah] . . . And the way they say that is by praising you or saying, "I like you" or being nice to you.

C: Mm-hm. See, I have glimpses of I'm OK, um, without that, y'know, at times, but I think that it has to be a fairly obvious situation. If there's any degree of judgment, I'm the "un-OK" one in the whole thing, y'know.

T: The glimpses are like little tastes of, "Oh, that's how I would like to feel all the time." Or to have that feeling—I'm a good person?

C: Yeah. Yeah. Well, it's things like, uh, at a meeting I had some ideas I had written down and I had expressed some of them but not all of them, and a person sitting a couple seats away expressed similar ones, and I thought, "Oh, well, he's thinking the same way I'm thinking. I can't be that bad." Y'know, I need to make those kinds of judgments all the time . . .

T: Even then it was something external that told you you were OK. [Mm-hm] You're not stupid [Mm-hm], somebody else thought the same thing. [Mhm] I see . . . what you want is . . .

C: I want something internal . . .

T: . . . to know that, that's right . . . without the always getting confirmation from somebody else that you're OK. No wonder you can't take any chances . . . with people. My God, they might get mad at you . . . implicitly tell you you're not a very good person. [Bad . . . yeah] And a core . . . that is somehow . . . you . . . you are your judge . . . that's what you want [Yeah] . . . You're in terrible conflict then, between, by God, wanting to be independent . . . and wanting to be so dependent and taken care of . . . somebody confirming you.

C: Yeah, like I'm almost a nonbeing without all those people around me . . .

T: I guess you almost can't stand to look at that about yourself.

C: No. I don't like it. [Uh-huh] Then I sometimes think that I overcompensate, especially with [name omitted] . . . overreact. That part of me . . . you're not going to get it . . . you're not going to control it, y'know . . . maybe I try and go too far the other way.

T: Uh-huh, I understand . . . that, uh, even stupidly the other direction. Or stupidly with some people you give in and let yourself be controlled out of fear . . . sort of to assert yourself and make up for it.

C: Yeah. I talked about that before too. Well, no . . . well, not on the same terms.

T: So with him you do irrationally controlling things. It all averages out.

C: Yeah, and it's just a crock of shit, eh? [Yeah, right] . . . So how do I get to feel OK? Where do I . . . My God, I'm 30 years old. Where do I get a deficit like that . . . to begin with?

T: You mean where does it come from or [Yeah] where do you get it overcome?

C: Well, both . . . I mean [OK] . . . I'm just wondering how does that kind of thing develop that you have to always be . . .

T: Always be praised . . . and not able to love yourself . . . or . . . I don't know what the word . . . that's the wrong word. [Yeah] Something like that. Love yourself . . . accept yourself . . . feel worthwhile. I guess that's closer [Yeah] . . . feel your own worth without somebody else giving it. Do you really mean that as a question? . . . like, how you get there? Forget it . . . I'm going to cop out anyhow, so I might just as well cop out now . . . um . . . I'm going to half cop out. Well, I can't answer that question, but I really think the process that we're engaged in is the [inaudible] . . . both the why, if it's important to know the why, and where you go from here.

C: Because I really think that . . . that that's probably what's happened to me all my life when I felt depressed or . . . or . . . what's the word? Just really like, really frustrated all the time with everything, y'know [Mm-hm], like . . . and that's probably where it's all coming from.

T: Yeah. You said that . . . no wonder you're angry all the time. Sort of always giving in. [Yeah. Yeah] You never get what you want, but you also don't feel good about yourself. You feel unhappy and depressed . . . and frustrated . . . It really makes a lot of sense. [Mm-hm]

C: It's almost like I have some . . . something's going to happen to me, y'know, in those situations . . . I . . . like what? I'll be a nonperson? I will die? They will reject me?

T: You seem clearly to fear they'll reject you.

C: Mhhm. Because you know . . . I was talking about . . . last night about people leaving me and how I felt really devastated when people left, and um [material omitted in which the client says she told a friend, "I've never forgiven you for leaving me," because the friend left their mutual place of employment], which is really significant I guess, you know [Mhm], and we were just talking about why I . . . you know . . . she was talking about the same kinds of . . . of feelings of rejection and stuff . . . just why . . . why is she just so much a part of me that when she leaves, like that's . . . the relationship didn't end, but something happened. It's not been the same.

T: And you felt it as a hurt [Yeah], as a . . . she did it to you.

C: Yeah, it was a personal affront. You know, she can't live her life. She has to live mine for me. She has to stay there. That whole . . .

T: Or something like that, but in any . . . or whatever, she rejected you. You were hurt that she left.

C: Yeah. Yeah. How can you leave me here and go away? [Yeah] And that happened with another girlfriend too that left there, who I was really emotionally close to y'know . . . almost like go through each day with them . . . and spend time with them . . .

T: Mm-hm. Hurt. Terribly hurt and, uh, depressed in a way that's like being rejected . . . [material omitted] and you feel awful about yourself. It's almost like you go through that a lot [Yeah] every time a friend leaves—so you're hurt and angry at them for doing it [Mhm] although I doubt you express the anger.

C: No, of course not—no, but that's what happens repeatedly with relation-ships, I mean the relationships don't end . . . I carry on with them. And I do think the only one I've never felt that with has been the one in [city name] . . . except . . . except when she was saying at one point, um, well, she's really into TA and uses that with her . . . in her own practice and stuff, and she said at one point, "You know, there's a lot of things happening with you, and maybe you should go talk with somebody and get some help." And I thought, "Oh, she doesn't want to talk to me anymore." You know, like she can't do it and . . . y'know . . . but, uh, and I know that, but I feel like it's, y'know . . .

T: Sure. Intellectually, you know she's . . .

C: . . . going to be there and . . .

T: . . . she's going to be there. She was saying, "Get some extra help." [Yeah] And your first thought is, "You don't want me anymore."

C: Yeah. That's awful. That's what I've always felt . . . just . . . even . . . we had a kid staying with us on one of these student exchange things in grade 11, and he was my brother's age, [material omitted] and he stayed for a week and . . . I was devastated for two days when he left. Just, y'know, I didn't feel hurt, but I just felt like, "Oh, he's gone," and I . . .

T: You didn't feel like he had hurt you [no, but just the whole . . .], but you just felt like somebody had died . . .

C: Yeah. Like everybody's left.

T: Yeah. When people leave, you feel . . . you mourn. You feel . . . abandoned.

C: Yeah. I wonder if my mother left me when I was young [laughs].

T: That word hit home?

C: What?

T: Abandoned? . . . Did it feel like people . . .

C: Yeah . . . it's like—what I—am I going to do? Like how can you leave me here? There's no plan for me, y'know? That . . .

T: Oh, I see. Who's going to take care of me now?

C: Yeah. That's it.

T: I need you . . .

C: Or I'll have to take care of me. Well, if that's the [inaudible] that I have felt . . . That's really awful . . . Because I know enough intellectually to know that I shouldn't be feeling this way, like I know [Yeah, I know what you're saying] . . . about relationships, and people don't dump people all the time and walk all over them and, y'know.

T: You should be able to trust that . . .

C: And it will continue, you know. They don't just all end, you know.

T: And you've had lots of experiences that haven't just ended.

C: Well, yeah. And good ones.

T: It seems like I should learn from those experiences. But you know what the book says—what you're supposed to be feeling—modern person . . .

C: But here I am. Like so wishy-washy and insecure that without all these people giving to me all the time, I can't survive. And I wonder how much I give back, if I need all this, am I really giving . . . Why are they sticking around? Y'know, what am I giving?

T: Mhm. Feel like you're just sucking all the time . . . taking, taking, taking [Yeah] . . . Um. Wait a minute . . . Up till this minute, you feel like you do give back—in a lot of relationships? Now are you saying, "How could I possibly be giving back if I'm always so needy?"

C: Yeah. Well, I don't think I have been recently. I've been taking. But this last while is . . . but like, see, even the girlfriend in [city name]. It's reciprocal. She'll call me with the same kinds of problems, and she'll say, "Gee, I feel great talking to you, and that's really helped," and like with the one I was talking to last night, she told me a lot of stuff that was going on in her life, and I listened and understood. Like it wasn't all focused on me.

T: That's what I'm wondering about yeah.

C: Like, but yeah . . . very . . . so conscious of saying things about me all the time—my problems—and I—and my life—and not giving. I'm wondering how much I'm really giving.

T: I see, right. OK, sometimes you do give. But you may give a lot less than you thought . . .

C: . . . than I'm getting. Or than I'm getting.

T: . . . that you're getting. [In some ways] Because if you need that much, you must be taking a lot . . . or looking for a lot . . . or seeking a lot.

C: And draining people. That's why I don't have any friends. [laughs] But I do . . .

T: Yeah, you do . . . That's something else you don't want to be true about yourself—is that you drain people?

C: . . . that I'm so self-focused or something.

T: I'm almost waiting for you to say "I need so much."

C: . . . I was thinking about yesterday: I had fun. I laughed . . . I mean I have fun . . . even. We can even laugh about tragic things. I guess a survival thing, but . . .

T: You had fun . . .

C: . . . at work. Monday [inaudible] . . . that's pretty good, eh [facetiously]?

T: Oh, that's wonderful . . . You do that in here too. You laugh . . .

C: I know. Well I . . .

T: Funny . . . I go along with it too . . .

C: Aren't I supposed to laugh?

T: That's fine. That's good. I'm just saying that we both . . .

C: Humor's my big defense too. I use humor a lot. You know—to sort of say what I mean. I think that's all right [Yeah] . . . Therapy can be fun.

T: As we know, it's not always, though. [inaudible]

C: . . . What were we talking about? Oh, draining people . . . It's almost recently, I have to consciously get talking about something other than me . . . y'know . . . I have to make an effort at it. Which I guess is OK as long as I do it. I'm really not . . .

T: At one level it's OK. You wish it came more naturally yeah because that's evidence to yourself almost that you are so needy . . . self-centered.

C: I have so much going on in me that I can't look at the other person and give to them . . . I just feel like this is all so, like, sort of overwhelming. You know? Like so much is going on in my head.

T: Today, you mean. [Yeah] Also, I was about to ask you . . . Oh, golly we're almost out of time. It really did fly by, the last part for me. [Yeah] A lot of this clearly is new for you . . . clearly . . .

C: The feeling isn't new but maybe the . . . thinking about it that way is.

T: That the perspective is different in a way [Yeah], and it's almost too much to handle . . . or assimilate or something.

C: Like it makes sense in terms of what I'm doing with my life and my interaction and my relationships. Yeah. It makes a lot of sense. But then I think, but, God, what do I do now? . . . You partially answered that . . .

T: Well, I did partially answer that before. Um, are you saying now, "My God, do I have to wait till next Friday to get back into this?" and would like to come in sooner? . . . come in a couple times next week . . . Are you saying that?

C: Well . . . I don't know what I'm saying. I'm saying I'm feeling like, God, there's so much going on and . . . Like I guess I'm just feeling like this . . . will I ever . . . will that ever get better [OK] . . . it's just so . . .

T: Is there anything that can be done about this? [Yeah] That I can . . . I'll tell you my feeling. I feel good. I'm sorry about the pain you go through, but I feel good about what we're doing . . . feel good about . . .

C: That we got through some of the crap . . . yeah . . . I was avoiding, yeah . . .

T: And you feel—does something like this ever change at 30, for heaven sakes. If it doesn't, I'd get out of this business.

C: I guess the frustrating thing is . . . intellectually I have that information—or I should have it. I do have some of it, but . . . how do you . . .

T: . . . if we do what we did today . . . remember that . . . 20 minutes ago, when I . . . I didn't know what else to say . . . just sort of, "Boy, something sure is goofed up." That's when it hit me how overwhelming and blocked up . . . and distorted—that's what it was—how distorted your understanding and knowledge of yourself is. Something's going on . . . that neither of us understands, but we'll get to it. I really believe in this process . . . I've really got to quit.

C: Do you . . . like with school being over, do you change your schedule at all, or will you be able to see me . . . for a while? [Oh, yeah] That's no problem?

T: That's no problem. I'll be around almost all summer. I'll go away for maybe ten days . . . but usually . . . I'm very flexible in the summer. I'll take a few days off here and there to go camping . . . whatever . . . so, sure, I'll be here.

C: Like I don't know if seeing you twice next week or something is going to . . .

T: You answered my question. That is not what you were saying. See you could have been saying, "My God, I can't wait till Friday to deal with this." Or you could have been saying, "Wow, is there any way out of this?"

C: OK . . . I . . . yeah . . . I can wait till Friday because I can avoid it for a few days . . .

T: Right. OK, we'll say Friday at 12: 30 . . .

C: . . . [Heartfelt sigh]

■ Observing Bill Coulson— College of Notre Dame, Belmont, California

Introductory Comments by Bill: The Glazed Look

Trying to communicate with a foreign person is good discipline for a counselor who may have gotten sloppy.

The glazed look in my clients' eyes announces my sloppiness. It appears when I am talking. When they are talking, by and large my clients look alert and interested. When I speak (particularly when I speak at length) is when the glazed look appears.

In a way, the look is a sign of respect. My clients are not so rude as to say, "Shut up, this is my hour, not yours." So they feign interest and comprehension. The glazed look gives away the deception. What it means is "I am trying to get what you're saying, but, really, I don't get it."

I saw the glazed look once too often in my private practice recently and realized I needed a tune up. I needed discipline. I needed to learn again to stay within my clients' frame of reference.

Fortunately, we had a number of Japanese people in town for a program of community building: long hours of daily nondirective encounter for two and a half weeks with a large international group. I decided to take advantage of their presence by asking one of them to speak to me for an hour. I realized this might turn out to be difficult for us both, since she did not consider herself to speak good English at all. I would have to strain to catch her meaning, and that was the point.

It was a very good experience for me. When she returned to Japan, she wrote, "I felt completely accepted and deeply understood by you." So I have reason to think it wasn't bad for her either (though I am aware of the Japanese reputation for politeness). She said the interview seemed to make the many disparate experiences of her weeks in La Jolla cohere. I was pleased, because what I look for in counseling is that a person might pull together loose ends, more nearly taking possession of his or her life.

In the interview itself, she chose not to ask for counsel so much as to tell me the story of her time in La Jolla, particularly about what she called her "language handicap." I had been prepared for this because of the experience of other Japanese in previous La Jolla programs. It was the reason I had asked her to talk and not an American. But it was important not to take her as a specimen of a language handicap or as a specimen of the Japanese people.

At the end of the taping session, she told me she wished she could have expressed herself better. I said the problem of expression wasn't hers alone. "Sometimes, when I want to understand what you are saying, I don't quite understand and say it wrong. Then that's my language barrier." The reason it was good discipline for me to try to catch her meaning (and what makes me want to start a Rent-a-Foreigner agency for other counselors) is that the glazed look was *immediate* when I didn't catch her. It didn't wait until I was three quarters through a long speech. If I exceeded her framework even in choosing a particular word, I could see that I had lost her and that counseling was momentarily over.

I want to comment on a few specifics of the interview.

Her laugh.   I think it is cultural: part of her native framework and therefore not to be questioned. Even if it were not cultural I would try to resist highlighting or asking about it. In general I want to avoid distracting clients (or myself) by noting their manner. My goal is to see the world through their habits, just as they do.

An easy interpretation of an embarrassed laugh is that it discounts oneself. The counselor's own manner, however, is usually sufficient to set the tone for counseling to occur in spite of client embarrassment. The counselor takes everything the client says seriously. This is not to say the counselor is stodgy, but it means that counseling is quite different from conversation. The counselor bears down, is figuratively on the edge of his or her chair, trying always to catch the client's exact intention. I think you could define the uniqueness of counseling by the counselor's attitude: "I take myself seriously here, and I take you very seriously indeed." Such an occasion—signified by the single-mindedness of the counselor's devotion to the client's meanings—is fraught with a significance the client might never before have openly faced. In itself it is a giant step toward healing.

Asking questions.   I learned in training that client-centered counselors don't ask questions. But when I don't understand I like to ask—if asking doesn't impede the flow. There are points in the interview where I ask too clumsily and find that I have gotten in the way and other points when asking was a good thing because it forestalled having to *pretend* I understood. My goal is to stick with the client and not fall too far behind, though (of course) I don't like to be just curious. Waiting often pays off, too. There is no rule. It is a matter of judgment.

Going for the feelings.   There is a point late in the segment when, in rehearing it now, it seems she might have been expressing a present sadness rather than talking about something past. I'm not sure. In either case, I am pleased I didn't exploit it. I used to count my clients" tears and wear them like medals. I don't seem to need to do this so much any more and am glad for the shift.

Going too fast.   At the very end, she describes the situation in her marathon group (a 24-hour, nonstop encounter) when everything went too fast. *Then* she felt herself to be Japanese (that is, foreign). I think people come to counseling precisely because of such experiences. So much is happening in their lives that they can't keep track of it. Life comes into them but lodges in some secret place. They don't gain possession of their own experience.

Taking pause can be as good for the counselor as for the client. I know it was good for me to listen and speak to this client. Often being with people goes too fast for me, too. I neither catch their meaning nor say my own, and I don't stop to ask for help; it seems I *assume* I have understood, when, if I were more attentive, I would realize I haven't.

This conversation with a foreign person slowed me down. Going slower in itself helps me understand—and to *know* that I understand. I think it is similar for the client: because we are taking such small steps, she realizes her counselor is still with her. To believe (on good evidence) that your counselor knows you—and yet has no mind to condemn you—is one of the effects that make counseling worthwhile.

The Interview

C: At first, I would like to say . . . yesterday I joined your group . . . yesterday afternoon . . .

T: Yes . . . on conviction . . .

C: I tried to listen to your lecture, but your English is . . . words . . .

T: . . . too fast . . .

C: Yes, and like music to me [laughs].

T: Not like words, but like . . . sounds [yeah] . . . like sounds, sure.

C: And sometimes words . . . some words . . . came into me. For example, *client-centered therapy . . . mother . . .* or something . . . and my imagination worked hard, but I had to give up.

T: Yes, I understand. Is it different when you listen in the groups—in the small groups—to people speaking in English of themselves and their feelings? Do you find that you hear more of what they mean than in a lecture? . . . Do you understand . . .

C: Yeah . . . easier . . .

T: Easier . . . yeah. And does . . . is it that your heart hears then . . . or how does it work . . . is it just your brain or what?

C: Ummm. Maybe heart.

T: I've heard that. Other Japanese have told me that they hear many feelings, but they don't understand the words, but they understand with their heart is what they . . .

C: Yeah, maybe. I experienced . . . in my first group and the second group . . .

T: That understanding what a person feels . . . is that what you're experiencing . . . ?

C: And I was very surprised—at me [Ahh] who could understand without words.

T: I see. You didn't expect that you could understand.

C: Um. Before I came here, I knew I had language handicap. So at first I didn't want too much from this program.

T: You didn't want . . . too much . . .

C: At first, I didn't want too much from this program. [OK] I didn't expect so much.

T: Uh-huh . . . because of the language handicap . . . yeah.

C: And, uh . . . astonished . . .

T: You were astonished?

C: Yeah. In the first group . . .

T: Astonished at how much you understood?

C: Yeah . . . of course, I couldn't understand the details . . . exactly . . . but I can imagine . . . I could imagine . . . what they are . . . what they were talking about there. And . . . I could feel the feelings . . .

T: Even without grasping every word, you could imagine their experience.

C: Of course, sometimes . . . a sentence, or some words came into me. [Yes] Of course they helped my imagination.

T: The words would help, yeah.

C: Of course. But, uh, in the first group, I always felt I was there—with them . . . [Mhm] So I was pretty comfortable with them. [Yes] . . . And at first, in the first group, a facilitator asked me about my language problem [Yes] and then I answered him . . . I couldn't understand the details, but . . . I would try to ask you when I could, and then, . . . since then they didn't worry me about my language handicap . . .

T: I see. They . . . they were able to relax and trust you to ask them if you didn't understand . . . yeah . . . and so they didn't have to worry about you . . .

C: [Laughs] Yeah, and that made me easier.

T: I see. You would have to worry about them worrying about you otherwise—yes, so when they said, "Now we will not worry," then you could relax too.

C: In the third day . . . that's . . . I'm sorry. My English is sometimes strange . . . In the third day . . .

T: Second day or third day?

C: Third day [third day] in my first group . . . they began to talk about our facilitator . . . and because our facilitator didn't move so much, and some people was angry with him . . . and, uh . . . and one of them got angry with him very strongly, and I couldn't understand why she was interested in him so much.

T: Puzzled you . . . her interest.

C: Yeah. Of course [inaudible].

T: But you didn't say that there . . .

C: And then I forgot my language handicap [Ahh], and I asked her, "Have you ever experienced a facilitator in a small group?" I asked her. I forgot my language handicap.

T: I see. You just spoke to her . . . not . . . uh-huh . . .

C: And then suddenly she cried. I was very surprised. And then she began to tell us about her problem. [Oh] She identified her father with the facilitator [I see] because facilitator . . . were not interested in us and maybe for a while the meeting time . . . in the meeting time . . . for a while he ignored us . . .

T: Yes . . . I think I understand what you're saying. You're . . . right now you're puzzled about what you want to say . . . is that right? . . . that right now you are trying very hard to say what was happening in the group . . . or there is some . . . are you a little confused right now . . . that's what I wanted . . .

C: No. [No?] It's hard to—for me to explain . . .

T: In English. I see. OK. I think I understand. Now let me see . . . let me see if I understand. You tell me if I have this . . . if my understanding is correct, OK? That when she got angry with the facilitator, then, to your surprise, you spoke right to her, forgetting that you didn't speak English, and you spoke to her . . . and to your further surprise, she started to cry. You had touched something in her . . . and it turned out that the facilitator reminded her of her father [Yeah] that her father was like the facilitator. And that the way he was like—that they were like one another was that the facilitator seemed not to be attentive to the group . . . or not to care . . . is that what . . .

C: She felt . . .

T: Yes, that was her impression.

C: So . . . I could understand her . . .

T: Ahh, surely. You could understand from your own experience? Is that what you mean? You could understand why she was angry with the facilitator.

C: Yeah, yeah. [Uh-huh] And after group . . . after group meeting, I confirmed my imagination and my experience to . . . I asked one of members of my group [Yes] . . . and then she told me . . . my question was good . . . sharp [Sharp question] and then I was surprised.

T: That was more than you expected. [Yeah] It was . . . yes, it's um . . . you know the word *remarkable*? [Remarkable] . . . As I understand it, that you came here not . . . not expecting much because of your language handicap, and in that moment, you were . . . you forgot about yourself, and you just spoke directly to her and it was a very facilitative question. Your friend said afterward it was a sharp question, and it seemed like you surprised yourself . . . yeah . . . that's a good feeling . . .

C: Highly exciting . . . experience . . . and, uh, in the second group, uh, our facilitator . . . the facilitator asked me about myself. He was interested in me . . . in my life in Japan. Then I could express myself.

T: You could be . . . unself-conscious then? [What?] Well, when he asked you about yourself, then you were free to speak up without thinking of yourself or your handicap—your language barrier? Or . . . I would like to understand what you . . . what you told me there.

C: Uh . . . If they are talking about themselves too fast, of course I try to listen to them, but sometimes I must give up. [Yes, you're tired] And sometimes I can't ask them, because I can't understand because of too fast English, and I can't ask them. I can't say . . . I can say nothing. [Yeah, you can say . . .] But he is . . . he was interested in me, and he asked me, and I had opportunity to express myself [Ah, yes], and I could . . . I could.

T: Yes, you could tell your story. It was your story then, and that you could say.

C: And after that meeting, one of members told me I could express myself . . . I could express myself better than I think . . . I thought.

T: Did that surprise you? [Yeah] Yes . . . and did you have to agree? [Yeah] that you did better than you thought you would do . . . Did that . . . what the person said to you . . . that [client's name] you can express yourself better than you think. [Yeah] And then did you say, "Yes I can" . . . or is that true . . . that you thought so then too?

C: Maybe. I said maybe.

T: Not so sure . . . I think you would like to express yourself even better. Is that correct? Did you wish that more people had asked you about yourself?

C: Yeah. I want to meet many people here. [Yes] At least . . .

T: At least here you would like to meet them?

C: I didn't want so much . . . I didn't expect so much because of the language problem, but at least I want to meet many people here. I know I can talk with some . . . with other people if they speak to me slowly [Yes] . . . I believe I can understand what they mean . . . so I know . . . I can understand them if I have time enough to talk.

T: Yes, I understand that. And were you . . . were you ever disappointed that more people did not give you time to talk and to understand?

C: Mmm, not . . . not so disappointed [OK].

T: Then did you . . . you did get to meet many people? [Yeah] Ahh . . . I'm glad.

C: I need much more time . . . to meet more people . . .

T: To stay longer.

C: I want to stay longer.

T: So that you have not been lonely while you have been here.

C: Yeah, but in . . . in the third group, I had a difficult time. In marathon group. Because maybe we were too tired. The members were too tired, and there were more people than in small group, and they were talking too fast, and . . . my imagination wasn't working. And I slept and maybe they were angry with me because I slept . . . very well.

T: And you slept very well, huh? [Laughter]

C: And in marathon group everything was too fast. We didn't have silence and . . . I felt they didn't try to accept a person . . . a member in marathon group, I felt so, it was very difficult for me to follow them or to catch their feelings.

T: They . . . you felt that they didn't accept a person . . . do you mean many persons or do you mean a certain person that they didn't accept? [Please, once more] OK, you said, if I understood you correctly, that there was not enough silence, and they talked too fast, and that they didn't accept a person. [Accept] Accept a person. [I felt . . .] Yes, you felt that they did not accept you either . . . is that correct? [Yeah] They did not accept one another, and they did not accept you . . . [Yeah, I felt . . .] Uh-huh . . . unaccepted.

C: So . . . and . . . and . . . they can express themselves . . . or their feelings . . . or their emotions . . . so strongly and so intensively . . . and I couldn't catch them. I wanted to escape.

T: You didn't want to be there with them when they were so heavy.

C: And then I felt I was a Japanese [Ahh]. I was different from them.

T: I see . . . that earlier, you had felt like a person . . . in your first group and your second group.

C: Yeah . . . yeah. I never felt I was a Japanese . . . in those two groups.

T: Uh-huh . . . but now, when they . . . then when they say too much too rapidly and do not take time to accept one another. Then you feel like a stranger . . . a foreign person.

C: In my case, I want . . . if a person . . . if a member . . . if a certain person . . . begins to talk about himself or herself, I want to taste her feelings . . . or her mind or her emotions, and I need enough silence . . . in the group . . .

T: . . . take it in and really taste what she says and feels.

C: Very big . . . I was about to cry.

T: It really did upset you that you couldn't feel what they said.

C: I couldn't catch . . .

T: . . . the person . . . and it hurt you. [Mhm?] It hurt you. [Mhm?] It hurt you? It made you feel like crying.

C: Yeah . . . I hurt sad.

T: Uh-huh, yeah, I understand.

■ Observing Joan Strachan— Catholic Pastoral Center, Winnipeg, Manitoba

Introductory Comments by Joan

About "M" in the therapy.   When "M" first arrived at my office she presented the image of defeat. Her large size, plain hairstyle and bulky clothing made her difficult to define physically—and she sat with her hands concealed beneath her rolled-up coat. Her speech faint and halting, seemed to convey that she was barely able to function, and her breathing was too shallow to lend any impetus to her words.

Something in her had died. Slowly, with encouragement, she began the painful story of her experience during and following a voluntary period in a mental hospital. While there, she had 39 shock treatments and the attention of three psychiatrists without, in her view, being given any understanding of what was "wrong" with her. Eventually, after leaving the hospital of her own volition and throwing away her pills, she tried to face the world again, only to find it less friendly to her than before. Confused and frightened, she retreated into a one-room apartment—her "box"—and stayed there, unable to work, to eat well, sleep well (she did not even own a bed), or finally to consider any real life outside her four walls.

Our contract became to experiment with movement—out and back into the box. "M" said she wanted me to help her find the courage to act. Yet, having come close to suicide, she could not face an expectation of consistent success. She needed to know she could "give up" in small doses and for short periods. Giving herself permission for forward movement and retreat, she began to reward herself for whatever she did, learning to measure movement in little steps and, finally, learning to celebrate the *self* that began to emerge. She took some charge of her therapy (which she had felt unable to do at the hospital)—bought a bed—had her hair styled—lost weight deliberately—exercised—reached out to others—began a project on recreation therapy—and started to feel *alive*.

About me in the therapy.   Before "M" could move, she had to deal with feeling stuck in her anger, hurt, and confusion. I saw my work beginning with listening to her story of what she experienced as betrayal at the hands of professional helpers. Since she felt the need to repeat this story like a broken record, to me and inside her head, I helped her gradually to add something new (from her) to the narrative, so that it began to sound different: for example, " . . . I did a smart thing for me and got out," and later " . . . I chose to leave, and I can keep on making choices."

I supported "M" in her choices, from the buying of the bed to an occasional move back into the box, which I reframed as "creative resting." The ideas came from her. If I got ahead of her (for example, using the word "celebrate" when it was too strong for her, or moving her to action too quickly), she began to put me straight in a positive way.

"M" is currently assuming more and more responsibility for her therapy—for her life. She is finding the courage to act.

About the Sessions

Below are brief segments from sessions 14 and 16. In session 14, she refers to her "project"—designing the kind of treatment program that might have helped her and sharing it with the professionals who might learn from her experience. She is planning a visit to one of the professionals at the hospital where she had had the experiences that seemed so destructive to her. She subsequently had this visit, and it went well. In session 16, she makes it clear to me that I had nearly sidetracked her in a previous session, by focusing on what was really my agenda—encouraging her to get a job. She, however, is going another direction, and I try to respond by staying with her and acknowledging that I had misheard her before—not by apologizing but by thoroughly understanding what she was saying to and about me.

Interview Fourteen

C: I had a good week. I didn't really do anything special. Just felt good during the week.

T: Am I right in thinking that's . . . that's new? It's new for me to hear you say that.

C: Yeah. It's new for me to say it. Before I would have just said . . . if you'd said, "How are you?" I would have said, "Fine." But it really was a good week. I don't know what made it good. Like I say, I didn't do anything different . . . differently than I did other weeks. I just enjoyed it.

T: Maybe you learned something about yourself: that you don't always have to be doing something different to feel good?

C: I think I knew that before. I think I knew that you didn't have to do something extra special, something fantastic, in order to feel well . . . just felt good. And when I was feeling good, it . . . maybe one thing I did differently was that I didn't get scared about feeling well . . . and turn it off and say, "You don't deserve this."

T: You didn't sabotage it.

C: Yeah. I just . . . I felt good and was grateful for that, and so when the next day came and I kind of wondered whether the feeling would continue, and it did, and I was willing to just let it continue. And I didn't . . . I had a few bad moments, but nothing that was too overwhelming. Nothing that lasted long.

T: So not only are you telling me that you felt good, but you're telling me that you felt good about feeling good.

C: Yes.

T: Huh! . . . Last week you said no matter what you did to feel good, you were always carrying around those thoughts—these negative thoughts.

C: Well, they were still there. I didn't get rid of those . . . just didn't let them bother me. I don't think they took up quite as much time in my brain as they normally do, but they were still there. It . . . maybe one of the things that made me feel good was that, uh, the last couple of weeks you've kinda of drummed into me that I have changed, so I sat down one day with a pen and a pencil, and I . . . pen and paper . . . and wrote down what I was like before and what I'm like now. And you're right. I've changed. You see, before when I was thinking, "change" would be a job, and a nice place to live, and a completely different lifestyle. That's what I wanted in change. I wasn't willing to accept the little things . . . like you said the first day I'd ever been here . . . the little accomplishments.

T: It's not easy just to accept those where you have such a wide vision of what you want to change, and you think there's so much you've got to do. [Right] And yet when you take great big chunks like that of expectations, it's very hard to be able to digest all that, and so it's easy to give up . . . You told me that you're going to see the one ally that you have at the mental hospital . . . going to see him on Thursday? [Mhm] Having just talked to him . . . you actually talked to him. [Mhm] Was that a good experience? Was that OK for you?

C: Yeah. That was fine. That never bothers me.

T: The making the phone call bothers you, but once you've got . . .

C: And worrying, will he answer it? Do I leave my name and number or . . . that worries me . . . getting to talking.

T: Yeah, I was going to say, getting through that hurdle of picking up the phone and calling like that would be a major—a really significant thing for you. Whatever happened at the other end, I would think that, uh, that would make you feel good, to have gotten across that. Then when he answered, it was OK. You could breathe again.

C: Right.

T: You set up an appointment?

C: Thursday. Meeting down the road. I won't go to the clinic. He didn't seem to mind at all. I am not too sure what we're going to talk about.

T: You . . . you sound like you need to be sure before you can . . .

C: Well, there must be a purpose in my going down there, other than just to say hello. I . . . I did that on the phone. I don't know what I'm going to say. I don't know what the topic of conversation is supposed to be. He wasn't too clear either, so we're going to be in a little bit of trouble. He said he didn't quite understand . . . understand things.

T: That's like when you come here, and I put you in charge of the agenda, you feel kind of anxious about that.

C: I don't like it, no.

T: It would be easier if I knew exactly what I wanted from you, and how I was going to go about getting it out of you.

C: Right, and I would willingly participate.

T: I know.

C: But just don't ask me to start.

T: Now when you go on Thursday, he's going to ask you to start.

C: Right . . . but the way I see it is that I'm supposed to be going down there to talk about my project, I think. I think that's the main idea.

T: Is that your idea?

C: Well, I'm not really sure. Last week, when we were talking, and I said, for my project I didn't know the right way—the proper way to approach it—from which angle to approach it. I said that I didn't understand the philosophy behind the mental institution—what they were trying to do and the ways they went about doing it. And it was almost as if I had said the magic word, and you just sort of jumped, and you offered to call him, and you've never offered to do anything before for me, so I took you up on it. And I guess I'm going . . . that's the idea to go down, but I don't know the questions to ask yet. "Could you please tell me the philosophy of the place that you work at."

T: That's one possibility.

C: I think I should be a little more specific. [OK] I don't know . . . I don't quite know how.

T: Well, would you be willing to practice that a little bit here? To just kind of talk it out a little bit here?

C: Sure. I think I'd probably end up saying much the same I've already said to you . . . Give it a try. [Yeah] . . . You're waiting for me to start?

T: Maybe I could say something to you like your friend is likely to say, such as, "It's good to see you again. It's really good to see you again." He'll probably say some other things too about what he, uh, notices about you. He may notice that you cut your hair. You could cut it again. Looks terrific.

C: Thank you.

T: He may notice that you're slimmer. He is bound to notice that you've made some moves just in your phone call and your agreement to meet him, and then he may say to you something like, "I understand that you're doing a project and you need some information about this place."

C: I would probably say, "Well, it's not really a project. It's just one of my fantasies." [OK] I'd explain to him what it is and why . . . and then . . . don't know . . . I'm lost from there on. See I think this week has been so good, I don't even know if I want to do this thing. Just another part of the problem.

T: Huh. So if you go down there, you might gather information to put in a file somewhere for a while in case you felt like doing it. Would that be fair?

C: Yeah. Yes. I still think it's a worthwhile way to spend my time.

T: Well, yeah.

C: I haven't really thought about it for two weeks now. Maybe that's what's making me feel real good, is not going back into what happened and thinking of ways to make it better.

T: Mm. Like, uh . . . let me see if I, if I'm getting with you. "I feel OK right now. I feel better than I've felt in quite a while. Would that even be fair to say? [Yes] And if I get into this project . . ."

C: I wouldn't . . .

T: "I'm going to go back to the hospital, and I'm going to go through all that stuff again."

C: Right.

T: "Do I really want to get into that crap?"

C: Right. I think it's worthwhile. Maybe . . . Maybe they know. It was . . . On the phone I told him the . . . I told him why. I explained the project very briefly and what I thought the benefits would be. And I told him eventually I'd probably just get into an argument with him about how rotten their program is and how this fantasy program of mine would change things. And he said, "That's OK." Said that was fine. He said, "We know we failed with you."

T: Huh! Wow!

C: Kind of knocked me off the chair, and, uh, I think he used the . . . when he said, "We know we failed." I think he meant to say, "He knows they failed."

T: That makes a difference to you.

C: You see, don't think he failed. I . . . I know he cared, and I feel that he tried. And you really can't ask for much more than that from anybody, but I don't feel that the others tried. I really don't feel that any of them put any sort of ingenuity or creativity into what they were doing.

Interview Sixteen

Note: this segment begins after the session has started.

C: I know that if I see something that upsets me or if I hear something or do something or something's done to me, I know now that I can't dwell on it or I'm just putting myself . . . moving myself backwards. And I'm . . . I don't want to do that.

T: It feels bad to do that.

C: Yes.

T: You don't deserve all that punishment . . . when you come right down to it.

C: No.

T: So that's one of the things that's made your week kind of good: the fact that you didn't get stuck in that box or whatever.

C: Right. It's been about three weeks now that it's been pretty good. I just don't seem to . . . it doesn't seem to bother me as much.

T: I'm going to ask you a kind of a funny thing. How do you feel about the fact that you don't feel so bad? Do you know what I'm saying?

C: Yes. Like that book. You have to create anxieties. I think that's a large part of it . . . that I feel good about feeling good. Last week when I was sitting here and I was really feeling frustrated. I didn't . . . There was something wrong, and I didn't know what it was. And you'd say to me a couple of times, "What are you thinking?" And I didn't know and I . . . I was walking back home; I thought about it and for the first time I really feel good about feeling good, and you were sitting here talking about going back to work. And here I am feeling so good, and the idea of working doesn't appeal to me in the least. And I wanted to celebrate.

T: You wanted to celebrate.

C: I wanted to celebrate, and I thought: this word celebrate. [inaudible] I wanted to do something that I haven't done, you know, for a long time. I just wanted to go away on a holiday or do something really interesting or exciting. Here we were sitting; you kept telling me . . . well, you kept saying, "Maybe this week you can inquire about a job." I kept saying, "I don't think so for this week." [Uh-huh] That's 'cause I . . . I still want to do something that's exciting and that's . . . I haven't done for a long time. Something that I'll enjoy.

T: You heard me say you should be applying for a job.

C: No. You didn't . . . you were just . . .

T: We were talking about some possibilities for . . .

C: Right. You said, "Maybe this week you could call . . . call a certain place." You said, "That's one of the possibilities for this week," and I said, "Forget it. It's not even a possibility."

T: Uh-huh. That's right. You put me straight.

C: I wanted to do something that's, you know like go away on a holiday. Just do something that's really fun.

T: As I remember it, it was like you weren't in touch with that—what you wanted to do—until maybe after you got out of here, because I didn't . . . I didn't hear that celebrative tone in you . . .

C: I didn't know it either.

T: I thought you were all business, but you . . . you're saying now, no wonder you were frustrated, because you were trying to express yourself on that level—that business level—but inside there was a little itch to get out and have fun.

C: Right, but I didn't realize that until I sat down and figured out well, why . . . what was wrong. What was it that I really didn't want to do? I didn't want to go out and look for a job. And that was the reason. I'm no further ahead in figuring out what I'm going to do to celebrate. I'm . . .

T: But even getting in touch with the fact that that's what you wanted to do and using that word for the first time . . .

C: Oh, I know. When it hit me, I just laughed.

T: Well, it would be fun to use your creativity to figure out what celebration would mean. How it would translate for you.

C: I think I would like to go out to the mountains and go camping. I would really enjoy that. I think that would be an appropriate celebration.

T: You haven't been camping for how long?

C: Five years.

T: When you were away? You mean? When you were overseas?

C: I camped with someone when I came back. I came back in the spring, and then I went camping that summer. Haven't been since.

T: Would you go back to the place where you were that summer?

C: I was . . .

T: I don't know where that was.

C: No. That was like a regular camp. I would like to just go out with a backpack on my back and go out into the mountains and pitch a tent. And I would like to do it with somebody, and therein lies the problem. I need somebody to do it with. I think that's what I would like to do to celebrate. Because before I wouldn't . . . no matter how much fun it was, I wouldn't let myself have fun. I wouldn't let myself enjoy it. And now I can. I can just forget about not expecting a good . . . forget about everything that's happened and just go out for a week or so and just have fun.

T: Well, spin that out a little bit, you know? Spin it out. What's . . . look at how you might put a little flesh on your dream. Is that what you want to do now? This time? I've got to check that out this time, so I don't make a mistake. [Shared laugh]

■ Observing Morgan Henderson— Full Circle Counseling, Inc., Staunton, Virginia

Introductory Comments by Morgan

This is my second session with a single mother (never married) in her 30s. Her 3-year-old son died about six weeks ago. She was holding him in her arms in the ambulance, on their way to a better hospital. His last words to her were, "No more machines, Mommy." She spent the last 68 days of his life sleeping at the hospital, there 24 hours a day. It appears from the autopsy that there was medical mismanagement, and the physician involved has had a number of children in his care die during this past year.

In our first session together, she spent much of the time expressing her pretty obvious rage at the doctor and the hospital and her desire to work in the field of death and dying, to do something to stop the needless death of children and to help grieving parents. In this session, there clearly are times when her statements include both anger and her struggle to survive and cope. I notice that I tend to respond more to the second part of the message; here I think I am doing this partly because of how intensely we dealt with her anger in the first session. I want her to know that I understand both her anger and her need. There were times in this interview, however, when it would have been more helpful to have articulated the anger a bit more than I did. In the session, she refers to Compassionate Friends, which is a support self-help group for parents of children who have died. As you will see, she is a very intelligent, sensitive, and gutsy woman. Her struggle to make it financially right now is taking any energy she might have left over from her grieving.

In our workshops and counseling on death and dying, we [Morgan and her husband, Steve] have been traveling full-time for the past four years. Thus, all of my counseling has been done on the run and I get out of town by sunset. That is, it has been crisis-oriented and intensive—maybe every day for a week, and then I don't see the person again for a year, or we work by phone after that. That means that all my long-term clients, like this woman, are new, and the trust and relaxation are just being built up.

I do want to comment that starting to tape-record sessions has been a big step. Sometimes I have been conscious of watching myself, which of course interferes with hearing the client. I also think that I responded more frequently than I usually do. There are times when I could have let her do more of the work. I seem to be more affected by this than my client is, but I am feeling quite convinced that taping will be a big part of my own growth as a counselor.

The Interview

T: I'm finally feeling back from the summer—summer off.

C: Yeah. You took the whole summer off?

T: More or less. I did some training workshops, one in Maine and one in California, but I more or less just vegetated. It was really nice.

C: I bet it was.

T: You didn't.

C: Huh-uh . . . I think, though, it was vegetating. [Yeah] . . . essentially it was that.

T: In the sense that it wasn't living. [Mm-hm] Is that what you mean?

C: Very definitely.

T: How are you doing now?

C: Um . . . I just . . . I don't know what to do. I don't feel like I'm in any way ready for a job, but I have to work . . .

T: Feeling pushed by the money?

C: Yeah. And it's hard to start moving and not know where you're going.

T: Kind of like you're not ready yet to move and . . .

C: And I'm not ready to stay there, but I can't . . . there's no way I can afford to keep the place. [The apartment?] Mhm . . . so . . . there's no choice in that.

T: She's gone up on the rent? . . . I'm not sure what . . .

C: Yeah, and uh . . . course it was in the subsidized housing also, and that will be shot . . . so . . .

T: Why will that be shot?

C: Well, (her son) qualified for subsidized.

T: Oh, I see. I see. Yeah . . . you . . . that's another loss . . . isn't it?

C: I don't . . . it's . . . how do you work when you just don't feel like you can do anything? And the only option is to go and live with my family, and that's not really an option.

T: So it means . . . neither choice is . . . They're both crummy choices right now and neither one is what you need to be doing.

C: Uh-huh. And I need to have a place to stay, in order to get, you know, to get a job. And I don't want to take a job that's too far away from what my ultimate goal is, and that's working with families of sick kids. Well, you know what that entails . . . back to school . . . more money. Blah . . .

T: Doesn't . . . it doesn't seem like there's any options right now . . . going to get you where you want to . . . where you want to go or what you need right now . . . I guess you must feel just kind of up against the wall. You've no choices that are good ones.

C: Really. Because . . . there's just . . . what can I do? [A male friend] really wants us to marry, and I love him . . . I'm not in love with him. But it seems so soon to take on the responsibility of loving someone again.

T: Yeah. You haven't finished . . . haven't finished this process, and it's . . . someone else is saying, "Now I need you to love me, and . . ."

C: And I think you do . . . just sort of need to shut down for a while after death.

T: Not love anybody. Just not have that responsibility . . . just want to check that [tape recorder] . . . Last week we didn't get anything, so that's why . . . no problem . . . Yeah, and I guess what I . . . one of the things I heard you saying last time was . . . "I need some time to just love myself . . . find out who that is and care for that person and . . ."

C: Or find out if there's anything there to love. And that's a real kicker.

T: "And if I . . . what if I take the time and there's nobody lovable there . . . it's really scary."

C: Oh, very . . . I don't know. I don't know, you know . . . people have a tendency to say, OK, you shouldn't do anything for a year . . . or no, you should make a clean break . . . or . . . and none of it seems right.

T: Their advice is so neat.

C: Mhm. And it, you know, you just wrap up everything . . . oh, OK, a year from now then I'll do so and so. What do you do in that year?

T: Telling you what you shouldn't do, but nobody's saying here's how to survive it . . . here's how to . . . yeah.

C: It's like get rid of everything of [child's name]'s. His clothes, his toys . . .

T: And that doesn't fit . . . yeah.

C: Mm-hm. You know—what if I want another kid?—that's my argument.

T: What if you want to just keep [child's name]'s things . . . just because . . .

C: And if . . . you don't . . . how do you give a whole life to Goodwill?

T: Just throw it away . . . just sort of . . . as if that would get rid of [child's name], or . . . sounds like you need to hold on to him and those things [Mm-hm] . . . in a good way.

C: It's not as painful as it was to see his things . . . um . . . but I can't just discard them either.

T: That would be like discarding him, I guess.

C: And I have to wonder if it's selfish . . . I'm just keeping them . . . what is it C. L. [sic] Lewis says—that incredible selfishness or laziness of grief.

T: You mean it's sort of . . . does this mean "I'm hanging on to my grief and not willing to go on . . ."

C: But I . . . I don't know . . . all I know is that I can't seem to get rid of the things.

T: Mm-hm . . . just doesn't feel right yet . . . yeah . . . hasn't been very long.

C: And his death itself I think I'm . . . you know . . . I think I'm accepting his death. What I can't accept is the medical information after the glaring lack of it and misdiagnosis and wondering why . . . in the hell has this happened.

T: The medical information is . . . is wrong?

C: Apparently the kid was misdiagnosed.

T: He didn't have renal failure.

C: Mm-hm. And the medications interfered with the renal functions so much for so long . . .

T: Ch- . . . it's like now you have to look at—did he have to die? Was it a medical mistake, or was there really an illness that was killing him?

C: Right . . . And that has really . . . it's better than not knowing.

T: Yeah . . . even the worst . . . even the worst is better than not knowing.

C: But processing the information is just impossible.

T: What do you do with that? What do you do with all that stuff [Yeah] that you've been . . .

C: To whom do you go . . . what, to his doctor and say, "What's happened here?" You're not going to get . . . why should I get any information now? I never got any when he was sick.

T: It's like going back to the same source that screwed it up.

C: So how do you find out? And it's never going to be resolved . . . not with the complications that . . . and it's really difficult for me to accept the lack of resolve there.

T: "It's like no end . . . there's no end. How do I ever let this go. How do I get rid of it?" And I guess I hear you saying that your friends are giving you these real neat solutions after a year, and you're saying—am I going to live with this uncertainty and this helplessness in the face of this injustice? How do I deal with that?

C: Yeah, because you're not . . . you not only have the whole psychic energy that's drained, but, you know . . . practical matters . . . I can't really even make a decision about practical matters . . .

T: Yeah . . . just the day-to-day garbage . . . moving and . . .

C: To where? I don't know. My things are in [town name], but I'm not there.

T: You don't even have a place right now . . . to hide out in to do this kind of work that you want to do.

C: It's a lot of pressure to get . . . I understand the need for people to see what they think is positive for their own sake—and I need positive things too—but I don't know how to find them.

T: They're not coming from those statements and platitudes, are they? Guess it's that feeling of—"so where do I turn and find . . . positive . . . find the good?"

C: Right. I can accept his death, and that's positive. I'm beginning to accept his absence. But, Lord, I can't take what's happened.

T: Why it happened and the way it happened . . . not right.

C: Mm-hm. Isn't anybody responsible? And they are but shifting responsibility or naming responsibility doesn't stop the whole process of this kind of horror.

T: That's like . . . you have this helplessness of—"am I the only one watching this horror and . . . everybody's busy shifting it around, and still children are dying."

C: Yeah, and you know the kind of credibility you get if you walk . . . if a layman walks in and says, "Hey. Look at this. You made a misdiagnosis." Oh, sure. That's really credible.

T: Just seems like some mother comes in . . . that makes you even feel more powerless, I guess.

C: And that only leaves the legal profession, and what is it to them?

T: They only . . . they see the black-and-white stuff, but they don't see the pain and . . . that you're carrying and what's happened to you.

C: Do they see the necessity to make it stop happening to kids or to anyone . . . and who does? Except the victims . . . who does?

T: When it happens to you then . . . you know in a way you can never know if you're just a lawyer or . . . so who do you find to be on your side?

C: Right.

Appendix B
On Being a Client

Jo Ann M. Unger

Many times over the course of my studies as a clinical psychology student, I have been advised to seek personal therapy, which I did. Below I discuss my impressions of being a client based on my firsthand experiences. I also share some conclusions I have drawn from these experiences.

Deciding to enter therapy can be a difficult decision for a client. There can be a perception that therapy and counseling are only for those who have serious problems and not for "someone like me." Therefore, clients will often wait until their life situation or negative feelings have gotten almost unbearable, and therapy is their last resort. Clients can come to therapy quite distressed, embarrassed about needing therapy, and anxious about the process. I remember trying a number of different strategies to work through personal issues before seeking therapy. While this may be a good thing, as it may lead to finding a solution and a sense of self-efficacy, part of the reason for engaging in these strategies was to avoid going to therapy. Often the strategies clients use to cope with their issues involve methods of avoiding the negative situation or feelings. The stigma associated with receiving therapy is so great that many people will wait until they are desperate or never go. However, avoidance does not work in the long term. In my case, the strategies I used did not seem to improve my situation. My painful feelings did not diminish. What I needed was someone to talk to who would accept me and provide a place to explore my feelings and emotions fully.

For many people the decision to receive therapy is a big one filled with conflicting emotions. Clients want relief from their pain but often are embarrassed by their inability to solve their problems on their own and may be afraid of what therapy may involve. For these reasons, it is important for therapists to be especially sensitive to clients' leading edge in the first session. The first session can be extremely anxiety provoking. The first time I attended therapy with my husband I remember standing at the therapist's door not wanting to go in. Both of us just stood there waiting for the other person to ring the doorbell. The fear was so great that neither one of us wanted to do it. Finally, the thought of us being seen just standing at the door, without ringing the doorbell, caused me to ring it. Entering through the therapist's door for the first time is like entering into an unknown universe. Often clients will have very little background or knowledge as to what therapy involves. Their information, unfortunately, often comes from unrealistic portrayals of therapy on television shows or in movies. They fear being judged, being verbally attacked, or being forced to do or say things they do not want to. In the first session, it is very important for a therapist to provide a safe and comfortable place for their clients. It is also important to help clients understand what they can expect in that session and in the sessions ahead. Making therapy less mystical and mysterious can help reduce anxiety and promote engagement.

After a person has made the decision to enter therapy, has made it through the door, and has a basic understanding of the therapeutic process, the development of trust begins. While clients certainly have some idea of what has brought them to therapy, getting the courage to discuss that issue may not happen immediately. Initially, clients can be very conscious of how the therapist will react to their story. Clients may start by presenting less distressing and difficult material in order to gauge whether they will be accepted by the therapist and whether the therapist can be trusted with more difficult and important material. Each time clients speak about something important or emotionally charged, they are taking a leap of faith. They are taking the therapist to a deep and vulnerable place where a sense of judgment could be excruciatingly painful. "What will my therapist think of me? Will I shock or disgust him/her? Will my therapist still want me for a client? Will I be acceptable?" Therapists who have not been clients cannot fully understand the fear clients must face and conquer in that moment of trust. In therapy, clients entrust their innermost thoughts and feelings to a person who has no vested interest in them. This can be both terrifying and freeing. In the moment before and during disclosure, clients may feel a sense of impending doom. And then there is the long and terrifying wait for the therapist's reaction.

When the reaction of the therapist is one of acceptance, understanding, and respect, there can be huge sense of relief and almost joy. "I am not disgusting. I am not unacceptable. I just am." I remember sharing a particularly difficult topic with my therapist. I took a huge leap of faith and waited for a response. There was no huge reaction of disbelief. There was no look of shock or surprise. There was no condemnation or judgment. I was still an acceptable human being working through a personal issue. I left that session feeling lighter than air. While my problem was not solved and my negative feelings had not dissolved, I left that session feeling blessed. Someone I barely knew listened to my story and accepted me. There is so much power in that moment. In most of our interpersonal relationships we do not just listen to each other; instead, we listen, judge, and give our opinions. It is rare to share our deepest and most personal emotions and have someone respond with simple listening, understanding, and acceptance.

I believe this is why therapy is so powerful. Much of the distress we feel in having a personal issue does not come from the issue itself but from the meaning and value we give to that issue. We are taught in our society that we need to be happy and content all of the time. When we do not feel that way, we think something is wrong with us and start to feel anxious and upset. We believe we are unacceptable and become distressed over having an issue. When a therapist accepts the client and his/her issue, the distress and anxiety about having an issue decreases. A client can learn from the therapist that having an issue does not make him/her disgusting or abnormal. Through the therapist's acceptance, the client can learn to accept her- or himself. Once the anxiety about having an issue can be reduced, the work of addressing the issue itself can take place with much greater ease.

While the goal of therapy is to reduce distress and solve problems, the therapeutic process itself is not distress free. Not only do clients have to learn to trust the therapist and face their fear of rejection, they must also do the work of self-reflection and self-discovery. The therapist creates a safe place to discuss and explore the client's thoughts and feelings. In that space, the client can learn things about him- or herself that are surprising, wonderful, discouraging, and distressing. Clients may have spent much of their lives trying to avoid these thoughts and feelings and now the therapist is asking them to voice those thoughts and feelings aloud, in front of another person. Clients either may not want to admit those thoughts and feelings to themselves, let alone another person, or may not have been aware of those thoughts and feelings until the very moment they were given the space they needed in therapy. For clients to explore what for a long time has been feared and avoided requires a tremendous amount of trust.

My therapist is a gifted person who is able to foster a trusting relationship with his clients. He is able to communicate a deep sense of interest and caring through his presence. This allowed me to feel comfortable and free to explore those uncharted parts of my soul. As a client, I felt my therapist was on my team. He was not going to judge me or ask me to do or be anything I did not want to do or be. This gave me the freedom to explore my thoughts and feelings—even those I did not like and had difficulty facing. His presence not only provided freedom, but it also provided extra courage. I was not facing my fearful thoughts and feelings alone. I had someone to walk with me, someone who genuinely accepted and cared for me, was not afraid, and provided me with extra courage. Having both the freedom to explore and the comfort of a strong team member, I was able to explore territories of myself that were previously unexplored, resulting in greater self-awareness. I said things in therapy I had not voiced aloud and things I did not know were there. I made discoveries about myself that were previously unknown. With this new knowledge, I was able to make steps and changes to improve myself and my relationships. My therapist took the time to make sure that he understood what I was saying as well as the emotions behind my words. I believe that it was the unique ability to understand the emotion being communicated that made my therapist so effective.

In my therapy sessions, however, my therapist did not always immediately understand exactly what I was trying to communicate. This is important information for beginning therapists to know, as we often feel the need to understand the client perfectly the first time. This expectation is unrealistic and impossible to achieve. As a client, I realized it was not essential that my therapist understand me immediately. What was important was that he took the time to listen and correct his understanding when necessary. His corrections enabled me to feel that he truly did understand me, that I was worth taking the time to be understood, and allowed me to continue the therapeutic process.

Therapy is an amazing, terrifying, wonderful, and growth-promoting experience. It increases self-awareness, self-acceptance, and emotional and social functioning. It allows clients to learn about themselves, accept themselves, and develop new skills to function more effectively in their lives. I think it is something everyone should experience.

I was given the opportunity to receive therapy, during the course of my clinical training as a clinical psychology student. This was a valuable experience both personally and professionally. It allowed me the opportunity to work on my own personal growth and receive therapy from an exceptionally gifted therapist who uses evocative empathy in his approach. Although I have learned about evocative empathy in my coursework, learning and understanding the principles of evocative empathy and effective therapy is almost nothing like experiencing them as a client. Receiving therapy helps the principles of effective therapy come alive. I could see how the principles of evocative empathy are actually practiced as well as understand how it feels to be the client. Being on the "receiving end" is also a good test of whether a therapist can feel comfortable adopting a particular therapeutic practice or principle.

By being a client I discovered three main benefits of undergoing therapy as a clinical psychology student. First, it gave me a better understanding of what clients go through as they enter therapy and engage in the therapeutic process. Entering therapy is often an uncomfortable experience. Engaging in therapy is often challenging, difficult, and emotionally taxing. Thus, in order to be empathic to this experience it is helpful for therapists to have had a similar experience. Second, therapy gives clinical psychology students the opportunity to work through issues that may influence their ability to be effective therapists. Such issues might include stereotypes about groups of people; doubts about our own effectiveness as therapists; our personal feelings, either positive or negative, toward our clients; and a variety of other issues that may arise as we work with clients. It is possible that many of these issues would surface and be addressed in the supervision stage of our training. But highly personal issues or ones that are not easily identified might be more effectively dealt with by seeing a trained therapist. Third, therapy provides a safe place to explore, heal, and grow as a human being. The therapeutic process allows all clients, including those of us who are therapists, to grow and develop into more mature and healthier people, no matter the starting point, and to become better people, better friends, better partners, better parents— and better therapists. We can be more present, more empathic, and more in tune with our clients' needs by giving our own issues a place to be heard and worked on. In my opinion, though therapy is not always comfortable and can be challenging and anxiety provoking, in the end, there just is no downside to being a client.

References

Ablon, J. S., Levy, R. A., & Katzenstein, T. (2006). Beyond brand names of psychotherapy: Identifying empirically supported change processes. *Psychotherapy: Theory, Research, Practice, Training, 43,* 216–231.

Ackerman, S. J., & Hilsenroth, M. J. (2001). A review of therapist characteristics and techniques negatively impacting the therapeutic alliance. *Psychotherapy, 38,* 171–185.

Alberta, A. J., & Wood, A. H. (2009). A practical skills model for effectively engaging clients in multicultural settings. *The Counseling Psychologist, 37,* 564–579.

Alexander, F. (1948). *Fundamentals of psychoanalysis.* New York: Norton.

Allport, G. W. (1969). Defining healthy personality. In H. Chiang & A. Maslow (Eds.), *The healthy personality: Readings.* New York: Van Nostrand Reinhold.

American Psychiatric Association. (2000). *Diagnostic and statistical manual of mental disorders* (DSM-IV-TR) (4th edition—text revision). Washington, DC: Author.

American Psychological Association. (2002). Ethical principles of psychologists and code of conduct. *American Psychologist, 57,* 1060–1073. Online at: http://www.apa.org/ethics.

American Psychological Association. (2003). Guidelines on multicultural education, training, research, practice, and organizational change for psychologists. *American Psychologist, 58,* 377–402.

Anderson, M. C. (2006). Repression: A cognitive neuroscience approach. In M. Mancia, (Ed.), *Psychoanalysis and neuroscience.* New York: Springer.

Angus, L. E., & Rennie, D. L. (1989). Envisioning the representational world: The client's experience of metaphoric expression in psychotherapy. *Psychotherapy, 26,* 372–379.

Aposhyan, S. (2004). *Body-mind psychotherapy: Principles, techniques, and practical applications.* New York: W. W. Norton.

Asay, T. P., & Lambert, M. J. (1999). The empirical case for the common factors in therapy: Quantitative findings. In M. A. Hubble, B. L. Duncan, & S. D. Miller (Eds.), *The heart and soul of change: What works in therapy.* Washington, DC: American Psychological Association.

Asli, O., Kulvedrosten, S., Solbakken, L. E., & Flaten, M. A. (2009). Fear potentiated startle at short intervals following conditioned stimulus onset during delay but not trace conditioning. *Psychophysiology, 46,* 880–888.

Audet, C., & Everall, R. D. (2003). Counselor self-disclosure: Client informed implications for practice. *Counseling and Psychotherapy Research, 3,* 223–231.

Aveline, M. (2005). The person of the therapist. *Psychotherapy Research, 15,* 155–164.

Bachelor, A. (1988). How clients perceive therapist empathy: A content analysis of "received" empathy. *Psychotherapy, 25,* 227–240.

Baer, R. A. (2003). Mindfulness training as a clinical intervention: A conceptual and empirical review. *Clinical Psychology: Science and Practice, 10,* 125–143.

Balconi, M. (2006). Exploring consciousness in emotional face decoding: An event-related potential analysis. *Genetic, Social, and General Psychology Monographs, 132,* 129–150.

Balconi, M., & Lucchiari, C. (2007). Conscious and emotional facial expression recognition: Subliminal/supraliminal stimulation effect on n200 and p300 ERPs. *Journal of Psychophysiology, 21,* 100–108.

Bandura, A. (1969). *Principles of behavior modification.* New York: Holt, Rinehart & Winston.

Bargh, J. A., & Chartrand, T. L. (2005). The unbearable automaticity of being. In D. L. Hamilton (Ed.), *Social cognition: Key readings.* New York: Psychology Press.

Barkham, M., & Shapiro, D. A. (1986). Counselor verbal response modes and experienced empathy. *Journal of Counseling Psychology, 33,* 3–10.

Barrett-Lennard, G. T. (1978). The relationship inventory: Later development and adaptations. *JSAS Catalog of Selected Documents in Psychology, 8,* 68. (Ms. No. 1732).

Barrett-Lennard, G. T. (1993). The phases and focus of empathy. *British Journal of Medical Psychology, 66,* 3–14.

Barrett-Lennard, G. T. (1997). The recovery of empathy—toward others and self. In A. C. Bohart & L. S. Greenberg (Eds.), *Empathy reconsidered.* Washington, DC: American Psychological Association.

Barron, J. W. (1998). *Making diagnosis meaningful: Enhancing evaluation and treatment of psychological disorders.* Washington, DC: American Psychological Association.

Barsalou, L. W. (2008). Grounded cognition. *Annual Review of Psychology, 59,* 617–645.

Becker, D. (2006). Toward a feminist ecological awareness. In L. T. Hoshmand (Ed.), *Culture, psychotherapy, and counseling.* Thousand Oaks, CA: Sage.

Bell, J. E. (1963). A theoretical position for family group therapy. *Family Process, 2,* 1–14.

Benish, S. G., Imel, Z. E., & Wampold, B. E. (2007). The relative efficacy of bona fide psychotherapies for treating post-traumatic stress disorder: A meta-analysis of direct comparisons. *Clinical Psychology Review, 28,* 746–758.

Bergin, A. E. (1963). The effects of psychotherapy: Negative results revisited. *Journal of Counseling Psychology, 10,* 244–250.

Bergin, A. E. (1966). Some implications of psychotherapy research for therapeutic-practice. *Journal of Abnormal Psychology, 71,* 235–246.

Bergin, A. E. (1970). The deterioration effect: A reply to Braucht. *Journal of Abnormal Psychology, 75,* 300–302.

Bergin, A. E. (1980). Negative effects revisited: A reply. *Professional Psychology, 11,* 93–100.

Bergin, A. E., & Garfield, S. L. (1994). Overview, trends, and future issues. In A E. Bergin & S. L. Garfield (Eds.), *Handbook of psychotherapy and behavior-change* (4th ed.). New York: Wiley.

Bergin, A. E., Payne, I. R., & Richards, P. S. (1996). Values in psychotherapy. In E. P Shafranske (Ed.), *Religion and the clinical practice of psychology.* Washington, DC: American Psychological Association.

Beutler, L. E. (2002). The dodo bird is extinct. *Clinical Psychology: Science and Practice, 9,* 30–34.

Beutler, L. E., & Bergan, J. (1991). Value change in counseling and psychotherapy: A search for scientific credibility. *Journal of Counseling Psychology, 38,* 16–24.

Beutler, L., & Malik, M. (2002). *Rethinking the DSM.* Washington, DC: American Psychological Association.

Beutler, L. E., Moleiro, C. M., & Talebi, H. (2002). Resistance. In J. C. Norcross (Ed.). *Psychotherapy relationships that work.* New York: Oxford University Press.

Bike, D. H., Norcross, J. C. & Schatz, D. M. (2009). Processes and outcomes of psychotherapists' personal therapy: Replication and extension 20 years later. *Psychotherapy: Theory, Research, Practice, Training, 46,* 19–31.

Bischoff, R. J. (2008). The research on emotion and couple functioning and what it means for clinical work. *Journal of Couple & Relationship Therapy, 7,* 363–368.

Blatt, S. J., Zuroff, D. C., Quinlan, D. M., & Pilkonis, P. A. (1996). Interpersonal factors in brief treatment of depression: Further analyses of the National Institute of Mental Health Treatment of Depression Collaborative Research Program. *Journal of Consulting and Clinical Psychology, 64,* 162–171.

Bohart, A. C. (1993). Experiencing: The basis of psychotherapy. *Journal of Psychotherapy Integration, 3,* 51–67.

Bohart, A. C., & Associates. (1996). Experiencing, knowing, and change. In R. Hutterer, G. Pawlowsky, R. F. Schmid, & R. Stipsits (Eds.), *Client-centered and experiential psychotherapy.* Frankfurt am Main: Peter Lang.

Bohart, A. C., Elliott, R., Greenberg, L. S., & Watson, J. C. (2002). Empathy. In J. C. Norcross (Ed.). *Psychotherapy relationships that work.* New York: Oxford University Press.

Bohart, A. C., & Rosenbaum, R. (1995). The dance of empathy: Empathy, diversity, and technical eclecticism. *The Person-Centered Journal, 2,* 5–29.

Bohart, A. C., & Tallman, K. (1997). Empathy and the active client: An integrative, cognitive-experiential approach. In A. C. Bohart & L. S. Greenberg (Eds.), *Empathy reconsidered.* Washington, DC: American Psychological Association.

Bohart, A. C., & Tallman, K. (1999). *How clients make therapy work: The process of active self-healing.* Washington, DC: American Psychological Association.

Bornstein, R. E, & Pittman, T. S. (Eds.). (1992). *Perception without awareness.* New York: Guilford.

Both, S., Spiering, M., Laan, E., Belcome, S., van den Heuvel, B., & Everaerd, W. (2008). Unconscious conditioning of sexual arousal: Evidence for the conditioning of female genital arousal to subliminally presented sexual stimuli. *Journal of Sexual Medicine, 5,* 100–109.

Bourbonnais, Y. (1980). An innovative approach for training beginning counselors and a definition of good interviewer behavior. Unpublished dissertation, University of Regina.

Bower, B. (2004). Neural road to repression. *Science News, 165*(2), 21.

Boy, A. V. (1989). Psychodiagnosis: A person-centered perspective. *Person Centered Review, 4,*132–151.

Bozarth, J. D. (1984). Beyond reflection: Emergent modes of empathy. In R. F. Levant, & J. M. Shlien (Eds.), *Client-centered therapy and person centered approach: New directions in theory, research and practice.* New York: Praeger.

Bozarth, J. D. (1997). Empathy from the framework of client-centered theory and the Rogerian hypothesis. In A. C. Bohart & L. S. Greenberg (Eds.), *Empathy reconsidered.* Washington, DC: American Psychological Association.

Braucht, G. N. (1970). The deterioration effect: A reply to Bergin. *Journal of Consulting Psychology, 75,* 293–299.

Breggin, P. R. (1997). *The heart of being helpful: Empathy and the creation of a healing presence.* New York: Springer.

Brewin, C. R. (1997). Clinical and experimental approaches to understanding repression. In J. D. Read & D. S. Lindsay (Eds.), *Recollections of trauma: Scientific evidence and clinical practice.* NATO ASI series: Series A: Life sciences (Vol. 291). New York: Plenum Press.

Brown, L. S. (2007). Empathy, genuineness—and the dynamics of power: A feminist responds to Rogers. *Psychotherapy: Theory, Research, Practice, Training, 44,* 257–259.

Bruner, J. (1962). *On knowing: Essays for the left hand.* Cambridge, MA: Harvard University Press.

Bryan, C. J., & Rudd, M. D. (2005). Advances in the assessment of suicide risk. *Journal of Clinical Psychology: In Session, 62,* 185–200.

Burlingame, G. M., Fuhriman, A., & Johnson, J. E. (2002). Cohesion in group psychotherapy. In J. C. Norcross (Ed.), *Psychotherapy relationships that work.* New York: Oxford University Press.

Burns, D. D. (1995). *Therapist's toolkit: Comprehensive assessment and treatment tools for the mental health professional.* Unpublished manuscript.

Burns, D. D., & Auerbach, A. (1996). Therapeutic empathy in cognitive-behavioral therapy. In P M. Salkovskis (Ed.), *Frontiers of cognitive therapy.* New York: The Guilford Press.

Burns, D. D., & Nolen-Hoeksema, S. (1991). Coping styles, homework compliance, and the effectiveness of cognitive behavioral therapy. *Journal of Consulting and Clinical Psychology, 59,* 305–311.

Burns, D. D., & Nolen-Hoeksema, S. (1992). Therapeutic empathy and recovery from depression in cognitive-behavioral therapy: A structural equation model. *Journal of Consulting and Clinical Psychology, 60,* 441–449.

Burum, B. A., & Goldfried, M. R., (2007). The centrality of emotion to psychological change. *Clinical Psychology: Science and Practice, 14,* 407–413.

Butler, J. M., & Rice, L. N. (1963). Audience, self-actualization, and drive theory. In J. M. Wepman & R. W. Heine (Eds.), *Concepts of personality.* Chicago: Aldine.

Cain, D. J. (2007). What every therapist should know, be and do: Contributions from humanistic psychotherapies. *Journal of Contemporary Psychotherapy, 37,* 3–10.

Cameron, N. (1963). *Personality development and psychotherapy: A dynamic approach.* Boston: Houghton Mifflin.

Campbell, B. A., & Church, R. M. (Eds.). (1969). *Punishment and aversive behavior.* New York: Appleton-Century-Crofts.

Carkhuff, R. R. (1969). *Helping and human relations.* New York: Holt, Rinehart & Winston.

Carkhuff, R. R., & Berenson, B. G. (1967). *Beyond counseling and therapy.* New York: Holt, Rinehart & Winston.

Carkhuff, R. R., & Berenson, B. G. (1977). *Beyond counseling and therapy* (2nd ed.). New York: Holt, Rinehart & Winston.

Castonguay, L. G., Constantino, M. J., & Holtforth, M. G. (2006). The working alliance: Where are we and where should we go? *Psychotherapy: Theory, Research Practice, Training, 43,* 271–279.

Chambless, D. L. (2002). Beware the dodo bird: The dangers of overgeneralization. *Clinical Psychology: Science and Practice, 9,* 13–16.

Chesler, R. (1972). *Women and madness.* New York: Avon Books.

Christianson, S., Saeisae, J., & Silfvenius, H. (1996). The right hemisphere recognizes the bad guys. *Cognition and Emotion, 9,* 309–324.

Chung, R. C., & Bemak, F. (2002). The relationship of culture and empathy in cross-cultural counseling. *Journal of Counseling & Development, 80,* 154–159.

Cirillo, L., & Crider, C. (1995). Distinctive therapeutic uses of metaphor. *Psychotherapy, 32,* 511–519.

Clark, A. J. (2007). *Empathy in Counseling and Psychotherapy: Perspectives and Practices*. Hillsdale, NJ: Erlbaum.

Clark, L. A., Watson, D., & Reynolds, S. (1995). Diagnosis and classification of psychopathology: Challenges to the current system and future directions. *Annual Review of Psychology, 46*, 121–153.

Clarke, H. K., Murdock, N. L., & Koetting, K. (2009). Predicting burnout and career choice satisfaction in counseling psychology graduate students. *The Counseling Psychologist, 37*, 580–606.

Clarke, I., Mackaness, W., Ball, B., & Horita, M. (2003). The devil is in the detail: Visualising analogical thought in retail location decisionmaking. *Environment and Planning B: Planning and Design, 30*, 15–36.

Cleckley, H. (1976). *The mask of sanity* (5th ed.). St. Louis: Mosby.

Cleeremans, A., & Dienes, Z. (2008). Computational models of implicit learning. In R. Sun (Ed.), *The Cambridge handbook of computational cognitive modeling*. Cambridge: University Press.

Coombs, M. M., Coleman, D., & Jones, E. E. (2002). Working with feelings: The importance of emotion in both cognitive-behavioral and interpersonal therapy in the NIMH Treatment of Depression Collaborative Research Program. *Psychotherapy: Theory, Research, Practice, Training, 39*, 233–244.

Copeland, J., & Snyder, M. (1995). When counselors confirm: A functional analysis. *Personality and Social Psychology Bulletin, 21*, 1210–1220.

Corteen, R. S., & Wood, B. (1974). Autonomic responses to shock-associated words in an unattended channel. *Journal of Experimental Psychology, 94*, 308–318.

Crits-Christoph, P. (1997). Limitations of the "Dodo Bird" Verdict and the role of clinical trials in psychotherapy research: Comment on Wampold et al. (1997). *Psychological Bulletin, 122*, 216–220.

Crits-Christoph, P., Baranackie, K., Kurcias, J. S., Carroll, K., Luborsky, L., McLellan, T., Woody, G., Thompson, L., Gallagher, D., & Zitrin, C. (1991). Meta-analysis of therapist effects in psychotherapy outcome studies. *Psychotherapy Research, 1*, 81–91.

Crowley, C., & Lodge, H. S. (2004). *Younger next year.* New York: Workman.

Crowne D. P (1979). *The experimental study of personality.* Hillsdale, N J: Erlbaum.

Csikszentmihalyi, M. (1990). *Flow: The psychology of optimal experience.* New York: HarperCollins.

Csikszentmihalyi, M. (1996). *Creativity: Flow and the psychology of discovery and invention.* New York: HarperCollins.

Csikszentmihalyi, M. (1997). *Finding flow.* New York: Basic Books.

D'Alessio, G. R. (1968). The concurrent use of behavior modification and psychotherapy. *Psychotherapy: Theory, Research and Practice, 5*, 154–159.

Dalai Lama, & Cutler, H. C. (1998). *The art of happiness.* New York: Riverhead Books.

Damasio, A. R. (1999). *The feeling of what happens: body and emotion in the making of consciousness.* New York: Harcourt Brace.

Davanloo, H. (1996). Management of tactical defenses in intensive short-term dynamic psychotherapy: Part II. Spectrum of tactical defenses. *International Journal of Short Term Psychotherapy, 11*, 153–199.

Dickerson, F. B., & Lehman, A. F. (2006). Evidence-based psychotherapy for schizophrenia. *The Journal of Nervous and Mental Disease, 194*, 3–9.

Dimidjian, S., & Linehan, M. M. (2003). Defining an agenda for future research on the clinical application of mindfulness practice. *Clinical Psychology: Science and Practice, 10*, 166–171.

Dollard J., & Miller, N. E. (1950). *Personality and psychotherapy: An analysis in terms of learning, thinking and culture.* New York: McGraw-Hill.

Domar, A. D., & Dreher, H. (2000). *Self-nurture: Learning to care for yourself as effectively as you care for everyone else.* New York: Penguin Books.

Dretske, F. (2006). Perception without awareness. In T. Gendler, T. S. Gendler, & J. Hawthorne (Eds.), *Perceptual experience.* New York: Oxford University Press.

Eaton, T. T., Abeles, N., & Gutfreund, M. J. (1988). Therapeutic alliance and outcome: Impact of treatment length and pretreatment symptomatology. *Psychotherapy, 25,* 536–542.

Egan, G. (2004). *The skilled helper* (7th ed.). Pacific Grove, CA: Brooks/Cole.

Eitam, B., Hassin, R. R., & Schul, Y. (2008). Nonconscious goal pursuit in novel environments: The case of implicit learning. *Psychological Science, 19,* 261–267.

Elliott, R., & Freire, E. (2007). Classical person-centered and experiential perspectives on Rogers (1967). *Psychotherapy: Theory, Research, Practice, Training, 44,* 285–288.

Ellis, A. (1994). *Reason and emotion in psychotherapy revised.* New York: Carol.

Ehrenreich, C. P. F., Buzzella, B. A., & Barlow, D. H. (2007). The role of emotion in psychological therapy. *Clinical Psychology: Science and Practice, 14,* 422–428.

Elvins, R., & Green, J. (2008). The conceptualization and measurement of therapeutic alliance: An empirical review. *Clinical Psychology Review, 28,* 1167–1187.

Enns, C. Z. (1997). *Feminist theories and feminist psychotherapies.* Binghamton, NY: The Harington Park Press.

Erdelyi, M. H. (1980). A new look at the new look: Perceptual defense and vigilance. *Psychological Review, 81,* 1–25.

Esteves, E., Dimberg, U., & Oehman, A. (1995). Automatically elicited fear: Conditioned skin conductance responses to masked facial expressions. *Cognition and Emotion, 8,* 393–413.

Eysenck, H. J. (1952). The effects of psychotherapy: An evaluation. *Journal of Consulting Psychology, 16,* 319–324.

Eysenck, H. J. (1969). Relapse and symptom substitution after different types of psychotherapy. *Behaviour Research and Therapy, 7,* 283–287.

Farber, B. A., & Lane, J. S. (2002). Positive regard. In J. C. Norcross (Ed.), *Psychotherapy relationships that work.* New York: Oxford University Press.

Farsimadan, F., Draghi-Lorenz, R., & Ellis, J. (2007). Process and outcome of therapy in ethnically similar and dissimilar therapeutic dyads. *Psychotherapy Research, 17,* 567–575.

Fauth, J. (2006). Toward more (and better) countertransference research. *Psychotherapy: Theory, Research, Practice, Training, 43,* 16–31.

Forster, R. M., & Govier, E. (1978). Discrimination without awareness? *Quarterly Journal of Experimental Psychology, 30,* 282–295.

Fouad, N. A., & Arredondo, P. (2007). *Becoming culturally oriented: Practical advice for psychologists and educators.* Washington, DC: American Psychological Association.

Fox, E. (1996). Selective processing of threatening words in anxiety: The role of awareness. *Cognition and Emotion, 10,* 449–480.

Franklin, C., & Jordan, C. (1999). *Family practice.* Pacific Grove, CA: Brooks/Cole.

Franklin, C., & Jordan, C. (2002). Effective family therapy: Guidelines for practice. In A. R. Roberts & G. J. Greene (Eds.), *Social workers' desk reference.* New York: Oxford.

Frankel, Z., Levitt, H. M., Murray, D. M., Greenberg, L. S., & Angus, L. (2006). Assessing silent processes in psychotherapy: An empirically derived categorization system and sampling strategy. *Psychotherapy Research, 16,* 627–638.

Franks, C. M., & Mays, D. T. (1980). Negative effects revisited: A rejoinder. *Professional Psychology, 11,* 101–105.

Friedman, N. (2005). Experiential listening. *Journal of Humanistic Psychology, 45,* 217–238.

Fromm-Reichmann, F. (1950). *Principles of intensive psychotherapy.* Chicago: Phoenix Books, University of Chicago Press.

Garfield, S. L. (1986). Problems in diagnostic classification. In T. Millon & G. L. Klerman (Eds.), *Contemporary directions in psychopathology.* New York: Guilford.

Gaston, L. (1990). The concept of the alliance and its role in psychotherapy: Theoretical and empirical considerations. *Psychotherapy, 27,* 143–153.

Gaston, L., Thompson, L., Gallagher, D., Cournoyer, L-G., & Gagnon, R. (1998). Alliance, technique, and the interactions in predicting outcome of behavioral, cognitive, and brief dynamic therapy. *Psychotherapy Research, 8,* 190–209.

Geller, J. D., Norcross, J. C., & Orlinsky, D. E. (2005). Research on conducting psychotherapy with mental health professionals. In J. D. Geller, J. C. Norcross, & D. E. Orlinsky (Eds.), *The psychotherapist's own psychotherapy: patient and clinician perspectives.* New York: Oxford University Press.

Gelso, C. J., & Hayes, J. A. (2002). Counter transference management. In J. C. Norcross (Ed.), Psychotherapy relationships that work. New York: Oxford University Press.

Gendlin, E. T. (1962). *Experiencing and the creation of meaning.* New York: Free Press.

Gendlin, E. T. (1969). Focusing. *Psychotherapy: Theory, Research and Practice, 6,* 4–15.

Gendlin, E. T. (1974). Client-centered and experiential psychotherapy. In D. A. Wexler & L. N. Rice (Eds.), *Innovations in client-centered therapy.* New York: Wiley.

Gendlin, E. T. (1978). *Focusing.* New York: Everest House.

Gendlin, E. T. (1991). On emotion in therapy. In J. D. Safran & L. S. Greenberg (Eds.), *Emotion, psychotherapy, and change* (pp. 255–279). New York: Guilford.

Gendlin, E. T. (1996). Focusing-oriented psychotherapy: A manual of the experiential method. New York: Guilford.

Gendlin, E. T. (1997). *A process model.* New York: The Focusing Institute: www.focusing.org.

Gere, S. H. (2006). A woman's view of clinical trauma theory and therapy. In L. T. Hoshmand (ed.). *Culture, psychotherapy, and counseling.* Thousand Oaks, CA: Sage.

Gladwell, M. (2005). *Blink: The power of thinking without thinking.* New York: Back Bay Books.

Gleaves, D. H. (1996). The evidence for "repression": An examination of Holmes (1990) and the implications for the recovered memory controversy. *Journal of Child Sexual Abuse, 5,* 1–19.

Glucksberg, S., & King, L. J. (1967). Motivated forgetting mediated by implicit verbal chaining: A laboratory analog of repression. *Science, 158,* 517–519.

Glucksberg, S., & Ornstein, R. A. (1969). Reply to Weiner and Higgins: Motivated forgetting is not attributable to a confounding original learning with retention. *Journal of Verbal Learning and Verbal Behavior, 8,* 681–685.

Gold, S. H., & Hilsenroth, M. J. (2009). Effects of graduate clinicians' personal therapy on therapeutic alliance. *Clinical Psychology and Psychotherapy, 16,* 159–171.

Goldfried, M. R. (1995). *From cognitive-behavior therapy to psychotherapy integration.* New York: Spring.

Goldfried, M. R., Castonguay, L. G. (1992). The future of psychotherapy integration. *Psychotherapy, 29,* 4–10.

Goldman, R. N., Greenberg, L. S., & Pos, A. E. (2005). Depth of emotional experience and outcome. *Psychotherapy Research, 15,* 248–260.

Gomes-Schwartz, B., Hadley, S. W., & Strupp, H. H. (1978). Individual psychotherapy and behavior therapy. *Annual Review of Psychology, 29,* 435–471.

Gordon, T. (1976). *P. E. T. in action.* New York: Wyden.

Grafanaki, S., & McLeod, J. (2002). Experiential congruence: Qualitative analysis of client and counsellor narrative accounts of significant events in time-limited person-centred therapy. *Counselling and Psychotherapy Research, 2,* 20–32.

Greenberg, L. S., (2007). Emotion coming of age. *Clinical Psychology: Science and Practice, 14,* 414–421.

Greenberg, L. S., Auszra, L., & Herrmann, I. R. (2007). The relationship among emotional productivity, emotional arousal and outcome in experiential therapy of depression. *Psychotherapy Research, 17,* 482–493.

Greenberg, L. S., & Elliott, R. (1997). Varieties of empathic responding. In A. C. Bohart & L. S. Greenberg (Eds.), *Empathy reconsidered.* Washington, DC: American Psychological Association.

Greenson, R. R. (1974). Loving, hating and indifference towards the patient. *International Review of Psychoanalysis, 1,* 259–266.

Grepmair, L., Mitterlehner, F., Loew, T., Bachler, E., Rother, W., & Nickel, M. (2007a). Promoting mindfulness in psychotherapists in training influences the treatment results of their patients: A randomized, double-blind, controlled study. *Psychotherapy and Psychosomatics, 76,* 332–338.

Grepmair, L., Mitterlehner, F., Loew, T., & Nickel, M. (2007b). Promotions of mindfulness of psychotherapists in training: Preliminary study. *European Psychiatry, 22,* 485–489.

Groth-Marnat, G., Roberts, R., & Beutler, L. E. (2001). Client characteristics and psychotherapy: Perspectives, support, interactions, and implications for training. *Australian Psychologist, 36,* 115–121.

Guerney, B. G. (1977). *Relationship enhancement.* San Francisco: Jossey-Bass.

Gurman, A. S. (1977). The patient's perceptions of the therapeutic relationship. In A. S. Gurman & A. M. Razin (Eds.), *Effective psychotherapy: A handbook of research.* Oxford, England: Pergamon Press.

Hafkenscheid, A., & Kiesler, D. (2007). Assessing objective countertransference: A comparison of two different statistical procedures in three different samples *Psychotherapy Research, 17,* 393–403.

Hall, M. H. (1967). A conversation with Carl Rogers. *Psychology Today,* December, 18–21 & 62–66.

Hammond, D. C., Hepworth, D. H., & Smith, G. (2002). *Improving therapeutic communication.* San Francisco: Jossey-Bass.

Hanley, J. L., & Deville, N. (2001). *Tired of being tired.* New York: G. P. Putnam's Sons.

Hassin, R. R., Uleman, J. S., & Bargh, J. A. (Eds.). (2005). *The new unconscious.* Oxford: Oxford University Press.

Hayes, J. A. (2004). The inner world of the psychotherapist: A program of research on countertransference. *Psychotherapy Research, 14,* 21–36.

Hayes, J. A., Riker, J. R., & Ingram, K. M. (1997). Counter-transference behavior and management in brief counseling: A field study. *Psychotherapy Research, 7,* 145–153.

Hebb, D. O. (1972). *A textbook of psychology* (3rd ed.). Philadelphia: Saunders.

Hefferline, R. E., & Keenan, B. (1963). Amplitude-induction gradient of a small-scale (covert) operant. *Journal of Experimental Analysis of Behavior, 6,* 301–315.

Hendricks, M. N. (2007). The role of experiencing in psychotherapy: Attending to the "bodily felt sense" of a problem makes any orientation more effective. *Journal of Contemporary Psychotherapy, 37,* 41–46.

Hendrix, H. (2008). *Getting the love you want: A guide for couples.* Twentieth Anniversary Edition. New York: Henry Holt and Company.

Henry, W. E., Schacht, T. E., & Strupp, H. H. (1990). Patient and therapist introject, interpersonal process, and differential psychotherapy outcome. *Journal of Consulting and Clinical Psychology, 58,* 768–774.

Hermans, D., De-Houwer, J., & Eelen, E. (1995). The affective priming effect: Automatic activation of evaluative information in memory. *Cognition and Emotion, 8,* 515–533.

Hersoug, A. G., Høglend, P., Havik, O., von der Lippe, A., & Monsen, J., (2009). Therapist characteristics influencing the quality of alliance in long-term psychotherapy. *Clinical Psychology and Psychotherapy, 16,* 100–110.

Hick, S. F. (2008). Cultivating therapeutic relationships: The role of mindfulness. In S. F. Hick & T. Bien, *Mindfulness and the therapeutic relationship.* New York: Guilford Press.

Hill, C. E., & Knox. S. (2001). Self-disclosure. *Psychotherapy, 38,* 413–417.

Hill, C. E., & Knox, S. (2002). Self-disclosure. In J. C. Norcross (Ed.), *Psychotherapy relationships that work* (pp. 249–259). New York: Oxford University Press.

Holmes, D. S. (1974). Investigations of repression: Differential recall of material experimentally or naturally associated with ego threat. *Psychological Bulletin, 81,* 632–653.

Holmes, D. S. (1990). The evidence for repression: An examination of sixty years of research. In J. Singer (Ed.), *Repression and dissociation: Implications for personality theory, psychopathology, and health.* Chicago: University of Chicago Press.

Horvath, A. O. (2006). The alliance in context: Accomplishments, challenges, and future directions. *Psychotherapy: Theory, Research, Practice, Training, 43,* 258–263.

Horvath, A. O. & Bedi, R. P. (2002). The alliance. In J. C. Norcross (Ed.), *Psychotherapy relationships that work* (pp. 37–69). New York: Oxford University Press.

Horvath, A. O., & Greenberg, L. S. (1994). *The working alliance: Theory, research and practice.* New York: Wiley.

Horvath, A. O., & Luborsky, L. (1993). The role of the therapeutic alliance in psychotherapy. *Journal of Consulting and Clinical Psychology, 61,* 561–573.

Horvath, A. O., & Symonds, B. E. (1991). Relation between working alliance and outcome in psychotherapy: A meta-analysis. *Journal of Counseling Psychology, 38,* 139–149.

Hoshmand, L. T. (Ed.). (2006). *Culture, psychotherapy, and counseling.* Thousand Oaks, CA: Sage.

House, J. S., Landis, K. R., & Umberson, D. (1988). Social relationships and health. *Science, 241,* 540–545.

Howard, K. I., Krause, M. S., Saunders, S. M., & Kopta, S. M. (1997). Trials and tribulations in the meta-analysis of treatment differences: Comment on Wampold et al. (1997). *Psychological Bulletin, 122,* 221–225.

Hsieh, D., & Kirk, S. A. (2004). The limits of diagnostic criteria: The role of social context in clinicians' judgments of mental disorder. In S. A. Kirk. (Ed.), *Mental disorders in the social environment.* New York: Columbia University Press.

Hunt, C., Keogh, E., & French, C. C. (2006). Anxiety sensitivity: the role of conscious awareness and selective attentional bias to physical threat. *Emotion, 6,* 418–428.

Irving, P., & Dickson, D. (2006). A re-conceptualization of Rogers' core conditions: Implications for research, practice, and training. *International Journal for the Advancement of Counseling, 28,* 183–194.

Jacobs, D. (1981). Successful empathy training. *Journal of Humanistic Psychology, 21,* 39–56.

Johnson, S. (2007). The contribution of emotionally focused couples therapy. *Journal of Contemporary Psychotherapy, 37,* 47–52.

Kabat-Zinn, J. (1990). *Full catastrophe living: Using the wisdom of your body and mind to face stress, pain and illness.* New York: Scribner.

Kabat-Zinn, J. (2003). Mindfulness-based interventions in context: Past, present and future. *Clinical Psychology: Science and Practice, 10(2):* 144–156.

Karon, B. P. (2003). The tragedy of schizophrenia without psychotherapy. *Journal of the American Academy of Psychoanalysis and Dynamic Psychiatry, 31,* 89–118.

Karon, B. P., & Vanden Bos, G. R. (1972). The consequences of psychotherapy for schizophrenic patients. *Psychotherapy: Theory, Research and Practice, 9,* 111–120.

Kashdan, T. B. (2007). Social anxiety spectrum and diminished positive experiences: Theoretical synthesis and meta-analysis. *Clinical Psychology Review, 27,* 348–365.

Kelly, E. W. Jr. (1997). Relationship-centered counseling: A humanistic model of integration. *Journal of Counseling and Development, 75,* 8–25.

Kessler, D. A. (2009). *The end of overeating.* Toronto: McLelland & Stewart.

Kiesler, D. J. (1966). Some myths of psychotherapy research and the search for a paradigm. *Psychological Bulletin, 65,* 110–136.

Kirk, S. A., & Kutchins, H. (1994). The myth of the reliability of DSM. *The Journal of Mind and Behavior, 15(1–2),* 71–86.

Klein, M. G., Dittmann, A. T., Parloff, M. B., & Gill, M. M. (1969). Behavior therapy: Observations and reflections. *Journal of Consulting and Clinical Psychology, 33,* 259–266.

Klein, M. H., Kolden, G. G., Michels, J., & Chisolm-Stockard, S. (2002). In J. C. Norcross (Eds.), *Psychotherapy relationships that work* (pp.191–211). New York: Oxford University Press.

Kopp, R. R. (1995). *Metaphor therapy: Using client-generated metaphors in psychotherapy.* New York: Bruner/Mazel.

Kopp, R. & Eckstein, D. (2004). Using early memory metaphors and client-generated metaphors in Adlerian therapy. *Journal of Individual Psychology, 60,* 163–174.

Kring, A. M., Johnson, S. L., Davison, G. C., & Neale, J. M. (2009). *Abnormal psychology,* 11th ed. New York: Wiley.

Krupnick, J. L., Elkin, I., Collins, J., Simmens, S., Sotsky, S. M., Pilkonis, P. A., & Watkins, J. T. (1994). Therapeutic alliance and clinical outcome in the NIMH treatment of depression collaborative research program: Preliminary findings. *Psychotherapy, 31,* 28–35.

Krupnick, J. L., Sotsky, S. M., Simmens, A., Moyer, J., Elkin, I., Watkins, J., & Pilkonis, P. A. (1996). The role of the alliance in psychotherapy and pharmacotherapy outcome: Findings in the National Institute of Mental Health treatment of depression collaborative research program. *Journal of Consulting and Clinical Psychology, 64,* 532–539.

Kuiper, N. A., & Martin, R. A. (1998). Laughter and stress in daily life: Relation to positive and negative affect. *Motivation and Emotion, 22,* 133–154.

Kurtz, R. (2005). *Body-centered psychotherapy: The Hamoki method.* Mendocino CA: Life Rhythm.

Lafferty, E., Beutler, L. E., & Crago, M. (1991). Differences between more and less effective psychotherapists: A study of select therapist variables. *Journal of Consulting and Clinical Psychology, 57,* 76–80.

Lambert, M. J., & Barley, D. E. (2002). Research summary on the therapeutic relationship and psychotherapy outcome. In J. C. Norcross (Ed.), *Psychotherapy relationships that work.* New York: Oxford University Press.

Lambert, M. J., & Bergin, A. E. (1994). The effectiveness of psychotherapy. In A. E. Bergin & S. L. Garfield (Eds.), *Handbook of psychotherapy and behavior change* (4th ed., pp. 143–189). New York: Wiley.

Lambert, M. J., Bergin, A. E., & Collins, J. L. (1977). Therapist-induced deterioration in psychotherapy. In A. S. Gurman & A. M. Razin (Eds.), *Effective psychotherapy: A handbook of research.* Oxford, England: Pergamon Press.

Lambert, M. J., DeJulio, S. S., & Stein, D. M. (1978). Therapist interpersonal skills: Process, outcome, methodological considerations, and recommendations for future research. *Psychological Bulletin, 85,* 467–89.

Lambert, M. J., & Simon, W. (2008). The therapeutic relationship: Central and essential in psychotherapy outcome. In S. F. Hick & T. Bien (Eds.), *Mindfulness and the therapeutic relationship.* New York: Guilford.

Lambie, J. A., & Marcel, A. J. (2002). Consciousness and the varieties of emotion experience: A theoretical framework. *Psychological Review, 109,* 219–259.

Lazar, S. W. (2005). Mindfulness research. In C. K. Germer, R. D. Siegel, & P. R. Fulton (Eds.), *Mindfulness and psychotherapy.* New York: Guilford.

Leproult, R., Van Reeth, O., Byrne, M. M., et al. (1997). Sleepiness, performance, and neuroendocrine function during sleep deprivation: Effects of exposure to bright light or exercise. *Journal of Biological Rhythms, 12,* 245–258.

Levitt, H. M. (2001). Sounds of silence in psychotherapy: The categorization of clients' pauses. *Psychotherapy Research, 11,* 295–309.

Lieberman, M. D., Eisenberger, N. I., Crockett, M. J., Tom, S. M., Pfeifer, J. H., & Way, B. M. (2007). Putting feelings into words: Affect labeling disrupts amygdala activity in response to affective stimuli. *Psychological Science, 18,* 421–428.

Lietaer, G. (2001). Being genuine as a therapist: congruence and transparency. In G. Wyatt (Ed.), *Rogers' therapeutic conditions: Evolutions, theory and practice. Volume 1: Congruence.* Ross-on-Wye: PCCS Books.

Ligiero, D. P., & Gelso, C. J. (2002). Countertransference, attachment, and the working alliance: The therapists's contributions. *Psychotherapy: Theory / Research / Practice / Training, 39,* 3–11.

Lipsey, M., & Wilson, D. (1993). The efficacy of psychological, educational, and behavioral treatment: Confirmation from meta-analysis. *American Psychologist, 48,* 1181–1209.

Littrell, J. (1998). Is the reexperience of painful emotion therapeutic? *Clinical Psychology Review, 18,* 71–102.

Loehr, J., & Schwartz, T. (2003). *The power of full engagement.* New York: Free Press.

London, P (1964). *The modes and morals of psychotherapy.* New York: Holt, Rinehart & Winston.

Luborsky, L. (2000). A pattern-setting therapeutic alliance study revisited. *Psychotherapy Research, 10,* 17–29.

Luborsky, L., Crits-Christoph, P., McLellan, A. T., Woody, G., Piper, W., Liberman, B., Imber, S., & Pilkonis, P. (1986). Do therapists vary much in their success? Findings from four outcome studies. *American Journal of Orthopsychiatry, 56,* 501–512.

Luborsky, L., Rosenthal, R., Diguer, L., Andrusyna, T. P., Berman, J. S., Levitt, J. T., Seligman, D. A., & Krause, E. (2002). The Dodo Bird Verdict is alive and well—mostly. *Clinical Psychology, Science and Practice, 9,* 2–12.

Luborsky, L., Singer, B., & Luborsky, L. (1975). Comparative studies of psychotherapies. *Archives of General Psychiatry, 32,* 995–1008.

Lutz, A., Dunne, J. D., & Davidson, R. J. (2007). Meditation and the neuroscience of consciousness. In P. D. Zelazo, M. Moscovitch, & E. Thompson (Eds.), *The Cambridge handbook of consciousness* (pp. 499–554). Cambridge, UK: Cambridge University Press.

Maas, J. B. (1998). *Power sleep.* New York: Villard.

Macran, S., & Shapiro, D. A. (1998). The role of personal therapy for therapists: A review. *British Journal of Medical Psychology, 71,* 13–25.

Magnavita, J. J. (2006). Emotion in short-term psychotherapy: An introduction. *Journal of Clinical Psychology: In Session, 62,* 517–522.

Mahrer, A. R., (1996). Lessons from 40 years of learning how to do psychotherapy. *Psychotherapy, 33,*139–141.

Malcolm, J. (1980). The impossible profession—II. *New Yorker, 56*(40), 54–152.

Martin, D. G. (1972). *Learning based client centered therapy.* Monterey, CA: Brooks/Cole.

Martin, D. G. (1991). *Psychology: Principles and applications.* Scarborough, Ontario: Prentice-Hall Canada.

Martin, D. G. (2003). *Clinical Practice with Adolescents.* Pacific Grove, CA: Brooks/Cole.

Martin, D. G., Hawryluk, G. A., Berish, C., & Dushenko, T. (1984). Selective forgetting of aversive memories cued in the right hemisphere. *International Journal of Neuroscience, 23,*169–176.

Martin, D. G., Stambrook, M., Tataryn, D. J., & Beihl, H. O. (1984). Conditioning in the unattended left ear. *International Journal of Neuroscience, 23,* 95–102.

Martin, D. G, Verman, S. H., & Miles, J. M. (1984). Selective inhibition of vocal reaction time to aversive words in the left visual field. *International Journal of Neuroscience, 23,*177–186.

Martin, D. J., Garske, J. P., & Davis, M. K. (2000). Relation of the therapeutic alliance with outcome and other variables: A meta-analytic review. *Journal of Consulting and Clinical Psychology, 68,* 438–450.

Martin, G., & Pear, J. (2006). *Behavior modification: What it is and how to do it* (8th ed.). Englewood Cliffs, NJ: Prentice-Hall.

Martinsen, E. W., & Morgan, W. P. (1997). Antidepressant effects of physical activity. In W. P. Morgan (Ed.), *Physical activity and mental health* (pp. 93–106). Washington, DC: Taylor & Francis.

Maslow, A. H. (1954). *Motivation and personality.* New York: Harper & Row.

Maslow, A. H. (1966). *The psychology of science: A reconnaissance.* New York: Harper & Row.

Masters, W. H., & Johnson, V. E. (1980). *Human sexual inadequacy* (2nd ed.). Boston: Little, Brown.

Masters, W. H., Johnson, V. E., & Kolodny, R. C. (1992). *Human sexuality.* New York: HarperCollins.

Mays, D. T., & Franks, C. M. (1980). Getting worse: Psychotherapy or no treatment—The jury should still be out. *Professional Psychology, 11,* 78–92.

McClure, F. H., & Teyber, E. (1996). The multicultural-relational approach. In F. H. McClure & E. Teyber (Eds.), *Child and adolescent therapy: A multicultural-relational approach.* Fort Worth, TX: Harcourt Brace.

McCullers, C. (1940). *The heart is a lonely hunter.* Boston: Houghton Mifflin.

McEwen, B. S. (1998). Protective and damaging effects of stress mediators. *New England Journal of Medicine, 338,* 171–179.

McMillan, D. (1976). SOC: An attempt at definition. Unpublished manuscript, George Peabody College for Teachers, Nashville, TN.

McNaughton, N., & Gray, J. A. (2000). Anxiolytic action on the behavioural inhibition system implies multiple types of arousal contribute to anxiety. *Journal of Affective Disorders, 61,* 161–176.

Menninger, K. (1958). Theory of psychoanalytic technique. New York: Harper & Row.

Messer, S. B., Wampold, B. E. (2002). Let's face facts: Common factors are more potent than specific therapy ingredients. *Clinical Psychology: Science and Practice, 9,* 21–25.

Messer, S. B., & Winokur, M. (1980). Some limits to the integration of psychoanalytic and behavior therapy. *American Psychologist, 35,* 818–827.

Miller, R. S., & Perlman, D. (2009). *Intimate relationships* (4th ed.). Boston: McGraw-Hill.

Miranda, J., Bernal, G., Lau, A. Kohn, L., Hwang, W., & LaFromboise, T. (2005). State of the science on psychosocial interventions for ethnic minorities, *Annual Review of Clinical Psychology, 1,* 113–142.

Mitchell, K. M., Bozarth, J. D., & Krauft, C. C. (1977). A reappraisal of the therapeutic effectiveness of accurate empathy, non-possessive warmth, and genuineness. In A. S. Gurman & A. M. Razin (Eds.), *Effective psychotherapy: A handbook of research.* Oxford, England: Pergamon Press.

Mitchell, R. M. (1971). Relationship between therapist response to therapist-relevant client expressions and therapy process and therapy outcome. Doctoral dissertation, Michigan State University, 1971. *Dissertation Abstracts International, 32,*1853B (University Microfilms No. 71–23, 216).

Mohr, D. C. (1995). Negative outcome in psychotherapy: A critical review. *Clinical Psychology: Science and Practice, 2,* 1–27.

Mullaney, D. J., Johnson, L. C., Naitoh, P., Friedman, J. K., & Globus, G. G. (1977). Sleep during and after gradual sleep reduction. *Psychophysiology, 14,* 237–244.

Naar, R. (1970). Client-centered and behavior therapies: Their peaceful co-existence—A case study. *Journal of Abnormal Psychology, 76,* 155–160.

Najavits, L. M., & Strupp, H. H. (1994). Differences in the effectiveness of psychodynamic therapists: A process-outcome study. *Psychotherapy, 31,* 114–123.

Nakamura, J., & Csikszentmihalyi, M. (2009). Flow theory and research. In C. R. Snyder & S. J. Lopez (Eds.), *Oxford handbook of positive psychology* (2nd ed.). New York: Oxford University Press.

Nelson, D. W., & Baumgarte, R. (2004). Cross-cultural misunderstandings reduce empathic responding. *Journal of Applied Social Psychology, 34,* 391–401.

Niedenthal, P. M. (2007). Embodying emotion. *Science, 316,* 1002–1005.

Nietzel, M. T., Bernstein, D. A., Kramer, G. P., & Milich, R. (2003). *Introduction to clinical psychology* (6th ed.). Upper Saddle River, NJ: Prentice-Hall.

Nolan, S. A., Strassle, C. G., Roback, H. B., & Binder, J. L. (2004). Negative treatment effects in dyadic psychotherapy: A focus on prevention and intervention strategies. *Journal of Contemporary Psychotherapy, 34,* 311–330.

Norcross, J. C. (2002). Empirically supported therapy relationships. In J. C. Norcross (Ed.), *Psychotherapy relationships that work.* New York: Oxford University Press.

Norcross, J. C., Bike, D. H., & Evans, K. L. (2009). The therapist's therapist: A replication and extension 20 years later. *Psychotherapy: Theory, Research, Practice, Training, 46,* 32–41.

Norcross, J. C., Bike, D. H., Evans, K. L., & Schatz, D. M. (2008). Psychotherapists who abstain from personal therapy: Do they practice what they preach? *Journal of Clinical Psychology, 64,* 1368–1376.

Norcross, J. C., & Goldfried, M. R. (2005). *Handbook of psychotherapy integration* (2nd ed.). New York: Oxford University Press.

Norcross, J. C., & Guy, Jr., J. D. (2007). *Leaving it at the office: A guide to psychotherapist self-care.* New York: Guilford Press.

Norcross, J. C., Hedges, M., & Castle, P. H. (2002). Psychologists conducting psychotherapy in 2001: A study of the Division 29 membership. *Psychotherapy: Theory, Research, Practice, Training, 39,* 97–102.

Norcross, J. C., Prochaska, J. O., & Farber, J. A. (1993). Psychologists conducting psychotherapy: New findings and historical comparisons on the psychotherapy division membership. *Psychotherapy, 30,* 692–697.

Norcross, J. C., Strausser-Kirtland, D., & Missar, C. D. (1988). The processes and outcomes of psychotherapists' personal treatment experiences. *Psychotherapy, 25,* 36–43.

Ogloff, J. R. P. (1995). Navigating the quagmire: Legal and ethical guidelines. In D. G. Martin & A. D. Moore (Eds.), *Basics of clinical practice.* Long Grove, IL: Waveland Press.

Ohman, A. (2002). Automaticity and the amygdala: Nonconscious responses to emotional faces. *Current Directions in Psychological Science, 11,* 62–66.

Ohman, A., Carlsson, K., Lundqvist, D., & Ingvar, M. (2007). On the unconscious subcortical origin of human fear. *Physiology & Behavior, 92,* 180–185.

Ohman, A., & Ursin, H. (1979). On the sufficiency of a Pavlovian conditioning model for coping with the complexities of neurosis. *Behavioral and Brain Sciences, 2,* 179–180.

Orlinsky, D. E., Grawe, K., & Parks, B. K. (1994). Process and outcome in psychotherapy—noch einmal. In A. E. Bergin & S. L. Garfield (Eds.), *Handbook of psychotherapy and behavior change* (4th ed., pp. 270–378). New York: Wiley.

Ornston, E. S., Cicchetti, D., Levine, J., & Fierman, L. B. (1968). Some parameters of verbal behavior that reliably differentiate novice from experienced psychotherapists. *Journal of Abnormal Psychology, 73,* 240–244.

Parks, B. K. (1997). "Flow," boredom, and anxiety in therapeutic work: A study of psychotherapists' intrinsic motivation and professional development. Unpublished dissertation, University of Chicago. (Available from UMI Microform, Ann Arbor, MI. UMI #9711210)

Patterson, C. H. (1974). *Relationship counseling and psychotherapy.* New York: Harper & Row.

Patterson, C. H. (1989). Foundations for a systematic eclectic psychotherapy. *Psychotherapy, 26,* 427–435.

Patterson, C. H., & Hidore, S. C. (1997). *Successful psychotherapy.* New York: Jason Aronson.

Pedersen, P. B., Crethar, H. C., & Carlson, J. (2008). *Inclusive cultural empathy: Making relationships central in counseling and psychotherapy.* Washington, DC: American Psychological Association.

Peebles, M. J. (1980). Personal therapy and ability to display empathy, warmth and genuineness in psychotherapy. *Psychotherapy: Theory, Research and Practice, 17,* 258–262.

Perls, E. S. (1970). Four lectures. In J. Fagan & I. L. Shepherd (Eds.), *Gestalt therapy now.* Palo Alto, CA: Science and Behavior Books.

Pessoa, L. (2005). To what extent are emotional visual stimuli processed without attention and awareness? *Current Opinion in Neurobiology, 15,* 188–196.

Peterson, Z. D. (2002). More than a mirror: The ethics of therapist self-disclosure. *Psychotherapy: Theory/Research/Practice/Training, 39,* 21–31.

Pfaffenberger, A. H. (2005). Optimal adult development: An inquiry into the dynamics of growth. *Journal of Humanistic Psychology, 45,* 279–301.

Phelps, E. A. (2006). Emotion and cognition: Insights from studies of the human amygdala. *Annual Review of Psychology, 57,* 27–53.

Phillips, E. L. (1956). *Psychotherapy: A modern theory and practice.* Englewood Cliffs, NJ: Prentice-Hall.

Posner, M. L., & Boies, S. J. (1971). Components of attention. *Psychological Review, 78,* 391–408.

Pinker, S. (2007). The mystery of consciousness. In *Time Magazine: Mind and Body Special Issue: The Brain: A User's Guide* (pp. 46–47). January 29, 2007, Volume 169, Number 5.

Rachman, S. T., & Teasdale, J. (1969). Aversion therapy: An appraisal. In C. M Franks (Ed.), *Behavior therapy: Appraisal and status.* New York: McGraw-Hill.

Raglin, J. S. (1997). Anxiolytic effects of physical activity. In W. P. Morgan (Ed.), *Physical activity and mental health* (pp. 107–126). Washington, DC: Taylor & Francis.

Rait, D. S. (2000). The therapeutic alliance in couples and family therapy. *Journal of Clinical Psychology, 56,* 211–224.

Reich, W. (1949). *Character analysis.* New York: Noonday Press.

Reik, T. (1948). *Listening with the third ear.* New York: Noonday Press.

Reisberg, D. (1997). *Cognition: Exploring the science of the mind.* New York: W. V. Norton & Company.

Remen, R. N. (1991). *Wounded healers.* Mill Valley, CA: Wounded Healer Press.

Rennie, D. L. (1994). Clients' deference in psychotherapy. *Journal of Counseling Psychology, 41,* 427–437.

Rennie, D. L. (1998). *Person-centered counselling: An experiential approach.* London: Sage.

Resnick, S., Warmoth, A., & Serlin, I. A. (2001). The humanistic psychology and positive psychology connection: Implications for psychotherapy. *Journal of Humanistic Psychology, 41,* 73–101.

Rice, L. N. (1974).The evocative function of the therapist. In I. A. Wexler & L. N. Rice (Eds.), *Innovations in client-centered therapy.* New York: Wiley.

Rice, L. N. (1984). Client tasks in client-centered therapy. In R. F. Levant, & J. M. Shlien (Eds.), *Client-centered therapy and the person-centered approach: New directions in theory, research and practice.* New York: Praeger.

Roback, H. B. (2000). Adverse outcomes in group psychotherapy: Risk factors, prevention, and research direction. *Journal of Psychotherapy Practice and Research, 9,* 113–122.

Robbins, A. (1998). Introduction to therapeutic presence. In A. Robbins (Ed.), *Therapeutic presence.* London: Jessica Kingsley.

Robinson, M. D., & Wilkowski, B. M. (2006). Loving, hating, vacillating: Agreeableness, implicity self-esteem, and neurotic conflict. *Journal of Personality, 74,* 935–978.

Robinson, M. D., & Wilkowski, B. M. (2008). Approach, avoidance, and self-regulatory conflict: An individual differences perspective. *Journal of Experimental Social Psychology, 44,* 65–79.

Rogers, C. R. (1942). *Counseling and psychotherapy.* Boston: Houghton Mifflin.

Rogers, C. R. (1957). The necessary and sufficient conditions of therapeutic personality change. *Journal of Consulting Psychology, 21,* 95–103.

Rogers, C. R. (1959). A theory of therapy, personality, and interpersonal relationships, as developed in the client-centered framework. In S. Koch (Ed.), *Psychology: A study of a science* (Vol. 3). New York: McGraw-Hill.

Rogers, C. R. (1961). *On becoming a person.* Boston: Houghton Mifflin.

Rogers, C. R. (1962). The interpersonal relationship: The core of guidance. *Harvard Educational Review, 32,* 416–429.

Rogers, C. R. (1975). Empathic: An unappreciated way of being. *Counseling Psychologist, 5,* 2–10.

Rogers, C. R. (1980). Client-centered psychotherapy. In H. I. Kaplan, B. J. Sadock, & A. M. Freedman (Eds.), *Comprehensive textbook of psychiatry* (Vol. 3). Baltimore: Williams & Wilkins.

Rogers, C. R. (1989). A client-centered/person-centered approach to therapy. In H. Kirschenbaum & V. L. Henderson (Eds.), *The Carl Rogers reader.* Boston: Houghton Mifflin.

Rogers, C. R., & Dymond, R. F. (1954). *Psychotherapy and personality change.* Chicago: University of Chicago Press.

Rogers, C. R., Gendlin, E. T., Kiesler, D. J, & Truax, C. B. (1967). *The therapeutic relationship and its impact: A study of psychotherapy with schizophrenics.* Madison: University of Wisconsin Press.

Rosenberg, J. L., & Rand M. L. (1991). *A boundary defines the self.* Atlanta, GA: Humanics Ltd.

Rosenthal, D. (1955). Changes in some moral values following psychotherapy. *Journal of Consulting Psychology, 19,* 431–436.

Rosenthal, R. (1994). Interpersonal expectancy effects: A 30-year perspective. *Current Directions in Psychological Science, 3,* 176–179.

Rosenthal, R. (2002). Covert communication in classroom, clinics, courtrooms, and cubicles. *American Psychologist, 57,* 839–849.

Ross, E. D., Homan, R. W., & Buck, R. (1994). Differential hemispheric localization of primary and social emotions: Implications for developing a comprehensive neurology for emotions, repression, and the subconscious. *Neuropsychiatry, Neuropsychology, and Behavioral Neurology, 7,* 1–19.

Roth, A., & Fonagy, E. (1996). *What works for whom? A critical review of psychotherapy research.* New York: Guilford Press.

Rudd, M. D. (2005). Suicidality in clinical practice: Anxieties and answers. *Journal of Clinical Psychology: In Session, 62,* 157–159.

Rudd, M. D., Mandrusiak, M., & Joiner, T. E. (2005). The case against no-suicide contracts: The commitment to treatment statement as a practice alternative. *Journal of Clinical Psychology: In Session, 62,* 243–261.

Ruegg, R. G., Haynes, C., & Frances, A. (1997). Assessment and management of antisocial personality disorder. In M. Rosenblatt & I. D. Yalom (Eds.), *Treating difficult personality disorders.* San Francisco: Jossey-Bass.

Santorelli, S. (2000). *Heal thy self: Lessons on mindfulness in medicine.* Toronto: Random House.

Schmidt, L. A. (1999). Frontal brain electrical activity in shyness and sociability. *Psychological Science, 10,* 316–320.

Schnellbacher, J., & Leijssen, M. (2009). The significance of therapist genuineness from the client's perspective. *Journal of Humanistic Psychology, 49,* 207–228.

Schneiderman, N., Ironson, G., & Siegel, S. D. (2005). Stress and health: Psychological, behavioral, and biological determinants. *Annual Review of Clinical Psychology, 1,* 607–628.

Schubert, J. (1977). *The therapeutic interview.* Unpublished manuscript, University of Regina.

Searleman, A., & Herrmann, D. (1994). *Memory from a broader perspective.* New York: McGraw-Hill.

Sears, S., & Kraus, S. (2009). I think therefore I Om: Cognitive distortions and coping style as mediators for the effects of mindfulness meditation on anxiety, positive and negative affect, and hope. *Journal of Clinical Psychology, 65,* 561–573.

Seeburger, F. F. (1992). Blind sight and brute feeling: The divorce of cognition from emotion. In V. Gecas (Ed.), *Social perspectives on emotion* (Vol. 1). Greenwich, CT: Jai Press.

Seligman, L. (1990). *Selecting effective treatments.* San Francisco: Jossey-Bass.

Seligman, M. E. R. (1995). The effectiveness of psychotherapy. *American Psychologist, 50,* 965–974.

Seligman, M., & Csikszentmihalyi, M. (2000). Positive psychology: An introduction. *American Psychologist, 55*(1), 5–14.

Selye, H. (1973). The evolution of the stress concept. *American Scientist, 61,* 692–699.

Sexton, T. L., Schofield, T. L., & Whiston, S. C. (1997). Evidence-based practice: A pragmatic model to unify counseling. *Counseling and Human Development, 30,* 1–18.

Shapiro, D. A., & Shapiro, D. (1982). Meta-analysis of comparative therapy outcome studies: A replication and refinement. *Psychological Bulletin, 92,* 581–604.

Shapiro, S. L. (2009). The integration of mindfulness and psychology. *Journal of Clinical Psychology, 65,* 555–560.

Shapiro, S. L., & Carlson, L. E. (2009). *The art and science of mindfulness: Integrating mindfulness into psychology and the helping professions.* Washington, DC: American Psychological Association Publications.

Shaw, R. (2004). The embodied psychotherapist: An exploration of the therapists' somatic phenomena within the therapeutic encounter. *Psychotherapy Research, 14,* 271–288.

Shlien, J. M., Mosak, H. H., & Dreikurs, R. (1962). Effect of time limits: A comparison of two psychotherapies. *Journal of Counseling Psychology, 9,* 31–34.

Shoham-Salomon, V. (1991). Introduction to special section on client-therapy interaction research. *Journal of Consulting and Clinical Psychology, 59,* 203–204.

Singer, B. A., & Luborsky, L. B. (1977). Countertransference: The status of clinical versus quantitative research. In A. S. Gurman & A. M. Razin (Eds.), *Effective psychotherapy: A handbook of research.* New York: Pergamon Press.

Skinner, B. F. (1969). *Contingencies of reinforcement.* Englewood Cliffs, NJ: Prentice-Hall.

Smith, M. L., & Glass, G. V. (1977). Meta-analysis of psychotherapy outcome studies. *American Psychologist, 32,* 752–760.

Smith, M., Glass, G., & Miller, T. (1980). *The benefit of psychotherapy.* Baltimore: Johns Hopkins University Press.

Solomon, G. F., et al. (1968). Early experience and immunity. *Nature, 220,* 821–822.

Solomon, G. F., Kemeny, M. E., & Temoshok, L. (1991). Psychoneuroimmunology aspects of human immunodeficiency virus infection. In R. Ader, D. L. Felton, and N. Cohen (Eds.), *Psychoneuroimmunology II.* New York: Academic Press.

Solomon, G. F., Temoshok, L., O'Leary, A., & Zich, J. (1997). An intensive psychoimmunologic study of long-surviving persons with AIDS. *Annals of the New York Academy of Sciences, 496,* 647–655.

Sonstroem, R. J. (1984). Exercise and self-esteem. *Exercise and sports sciences reviews, 12,* 123–155.

Sonstroem, R. J. (1997). Physical activity and self-esteem. In W. P. Morgan (Ed.), *Physical activity and mental health* (pp.127–143). Washington, DC: Taylor & Francis.

Sorenson, R. L., Gorsuch, R. L., & Mintz, J. (1985). Moving targets: Patients' changing complaints during psychotherapy. *Journal of Consulting and Clinical Psychology, 53,* 49–54.

Spiegler, M. D., & Guevremont, D. C. (2010). *Contemporary behavior therapy* (5th ed.). Pacific Grove, CA: Brooks/Cole.

Stadler, M. A., & Frensch, F A. (Eds.). (1998). *Handbook of implicit learning.* Thousand Oaks, CA: Sage Publications.

Stambrook, M., & Martin, D. G. (1983). Brain laterality and the subliminal perception of facial expression. *International Journal of Neuroscience, 18,* 45–58.

Strupp, H. H. (1979). A psychodynamicist looks at modern behavior therapy. *Psychotherapy: Theory, Research and Practice, 16,* 124–131.

Strupp, H. H. (1993). The Vanderbilt psychotherapy studies: Synopsis. *Journal of Consulting and Clinical Psychology, 61,* 431–133.

Strupp, H. H. (1996). Some salient lessons from research and practice. *Psychotherapy, 33,*135–138.

Strupp, H. H., & Bergin, A. E. (1969). Some empirical and conceptual bases for coordinated research in psychotherapy: A critical review of issues, trends, and evidence. *International Journal of Psychiatry, 7,* 23–115.

Strupp, H. H., Hadley, S. W., & Gomes-Schwartz, B. (1977). *Psychotherapy for better or worse: The problem of negative effects.* New York: Jason Aronson.

Stubbs, J. P., & Bozarth, J. D. (1994). The Dodo Bird revisited: A qualitative study of psychotherapy efficacy research. *Applied & Preventive Psychology, 3,* 109–120.

Sue, D. W., & Sue, D. (2003). *Counseling the culturally diverse: Theory and practice* (4th ed.). Hoboken, NJ: John Wiley.

Sue, S. (2003). In defense of cultural competency in psychotherapy and treatment. *American Psychologist, 58,* 964–970.

Sue, S. (2006). Cultural competency: From philosophy to research and practice. *Journal of Community Psychology, 34,* 237–245.

Sue, S., Zane, N., Hall, G. C. N., & Berger, L. K. (2009). The Case for Cultural Competency in Psychotherapeutic Interventions. *Annual Review of Psychology, 60,* 525–548.

Sullivan, H. S. (1962). *Schizophrenia as a human process.* New York: Norton.

Sweet, A. A. (1984). The therapeutic relationship in behavior therapy. *Clinical Psychology Review, 4,* 253–272.

Taub, J. M., & Berger, R. J. (1973). Performance and mood following variations in the length and timing of sleep. *Psychophysiology, 10,* 559–570.

Taylor, K. (1995). *The ethics of caring* (2nd ed.). Santa Cruz, CA: Hanford Mead.

Temerlin, M. K. (1970). Diagnostic bias in community mental health. *Community Mental Health Journal, 6,* 110–117.

Tesser, A., & Rosen, S. (1972). Similarity of objective fate as a determinant of the reluctance to transmit unpleasant information: The MUM effect. *Journal of Personality and Social Psychology, 23,* 46–53.

Timulak, L. & Lietaer, G. (2001). Moments of empowerment: A qualitative analysis of positively experienced episodes in brief person-centred counseling. *Counselling and Psychotherapy Research, 1,* 62–73.

Toth, J. E., & Reingold, E. M. (1996). Beyond perception: Conceptual contributions to unconscious influences of memory. In G. Underwood (Ed.), *Implicit cognition.* Oxford: Oxford University Press.

Trenholm, S., & Jensen, A. (1996). *Interpersonal communication.* Belmont, CA: Wadsworth.

Truax, C. B., & Carkhuff, R. R. (1967). *Toward effective counseling and psychotherapy.* Chicago: Aldine.

Truax, C. B., & Mitchell, K. M. (1971). Research on certain therapist interpersonal skills in relation to process and outcome. In A. E. Bergin & S. L. Garfield (Eds.), *Handbook of psychotherapy and behavior change.* New York: Wiley.

Tryon, G. S., & Winograd, G. (2002). Goal consensus and collaboration. In J. C. Norcross (Ed.), *Psychotherapy relationships that work* (pp. 106–122). New York: Oxford University Press.

Underwood, G. (Ed.). (1996). *Implicit cognition.* Oxford: Oxford University Press.

Vanaerschot, G. (1997). Empathic resonance as a source of experience-enhancing interventions. In A. C. Bohart & L. S. Greenberg (Eds.), *Empathy reconsidered.* Washington, DC: American Psychological Association.

Vanaerschot, G., & Lietaer, G. (2007). Therapeutic ingredients in helping session episodes with observer-rated low and high empathic attunement: A content analysis of client and therapist post-session perceptions in three cases. *Psychotherapy Research, 17,* 338–352.

Vasquez, M. J. T. (2007). Cultural difference and the therapeutic alliance: An evidence-based analysis. *American Psychologist, 62,* 878–885.

Vasquez, M. J. T., Bingham, R. P., & Barnett, J. E. (2008). Psychotherapy termination: Clinical and ethical responsibilities. *Journal of Clinical Psychology: In Session, 64,* 653–665.

Von Wright, J. M., Anderson, K., & Stenman, U. (1975). Generalization of conditioned GSR's in dichotic listening. In R. Rabbit and S. Dornic (Eds.), *Attention and performance* (Vol. 5). Oxford and Stockholm: Academic Press.

Waldinger, M. D., & VanStrien, J. W. (1995). Repression and cerebral laterality: A study of selective hemispheric activations. *Neuropsychiatry, Neuropsychology, and Behavioral Neurology, 8,* 1–5.

Walker, M. (2008). How therapy helps when the culture hurts. *Women & Therapy, 31,* 87–105.

Walters, G. C., & Grusec, J. E. (1977). *Punishment.* San Francisco: W. H. Freeman.

Wampold, B. E. (2001). *The great psychotherapy debate.* Mahwah, NJ: Erlbaum.

Wampold, B. E. (2006). Do therapies designated as empirically supported treatments for specific disorders produce outcomes superior to non-empirically supported treatment therapies? In J. C. Norcross, L. E. Beutler, & R. F. Levant (Eds.), *Evidence-based practices in mental health: Debate and dialogue on the fundamental questions.* (pp. 299–328). Washington DC: American Psychological Association.

Wampold, B. E. (2007). Psychotherapy: The humanistic (and effective) treatment. *American Psychologist, 62,* 857–873.

Wampold, B. E., Minam, T., Baskin, T. W., & Tierney, S. C. (2002). A meta-(re)analysis of the effects of cognitive therapy versus "other therapies" for depression. *Journal of Affective Disorders, 68,* 159–165.

Wampold, B. E., Mondin, G. W., Moody, M., & Ahn, H. (1997). The flat earth as a metaphor for the evidence for uniform efficacy of bona fide psychotherapies: Reply to Crits-Christoph (1997) and Howard et al. (1997). *Psychological Bulletin, 122,* 226–230.

Wampold, B. E., Mondin, G. W., Moody, M., Stich, F., Benson, K., & Ahn, H. (1997). A meta-analysis of outcome studies comparing bona fide psychotherapies: Empirically, "all must have prizes." *Psychological Bulletin, 122,* 203–215.

Watson, D., & Clark, L. A. (2006). Clinical diagnosis at the crossroads. *Clinical Psychology: Science and Practice, 13*, 210–215.

Watson, J. C., & Geller, S. M. (2005). The relation among the relationship conditions, working alliance, and outcome in both process-experiential and cognitive-behavioral psychotherapy, *Psychotherapy Research, 15*, 25–33.

Weiner, B., & Higgins, J. (1969). A mediational paradigm for a study of motivated forgetting: A critical analysis. *Journal of Verbal Learning and Verbal Behavior, 8*, 677–680.

Welkowitz, J., Cohen, J., & Ortmeyer, D. (1967). Value system similarity: Investigation of patient-therapist dyads. *Journal of Consulting Psychology, 31*, 48–55.

Whalen, P. J., et al. (2004). Human amygdala responsivity to masked fearful eye whites. *Science, 306*, 2061.

Whelton, W. J. (2004). Emotional processes in psychotherapy: Evidence across therapeutic modalities. *Clinical Psychology and Psychotherapy, 11*, 58–71.

Whiston, S. C., & Sexton, T. L. (1993). An overview of psychotherapy outcome research: Implications for practice. *Professional Psychology: Research and Practice, 24*, 43–51.

White, M. (1996). Automatic affective appraisal of words. *Cognition and Emotion, 10*, 199–211.

Whitmire, A. J. (1991). Correlation of optimal experience and counselor development. Research report: ERIC Document #ED 375 337 CG 025 538.

Wills, T. A. (1998). Social support. In E. A. Blechman & K. D. Brownell (Eds.), *Behavioral medicine and women: A comprehensive handbook* (pp. 118–128). New York: Guilford.

Wilson, K. G., & Murrell, A. R. (2004). Values work in acceptance and commitment therapy: Setting a course for behavioral treatment. In S. C. Hayes, V. M. Follette, & M. Linehan (Eds.), *Mindfulness and acceptance: Expanding the cognitive-behavioral tradition*. New York: Guilford.

Winkielman, E., Zajonc, R. B., & Schwarz, N. (1997). Subliminal affective priming resists attributional interventions. *Cognition and Emotion, 11*, 433–465.

Yalom, I. D. (2002). *The gift of therapy*. New York: HarperCollins.

Yalom, I. D., & Leszcz, M. (2005). *The theory and practice of group psychotherapy* (5th ed.). New York: Basic Books.

Yalom, I. D., & Lieberman, M. H. (1971). A study of encounter group casualties. *Journal of Abnormal Psychology, 25*, 16–30.

Younggren, J. N., & Harris, E. A. (2008). Can you keep a secret? Confidentiality in psychotherapy. *Journal of Clinical Psychology: In Session, 64*, 589–600.

Zajonc, R. B. (1980). Feeling and thinking: Preferences need no inferences. *American Psychologist, 35,*151–175.

Zajonc, R. B. (1981). A one-factor mind about mind and emotion. *American Psychologist, 36,*102–103.

Name Index

Subject Index

Respect, 88–91
Response(s)
  acknowledgment, 16
  approach, reinforcing in
    client, 241
  concise and vivid, 44–45
  confrontive, 57
  connotative, 44
  empathic, 40–41,
    113–114
  frequency of, 38
  metaphoric, 44–45
  particularity in, 43
  real-time, 34–35
  reciprocal/mainte-
    nance, 16–17
  recording/analyzing
    role-play sessions to
    improve, 35
  subjective, 43–44
  therapist, 7, 12–14
Role conflicts, ethical issues
  concerning, 164–166
Role-playing, 33–35, 114
Rules, learning and unlearning, 120, 232

"Safe emergency," therapy
  as, 54
Schemes
  breaking/reorganiza-
    tion of, 242
  memory distortion
    imposed by, 53
  for processing of new
    information, 233–234
Schizophrenia, 157
Schools of therapy, 149–150,
  250–251
Selective hearing, 25–30, 77
Self-awareness, 3, 190–191
Self-care, 202–214
Self-confrontation
  advantages of, 60
  by the client, 37–38, 49,
    53
  facing fear and joy, 53
  fear reduction through,
    52–53
  MUM effect preventing,
    56
  painful feelings evoked
    through, 56
  by the therapist, 35

Self-consciousness, disap-
  pearing in "flow" state,
  139
Self-defeating behavior
  anxiety reduction as
    source of, 229, 234
  habits based on former
    conflicts, 148
  intense emotional con-
    flict as necessary for,
    225
  neurotic stupidity as a
    synonym for, 69
Self-disclosure, benefits and
  dangers of, 92–94, 99
Self-esteem, 244, 246–247
Self-experiencing, accurate,
  245
Self-exploration, 68–69
Self-fulfilling prophecies, 25,
  77, 110, 176
*Self-nurture: Learning to Care
  for Yourself as Effectively
  as You Care for Everyone
  Else* (Domar & Dre-
  her), 201
Self-understanding, 69–70
Sensing others' experienc-
  ing, 124
Sensitivity, empathic, 9
Sex, as a relationship issue,
  104, 109
Shaded meaning, 97
Shadings, vocabulary of,
  46–47
Shame, power of, 228–229
Silence
  categories of, 7, 28–30
  as empathic response,
    127
  listening to, 27–30
Skillful tentativeness, 38–41,
  48
Skinner's analysis of aware-
  ness, 232
Sneaky interpretation, 27,
  39–40, 74–75
Social cognition and automa-
  ticity, research on, 126
Social needs vs. individual
  needs, 164
Social support, 211–212
Sociopathy. *See* Antisocial
  personality disorder

Spiritual renewal and prac-
  tice, 213
Step-by-step progress, 241
Stereotyping, 191, 193
Strength words, 47
Stress reduction, 131–132,
  205
Structure and focus, 35–38
Structure, need for, 120
Subjective countertransfer-
  ence, 106
Subjectivity, 43–44
Successive approximations,
  45–46, 96–97
Suicides, potential, 151–153
Summarizing, 37–38
Supervision, 35
Suppression, definition of,
  230
Symbolization of experi-
  ences, 123
Sympathy vs. empathy, 8
Symptom substitution,
  243–244

Technique, 120–121
Tentativeness, bold/forth-
  right/skillful, 38–41
Termination, 177–179
Tests/testing, for assessment
  purposes, 161
Theory(ies)
  importance of, 217–218
  as line drawings of dif-
    ferent parts of reality,
    219
  little/personal, 25–26,
    39–40
Therapeutic alliance
  in couple and family
    therapy, 185–186
  cross-cultural counsel-
    ing and, 194
  relationship issue of,
    86–88
  research on, 252–253
Therapeutic Presence (Robbins), 136
Therapeutic relationship.
  See Relationship issues;
  Therapeutic alliance
Therapeutic skills
  gaining through practice,
    113

About the DVD
"Observing Therapy"

There is much you can't learn about therapy by reading a book, and so in order to give readers a more complete understanding of conducting therapy focused on evocative empathy and the therapy relationship, I have created a DVD called "Observing Therapy." The DVD contains an introduction and videotaped excerpts from actual therapy sessions with three clients. I saw these clients for about ten sessions each over the course of three months. On the DVD, there are 14 excerpts that show you a total of one-and-a-half to two hours of each client's therapy, and each excerpt varies in length from about 12 minutes to 30 minutes. The total length of the DVD, including the introduction, is five hours. (You may notice that, in order to get five hours of material on the DVD, we sacrificed a bit of sharpness of resolution on the video.)

I suggest that you start with Session One for a particular client and watch the excerpts of that person's therapy in chronological order so that you get a sense of the progression of therapy. You'll see that I say less in the beginning sessions, because at this point in the therapy I'm trying to know the person and his or her story.

One way you can use the DVD as a learning tool is to click on the pause button when you want to respond to a client's statement, as though you were the therapist. Many people are surprised to find how difficult it can be to come up with a helpful response quickly; pausing the DVD allows a low-pressure way for you to respond, as well as a way to try out a variety of responses. Then, when the DVD resumes, you can hear what I said (or didn't say); my response can serve as a *comparison* to your response. Keep in mind that what I said isn't the only or best way to respond. You know from reading the book that there are many ways to respond helpfully and make the client feel both *deeply understood and accepted*; this is the essence of what makes therapy work. Techniques are important but are secondary. If the client feels emotionally safe and deeply understood, many techniques work, and almost no techniques work if that safety and understanding are not present.

The therapist's goal is not to produce "a high count of good responses." The goal is for the client to feel deeply understood. As you watch the video, I

337

think you will notice many places where I could have articulated a response and didn't. But even when I didn't say something, I hope that I was "present" with the clients and that they felt listened to. I also hope that I was accurately sensing when it would be helpful to articulate a response. In watching myself on video, I became aware that my responses were a mixture of both "moment-to-moment" understanding and "big picture" understanding. My goal is that the client has a sense of "he gets it . . . he gets me . . . he knows me." That sense comes from *moment-to-moment experiences* of the client feeling, "Yes, exactly; that's what I was trying say just now. . . ." and from *big-picture experiences* of, "Yes, that's how it is for me. And seeing it like that helps me move forward to new understanding."

One therapist in training who saw this video remarked that it was helpful to "see what therapy actually 'looks like.'" Another said that the sessions were more "like a conversation" than he had expected. I do think that these sessions show what therapy "looks like," but you need to remember that every therapist has a somewhat different style, and this video shows one particular therapist with three particular clients. You won't sound just like me in therapy because you will find a style that is most comfortable for you. In fact, I'm somewhat different with each of these three clients.

I am deeply grateful to the three clients, GR, AR, and HP, for their willingness to share their therapy in this way. For their helpful feedback on the video, I would also like to thank Patti Barss, Daniel Buchanan, Tracy De Boer, Chad Graves, Ed Johnson, Luella Jonk, Ross McCallum, Darren Neufeld, and Uliana Nevzerova.

I hope that you benefit from watching the video and wish you well on your path to becoming a great therapist.